THE INFLUENCE OF COGNITIVE
PSYCHOLOGY ON TESTING

Buros-Nebraska Symposium
on
Measurement & Testing

Volume 3

Series Editor

JANE CLOSE CONOLEY

**Buros Institute of Mental Measurements
and
Department of Educational Psychology
University of Nebraska-Lincoln**

THE INFLUENCE OF COGNITIVE PSYCHOLOGY ON TESTING

Edited by

Royce R. Ronning
John A. Glover
Jane C. Conoley
University of Nebraska-Lincoln

Joseph C. Witt
Louisiana State University

LEA LAWRENCE ERLBAUM ASSOCIATES, PUBLISHERS
1987   Hillsdale, New Jersey   London

Lawrence Erlbaum Associates, Inc., Publishers
365 Broadway
Hillsdale, New Jersey 07642

Library of Congress Cataloging-in-Publication Data

Buros-Nebraska Symposium on Measurement & Testing (3rd   :
  1984 : University of Nebraska-Lincoln)
  The influence of cognitive psychology on testing.

  (Buros-Nebraska Symposium on Measurement & Testing ; v. 3)
  "Buros-Nebraska Symposium on Measurement & Testing"—p. facing t.p.
  Held in Oct. 1984 at the University of Nebraska-Lincoln.
  Includes bibliographies and indexes.
  1. Psychological tests—Congresses.   2. Psychometrics—
Congresses.   3. Cognition—Congresses.   I. Ronning, Royce R.
  II. Title.   III. Series: Buros-Nebraska Symposium on Measurement & Testing (Series)
; v. 3)

[DNLM: 1. Cognition—congresses.   2. Psychological Tests—
congresses.   3. Psychometrics—congresses. W3 BU998 v.3 / BF 311 D967 1984i]
BF176.B87 1984   153.9'3   87-6803
ISBN 0-89859-898-2
10 9 8 7 6 5 4 3 2 1
Printed in the United States of America

Contents

Foreword   **ix**

1. **Introduction: The Implications of Cognitive Psychology for Testing**   **1**
    Royce R. Ronning, Jane C. Conoley, and John G. Glover

    Overview of Chapters   *3*
    Concluding Comments   *8*
    References   *8*

PART I: THE COGNITIVE-PSYCHOMETRIC CONNECTION

2. **Science, Technology, and Intelligence**   **11**
    Earl Hunt

    The Present Status of Psychometric Theory   *13*
    The Cognitive Psychology Approach   *18*
    The Union of the Camps   *34*
    Conclusion   *36*
    References   *37*

3. **Toward a Cognitive Theory for the Measurement of Achievement**   **41**
    Robert Glaser, Alan Lesgold, and Susanne Lajoie

    Introduction   *41*
    Cognitive Research Relevant to the Measurement
      of Achievement   *43*
    Cognitive Research Applied to Testing
      Methodology   *60*
    Intelligent Tutoring Systems: Laboratories
      for Integrating Testing and Instruction   *69*
    Summary: General Dimensions for a Cognitive
      Approach to the Measurement of Achievement   *77*
    References   *82*

4. **The g Beyond Factor Analysis**   87
Arthur R. Jensen

Some Definitions   *87*
Some Facts of Nature   *88*
Factor Analysis and the Highest Order
   Factor   *90*
Fluid and Crystallized Ability   *96*
Size and Invariance of g *97*
Practical External Validity of g *99*
The "Reality" of g *100*
Refining g *107*
Task Complexity and g *111*
Theories of g *119*
References   *136*
Appendix   *139*

PART II: COGNITIVE APPROACHES TO PSYCHOMETRIC ISSUES: APPLICATIONS

5. **The Assessment of Cognitive Factors in Academic Abilities**   145
Stephen L. Benton and Kenneth A. Kiewra

Declarative Knowledge   *146*
Procedural Knowledge   *148*
Control Processes   *149*
Cognitive Strategies   *150*
Metacognition   *152*
Reading   *153*
Writing   *163*
Mathematics   *175*
Science   *179*
Conclusion   *182*
References   *184*

6. **Theoretical Implications from Protocol Analysis on Testing and Measurement**   191
K. Anders Ericsson

An Outline of the Chapter   *193*
Protocol Analysis and Verbal Reports   *194*
Implications of Verbal Reports for Measurement
   and Theoretical Abstractions   *200*
Exceptional Ability Vs. Acquired Skill   *216*
Concluding Remarks   *221*
References   *223*

PART III: METHODOLOGICAL ISSUES

7. **Structure and Process in Cognitive Psychology Using Multidimensional Scaling and Related Techniques**   **229**
    Edward J. Shoben and Brian H. Ross

    Introduction   *229*
    Distinguishing Theories: An Illustrative
       Example   *230*
    Kinds of MDS and Related Procedures   *231*
    MDS as a Method for Determining Structure   *232*
    Applications of MDS to Cognitive Tasks   *235*
    MDS Results as a Source of Processing
       Explanations   *235*
    MDS and Constraints on Semantic Memory   *237*
    Music Perception   *238*
    Measurement of Change in Structure   *241*
    Contextual Effects   *243*
    Context and Increased Dimensionality   *245*
    MDS and the Underlying Representation   *247*
    Problems with Categories   *249*
    Selecting a Representation   *251*
    Minkowski *r* Metrics   *252*
    MDS and Memory Theories   *254*
    The Promise and Limitations of MDS for
       Cognitive Psychology   *262*
    References   *263*

8. **New Perspectives in the Analysis of Abilities**   **267**
    John B. Carroll

    Introduction   *267*
    What is an Ability?   *268*
    The Person Characteristic Function (PCF)   *275*
    Cognitive Psychology and Task Difficulty   *279*
    Application of the Theory to Cognitive
       Ability Factors   *280*
    Discussion   *282*
    References   *283*

    Author Index   **285**
    Subject Index   **293**

Foreword

For over 40 years Oscar K. Buros was Director of the Buros Institute of Mental Measurements and Editor of the *Mental Measurements Yearbooks*. He was a crusader, and he devoted his entire career to his crusade. He was a crusader for better tests and the more effective selection and use of tests, and he used the *Mental Measurements Yearbooks* as the principal instrument in this crusade. Buros passed away in 1978, and his widow, Luella Buros, worked tirelessly to find a new home for the Institute. As a result of her efforts the Institute was relocated at the University of Nebraska-Lincoln.

The new Buros Institute has sponsored an annual symposium called the Buros-Nebraska Symposium on Measurement and Testing. The prominence of the name of Buros in the symposium title attests to our interest in using the symposium as still another vehicle for contributing to the Buros crusade. There is always the hope the events of the symposium will have some influence on the development of better tests or the more effective selection and use of tests. At our second symposium, for example, Dr. Gene Glass, the keynote speaker, emphasized the field of measurement had become too isolated from its roots in psychology and had suffered grievously from lack of theoretical relevance to other fields and from the contributions that other fields could make to its development. His plea was reminiscent of that made earlier by Anne Anastasi. The theme for the third Buros-Nebraska symposium might be said to have taken this lament in the most serious manner possible. As we planned the third symposium, there were several people in the planning committee who felt the field of cognitive psychology had done much in recent years that had important implications for how and what we should measure and for the improvement of measurement instruments. And thus was born the theme of our third symposium and the basis for this third symposium book: The Influence of Cognitive Psychology on Testing.

The development of the theme and plans for this third symposium and book is an interesting history of the stage-setting influence of the Buros "crusade" for better tests combined with the search in all of our symposia for the best ways to improve those tests. It is obviously our hope that the reader will find the results of this theme development to be both interesting and illuminating.

James V. Mitchell, Jr.
Director of the Buros Institute of Mental Measurements and Editor of the *Mental Measurements Yearbook*

Volume Acknowledgments

An edited volume such as this one requires substantial support and effort from many persons. The following individuals provided valuable time and professional judgment to review and comment on the various chapters of the book. The volume editors acknowledge Drs. Douglas K. Detterman, John Flowers, H. D. Day, Bruce Britton, Harold F. O'Neill, Jr., James Royer and David F. Lohman. We are deeply grateful for their efforts.

James V. Mitchell, Jr., Director of the Buros Institute of Mental Measurements gave generously of his time and expertise whenever asked. Linda Murphy of the Buros Institute provided a variety of essential services to the project. Lawrence Erlbaum and his staff provided their usual fine services in supporting our efforts in production of the volume.

Finally, we wish to recognize our respective families as well as our Departments for their patience over the long period necessary to produce this volume.

Royce R. Ronning
John A. Glover
Jane C. Conoley
Joseph C. Witt

Contributors

STEPHEN L. BENTON
Kansas State University

JOHN B. CARROLL
University of North Carolina, Chapel Hill

K. ANDERS ERICSSON
University of Colorado

ROBERT GLASER
University of Pittsburgh

EARL HUNT
University of Washington

ARTHUR R. JENSEN
University of California, Berkeley

KENNETH A. KIEWRA
Kansas State University

SUSANNE LAJOIE
University of Pittsburgh

ALAN LESGOLD
University of Pittsburgh

BRIAN H. ROSS
University of Illinois

EDWARD J. SHOBEN
University of Illinois

THE INFLUENCE OF COGNITIVE PSYCHOLOGY IN TESTING

1 Introduction: The Implications of Cognitive Psychology for Testing

Royce R. Ronning
Jane C. Conoley
John G. Glover
University of Nebraska

The 1985 Buros-Nebraska Symposium was developed to address the broad issue of the influence of cognitive psychology on testing and measurement. In the planning process, four topics were formulated that we asked contributors to address. The following four issues provided the focus for the Symposium and hence for the present volume. We explore:

1. Cognitive psychology as a basis for questioning some of our assumptions about the nature of mental abilities;
2. The influence of cognitive psychology on test development;
3. Cognitive psychology influences on test validity;
4. Cognitive psychology as a means to provide a linkage between testing and measurement.

Each contributor, of course, responds to the four issues in a variety of ways and with differing emphases. Although examination of the chapters reveals all four issues are at least implicitly touched on, it is clear that issues one, two, and three were addressed most directly.

Why such a set of symposium themes? The explosive growth of cognitive psychology since 1950 has been widely noted. Cognitive psychologists claim a purview far beyond psychometric issues and take as their domain a rather breathtaking range of topics dealing with human behavior. For example, Donald Norman (1980) suggests the following range of topics as the domain for cognitive science: belief systems, consciousness, development, emotion, interaction, language, learning, memory, perception, performance, skill and thought. Psychometric theory and practice are now addressing the need to find methods for measuring increasingly varied and complex levels of behavior. The breadth

1

of topics cognitive science sets out to address suggests its appropriateness as a source of information and data for examining such complex behaviors.

In 1984, Robert Sternberg (see Volume I of this series) briefly mentioned his sense that the boundaries between cognitive psychology and psychometrics are arbitrary and capricious. However, his description of the basic research strategy of the cognitive psychologist—intensive examination of performance on the particular task—suggests an important difference in perspective. It is this difference upon which the present volume capitalizes. Existing psychometric test development techniques are largely empirical, arising out of a history of test development dominated by correlational methods. These methods have led to heavy emphasis on description of tests by factor analytic techniques or examination of predictive validity. Factor analytic studies have resulted in clearer descriptions of the nature of test content and relationships among items within tests. Predictive validity studies provide an estimate of test value in predicting some external criterion. Neither perspective, however, provides information leading to clearer descriptions of the specific human behaviors upon which successful test performance is based.

In the same chapter Sternberg described the range of cognitive tasks studied by cognitive psychologists. He recognized that most of these tasks have not been used to predict conventional psychometric criteria such as grades. Nonetheless, substantial progress has been made in use of relatively novel tasks to predict general, as well as crystalized and fluid intelligence. This effort was only briefly addressed by Sternberg (1984). If a comprehensive picture of the contributions of cognitive psychology to the testing movement is to be understood and appreciated, a more substantial development of the four themes mentioned earlier must be provided.

At the same time that cognitive psychology has been expanding its contributions to issues close to those traditionally deemed psychometric, increasing demands have been placed upon the test movement to develop instruments that assess more complex levels of knowledge and performance. Glass (1986), in the second Buros Symposium volume, roundly criticized the current state of psychometric theory and practice. He asserted that beginning in about 1940 psychometrics began to move away from psychology and that by the 1960s, ". . . testing in psychology and education was severed from its roots in the study of human behavior" (p. 13). Others, (e.g., Glaser, 1981, and Hawkins, 1977) criticize extant tests for their lack of value in helping educators decide *how* children should be educated. Such criticisms, coupled with the press for increased sensitivity to assessment issues in testing groups such as ethnic minorities, women, and the varieties of disabled persons, lead to the realization that current psychometric theory and practice is inadequate to meet such varied demands. While Glass pressed the field of psychometrics to meet the challenge of psychoanalytic psychology, others, (Anastasi, 1967) have raised the issue more generally. Can testing methods be developed that appraise performance in such a way that test givers may not only make selection decisions, but also acquire information basic to developing methods to help educators facilitate change in individuals and groups? Can cognitive psychologists provide descriptions of the structure of human information processing in ways that permit improved test construction as well as, ultimately, improved methods of education?

What is the current status of attempts to use "cognitive" tasks and cognitive research methods to assess performance in so-called "achievement" areas such as reading and writing? Are there upper limits to the information that these "new" methods can give us? Following the logic of Gene Glass, it seems clear that new conceptions of assessment are required, assessments that not only lead to improved selection decisions, but that also directly inform practice. Cognitive psychology may provide one source of ideas for these new assessment methods. However, differences in goals between psychometricians and cognitive psychologists may mask the significance of the information cognitive psychology can supply to performance appraisal. For example, concerns for selection and classification on the part of psychometrists may conflict with cognitive psychologist's desire to examine the processes humans use in responding to both simple and complex stimuli.

The present volume, then, represents an approach to measurement from a cognitive perspective. The rather varied chapters provide perspectives on the role cognitive psychology may play in developing means for both understanding and assessing human behavior. Taken together, they suggest the potential for fruitful collaborative work between psychometricians and cognitive psychologists.

OVERVIEW OF CHAPTERS

Part I: The Cognitive-Psychometric Connection

The boundaries between cognitive psychology and psychometrics are not clear. The three approaches taken by the chapter writers in this section demonstrate the fuzziness of the distinction. Hunt, as well as Glaser, Lesgold, and Lajoie address the distinction by directly examining potential situations where the measurement issues and cognitive issues impinge upon each other. Jensen, on the other hand, addresses a larger issue, the extent to which human performance may, or should be, explained at a physiological rather than a psychological level.

In the second chapter, the initial conference presentation, Professor Earl Hunt re-examines the issue Cronbach raised in his 1957 American Psychological Association presidential address: the need to unite experimental and correlational approaches to understand human behavior. Hunt's chapter, "Science, Technology, and Intelligence," demonstrates that at some levels such unification has already taken place, (i.e., some cognitive experimental approaches now *are* studying individual differences in process behaviors, while some individual difference approaches *are* concerned with process issues). At the same time, Hunt describes situations where the "costs," financial and otherwise, of measuring specific cognitive behaviors in situation specific settings may be higher than psychometric consumers are willing to pay. He also points out that current pschometric devices meet criteria of financial cost and prediction to certain settings, such as educational success, remarkably well.

Finally, Hunt rephrases the issue in a more complex way by questioning the appropriateness of a union of the two camps at a level where one might wish to " . . derive the dimensions of psychometric Euclidean representation of abilities from an underlying process theory." Hunt's question does not suggest that either approach is correct or incorrect, but rather that each was devised to answer different questions. Thus, the one approach deals with legitimate and important issues of prediction and classification while the other deals with the significant task of understanding cognitive performance in a wide variety of domains. In effect, Hunt seems to suggest a symbiotic relationship rather than a synthesis of approaches. This somewhat less positive view of the relationship between the two approaches is not shared by the writers of chapter three.

In chapter 3, "Toward a Cognitive Theory for the Measurement of Achievement," Professors Glaser, Lesgold, and Lajoie consider the division between psychometric and cognitive approaches from the perspective of the psychologically oriented practitioner-educator. They describe the strengths of the psychometric approach in areas of aptitude testing and selection, while stressing its weakness in providing an understanding of instructional and learning processes. Because typical achievement measures fail to provide an understanding of process, Glaser et al., report on progress in developing means for appraising knowledge structures and cognitive processes underlying differential performance in specific fields or domains of study.

Although admitting that knowledge of such structures and processes is limited, the authors assert that new perspectives in achievement testing will grow from the study of cognitive processes in learning and development examined in the context of instructional method. The use of the computer as a tool to provide intelligent, responsive tutoring systems illustrates, they believe, one technique that will not only gather psychometric data on learner behavior, but will also permit comparison of novice learner behavior to that of experts, thus permitting examination of process data. Knowledge obtained through use of computers to retain task processes permits assessment of present level attainment, and in addition, reveals forms of error, gaps in knowledge, etc., that require instructional attention.

The chapter concludes with identification of a set of dimensions that present components of achievement competency developed over time. The eight dimensions, knowledge organization and structure, depth of problem representation, quality of mental models, efficiency of procedures, automaticity, proceduralized knowledge, and procedures for theory change and metacognitive skills, provide a fresh perspective from which to examine traditional achievement assessment. In contrast to Hunt, Glaser et al. express considerable optimism for the value of cognitive approaches in broadening the instrumentation through which achievement behaviors are assessed.

In chapter 4, "The g Beyond Factor Analysis," Professor Jensen describes a process that may help us to understand cognitive and psychometric issues by considering them as subprocesses of a more fundamental process. He examines the problem of the basis of intelligent performance from examination of the g factor derived from factor analyses of a wide variety of psychometric and cognitive tasks. In contrast to the preceding chapters, Jensen presents an argument for explanation of behavior at the level of biological rather than psychological constructs.

In a carefully developed argument, Jensen deals with three increasingly complex issues: (1) He attempts to demonstrate that g is a stable entity and not a statistical artifact; (2) He builds a case that g carries the bulk of the reliable variance in intelligence (and by extension in many other "cognitive" tasks) in a way suggesting a biological basis for g leading him to conclude that the most viable explanation for g will be found not in psychological but ". . . in genuinely physiological terms." This argument, whether in the final analysis correct or incorrect, formulates the issue of understanding intelligence in such a way that in the words of a reviewer, it " . . . will occupy researchers in intelligence for the next decade or longer." Clearly an argument leading to such a strongly biological conclusion will spark substantial interest to both psychometricians and cognitive theorists.

Part II. Cognitive Approaches to Psychometric Issues: Applications

Part II gives the reader a perspective on the success of current attempts to use cognitive approaches in understanding "standard" achievement areas such as reading and writing. The reader is invited to consider the adequacy of present explanations based on cognitive analyses for describing both process and outcome of such complex tasks as reading and writing. At the same time, one may reasonably question the applicability of existing cognitive research techniques to issues of understanding domains typically measured by conventional psychometric devices. The degree of care necessary to adapt cognitive techniques to the understanding of complex tasks is also delineated.

In chapter 5, "The Assessment of Cognitive Factors in Academic Abilities," Professors Benton and Kiewra list a series of interrelated cognitive factors that appear to contribute to successful scholastic achievement. These factors, declarative and procedural knowledge, control processes, and cognitive and metacognitive strategies are assumed to underlie successful performance in subject domain areas such as reading, writing, mathematics, and science. Cognitive research in several domain areas is outlined in considerable detail. Research support for the usefulness of the cognitive perspective is described and an assessment of its present status is attempted.

Benton and Kiewra examine research and theory in the subject matter domains based in cognitive psychology. To the psychometrician, the extent and size of this literature may be surprising. Their review suggests a significant new direction in cognition is the study of complex processes necessary for success in domain specific areas. Such an examination seems fruitful not only in confirming cognitive principles derived from simpler and perhaps more artificial laboratory tasks, but in discovering additional principles growing out of the interactions observed when domain specific knowledge, such as skill in geometry, is acquired using more general cognitive skills.

Professor Ericsson's chapter, "Theoretical Implications from Protocol Analysis on Testing and Measurement," takes a technique associated with the study of complex problem solving, protocol analysis, and builds a careful, logical argument for the value of the technique in illuminating the nature of the problem-solving process. He documents the value of protocol analysis as a particularly useful technique to provide psychometricians with descriptions of the nature of the cognitive processes required for successful performance on a psychometric test. This information differs widely from that gained through examination of the psychometric structure of a test using statistical procedures such as factor analysis.

Ericsson's descriptions of existing research and theory in protocol analysis provide convincing support for the value of verbal reports to the psychometrist. Analysis of the verbal reports made while carrying out such diverse activities as algebra, spatial ability, and digit-span memory tasks reveal the flexibility and usefulness of protocol analysis techniques in adding to our understanding of *how* subjects solve problems. Of equal importance, are the implications this approach has on test construction.

Part III. Methodological Issues

The last section of the volume reminds the reader of the gap between theory and practice. In both chapters, the writers raise, directly or indirectly, issues of methodology and definition. The optimism Glaser et al. express about the potential of studies of cognitive process to inform practice must be tempered by recognition of the need to find means to choose among the many competing models in cognitive psychology. Similarly, those cognitive or psychometric theorists who desire to understand cognitive behaviors that may underlie expression of some ability must have a very clear sense of how the ability is to be defined. Thus, if we wish to examine verbal ability, we need to determine precisely what we mean by the term before we can hope to successfuly discover underlying processes that lead to performance reflecting degrees of that ability.

The extensive research and theoretical activity occurring in cognitive psychology has resulted in the generation of a large number of competing models of cognitive structure and process. In chapter 7, "Structure and Process in Cognitive Psychology Using Multidimensional Scaling and Related Techniques," Professors Shoben and Ross present a rationale and a number of research examples suggesting the use of multidimensional scaling (MDS) as a method to provide a basis for choice among competing models. When a structure or model is assumed to vary across individuals, such methods of providing constraint in choice are valuable to psychometricians as well as to cognitive psychologists. As is the case when dealing with many methodological approaches, the method by no means provides final answers to the choices among structures cognitive psychologists face. Yet, Shoben and Ross nicely demonstrate the value of MDS techniques in providing as clear a set of constraints as is consistent with the level of development of cognitive psychology.

The final chapter in the volume, "New Perspectives in the Analysis of Abilities," returns to a somewhat more psychometric approach. Professor Carroll attacks the problem of definition of specific abilities by providing empirical data on a seemingly simple aptitude, human pitch discrimination. Carroll examined data on a large number of college students, looking particularly at differences between successful and less successful performance. His psychometric approach, examination of high and low scores, contrasts to the protocol approach described by Ericcson. Thus Carroll wishes to examine performance by analysis of scores of persons performing well or poorly on the pitch discrimination task. From Ericsson's perspective one might attempt to find a way to permit subjects carrying out pitch discrimination tasks to describe the process they use to make difficult pitch discriminations. His examination of high and low scores revealed the seemingly obvious finding that difficulty on the task was dependent upon the size of the pitch difference between two tones. High ability individuals have smaller pitch difference thresholds than less able persons.

Generalizing this finding to all aptitudes, Carroll argues that one definition of ability is the difference in individual thresholds of that ability. Carroll supports his case with several other examples. While he does not make the argument, a clear implication for the cognitive psychologist is the need to study the *basis* for the empirical finding. To what process(es) do we attribute the differential difficulty? Carroll provides an example of a Block Counting test used to study development of spatial ability. He identifies the chief source of difficulty as that of "visualization." A study (through protocol analysis) of the procedures subjects use to attempt that visualization might provide an interesting addition to Carroll's approach. Yet his argument is clear: In order to describe the process used in carrying out an act representative of some ability, the description is only useful if the ability is very clear and tightly described.

CONCLUDING COMMENTS

Demands by consumers for increasingly valid assessments of performance in a wide set of arenas pose a continuing challenge to test constructors. Some psychometricians argue that sophisticated measurement techniques have extracted as much useful information as exists from existing psychometric instruments. If these experts are correct, the demand for increased test validity cannot be met with existing instruments or measurement techniques.

Cognitive psychology appears to offer an attractive alternative to meet consumer demands. Cognitive theory has spawned a variety of theories of complex human intellective functioning moving beyond the study of purely laboratory tasks to the study of real world performance in activities that are significant to consumers. This volume demonstrates, we believe, the presence of a considerable body of theory and data about human cognitive processes valuable in meeting consumer concerns. Combined efforts of cognitive psychologists and psychometricians may well result not only in new tests and testing formats but substantially different conceptions of scoring and test use.

REFERENCES

Anastasi, A. (1967). Psychology, psychologists and psychological testing. *American Psychologist, 22*, 297–306.

Glaser, R. (1981). The future of testing: A research agenda for cognitive psychology and psychometrics. *American Psychologist, 36*, 923–936.

Glass, G. (1986). Testing old, testing new: Schoolboy psychology and the allocation of intellectual resources. In B. S. Plake & J. C. Witt (Eds.), *The future of testing* (pp. 9–27). Hillsdale, NJ: Lawrence Erlbaum Associates.

Hawkins, D. (1977). *The science and ethics of equality.* New York: Basic Books.

Norman, D. (1980). Twelve issues for cognitive science. *Cognitive Science, 4*, 1–32.

Sternberg, R. (1984). What cognitive psychology can (and cannot) do for test development. In B. S. Plake (Ed.), *Social and technical issues in testing* (pp. 39–60). Hillsdale, NJ: Lawrence Erlbaum Associates.

THE COGNITIVE-PSYCHOMETRIC CONNECTION

2 Science, Technology, and Intelligence[1]

Earl Hunt
The University of Washington

The intelligence test has been cited as psychology's most important technological contribution to society. Whether this is good or ill can be debated (Eysenck, 1979; Gould, 1981; Herrnstein, 1971; Kamin, 1974). Certain facts are not really subject to debate. Psychologists can and have developed "standardized interviews" that, on a population basis, provide a cost effective technique for personnel classification in industrial, military, and some government settings. However, the tests are very far from perfect indicators. Validity coefficients between tests and performance ratings typically range in the .3 to .5 range (i.e., from 10 to 25% of the variance in performance is predictable from test scores). While such correlations may be high enough to justify testing in many situations, there is a nagging feeling that better tests can be found.

The popular view is that a technology must be rooted in a science; in this case psychological tests must be rooted in a science of mental competence. In fact, the situation is not quite that simple. Psychology has two distinct sciences of mental power. One, the psychometric study of intelligence (henceforth *psychometrics*), (2) is closely interwined with the development of testing itself. The other tradition, Cognitive Psychology, has historically stood apart from the study of individual differences. Yet, both study the human mind, in the human brain.

A number of years ago Cronbach (1957) urged psychologists to unite these two disciplines. At one level the uniting took place. Cognitive psychologists do

---

[1]The term "psychometrics" will be used throughout this paper to refer to the psychological theories of mental competence that have been developed by applying correlational analysis methods to test scores. The alternative meaning of psychometrics, as a branch of applied mathematics, will not be used.

look at individual variations, and the techniques of Cognitive Psychology are used to study individual differences. The resulting research, however, has had rather little influence on the technology of testing. Is this because there is always too long a lag between science and technology? Or is there a deeper reason? And if there is a deeper reason, is there cause for alarm? Should something be done to accelerate the application of new scientific findings to psychological technology?

These questions are particularly apt today because Cognitive Psychology and a group of related disciplines, collectively called the "Cognitive Sciences," are perceived as being extremely active intellectually. This is in marked contrast to psychometrics, where the questions currently being debated are not terribly different from those that were debated over 50 years ago (Hunt, 1986a). Interest in the technological potential of the Cognitive Sciences has been expressed at as high a level as the Office of the President of the United States (Holden, 1984). The interest in Cognitive *Science* has a strong technological bias. It is hoped that advances in the study of laws of cognition will lead to the development of a technology of intelligent devices. These devices may expand the power of human intelligence. They may also expand the efficiency of our society's very large program of formal education, which is perceived as having substantial defects. It is logical to believe that the development of better methods to improve mental competence will be closely linked to better methods of evaluating competence.

This view may be too optimistic. The current fervor in the Cognitive Sciences is based on real changes in our views of the mind. However, these changes are derived from theories about cognition that are almost intellectually orthogonal to psychometric theories of intelligence on which modern intelligence testing is founded. Previous writers have urged that psychometricians and experimental psychologists unite in their study of the mind (Cronbach, 1957; R. J. Sternberg, 1977a,b; Underwood, 1975). They have proposed that the personal ability measurements of the psychometricians be added to the design variables manipulated by the experimentalists, so that the interactions between the two could be studied. This logic is epitomized by the phrase "aptitude × treatment interaction." The same logic is found, slightly muted, in studies of *cognitive correlates* between psychometric and Cognitive Science measures (Pellegrino & Glaser, 1979). In both cases there is an implicit assumption that discovering the correlations between measures that have been developed in different intellectual traditions will further our understanding in both fields. In this paper some questions are raised about the approach. Two traditions can seldom be rammed together by statistics. What is required is a theoretical synthesis that fuses them. If the synthesis cannot be made the theories will probably co-exist, each covering slightly different domains.

Is the synthesis on the separate theory approach appropriate for the study of individual differences in cognition? This question can be only answered by considering the present status of the psychometric and Cognitive Science views of the mind, and asking whether they are compatible. This question is explored below. The sort of answer to be expected should be made clear. It is not a question of one approach being right and one being wrong. Neither is it a question of technology versus science. The question is whether psychometrics and cognitive science can be synthesized into a single view. If they can, then the technology can be developed from a uniform scientific basis. If Cronbach's two "camps of scientific psychology" are inevitably separate camps each may develop its own technology, which may be useful for different purposes.

THE PRESENT STATUS OF PSYCHOMETRIC THEORY

Since its inception psychometrics has been beholden to technology. Where would test theory be without the number 2 lead pencil, the mark sense form, and the calculating machine? The digital computer, which came somewhat later, really did little more than cement intellectual trends that had already developed in response to what, collectively, will be called the "paper and pencil technology."

The paper and pencil technology made it easy to record the products of cognition. Note the stress on product. The paper and pencil technology is at its best when large numbers of fairly short questions are presented and when the respondent must choose from a fixed set of alternatives. The paper and pencil technology is not well suited to recording how a person chooses the answers, and is worse suited for situations in which free form responding is required. Perhaps most important, the paper and pencil technology emphasizes counting the total number of correct items or, in more recent applications, determining the most difficult item that a person can consistently answer correctly. Thus, the conditions of the measurement procedure rule out observation of some psychologically interesting behavior, and no amount of theorizing can put them back in.

The paper and pencil testing process has also been influenced by the economic constraints imposed on personnel evaluation, largely in military and educational settings. Because the test has been thought of as a one-time only measure on which to base a long term prediction of a vaguely specified criterion, great stress has been laid on measuring traits that are stable over repeated test administrations. Indeed, in many discussions of testing the correlations between test scores taken at different times are regarded as measures of test reliability rather than as measures of the stability of the examinee's ability to do whatever the test requires.

These are reasonable strategies if the goal of prediction is accepted. The decision to concentrate on stable mental traits does, however, rule out of consideration broad classes of behavior that could be considered part of intelligence. In particular, measures of learning and of individual variability of performance will not be measured. However, learning and personal stability could easily be regarded as part of a person's mental competence.

While any testing technology will be appropriate for some behavior and not for others, the very success of paper and pencil testing has made its shortcomings unusually serious. The behaviors measured on the tests have become the accepted definition of intelligence. The extent of this belief has been shown by reactions to some of the attempts that experimental psychologists have made to establish theories of individual differences in cognition. Although these attempts proceed from a very different tradition, and although atempts to reproduce correlations with traditional tests were specifically disavowed in one of the earliest papers on these attempts (Hunt, Frost, & Lunneborg, 1973) people still evaluate both their own (Keating, 1984) and other's (R. J. Sternberg, 1984, but for a more balanced view see R. J. Sternberg, 1985) work in terms of correlations with existing tests.

The paper and pencil technology has led to a particular type of theorizing. The volume of data produced by giving batteries of tests to large numbers of people has forced psychometricians to develop sophisticated statistical procedures for data summarization and analysis. The natural way to represent a person's test scores is by a vector, and the natural way to summarize a vector is by a smaller vector. Hence factor analysis, the art of extracting the small factor score vector from the bewilderingly large vectors of test scores. The summary is well defined mathematically. A person's abilities are represented by a point in a Euclidean space of "mental abilities." The point is then mapped on a line representing the (usually vaguely defined) ultimate criteria. As shown in Fig. 2.1, this is a perfectly respectable way of making classification decisions.

The Euclidean representation has been used as a psychological theory of intelligence, by interpreting the dimensions of the Euclidean space as basic mental traits. The method is well known, so no further description is needed here. (See Nunnaly, 1978, for a good introduction.) This is where the problem lies. Factor analytic based theories do not provide an adequate conceptual basis for thinking about individual differences in mental competence, except for the restricted purpose of classification. Why is this?

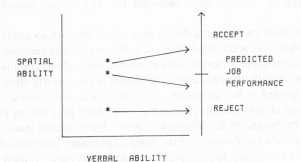

FIG. 2.1.   The Euclidean model of mental ability. A person is conceptualized as a point in a space of spatial and verbal mental traits. Each point on the space can be mapped into an acceptance or rejection interval on a one-dimensional criterion variable.

The usual objection to factor analytic theories is that the factor analysis as a mathematical procedure does not lead to a unique Euclidean representation of the data. Therefore subsidiary mathematical assumptions are made that, in effect, dictate the psychological theory to be accepted (Gould, 1981). The biggest argument is over whether one should insist that the dimensions, when interpreted as traits, be mathematically orthogonal. The argument is not trivial, because the orthogonality requirement *mathematically* precludes the discovery of separate but correlated psychological traits. This and similar indeterminancies in the mathematical solutions to the data analysis problem set the stage for a confusing play of empirical observations. Different investigators applied different mathematical techniques to different data sets; producing a variety of claims for models that vary from Spearman's (1927) classic "general" theory of intelligence through hierarchial model of "general intelligence" of varying degrees, and finally to the orthogonal specific abilities models exposed by Thurstone (1938) and Guilford (1967).

The trees may have obscured the forest. Carroll (1984) has done the field a considerable service by applying consistent factor analytic procedures to some of the major data sets reported in the literature. In it's simplest form, what Carroll found is that most of these data sets can be fit by a "hierarchial general factor" model of human abilities. Examples of such models are those espoused by Cattell and Horn (Cattell, 1971; Horn & Donaldson, 1980) or by Vernon (1961). The Cattell-Horn model seems to be the most accurate. It assumes that there are three major classes of abilities. These are the "crystallized," and usually highly verbal, ability to apply previously learned solutions to current problems (Gc), the "fluid intelligence" ability to apply general problem solving methods to new situations (Gf), and a "visualization" ability to deal with problems involving visual-spatial relations (Gv). (There is some evidence for an analagous ability to deal with auditory relations [Stankov & Horn, 1980]). There is ample evidence that these abilities are distinct, although Gc and Gf are correlated in most populations.

One of the most encouraging things about the Cattell-Horn model is that it fits reasonably well with neuropsychological analyses of brain function. These analyses are based on quite different sorts of observations about cognition; extensive examinations of pathological cases. The match is particularly strong for Gv and for Gc, interpreted as verbal ability, for there is massive evidence that spatial-visual and verbal information processing take place in different physical locations in the brain (Kolb & Whishaw, 1980). There is also some evidence for selective forebrain involvement in the sorts of planning functions that appear to be involved in the ability to plan and coordinate activities. At least superficially this sounds like Gf, although it should be realized that the sorts of failures of planning described for frontal lobe patients are much more extreme than those associated with low Gf.

In summary, hierarchial models provide good summaries of the abilities tapped by paper and pencil testing. To a limited extent, we can make a guess about where some of the information processing that underlies the traits identified in the models takes place in the brain. Clearly there is some reality to the model, as a Euclidean description of human abilities. The problem is that it is difficult to go further with *any* Euclidean model of cognition, because such models provide relative descriptions of the products of thought without any commitment to a model of the process of thinking.

Since this point is crucial, a hypothetical illustration will be given. Consider the task of predicting how a person might perform on a test paragraph comprehension. A psychometrician could predict the total test score, by using a formula something like:

Predicted test score = a x (Examinee's Gf trait score)
          + b x (Examinee's Gc trait score),

where a and b are appropriately valued coefficients. But this predicts *how well* the person will perform, not *how*.

To describe performance on the test one has to have a model of how a person merges his or her general knowledge with the information in the text, in order to construct a representation of the information in the paragraph, and then one has to have a model of how the examinee interprets questions and interrogates the internal representation of the text. These models deal with processes, not relative outcomes.

Psychometricians are certainly aware of this problem. Their approach has been to examine tests that appear, by mathematical criteria, to be relatively pure tests of a trait. The hope is that an examination of such tests will lead to a better understanding of what the trait means. This has worked relatively well for spatial-visual reasoning (Gv), which seems to be composed of several definable actions; holding bits of visual images in one's head, and moving images about ''in the mind's eye'' (Lohman, 1979; McGee, 1979). The approach has worked much less well in the case of the more general ''crystallized'' and ''fluid'' intelligence traits. The relevant findings are very well summarized by recent work by Snow and his colleagues (Marshalak, Snow, & Lohman, 1984; Snow, 1986). They used multidimensional scaling methods to construct a space of various tests in which distances between tests approximated correlations between them. Hence tests that define a factor will be grouped in tight clusters. A graphic summary of some of their results is shown in Fig. 2.2. As the figure shows, there are clusters that define the Gf and Gc factors. However the tests in these clusters tend to be complex ones. Therefore people differ in their interpretation of the behavioral capabilities needed to attack them. The well known Raven Progressive Matrix test (Raven, 1965), which is widely regarded as a good Gf measure, is a good example. The test contains problems that yield to several

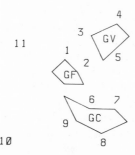

FIG. 2.2.   An abstraction of the two dimensional space of mental tests developed by Marshalek, Snow, and Lohman (1983). Tests were located by a multidimensional scaling in which the distance between tests in the space is roughly proportional to the correlation between them; the higher the correlation the less the distance between test points. Some of the tests shown in this figure are 1-Raven Matrices, 2-Letter Series, 3-Hidden Figures, 4-Paper Form Board, 5-Object Assembly, 6-Vocabulary, 7-Information, 8-Comprehension of verbal statements, 9-Arithmetic problem solving, 10-Digit span, and 11-Locating A's in a line of text. Three groups of tests are shown, corresponding to fluid intelligence (GF), crystallized intelligence (GC), and visualization (GV).

alternative strategies, each of which utilizes distinct elementary processing steps (Hunt, 1974). Therefore one cannot easily summarize the processes that the Raven Matrix test tests. A summary that one person finds adequate will displease another, and there is no way to resolve the issue.

R. J. Sternberg (1977a,b) has developed an alternative approach to the problem of definition of what a trait means. The technique is called "component analysis." One assumes that an examinee's overall test performance can be broken down into components, where a component is defined as a process that begins with a defined input from previous components and ends with a defined output to be delivered to the next component in line. Consider analogy tests. Each item is of the form

"A is to B as C is to D1, D2, D3, D4"
e.g.,
"Cat is to Dog as Wolf is to (Lion, Giraffe, Elephant, Penguin)"

Such a problem can be solved in the following steps.

1. Code the meaning of the terms.
2. Establish the relation between the A and B terms.
3. Apply that relation to map from the C term into an ideal answer.
4. Locate that answer amongst the D terms that most closely approximates the ideal answer.

The time required to answer a test item is assumed to be a linear function of the time required to execute each component process, plus a "junk" term representing "all other processes involved." A similar model can be constructed for estimating the probability of producing the correct answer as a function of the probability of correctly executing each component process. A person's ability to execute individual components can be estimated in two ways; by designing modified test items that isolate one of the components (as was done in Sternberg's original work) or by constructing a factorial experiment in which the experimental variables are chosen to modify the difficulty of one and only one of the component processes (e.g., Pellegrino & Kail, 1982).

Componential analyses can produce very accurate partitions of variation in performance on different problems within a particular type of test, averaged across individuals. On the other hand, no one of the component process measures seems to account for very much of the variance in inter-individual test performance. The "junk" parameter, which represents "encoding plus everything else" is consistently the most accurate estimate of general performance in other areas. This is disconcerting, for the processes contributing to the junk parameter are not defined by the experimental variations. As a result, componential analysis does provide a better idea of what behaviors are required to take a conventional test, but componential analysis has not related these behaviors to a theory of cognition, nor has it explained why some tests work as predictors in some situations.

The criticisms that have been directed at the hierarchial model are not specific to it. They can be directed at any trait theory of cognition. This does not mean that trait theories are false, just that they have inherent deficiencies. Can these deficiencies be remedied by combining psychometrics with cognitive psychology? To answer this question, let us take a look at the Cognitive Psychology view.

THE COGNITIVE PSYCHOLOGY APPROACH

Cognitive psychology is based on an approach to the mind that is markedly different from the Euclidean representation approach taken by psychometrics. The modern (post 1970) approach has been strongly influenced by a variety of other disciplines, notably by linguistics, neuropsychology, artificial intelligence, psychology, and to a lesser extent cultural anthropology. These branches of each of these disciplines that are concerned with thinking have come to be referred to, collectively, as the "Cognitive Sciences." This is an umbrella term for a collective movement toward the development of a unified theory of mind rather than to multiple, discipline-specific models. Since modern cognitive psychology is best underscored as part of this movement a few words about it are in order. The basic assumption of the cognitive sciences is that there are laws that govern physical symbol manipulating systems, somewhat akin to laws that govern physical phenomena. At a very general level, Shannon & Weaver's (1949) theory of information transmission would be an example of such a law. The term "physical symbol manipulating system" is important. The cognitive science approach assumes cognition is achieved by the manipulation of symbols that represent some external world. However the act of symbol manipulation requires some sort of physical system. What cognitive science studies is the restraints placed on symbol manipulation by the nature of the external world being represented, by the nature of symbol manipulation itself, and by the physical character of the system doing the manipulation.

Pylyshyn (1983) has identified three levels of cognitive science studies. The first is the study of the influence of physical mechanisms upon cognitive processing. This can be done by analyzing the one device that we know is capable of thought; the mammalian brain. The cognitive and neurosciences merge here. A complementary approach is to analyze the performance of hypothetical physical devices, to see if they could perform the computations that are required to achieve certain cognitive actions. Examples of such work are the study of the learning and memory capacities of networks of idealized, neuron-like devices (Hinton & Anderson, 1981; Minsky & Papert, 1969) and analyses of the networks that can realize computations required in vision (Marr, 1982).

Pylyshyns's second level of cognitive science research deals with *pure* symbolic processing capabilities defined without concern for the external referents of the symbols being processed. An example would be the well known studies of the scanning of information in short-term memory (S. Sternberg, 1969, 1975) or studies of the process of moving visual images "in the mind's eye" (Shepard & Cooper, 1982).

At the highest level are studies of thought processes that are controlled by people's understanding of the referents of symbolic processing. Examples of work at this level are studies of problem solving and text comprehension. Johnson-Laird (1983) has described this level of research as research on the mental models that people construct and manipulate in the course of problem solving.

For brevity let us refer to these levels as the physical, information processing, and referential levels of cognition. Clearly the physical level is the most concrete, for an action of the mind must ultimately be an action of the brain. The referential level is what we normally think of as conscious thought. The most abstract of the three levels is the information processing level. Pylyshyn presented the levels as analogically similar to the study of computer circuitry, system design, and programs within computer science. A related, and perhaps somewhat clearer, analogy is to think of studies at the physical (brain) level in humans as being analogous to the study of computer hardware, studies at the representational level as being analogous to the study of the actions of particular programs, and studies at the information processing level as being analagous to studies of the operations permitted in a computer language in which the representational "programs" are written.

To provide a more specific illustration, consider the study of human verbal comprehension. At the physical level there have been numerous studies showing that language processing in the brain takes place largely in the left hemisphere (Kolb & Whishaw, 1980). At the representational level we find studies of how the information people extract from a text is influenced by their level of knowledge of the topic, the text, and their beliefs about the use they will have to make of the text-based information (Johnson & Kieras, 1983; Chiesi, Spillich, & Voss, 1979).

The information processing level is the hardest level to define, because it refers to processes rather than to physical structures, but the processes are not open to conscious inspection. Continuing the analogy to computation, unraveling the information processing elements of cognition is a bit like attempting to infer the basic operations of a computer programming language by observing the performance of programs written in that language. The problem can be illustrated by considering the logic of the *sentence verification* paradigm developed by Clark and Chase (1972). This procedure will be considered in some detail because it has been the vehicle for a reasonable amount of research on individual differences. The procedure is shown in Fig. 2.3.

First a simple sentence is shown. The sentence is followed by a picture. The participant must indicate whether or not the sentence correctly describes the picture. Since errors are infrequent, the dependent variables are the time a person requires to comprehend the sentence ("comprehension time") and the time required to determine whether or not the sentence correctly describes the picture ("verification time"). These can be altered by varying the truth value and syntactic-semantic form of the sentence. For instance, it takes longer to verify negations than affirmations ("Plus above star" versus "Plus not above star") and longer to verify sentences containing marked terms ("below") than unmarked ones ("above"). The time required to carry out basic steps in linguistic

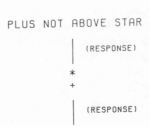

PLUS NOT ABOVE STAR

| (RESPONSE)

*
+

| (RESPONSE)

FIG. 2.3. The Sentence Verification paradigm. A phrase is displayed. When the participant indicates that the phrase is understood the picture is displayed. The participant then determines whether or not the phrase correctly described the picture. The dependent variables are the times between phrase display and comprehension (comprehension time) and picture display and verification (verification time).

information steps can be measured by observing how verification times change when sentence forms are altered systematically. The logic can be extended to individual difference research by determining how (or whether) the time required to execute a specific linguistic process varies across people.

Harking back to my earlier discussion of Psychometrics, two major differences between the cognitive psychology and the psychometric approaches are apparent. Both are particularly striking in studies at the information processing and representational level. Cognitive psychology is interested in the process of cognition, rather than the product. This can be seen in the studies of verbal comprehension just described, where the emphasis is on building a model of how a linguistic statement is understood, rather than on specifying how likely a person is to understand an arbitrary statement. The second difference, which follows from the first, is that a cognitive psychology theory of individual differences must fit into a process model of the cognitive action being studied. The cognitive psychologist is not particularly interested in determining the dimensions of the Euclidean space adequate to describe individual's ability, relative to each other. The cognitive psychologist is interested in knowing how variables related to the individual impinge upon the process of that individual's cognition.

This can be illustrated by looking at a series of studies on the role of short-term memory in reading. There is a positive correlation between measures of memory span and scores on omnibus written tests of verbal ability (Daneman & Carpenter, 1980; Palmer, MacLeod, Hunt, & Davidson, 1985). Daneman and her colleagues (reviewed in Daneman, 1984) asked why this is so. First it was shown that higher correlations can be achieved if the measure of memory span is one that directly reflects the ability to hold information in memory while processing intervening linguistic statements, rather than one that reflects the "passive" capacity to hold words in memory without doing some intervening activity. (The memory span subjects of most intelligence batteries are of the latter sort.) Next, it was shown that the ability to hold information in memory exerts its effect on certain steps in linguistic processing, such as the ability to resolve anaphoric references or to recall previously presented information when some reference to it is required. Instead of stopping with the observation that reading comprehension and short-term memory tests load on the same factor, Daneman and her colleagues examined the process of reading in order to determine what produced the loading.

Because the emphasis of cognitive psychology is on process, experimenters try to construct laboratory situations that isolate process. A cognitive psychologist may find performance in an isolated situation extremely interesting, on theoretical grounds, even though that isolated situation does not draw upon behaviors that are called upon a great deal in the everyday world. Prediction is not the point.

Measures of individual differences that relate to a theory of process are always of interest, in the framework of that theory, even though variations in the measures may not be highly related to variations in performance in any important socioeconomic activity. Indeed, from a theoretical view some of the most important measures on an individual may be those measures that reflect constancies. Years ago, Miller (1956) observed that there is very little absolute variation in the human abilities to make perceptual judgments and to hold information in short-term memory. The importance of these constancies for perception and language comprehension is immense. Yet measures with low variability are not good predictors.

Given the difference in philosophy, it is not clear that cognitive psychology and psychometrics can be united. On the other hand, it is not clear that they cannot. The problems are somewhat different at each of Pylyshyn's three levels of the study of the mind.

The functioning of the mind depends on the functioning of the brain, so questions about the relation between brain processes and mental processes are of interest. The famous issue of hemispheric localization of function is an example. So are studies of the influence of specific chemicals upon mental functioning; e.g., the role of alcoholic intoxication upon memory. A great deal of technological development has gone into the construction of measures of functioning of the physical brain, ranging from neuropsychological observations of behavior to such exotica as tomographic scans (Mazziotta, Phelps, Carson, & Kuhl, 1982). The technology provides an excellent way to study two things; the general physical substrate of the normal mind and aberrations in mind that are produced by specific, usually physical alterations in the brain.

The fact that the dimensions of individual variation uncovered by psychometrics do map reasonably well upon the brain functions discovered by neuropsychology is an important observation. The neuropsychological observations are almost all based on the study of extreme cases, while the psychometric data rests very largely upon the study of normal variation in mental competence within a normal population. This suggests that there are sufficient differences in brain functioning in the normal population to make a difference in at least some of our behaviors, specifically those actions required by a conventional aptitude test. In terms of the Euclidean representation of the psychometrician, the question is whether or not measures of brain functioning are sufficiently close to psychometric measures to fit into the psychometric dimensional representation of the mind. In more pragmatic terms whether or not brain function measures can be related to everyday functioning in normal individuals depends on whether the measures are related to behaviors shared by test taking and everyday cognitive actions, or whether the brain function measures are mainly associated with cognitive epiphenomena of the test itself.

From time to time there are reports that there are "substantial correlations" between measurements of brain functioning and some extremely complex behavior, such as a general intelligence test. (See Hendrickson, 1982, for a recent example.) The vast majority of these reports have simply failed the crucial test of independent replication. This is not to deny that the proposition that individual differences in brain functioning have something to do with individual cognitive behavior. I am sure that they do, especially in extreme cases. As a matter of scientific interest, studies of the relation between brain functioning and cognitive behavior should and will be repeated. However it is not at all clear what will be learned by studies that are confined to reporting correlations between gross measures of brain function and gross measures of mental function; e.g., a correlation between a measure of the variability of the brain's overall response to a repeated stimulus and performance on a general intelligence test. Unless the correlations were extremely high (and again I repeat my caution about independent replication) all this tells us is that the general functioning of the brain is related to general cognitive functioning. Did anyone doubt this?

Brain-cognition questions have a seductive physical concreteness. If tomographic scans reveal metabolic activity in a particular brain region during certain sets of cognition (e.g., activity in the right hemisphere during spatial-visual reasoning) then surely this must tell us how we think. Unfortunately, it does not. It tells us where we think. Brain function measures do not answer the questions posed by the cognitive psychologist unless measures on the brain can be associated with specific processes. To some extent this has been done, especially in the analysis of language comprehension, where the processes of word and sentence comprehension have been disassociated at an anatomical level. It is even possible that physical disassociations between different techniques for word analysis will be discovered (Coltheart, 1985). Such work is certainly exciting, but it is probably not going to have much influence on the relation between psychometrics and cognitive psychology, since neuropsychology rests upon evidence from pathological cases. One must also remember that a process may be distributed over several anatomical loci. So a failure to identify an anatomical location for a process tells us little. There would be a need for information processing studies even if we knew all there was to know about neuropsychology.

Early theories of information processing emphasized the isolation of stages of symbol manipulation. In Fig. 2.4 is an example, taken from an early paper by Smith (1968), in which the act of selecting a response to a stimulus was broken up into two stages of stimulus analysis and two stages of response execution. In fact, this approach is the historic progenitor of R. J. Sternberg's (1977a,b) component analyses of intelligence tests. The strongest interpretation of Smith's model is that there are distinct stages of information processing, that activity in one stage is independent of activity in the other stages, and that the stages pass information to each other in a serial manner. Thus a model like that shown in Fig. 2.4 is really quite a strong statement about information processing. A more general view is to regard thought as depending upon isolable subsystems, or modules, of information processing actions that operate independently of each other (Fodor, 1983; Posner, 1978). Each of the modules contains its own view of some aspect of the external world. These views are eventually integrated into an overall representation of what is going on. As an example of modular processing,

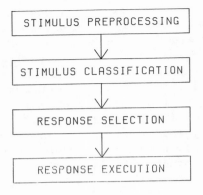

FIG. 2.4. Smith's (1968) stage model of stimulus classification and response production. Each box is assumed to represent a distinct psychological process. The processes take place in series, progressing from the top downward.

consider what must happen when an automobile driver is told, verbally, by a passenger, that the passenger would like to stop for dinner at the next restaurant. Figure 2.5 shows the exchange of information between modules that must go on inside the driver's head if the car is to be maneuvered into the nearest restaurant parking lot.

The current "wisdom" is that the integration of modular processing that occurs in cognition can be modeled by the use of a conceptual device known as a production execution system. The basis of production execution systems is the *production*, that is, a pattern and an action to be taken if that pattern is executed. In Fig. 2.6 is a slightly whimsical set of productions for driving a car. Each module of thought can be conceptualized as the set of patterns and primitive actions that are effected within by that module. Intermodule communication is achieved by allowing modules to place their output either into the pattern area of other modules or (more usually) by assuming a common "blackboard" area that can contain patterns appropriate to any of the separate modules. This is illustrated in Fig. 2.7, which shows the organization of an hypothetical modular

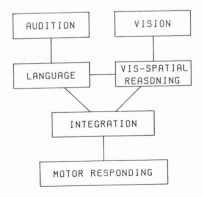

FIG. 2.5. A modular approach to cognition. Each box represents a class of mental processing, analogous to a specialized work shop. In integrated thinking information is passed back and forth between the different modules, and finally represented as a coherent internal picture of the external world. Processing is not necessarily serial.

CONDITION	ACTION
IF THE LIGHT IS RED	THEN BRAKE
IF THE LIGHT IS GREEN	THEN CONTINUE
IF THE LIGHT IS YELLOW AND CARS ARE IN THE INTESECTION	THEN BRAKE
IF THE LIGHT IS YELLOW AND NO CARS ARE IN THE INTERSECTION	THEN ACCELERATE

FIG. 2.6. Fragments of a set of production rules for driving an automobile.

system of productions that might be required to execute the logical production system stated in Fig. 2.6.

Thinking of thinking as organized modularity leads to an emphasis upon certain classes of information processing functions. The first is the definition of the modules themselves. Modules should not be thought of as stages in component processes (as described previously in discussing R. J. Sternberg's work), but rather as specialized workshops containing resources to be assembled into component processes. The distinction is roughly analogous to the distinction between a hardware manufacturer, such as the Boeing Aircraft Company, that is capable of doing certain things, provided its shops are not overloaded, and the stages in the process of constructing a specific aircraft, missile, or space vehicle.

Information processing research attempts to identify the modules and the actions of which the modules are capable. This is done by inferring the existence of a module, or of a process within a module, and by observing the selective action of variables on certain types of performance. An example is a widely cited study by Biederman and Kaplan (1970) which demonstrated selective effects of stimulus discriminability and response compatibility upon visual encoding and motor response production systems. An alternative technique for inferring the existence of separate modules is to show that action within one module does not interfere with action in another module. This sort of reasoning is exemplified by

FIG. 2.7. The organization of an information processing system for executing productions. The productions reside in long term memory. Information is presented to the system on auditory and visual channels that are connected to the external world. The system can "keep notes for itself" by placing temporary information in working memory, and using this information to guide production selection.

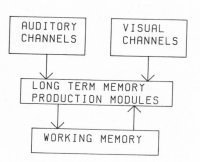

dual task studies, in which people are asked to do ostensibly independent tasks. If the tasks are done by separate modules it should be possible to time share the tasks without interference. A good illustration is a study by Kerr et al. (1985) in which maintaining one's posture was found to interfere with visual but not with verbal memory tasks.

Once modules have been identified one can investigate the extent to which each module displays variation across individuals. Similar studies can be made of processes within a module. Logically, individuals are treated as factors in an experiment, and one observes when differences associated with individuals (e.g., age, sex, or sometimes simply individual identity) make a difference in the performance of a task that is *already* known to involve a particular module. The fact that the modules have been defined independently is what distinguishes the experimental psychology of individual differences from psychometric investigations. In psychometric theory a "good" measure is defined by the pattern of correlations involving it and other tests. In cognitive psychology the meaning of the testing procedure will already have been defined, with respect to a particular theory of cognition, and will have been justified by the nomothetic experiments done to validate that theory. The pattern of individual differences is something to discover, but the pattern does not validate the measure.

The approach can be illustrated by a further consideration of linguistic information processing. The modular character of linguistic processing has been established by psychometric, neuropsychological, and experimental psychological criteria. In order to process language one has to know words. This is reflected in the well known fact that (at least in young adults) vocabulary size is an excellent indicator of one's general ability to deal with language. This is the reason that vocabulary tests are often used as "markers" for verbal ability. Tests of the speed of retrieval of the meaning of common words identify a reliable dimension of individual differences. Furthermore, this dimension of ability is distinct from the ability to manipulate strings of words, as tested in the sentence verification paradigm (Hunt, Davidson, & Lansman, 1981; Palmer et al., 1985). These findings indicate that the language processing module contains two somewhat separate mechanisms, one for retrieving word information from long-term memory and one for manipulating information after it has been retrieved. The conclusion is buttressed by neuropsychological findings indicating that different brain structures are involved in retrieval of word meaning and sentence analysis (Kolb & Whishaw, 1980). Because sentence and word processing are not perfectly correlated they evidently make a distinct contribution to the psychometrician's verbal comprehension trait. Note the implied causality. Sentence and word processing measures are not regarded as loading on an underlying trait of verbal comprehension ability, they are thought of as producing that ability. On the other hand, from the point of view of someone interested in prediction, a test that mixed sentence and word processing into a general test of the ability to comprehend language might be far more useful than isolated tests of the separate processes.

Verbal comprehension depends on the integration of word information into sentence structure, and sentence structure into discourse structure. Detailed models for both processes have been proposed (Kintsch & van Dijk, 1978; Schank, 1975). Both assume that what a comprehender does is to construct a structure representing the meaning of the message being received. This is not a trivial task, since the meaning of words and sentences will often be determined largely by context. Substantial individual differences in the ability to define words in context have been observed, indicating that variation in fitting semantic meaning to pragmatic context is a major source of variation in verbal comprehension (Hunt, 1985).

Positive findings such as these fit well into hierarchial psychometric models because they suggest that broad dimensions, such as "verbal ability," can be broken down into more tightly defined traits. But what about negative findings? One of the processes that facilitates the integration of words into sentences is a nonselective "printing" process, in which topics that have already been identified increase a person's sensitivity to the recognition of related words (Foss, 1982). The usual example is that people shown the word "Doctor" are quick to recognize the following word "Nurse." There is no doubt about the existence of this mechanism or about its role in the processing of normal discourse. However the priming mechanism appears to show little variation across individuals, and therefore measures of it are poor predictors of *relative* verbal comprehension ability (Hunt, 1985).

From a cognitive science view, findings showing that there is a linguistic information processing module, that it has subprocesses, and that the subprocesses sometimes show individual variation represent a start towards an information processing theory of verbal ability. Mapping the distribution of individual differences, per se, (i.e., constructing the appropriate Euclidean representation) is not a high priority next step. Studies that relate theoretically defined measures to specific individual characteristics are far more interesting. For instance, it appears that adult aging harms linguistic information processing at the level of sentence and text integration (Cohen, 1979; Light, Zelinski, & Moore, 1982). This is somewhat contrary to the psychometric observation that "verbal ability," as defined by certain psychometric tests, is relatively impervious to aging (Botwinick, 1977). How is this discrepancy to be resolved? Questions such as this are central to a scientific understanding of individual differences, but may be much less central to prediction of performance in wide-range situations.

The discussion of verbal comprehension illustrates how cognitive psychologists think about individual differences within an area of information processing module. Cognitive psychology also stresses the process of integration of information across different modules, or across different sources of input. The distinction is important. Studies of the exchange of information between processes deal with the passage of information from one representation to another. Studies of the way in which people deal with multiple sources of information focus more upon people's ability to control the way in which attention highlights first one, and then another, aspect of the current situation. Both of these concerns present challenges for the psychometric approach, but for somewhat different reasons.

Virtually everyone who has examined problem solving has stressed the importance of forming a good problem representation. Perhaps the clearest example is in high school geometry. Strictly speaking, geometric problem solving is an exercise in syntactical analysis; well formed strings of symbols are to be written into other well formed strings using a finite set of rules. Problem diagrams are not logically necessary, but they certainly help. It is quite easy to show that people differ in the representations that they use. Consider the sentence verification task. Most people solve this problem by comparing the meaning of linguistic descriptions of the picture to the meaning of the sentence. These are people who will use the sentence to construct an image of the picture they expect to see and then compare it to the picture that they are actually shown (MacLeod, Hunt, & Mathews, 1978). Regularities in representation use can also be shown across cultures. Children raised in a western European culture will attack an object memorization task similar to the game "concentration" by developing a verbal strategy of where the objects are. Desert dwelling Australian aboriginal children treat the same task as one of memorizing a visual image (Kearins, 1981).

The fact that different people use different representations poses a major problem for any trait model of cognition. Changes of representation may change the type of information processing that is required to take a particular test. This challenges a basic assumption of all psychometric methods; that the same linear combination of abilities can be used to predict the test score of every examinee. More colloquially, if representations change then there will be "representation optional" tests that are verbal tests to some and visual-spatial tests to others. When representation optional tests are included in psychometric batteries they will give erratic results, because their loadings will depend on the frequency of use of different representations in the population being tested. (Sentence verification tests provide mixed results when used with college students, but seem to be purely verbal tests in populations of older people [Hunt & Davidson, 1981].) By a sort of Darwinian logic, representation optional tests drop out of intelligence testing, because they do not fit well into the Euclidean model of ability description. But, from a cognitive science view, knowing the sort of representations a person likes to use is one of the most important pieces of information that you can have about problem solving ability.

Colloquially, we sometimes say that a person failed to solve a problem because their attention wandered. The ability to control attention during problem solving appears to be an important source of individual difference. This ability is usually tested by giving people several tasks to do in a short time period, and seeing how well they are able to cope with streams of information from different tasks. The tasks involved are almost always very simple ones, such as detecting whether or not a particular word has occurred in a string of words presented to the right or left ear (dichotic listening), or determining whether a signal has been presented at a particular location in the visual field. These simple tasks are studied because they are believed to be key components in a variety of very complex machinery operating tasks, such as flying an airplane.

Early research suggested that there are no reliable individual differences in the ability to do several things at once, apart from the ability to do each of the tasks singly. This early work has been criticized, however, on methodological grounds, and a reanalysis of key studies indicates that the ability to share one's attention across several tasks ("time sharing ability") is a reliable dimension of individual differences (Ackerman, Schneider, & Wickens, 1984; Stankov, 1983). Research identifying just what time sharing ability is, is in its infancy. However, we do have some indications of its nature.

Time sharing must involve some capacity for controlling attention. People who are good either at focusing attention on one *auditory* channel (e.g., listening to a speech against a background of conversation) or splitting attention across two auditory channels (listening to a conversation while talking on the telephone) are not necessarily the people who can focus or split attention across the visual field, but there is a substantial (.60) correlation between measures of control of attention within each modality. This suggests that there are both inter and intra modality mechanisms involved (Lansman, Poltrock, & Hunt, 1983). There also seems to be a reliable dimension of individual differences in the ability to shift attention from one stream of input to another. Examples are the task of shifting from listening to one ear in a dichotic presentation to listening in another, or shifting from following one sequence of visual symbols to following another (Hunt, 1986b; Hunt & Farr, 1984). We do not know the relation between "attention shifting" ability and the "attentional control" ability identified by Lansman et al. (1983).

The ability to control attention is not tested by conventional psychometric procedures. There are two reasons why. One is that the motivation for studying individual differences in the control of attention is based partly on a desire to predict how well people will operate machinery in highly demanding, time limited situations. Again aircraft operation is the best example. The sorts of processes being tapped in attentional control studies are simply not an issue in the educational and business settings applications that fuel many psychological studies of intelligence. There is also an intentionally practical reason for avoiding studying attention in a psychometric framework.

The procedures required to evaluate the control of attention are, to put it mildly, not easily included in the usual psychometric testing situation. The tasks are complicated so the participants must receive a careful explanation of them. In some cases up to several *hours* of practice may be needed before a person's performance is stable enough so that he or she can be tested. All of these considerations mitigate against the ''large N'' studies upon which psychometric technology depends. However, there is no way to shortcut the precautions. As was pointed out earlier, cognitive psychology develops procedures that are justified by their relevance to a theoretical model. Any use of these procedures must contain internal checks to make sure that the model still applies. In the case of studies of attention, the procedures and the internal checks will often be so onerous as to preclude their use in conventional personnel evaluation settings. This pragmatic fact does not diminish the theory, nor does it diminish our scientific interest in individual differences in attention.

Previous remarks have focused on the conceptual limits of the psychometric approach. It is worth noting that in the case of studies of attention, cognitive psychology has also been myopic. ''Attention'' has been conceived of as something that a person throws from one place to another, in response to an environment that demands an instantaneous response. This is a realistic model for skateboarders, all the time, and for airplane pilots some of the time. In most human endeavors, though, the cognitive environment demands responses within minutes, hours, or even days. The person doing the thinking usually has a good deal of freedom in scheduling the order if different cognitive tasks are to be done. This is a very different situation to study within the technologies of both psychometrics and cognitive psychology, because it means giving control of the situation over to the participant. And once this is done, the examinee has control over what is to be measured. Understandably both psychometricians and experimental psychologists avoid such situations. However difficult to measure, the ability to structure one's environment may be the key to successful thinking. This becomes apparent when we consider the topmost level of cognitive psychology, the study of conscious, specialized problem solving.

Complex problem solving is very much influenced by the representations that problem solvers choose to use, so understanding the process by which representations are developed, selected, and chosen for use has become a central goal of cognitive psychology. Because the choice of optional representations is very heavily influenced by learning, any theory of representation in problem solving has to be, in effect, a theory of how a person acquires and uses knowledge. The effects of representation owning on representation having are multiplicative, not additive.

This point has been illustrated in a striking way in studies that show how the information that a person extracts from a situation depends upon the person's representation of the situation itself. Chiesi, Spillich, and Voss (1979) offered a good illustrative study in a rather trivial field, recalling an account of a baseball game. People who were familiar with baseball could construct a representation of the plays being described. This caused them to focus on game relevant information, which they were subsequently able to recall. People not familiar with baseball were not able to do this, although they were able to recall game irrelevant information contained in the broadcast.

At one level, such an observation is hardly surprising. "Everyone" knows that people recall more about events that they understand. But this is precisely the point. Understanding and learning are problem solving situations, in which a person's current knowledge is used to structure new knowledge. The topic of Chiesi et al. experiment may have been trivial. The principle was not. Exactly the same point can be made (after a much more complicated analysis) by studying the way in which students acquire knowledge of plane geometry, or of computer programming (Anderson, Boyle, Farrell, & Reiser, 1984). And consider a still more detailed analysis of a very important activity. Carbonell (1978) was able to simulate conservative and liberal interpretations of political events using a program that applied identical information processing mechanisms to merge the statements with different representations of political and social forces. What one gets from experience depends very heavily upon one's interpretation of it.

The psychometric view is quite unsatisfactory here. Saying that people differ in their ability to use common, culturally defined solution methods (the definition of Gc) hardly captures the process of representation use. Amplifying the statement by saying that content knowledge extends Gc in specific fields is only a small step forward, for the psychometrician is still operating within the Euclidean representation of cognition. Regarding 'applying knowledge' as a trait does not discriminate between the possession of knowledge and the ability to see that a particular piece of knowledge is relevant to the problem at hand. It is fairly easy to demonstrate that the two are not synonymous. People can be given exactly the appropriate knowledge to use in problem solving, but in a slightly different context, and be unable to apply it. Some people see connections where others do not (Gick & Holyoak, 1983), but why? What processing differences are there between people who do and don't make generalizations? This is another example of a question that is central to a science of individual differences but not particularly crucial to a technology for prediction.

The issue being raised here is quite a broad one, for it has to do with the way in which "culturally acquired knowledge" is used. While some knowledge consists of ready-made answers to questions of fact, for example, much cultural knowledge consists of ways of representing problems so that their solution can be achieved. The representations form skeletons that guide thought, directing one's attention to key aspects of the problem at hand and suggesting particular solutions. Different theorists have used the terms "schema," "frame," and "script" to describe this process. These terms all reflect what seems to be a universal characteristic of human thought. The world is often ambiguous or overwhelmingly complicated. People bring order into this chaos by assuming that the world satisfies the constraints implicit in their world view. Successful problem solving is largely a process of trying out one or another constraining representation until one is found that works. To give a concrete example, consider the problem solving process of expert physicists. They recognize specific problems as instantiations of a generalized class of problems (e.g., balance of force problems). Once recognition has been achieved problem solving methods associated with the general class can then be applied to solve the specific problem. Novices are likely to focus on aspects of a problem that are not relevant to the general classification principles (e.g., is a sliding block involved?), leading to the use of general, but clumsy problem solving methods. (Chi, Glaser, & Reese, 1981; Larkin, McDermott, Simon, & Simon, 1980).

The realization that most problem solving is achieved by context specific methods marks a major change in Cognitive Science. Early work on artificial intelligence and human problem solving placed great emphasis on the discovery of general problem solving methods (Hunt, 1975). More recent studies have emphasized area specific knowledge (Feigenbaum, 1977; Hayes-Roth, Waterman, & Lenat, 1983). The same trend has been evident in cognitive psychology, where research has shown the extreme importance of topic specific schemata as guides in problem solving.

If this trend was to be taken to its extreme, generalized psychometrics would be, if not impossible, at least greatly changed. The whole idea of "intelligence" is that there is some mental characteristic of the individual that applies to many problem solving situations. An emphasis on the use of schema in problem solving does not completely deny this notion, for some schema will have wide applicability, especially in educational settings. Arguing again by illustration, Van Dijk and Kintsch (1983) have shown that understanding of a text is driven by schema that specify the form of argument in different types of text (stories, scientific reports, etc.). Obviously, it is possible to design tests to see whether or not people possess these general schema. Such tests are likely to be useful predictors of ability to function in places where general schema are used. Educational settings immediately spring to mind. Tests of general schema use are not likely to be of much use in predicting performance in situations in which effective local schema operate. People appear to be able to function quite well with a local schema even though they are not terribly comfortable with a related, more general problem solving procedure.

Some recent studies of the learning and the use of mathematics and logic provide excellent examples of this point. Mathematics and logic are often thought of as the purest, most abstract, and most general problem solving methods. At least in academic circles, an argument can be justified solely by appealing to its logical purity. When children learn mathematical problems they learn them as schema (Riley, Heller, & Greeno, 1983). Much of the difficulty in mathematics appears to be in translating from a nonmathematical statement of a problem into the appropriate schema (Kintsch & Greeno, 1985). At a grander level, the abstract schema of mathematics are so hard to learn that the ability to do so is often considered in itself a hallmark of intelligence.

If mathematical reasoning is so difficult, how does the modern world function? To take a specific example, how do people calculate the price of products in a supermarket? People are quite good at doing so, even though pricing information is not always presented in the most straightforward way (Lave, Murtagh, & De la Roche, 1984). The same people are not good at solving simple arithmetic problems, when those problems are presented outside of the shopping context. Lave et al. found that shoppers made errors on only 2% of the pricing problems presented in an actual shopping context and on 41% of the problems presented in an abstract arithmetical context. This was true even though the same arithmetic operations were used in each case. Furthermore the two tests were not reliably correlated! Further probing showed that the shoppers had a variety of problem solving procedures that were specialized for shopping and that were quite adequate for problem solving in that context.

Shopping is not the only place where people exhibit context-specific specializations of a logic that, in some abstract sense, they really do not understand. Ceci and Liker (1985) have reported a study similar to Lave's using an even higher order skill, statistical decision making. Inveterate horse race bettors have to determine whether the odds offered by the track are actually a good estimate of whether or not a horse will win. (The racetrack odds are determined solely by the amount of money bet on each horse, and do not reflect an explicit analysis of the horse's ability vis a vis its competitors.) Some individuals can "beat the odds" reliably. It is possible to formulate what they do as a complicated statistical estimation problem. But the racetrack handicappers were far from being untutored, brilliant mathematicians. In fact, their formal intelligence test scores were well below undergraduate norms. The skilled handicappers had developed complicated, race-track specific techniques for handling an unusually complex problem in decision making.

None of these remarks will be new to those familiar with studies of cross cultural cognition. Specialists in this field have long pointed out that the Western emphasis on "intelligence" emphasizes the ability to do problem solving in the abstract. The very idea of abstract problem solving seems to be related to Western European schooling (Cole & Scribner, 1974). While this may be true, it does beg a very important point. The Western European schooling situation, with its emphasis on abstract problem solving, may indeed be a cultural phenomenon. However, it is an important, useful phenomenon. Skills in logic, mathematics, and general problem solving are an important part of our culture, even these skills are then specialized as people find their niche in society. Therefore identifying people who are likely to become good general problem solvers is a reasonable endeavor.

This is where the concepts of Gc and, to a lesser extent, Gf, are likely to be useful. Let us accept the fact that high scores on Gc tests identify those people who have acquired the problem solving schemata of our society. Those are the very schemata that are going to be used in the classrooms, to aid people in acquiring further decontextualized knowledge. Perhaps we could design better tests is we had a better idea of how the educational process proceeds, because we would then know what schemata are going to be required, when, and (perhaps) how they should be learned. Furthermore, at least in theory Western schooling is supposed to develop an ability to generalize; that is to see how problem solving schemata learned in one setting can be applied in another. It may be that tests of Gf *identify* people who can make such generalizations. If we had a better understanding of the process of schemata generalization we would know what it is that these people are doing, and then could develop better tests for their identification.

THE UNION OF THE CAMPS

Cronbach (1957) sought a uniting of two camps of *scientific* psychology; the study of individual differences and the study of nomothetic influences on cognition. The prospects for uniting *these* camps is excellent. However, the study of individual differences is not identical to the use of a Euclidean representation of mental abilities. The prospects for uniting psychometrics and cognitive psychology are mixed, and for perfectly good reasons.

The paper and pencil testing technology and its accompanying Euclidean representation are hard to beat, so long as one's criteria are cost effective evaluation, and predicting is to a situation that involves very general behavior that depends on decontextualized reasoning processes. Education and, to a lesser extent, military life are examples of such situations. Traditional psychometric evaluation has not, and probably will not, be extended successfully to the prediction of performance in more specific situations, where adequacy depends upon the ability of an individual to execute situation specific, schema based, and perhaps complex information processing sequences. Note that the problem here is not that the paper and pencil technology is inadequate to construct such situations. The problem is that the underlying Euclidean representation of mental abilities cannot be used to formulate a process model of cognition.

Enter the computer. My frequent references to "paper and pencil technology" may have sounded archaic to those who are already programming computer presentations of the Wechsler Adult Intelligence Scale, the Armed Services Vocational Battery, and any number of other intelligence tests. Doing so will certainly make testing more efficient, as witnessed by current developments in "item banking" and latent trait theory (Green et al., 1982). Furthermore, computer presentations are more flexible than paper and pencil presentations, so the Euclidean model can be extended to new domains. Some possibilities are extensions of spatial-visual testing to the situations involving moving visual displays (Hunt & Pellegrino, 1985) and the development of practical tests of auditory information processing (Stankov & Horn, 1980). We may have to add a few dimensions to the Euclidean model, or we may not. Either way, the expansion of the traditional model via computerized testing will be a useful exercise. In itself, though, computerized testing will not address the conceptual issues that have been raised here. There is every reason to believe that a theory of individual differences can be developed as a subtheory of a general theory of cognitive psychology and will result in a better understanding of how individual variables such as age, education, sex, and genetics influence the processes of problem solving. To what extent will or will not this theory influence the technology of testing?

It is now technically possible to develop automated laboratories, so that the experimental psychologist can collect data on enough individuals to study individual differences. In the abstract, one could conceive of the development of even larger laboratories devoted to assessment and prediction. Such laboratories would immediately encounter another economic limit; the expense of the evaluation to the examinee. The sorts of measurements required by cognitive process theories are often extremely time consuming. The equipment is relatively complex, so that the examinee must spend considerable time learning to use it before any data can be collected. This and several related problems are very well discussed in Longstreth's (1984) excellent critique of the misuse that has been made of choice reaction time paradigms in order to fit them into an evaluation setting. A point that was made earlier is more than worth repeating. The measures developed from cognitive process theories are valid only when the boundary conditions for measurement are met. This requirement may forever prevent developing cognitive psychology analogs to the ten to twenty minute tests so common in psychometric batteries.

These remarks apply with particular force to any testing program based on the information processing aspect of cognitive science. Because such tests are likely to be expensive, testing itself will of necessity be limited to those situations in which prediction is important and in which performance is limited by a person's information processing capacity, once that person has acquired the specific knowledge required to perform at all. This suggests two guidelines for applied research. If information processing models are to be useful, then the test constructor must have a good idea of how information processing limits performance in the situation to be predicted. Two cases can be imagined. In one the key information processing requirements are not situation specific, and hence may be tested using some manageable testing paradigm. In the other case the information processing limits may be definable only in context, and hence can be tested only in the actual situation or an adequate simulation of it. If this is so it may not be possible to test examinees who do not already have a good understanding of the job for which they are applying. In either case the test constructor cannot proceed without a situational model. One can imagine such a model for specific situations, such as aircrew or radar operation. A detailed model of the information processing required in high school is unlikely.

At first glance a theory of the use of representations might seem to be of little use in personnel evaluation because, by definition, representations are used by people who have already acquired expertise in some field of endeavor. Ergo they must have already been permitted entry to the field. Fortunately this logic can be reversed. If "becoming an expert" means acquiring certain problem solving schema, why not evaluate a student by determining the extent to which the expert's problem solving schema have been internalized? Developments in Artificial Intelligence have led to at least the claim that we can represent expert knowledge inside a computer (Hayes-Roth et al., 1983; but see Dreyfus & Dreyfus 1984 for questions about some of the evidence on which the claim is based). "All" that needs to be done is to apply the interview methods used to extract knowledge from an expert to extract (faulty) knowledge from a student. To aid teaching, the evaluation process can be made the basis for further specialized instruction.

Efforts are underway to develop just this sort of intelligent computer aided instruction system (Anderson et al., 1984). The teaching goals appear to be in reach in nontrivial fields (computer programming and geometry). Whether or not the evaluation goal is feasible remains to be determined. The present intelligence tutoring programs seem to make a rather general guess at the student's current state of knowledge, and use that guess to select problems that are most educational for that student. Whether or not the program's guess about the student's representation is sufficiently accurate to be predictive remain to be seen.

CONCLUSION

Cronbach thought that general theories of psychological process ought not to ignore individual differences, and vice versa. He was right, and in a general sense the union of the camps is well underway. In my opinion (and here there may be a violent difference of opinion!) the way to achieve the *scientific* union is to concentrate on understanding how individual differences variables, such as age, sex, genetic constitution, and education, influence the processes of cognition. It does not seem particularly fruitful to try to derive the dimensions of the psychometric Euclidean representation of abilities from an underlying process theory.

This does not mean that the Euclidean model is wrong, within the context in which it has been developed. Consider an analogy to what we know about expertise. Experts develop local schema that apply to their local problems. The psychometric Euclidean model is an excellent way to deal with personnel prediction and classification. But it does not generalize well to understanding cognitive actions. Einstein was certainly intelligent, in the psychometric sense. However he did not develop a single one of his intellectual conceptualizations because he was high on Gc or Gf. He developed them because he had certain schema for problem solving and because he had the information processing capacity to apply these schema.

Eventually there may be a "Grand Unified Theory" of psychology, similar to those now being developed for physics. But will we understand it? There seems to be a role for Newtonian mechanics even after quantum theory. Engineers use the limited Newtonian notions all the time. Psychometric and cognitive process theories may similarly co-exist for many years. Practical application and power of conceptualization are both worthwhile goals. They are not necessarily synonymous.

ACKNOWLEDGMENT

The preparation of this paper was partially supported by the Office of Naval Research, Contract N00014-84-K-5553 to the University of Washington. The opinions expressed are the author's and do not reflect policies of the Office of Naval Research or any other U.S. government agency.

REFERENCES

Ackerman, P. L., Schneider, W., & Wickens, C. D. (1984). Deciding the existence of a time-sharing ability: A combined methodological and theoretical approach. *Human Factors, 26*, 2–27.

Anderson, J. R., Boyle, C. F., Farrell, R., & Reiser, B. J. (1984). *Cognitive principles in the design of computer tutors* (Tech. Rep.). Carnegie-Mellon University. Department of Computer Science.

Biederman, I., & Kaplan, R. (1970). Stimulus discriminability and S-R compatibility: Evidence for independent effects in choice reaction time. *Journal of Experimental Psychology, 86*, 434–439.

Botwinick, J. (1977). Intellectual abilities. In J. Birren & K. Schaie (Eds.), *Handbook of the psychology of aging*. New York: Van Nostrand Reinhold.

Carbonell, J. G. (1978). Politics: Automated ideological reasoning. *Cognitive Science, 2*,(2), 27–52.

Carroll, J. (1984, December). *Psychometric approaches to cognition and cognitive ability*. Lecture presented to NATO Advanced Study Institute on Intelligence and Cognition, Athens.

Ceci, S., & Liker, J. (1985). Academic and non-academic intelligence: An experimental station. In R. J. Sternberg & R. K. Wagner (Eds.), *Practical intelligence: Origins of competence in the everyday world*. New York: Cambridge University Press.

Cattell, R. B. (1971). *Abilities: Their Structure, growth, and action*. Boston: Houghton-Mifflin.

Chi, M., Glaser, R., & Reese, E. (1981). Expertise in problem solving (Tech. Rep. #5). University of Pittsburg.

Chiesi, H. L., Spillich, G. J., & Voss, J. F. (1979). Acquisition of domain-related information in relation to high and low domain knowledge. *Journal of Verbal Learning and Verbal Behavior, 18*, 257–274.

Clark, H., & Chase, W. (1972). On the process of comparing sentences against pictures, *Cognitive Psychology, 3*, 472–517.

Cohen, G. (1979). Language comprehension in old age. *Cognitive Psychology, 11*, 412–429.

Cole, M., & Scribner, S. (1974). *Culture and thought*. New York: Wiley.

Coltheart, M. (1985). Cognitive neuropsychology and the study of reading. In M. I. Posner & O. S. M. Marin (Eds.), *Attention and Performance XI* (pp. 3–40). Hillsdale, NJ: Lawrence Erlbaum Associates.

Cronbach, L. (1957). The two disciplines of scientific psychology. *The American Psychologist, 12*, 671–684.

Daneman, M. (1984). Why some people are better readers than others: A process and storage account. In R. J. Sternberg (Ed.) *Advances in the psychology of human intelligence, Vol. 2.* Hillsdale, NJ: Lawrence Erlbaum Associates.

Daneman, M., & Carpenter, P. A. (1980).Individual differences in working memory and reading. *Journal of Verbal Learning and Verbal Behavior, 19,* 450–466.

Dreyfus, H., & Dreyfus, S. (1984). Mindless machines. Computers don't think like experts, and never will. The Sciences 24(6): 18–22.

Eysenck, H. (1979). *The structure and measurement of intelligence.* Berlin: Springer-Verlag.

Feigenbaum, E. A. (1977). Art of artificial intelligence: Themes and case studies of knowledge engineering. *Proceedings of 5th Artificial Intelligence Conference.* 1014–1029. Aug., Cambridge, MA. (MIT)

Foder, J. (1983). *Modularity of mind,* Cambridge, MA: MIT Press/Bradford.

Foss, P. J. (1982). A discourse on sentence priming. *Cognitive Psychology, 14,* 590–607.

Gick, M. L., & Holyoak, K. J. (1983). Schema induction and analogical transfer. *Cognitive Psychology, 15,* 1–30.

Green, B. F., Bock, R. D., Humphreys, L. G., Lin, R. L., & Reckase, M. D. (1982). Evaluation plan for the computerized adaptive vocational aptitude battery (Tech. Rep.). John Hopkins University.

Gould, S. (1981). *The mismeasure of man.* New York: Norton.

Guilford, J. P. (1967). *The nature of human intelligence.* New York: McGraw-Hill.

Hayes-Roth, F., Waterman, D., & Lenat, D. B. (1983). *Building expert systems.* Reading, MA: Addison-Wesley.

Hendrickson, D. E. (1982). The biological basis of I.Q., Part 2: Measurement. In H. Eysenck (Ed.), *A model for intelligence* (pp. 197–228). Berlin: Springer-Verlag.

Herrnstein, R. J. (1971). *I.Q. in the meritocracy.* Boston: Atlantic-Little, Brown.

Hinton, D., & Anderson, J. A. (1981). *Parallel models of associative memory.* Hillsdale, NJ: Lawrence Erlbaum Associates.

Holden, C. (1984). Reagan versus the social sciences. *Science, 215,* 1054–1057.

Horn, J. L., & Donaldson, G. (1980). Cognitive development II: Adulthood development of human abilities. In O. B. Brim & J. Kagan (Eds.), *Constancy and change in human development.* Cambridge, MA: Harvard University Press.

Hunt, E. (1974). Quote the raven? Nevermore! In L. Gregg (Ed.), *Knowledge and Cognition.* Hillsdale, NJ: Lawrence Erlbaum Associates.

Hunt, E. (1975). *Artificial intelligence:* Orlando, FL: Academic Press.

Hunt, E. (1985). Verbal ability. In R. J. Sternberg (Ed.), *Human abilities: An information processing approach* (pp. 31–58). New York: W. H. Freeman.

Hunt, E. (1986a). The heffalump of intelligence. In R. J. Sternberg & D. K. Detterman (Eds.), *What is intelligence? Contemporary viewpoints on its nature and definition* (pp. 101–107). Norwood, NJ: Ablex.

Hunt, E. (1986b, December). The information processing approach to intelligence. In S. Newstead, S. Irvine, & P. Dann (Eds.), *Human assessment: Cognition and motivation* (pp. 27–42). Dordrecht: Martinus Nijhoff.

Hunt, E., & Davidson, J. (1981, November). *Age related changes in strategies for sentence verification.* Paper presented to the annual meeting of the Psychonomic Society.

Hunt, E., Davidson, J., & Lansman, M. (1981). Individual differences in long-term memory access. *Memory & Cognition, 9,* 599–608.

Hunt, E., & Farr, S. (1984, November). *Individual differences in attention.* Paper presented to Psychonomic Society meeting, San Antonio, TX.

Hunt, E., Frost, N., & Lunneborg, C. (1973). Individual differences in cognition: A new approach to intelligence. In G. Bower (Ed.), *Advances in learning and motivation, 7,* Orlando, FL: Academic Press.

Hunt, E., & Pellegrino, J. (1985). Using interactive computing to expand intelligence testing. *Intelligence, 9*(3), 207–236.

Johnson, W., & Kieras, D. (1983). Representation-saving effects of prior knowledge in memory for simple technical prose. *Memory and Cognition, 11,* 456–466.

Johnson-Laird, P. (1983). *Mental models.* Cambridge, MA: Harvard University Press.

Kamin, L. (1974). *The science and Politics of I. Q..* Hillsdale, NJ: Lawrence Erlbaum Associates.

Kearins, J. M. (1981). Visual spatial memory in Australian children. *Cognitive Psychology, 13,* 434–460.

Keating, D. P. (1984). The emperor's new clothes: The "new look" in intelligence research. In R. J. Sternberg (Ed.) *Advances in the psychology of human intelligence, Vol. 2.* Hillsdale, NJ: Lawrence Erlbaum Associates.

Kerr, B., Connon, S., & McDonald, L. A. (1985). Cognitive spatial processing and the regulation of posture. *Journal of Experimental Psychology: Human Perception and Performance, 11*(5), 617–622.

Kintsch, W., & Greeno, J. (1985). Understanding and solving word arithmetic problems. *Psychological Review, 92,* 109–129.

Kintsch, W., & Van Dijk (1978). Toward a model of text comprehension and production. *Psychological Review, 85,* 363–394.

Kolb, B., & Whishaw, I. Q. (1980). *Fundamentals of human neuropsychology.* San Francisco: Freeman Press.

Lansman, M., Poltrock, S., & Hunt, E. (1983). Individual differences in the ability to focus and divide attention. *Intelligence, 7,* 299–312.

Larkin, J., McDermott, J., Simon, D., & Simon, H. (1980). Expert and novice performance in solving physics problems. *Science, 208,* 1335–1342.

Lave, J., Murtagh, M., & De la Roche, O. (1984). The dialectic of arithmetic in grocery shopping. In B. Ragoff & J. Lave (Eds.), *Everyday cognition: Its development in social context.* Cambridge, MA: Harvard University Press.

Light, L. L., Zelinski, E., & Moore, M. (1982). Adult age differences in reasoning from new information. *Journal of Experimental Psychology: Learning, Memory and Cognition, 8,* 435–447.

Lohman, D. (1979). Spatial ability: A review and reanalysis of the correlational literature (Tech. Rep. #8). Stanford University, Department of Educational Psychology.

Longstreth, L. E. (1984). Jensen's Reaction-time investigations of intelligence: A critique. *Intelligence, 8*(2), 139–160.

MacLeod, C., Hunt, E., & Mathews, N. (1978). Individual differences in the verification of sentence-picture relationships, *Journal of Verbal Learning and Verbal Behavior, 17,* 493–507.

Marr, D. (1982). *Vision.* San Francisco: W. H. Freeman.

Marshalek, B., Snow, R. E., & Lohman, D. F. (1984). The complexity continuum in the radex and hierarchial models of intelligence. *Intelligence, 7*(2), 107–128.

Mazziotia, J. C., Phelps, M. E., Carson, R. E., & Kuhl, D. E. (1982). Topographic mapping of human cerebral metabolism: Auditory stimulation. *Neurology, 32,* 921–937.

McGee, M. G. (1979). Human spatial abilities: Psychometric studies and environmental, genetic, hormonal, and neurological influences. *Psychological Bulletin, 86,* 889–918.

Miller, G. A. (1956). The magic number seven, plus or minus two: Some limits on our capacity for processing information. *Psychological Review, 63,* 81–97.

Minsky, M., & Papert, S. (1969). *Perceptions.* Cambridge, MA: MIT Press.

Nunnaly, J. (1978). *Psychometric theory.* New York: McGraw-Hill.

Palmer, J., MacLeod, C., Hunt, E., & Davidson, J. (1985). Information processing correlates of reading. *Journal of Memory and Language, 24,* 59–88.

Pellegrino, J. W., & Glaser, R. (1979). Cognitive correlates and components in the analysis of individual differences. *Intelligence, 3,* 187–214.

Pellegrino, J. W., & Kail, R., Jr. (1982). Process analysis of spatial aptitude. In R. J. Sternberg (Ed.) *Advances in the psychology of human intelligence, Vol. 1.* Hillsdale, NJ: Lawrence Erlbaum Associates.

Posner, M. I. (1978). *Chronometric explorations of mind.* Hillsdale, NJ: Lawrence Erlbaum Associates.

Pylyshyn, Z. (1983). *Computation and cognition.* Cambridge, MA: Bradford Books.

Raven, J. C. (1965). *Advanced progressive matrices, Sets I and II,* London: Lewis Company.

Riley, M. S., Heller, J., & Greeno, J. (1983). Development of children's problem-solving ability in arithmetic. In H. P. Ginsburg (Ed.), *The development of mathematical thinking* (pp. 153–196). New York: Academic Press.

Schank, R. C. (1975). *Conceptual Information Processing.* New York: American Elsevier.

Schank, R. C. (1971). Finding the conceptual content and intention of an utterance in natural language conversation. *Proceedings of 2nd International Joint Conference on Artificial Intelligence,* 444–454.

Shannon, C., & Weaver, W. (1949). *The mathematical theory of information.* Urbana, IL: University of Illinois Press.

Shepard, R. N., & Cooper, L. A. (1982). *Mental images and their transformation.* Cambridge, MA: MIT Press.

Smith, E. E. (1968). Choice reaction time: An analysis of major theoritical positions. *Psychological Bulletin, 69,* 77–110.

Snow, R. E. (1986). A framework for aptitude theories. In S. E. Newstead, S. H. Irvine, & P. L. Dann, (Eds.), *Human assessment: Cognition and motivation,* (pp. 125–135). Dordrecht: Martinus Nijhoff Publishers.

Spearman, C. (1927). *The abilities of man.* New York: Macmillan.

Stankov, L. (1983). The role of competition in human abilities revealed through auditory tests. *Multivariate behavioral research monographs, 83–1.*

Stankov, L., & Horn, J. (1980). Human abilities revealed through auditory tests. *Journal of Educational Psychology, 72,* 21–44.

Sternberg, R. J. (1977a). Component process in analogical reasoning. *Psychological Review, 84,* 353–378.

Sternberg, R. J. (1977b). *Intelligence, information processing and analogical reasoning.* Hillsdale, NJ: Lawrence Erlbaum Associates.

Sternberg, R. J. (1984). Toward a trearchic theory of human intelligence, *Behavioral and Brain Sciences, 7*(2), 269–287.

Sternberg, R. J. (1985). *Beyond I.Q.* Cambridge: Cambridge University Press.

Sternberg, S. (1969). Memory scanning: Mental processes revealed by reaction time experiments. *American Scientist, 57,* 421–456.

Sternberg, S. (1975). Memory scanning: New findings and current controversies. *Quarterly Journal of Experimental Psychology, 27,* 1–32.

Thurstone, L. L. (1938). *Primary mental abilities.* Chicago: University of Chicago Press.

Underwood, B. J. (1975). Individual differences as a crucible in theory construction, *American Psychologist, 30,* 128–134.

Van Dijk, T. A., & Kintsch, W. (1983). Strategies of discourse comprehension. Orlando, FL: Academic Press.

Vernon, P. E. (1961). *The structures of human abilities.* London: Methuen.

3

Toward a Cognitive Theory for the Measurement of Achievement

Robert Glaser
Alan Lesgold
Susanne Lajoie
*Learning Research and Development Center,
University of Pittsburgh*

INTRODUCTION

Given the demands for higher levels of learning in our schools and the press for education in the skilled trades, the professions, and the sciences, we must develop more powerful and specific methods for assessing achievement. We need forms of assessment that educators can use to improve educational practice and to diagnose individual progress by monitoring the outcomes of learning and training. Compared to the well-developed technology for aptitude measurement and selection testing, however, the measurement of achievement and diagnosis of learning problems is underdeveloped. This is because the correlational models that support prediction are insufficient for the task of prescribing remediations or other instructional interventions. Tests can predict failure without a theory of what causes success, but intervening to prevent failure and enhance competence requires deeper understanding.

The study of the nature of learning is therefore integral to the assessment of achievement. We must use what we know about the cognitive properties of acquired proficiency and about the structures and processes that develop as a student becomes competent in a domain. We know that learning is not simply a matter of the accretion of subject-matter concepts and procedures; it consists rather of organizing and restructuring of this information to enable skillful procedures and processes of problem representation and solution. Somehow, tests

41

must be sensitive to how well this structuring has proceeded in the student being tested.

The usual forms of achievement tests are not effective diagnostic aids. In order for tests to become usefully prescriptive, they must identify performance components that facilitate or interfere with current proficiency and the attainment of eventual higher levels of achievement. Curriculum analysis of the content and skill to be learned in a subject matter does not automatically provide information about how students attain competence about the difficulties they meet in attaining it. An array of subject-matter subtests differing in difficulty is not enough for useful diagnosis. Rather, qualitative indicators of specific properties of performance that influence learning and characterize levels of competence need to be identified.

In order to ascertain the critical differences between successful and unsuccessful student performance, we need to appraise the knowledge structures and cognitive processes that reveal degrees of competence in a field of study. We need a fuller understanding of what to test and how test items relate to target knowledge. In contrast, most of current testing technology is *post hoc* and has focused on what to do after test items are constructed. Analysis of item difficulty, development of discrimination indices, scaling and norming procedures, and analysis of test dimensions and factorial composition take place after the item is written. A theory of acquisition and performance is needed before and during item design.

Recent work in cognitive psychology is a good start toward a theory to underpin such measurement. Modern learning theory is taking on the characteristics of a developmental psychology of performance changes—the study of changes that occur as knowledge and complex cognitive strategies are acquired, and the study of conditions that can influence these transitions in competence. Achievement measurement must be designed to assess these performance changes. It must be cast in terms of development, or levels of acquisition, and must be informed by knowledge of sources of difficulty and facilitators of the growth of competence.

In essence, the theme of this chapter is that the measurement of achievement should be based on our knowledge of learning and of the course of acquisition of competence in the subject matters that we teach. We begin by sketching some findings of cognitive psychological research that have implications for achievement test design. We then give additional research examples from various subject-matter fields. A third section describes several analytic methods from our work that we think can be extended into new testing formats. Throughout, we emphasize the necessary inseparability of instruction and assessment and we consider, in this connection, the design of intelligent computer tutors, which require both an instructional and a testing capability. We conclude with suggested ingredients for a set of cognitive principles for achievement measurement.

COGNITIVE RESEARCH RELEVANT TO THE MEASUREMENT OF ACHIEVEMENT

A psychology of learning that can inform testing must address two central problems.

- First, we must understand how subject-matter knowledge is structured and how it changes with learning. That is, we need to understand the knowledge structure indicators of achievement.

- Second, we must understand how a particular piece of knowledge, a single performance rule, or a part of a procedure, becomes more reliable, flexible, adaptive, and automatic with practice. That is, we need to understand the performance indicators of achievement.

Knowledge Structures

A substantial body of research has been carried out on the knowledge structures that characterize experts in a domain. Unlike past research, which tended to concentrate on the prerequisites of learning, this work attempts to determine the nature of competent performance by examining the underlying cognitive structures of the expert. It therefore has the potential to reveal how processes are transformed in the course of a person's progress from the novice to the expert state of performance. The research shows that, compared to novices' knowledge structures, experts' knowledge structures are both wider and deeper. That is, they contain more concepts, with more detail about each and with more interconnections among them. However, since it appears that little can be learned without at least a partial theory to lend it coherence (Murphy & Medin, 1985), we can assume that the understanding even of novices is held together by at least a primitive organizational structure, or *personal theory*. Since personal theories evolve as more is learned, bootstrapping further learning, the type of theory a person currently holds for a domain can serve as an index of and basis for his progress in acquiring the knowledge of that domain.

Carey (1985) has studied the evolution of theories that children hold at different points in their cognitive development, concentrating on such domains as basic biology. Her work suggests that related reasoning and problem solving are greatly influenced by experience with new information. In her research on animistic thinking in children, she has shown how children's knowledge influences their conceptualization of being "alive" and how such a concept becomes more differentiated with time through school learning and experience in the world. For instance, a 5-year-old's knowledge of biological properties is organized in terms of the child's knowledge of human activities, whereas a 10-year-old's knowledge is organized in terms of biological functions. Asked whether worms or plants breathe, the younger children respond based on their experience of how human beings breathe and say "no," since they see nothing like a moving chest in a worm or plant; older children, who have been exposed to school-taught notions of respiration, are more likely to answer that worms and plants do breathe. Such abstract pervasive changes in the child's reasoning and learning abilities are repeated as knowledge is gained in various domains.

The theories that we have for domains that are acquired partly on the basis of everyday experience are extremely stable. They are not easily rejected in the face of counterevidence, especially if that counterevidence comes from a textbook or lecture. This has been noted in a variety of studies showing that students do not relinquish their naive views about force and motion even after a physics course (Champagne, Klopfer, & Anderson, 1980; Larkin, 1983), and Carey has made similar observations. For example, after a long interview in which many internal organs were discussed, children of ages 4 through 6 were asked what part of their body was most important. In spite of all the new information about internal organs, they tended to name an external feature such as nose, toes, or hair, something related to their self-observations of their activity, consistent with their activity-based theories about life.

Personal theories seem to have the same sort of resilience and ability to withstand counterevidence that are seen in scientific theories that are socially shared, and the abandonment of one personal theory for another may well be revolutionary rather than evolutionary, just as seems to be the case with scientific theories (Kuhn, 1962). The robustness of personal theories implies that in order to facilitate learning, i.e., transitions in knowledge structures, it is necessary to confront a person's theories with specific challenges and contradictions. Understanding how counterevidence and knowledge confrontation assist in the transition between levels of competence, we should be able to design instruction that will help students build from their existing repertoires. The research on personal theory building that will be most useful to an improved technology of measurement aims at (1) understanding the stages through which personal theories pass well enough to be able to detect them, and (2) being able to prescribe forms of instructional intervention that are appropriate to those stages.

Automaticity, Proceduralization, and Practice

John Anderson (1983) has developed a theory of the development of skilled performance based on the work of Fitts (1964). It divides the course of learning into three parts: the declarative stage, the knowledge compilation stage, and the procedural stage. Initial performance in a novel situation involves the operation of general strategies that use declarative knowledge to guide performance. *Declarative knowledge* refers to verbal rules or facts regarding a task. Accessing these bits of information may be a slow process in this stage, and the task procedure is slow, laborious, and requires conscious attention. A child learning to tie a shoe or to do subtraction, possibly verbalizing aloud, losing track if he or she is interrupted, is probably in the declarative stage of acquiring a skill.

The conversion of slow declarative knowledge into faster compiled procedures occurs in the second stage of acquisition, *knowledge compilation.* Knowledge compilation is analogous to compilation of a computer program, the translation of that program from an understandable verbal form to commands, in the form of bit patterns, that can be directly executed by the computer hardware. Compiled knowledge, like a compiled program, runs faster but at the cost of greater difficulty in modification. Compiled procedures are relatively automatic. They can be represented as systems of condition-action pairs called *productions,* which state an action to be performed whenever its associated condition, which is a specific memory state, is attained. A production normally proceeds without conscious control except when one of the conditions for productions is a goal state that has to be set consciously. For example, anyone who, after years of tying shoes, has tried to give verbal directions to a child realizes that even though he now ties shoes very efficiently, he no longer remembers the instructions he was once given and doesn't quite know what to say to the child. Knowledge compilation consists of two processes, *proceduralization* and *composition. Proceduralization* can be compared to the primary activity of compilation in a computer, but it is driven by experience-established connections rather than by a parsing process alone. If one successfully uses specific declarative-knowledge in a specific setting, then the conditions at the time of the successful action are combined with the memory state needed to produce the action and stored in memory as a production. *Composition* takes place when two productions execute successfully in immediate sequence and thus become combined into a single production. It is similar to local optimization in a computer compiler. Proceduralization, then, is an automation process, whereas composition is an abbreviation process.

In Anderson's third stage the newly acquired productions become *tuned.* That is, they become strengthened, so that they prevail over other conflicting productions whose conditions may also match the same memory states, and their conditions for execution are more completely specified, through generalization and discrimination processes reminiscent of those described by Hull (1943) and Spence (1956).

A theory of skill acquisition such as this one has implications for test developers, since it identifies stages of learning and practice that are informative for instructional purposes. Lesgold (1984a; Lesgold, Rubinson, Feltovich, Glaser, Klopfer & Wang, in press) provided an example of how such a theory describes one aspect of the acquisition of expertise in medical diagnosis. Consider a resident who makes a faulty diagnosis during patient rounds. The attending physician may ask a series of questions that essentially walk the resident through the correct diagnosis. In spite of demonstration that this resident has the correct declarative knowledge, he or she is unable to organize the information in a manner that would lead to the correct solution because proceduralization has not taken place. The assessment of what knowledge needs to become organized and how to facilitate the proceduralization of such knowledge can greatly enhance instruction.

Of course, learning involves more than the proceduralization of declarative knowledge. Recall that we asserted in the previous section that new knowledge is acquired through the filter of one's personal theory. There are strong constraints on the verbal knowledge the student constructs from the things he experiences and is told. Consequently, a cognitive psychology of learning that deals only with what happens after the knowledge is already developed (albeit in fragile, declarative form) is not sufficient. Nonetheless, just as we have stated goals relating to the initial construction of knowledge, we can state some goals that a cognitive theory of measurement ought to have for dealing with practice and the automation of knowledge.[1]

A major emphasis in assessment should be to understand how the successive stages of learning, declarative, compiled, and tuned, manifest themselves in measurable performances. Combined with knowledge of how to foster progress from one stage to the next, this understanding will enable us to diagnose, to measure performance and to prescribe instruction based on those measurements. If we can develop both the capability to measure the stage of learning and the ability to assess which level of personal theory a student holds in a domain, then we should be able to make even stronger diagnoses.

Instruction might then guide the development of both the necessary declarative knowledge and its subsequent proceduralization and tuning. An emphasis on the conditions that foster the development of procedures, both simple and composite, will be necessary. Presumably, when teaching beginners we must build from their initial knowledge structures. This might be accomplished by assessing and using relevant prior knowledge, or by providing obvious organizational schemes or temporary models as scaffolds for new information. These temporary theories could be incorporated systematically into instruction. Such structures, when they are used, tested, and perhaps falsified by novices in the course of learning and experience, should lead to organizations of knowledge that are the basis for the more complete theories of experts. As well as assisting in developing theories, instruction can also systematically provide learners with the practice necessary for knowledge compilation and can encourage tuning by providing multiple contexts affording a chance to learn where certain procedures are applicable. This instructional emphasis should encourage discrimination and generalization of productions, leading to more robust, flexible, and efficiently

---

[1]We concede, of course, that these are not necessarily totally separate enterprises. How well certain components of a personal theory are automated may play a role in how resistant it is to being overthrown.

organized schemata[2] that allow the individual to perform appropriately under a variety of conditions. Acquiring expertise is to be seen as the successive development of efficient, tuned knowledge structures that facilitate the development of higher levels of competence.

A somewhat different approach to understanding the development of skilled performance is found in the work of Schneider (1984), whose research on the role of practice in training high levels of skilled performance also has several implications for assessment and instruction. We see Schneider's research as consistent with Anderson's theory of acquisition. Schneider, however, concentrates on an account of the development of automaticity, corresponding in particular with the knowledge-compilation stage. Environments must be designed, he asserts, to provide for the development of simple procedures. Once such procedures are developed, the sequence of instruction can facilitate a generalization between congruent procedures, fostering the composition and compilation process. He also suggests that construction of hierarchical knowledge structures can be facilitated by providing practice opportunities in multiple contexts, controlling the sequencing of levels of difficulty, and providing sufficient challenge and opportunities for success.

The areas of his investigations that could influence more diagnostic forms of achievement measurement to aid instruction include work on (1) identifying and training subskills rather than concentrating exclusively on total task instruction; (2) assessing levels of skill acquisition in order to facilitate the proper sequencing of instruction; (3) assessing individual differences in ceiling performance on a task; and (4) assessing the motivational aspects of learning the material under consideration.

In designing practice that is sufficient to produce high skill levels, Schneider suggests an emphasis on practicing consistent components of the task before practicing the task as a whole, even before the student understands a consistent mapping of required actions onto conditions. In other words, it is not just the amount of practice but also the focus of practice that matters. Schneider's approach places great importance on another goal for cognitive measurement theory: to formulate rules for deciding when a component skill is practiced enough to be integrated with other components to form a higher-order skill.

These contributions to theories of learning dealing with the role of practice have provided guides to the shaping of a diagnostic theory for the measurement of learning. For example, Schneider has suggested that goals for the level of proficiency to be attained must be set individually for different students, that different people show different cost-benefit functions for the marginal utility of

---

[2]Schemata are modifiable knowledge structures in memory that represent abstractions of experiences, including generic concepts, procedures, and situations (Glaser, 1984). They are used to interpret new instances of related knowledge (Rumelhart, 1975, 1981).

additional practice at different points in the course of learning. That is, not only the rate of learning but also the asymptote may vary from student to student. This poses another goal for diagnostic measurement, the assessment of potential for benefiting from particular components of an instructional program.

The bulk of the work in developing such a theory remains to be done. What we have now are some indicators of what a cognitive theory of measurement must be like. It must articulate with theories of learning and concentrate on shaping how we teach rather than whom we teach.

The Zone of Proximal Development

The idea of measurement techniques to measure the potential payoff of different instructional approaches is reminiscent of Vygotsky's theory of the zone of proximal or potential development, which was developed in the course of work on learning disabilities in the Soviet Union (Brown & French, 1979; Vygotsky, 1978). In this work, a distinction has been made between a child's actual developmental level (the level of mental functioning revealed in solo performance on a standardized test), and the child's level of potential development (the level of development that the child can achieve when offered certain forms of assistance). Both measures are considered essential for diagnosis and instruction. Vygotsky called the difference between these two levels the "zone of potential development," or "proximal development."

This zone of potential development is conceived of as an indication of learning potential. Thus, individuals with the same score on a mental ability test may vary in terms of their cognitive potential.[3] The relationship between assessments of the zone of potential and instructional strategies merits further research. The question is whether we could prescribe differential instructional treatment based on such a measure. Perhaps students with a large zone would do best being moved quickly through curricula, even skipping some units, while students with a small zone might require a slower, more complete treatment. In this manner, instruction might be prescribed so that learning neither lags behind potential nor pushes students beyond their capabilities. Presumably, motivation would be improved, too, if students were less likely to be overtaxed or bored. Extensions of Vygotsky's work (cf. Bransford, Delclos, Vye, Burns, & Hasselbring, 1986, and the chapters in Lidz, in press) represent an important step toward a cognitive instructional science of measurement.

---

[3]The distinction between crystallized and fluid intelligence (cf. Cattell, 1963) also seems to get at this issue.

Self-Regulatory and Metacognitive Skills

Metacognition has been defined in a number of ways across numerous subject domains and diverse populations. In general, though, metacognitive skills are generalized skills for approaching problems and for monitoring one's performance such as knowing when or what one knows, predicting the correctness of outcome of one's performance, planning ahead, efficiently apportioning one's time, and checking and monitoring one's thinking and performance (see Brown, 1978; Belmont & Butterfield, 1977; Borkowski, Cavanaugh, & Reichart, 1978; and Brown, Bransford, Ferrara, & Campione, 1983; for more extensive reviews). These skills, which act as control processes for cognitive performance, develop with maturity, and seem to be less developed in children with learning disabilities or those who are retarded. Brown (1978) suggests that these "executive processes" are a significant aspect of intelligence, since they determine when and where particular knowledge is used. Metacognitive skills are presumed to facilitate transfer of training to new situations.

In a sense, metacognitive skills represent, in part, performances that would be needed to realize the potential represented by the student's zone of proximal development. If we assess the zone of proximal development and attempt to specify and encourage the development of metacognitive skills, we are taking the first step toward trying to teach people to have larger zones. Thus, the movement toward task-analytic and instructional work on metacognitive skill is at the core of our aspirations for a technology of achievement assessment grounded in a cognitive instructional science.

Expert Performance

Understanding expertise is difficult because skillful performers appear to observe a set of rules that they themselves have difficulty verbalizing. This follows from the distinction made by J. Anderson between declarative and proceduralized knowledge (see p. 45), since experts can be assumed to have highly practiced repertoires of mental operations for tasks within their fields of competence. Seminal efforts to understand the nature of expert performance involved the study of skill in chess (Chase & Simon, 1973; de Groot, 1965, 1966; Simon & Chase, 1973). A series of experiments showed that the master chess player has a large repertoire of specific patterns that can be accessed in memory and quickly recognized. Chess expertise, to a large extent, is driven by rapid recognition processes that tap acquired structures of knowledge rather than by deep analytical thinking processes. Chess masters recognize the exact board situation they encounter and the strategies it entails; they do not excel by thinking ahead dozens of moves, as commonly thought; indeed they think ahead fewer moves than advanced players who are not yet at the master level (Chase & Simon, 1973).

Chess masters seem to have the ability to construct a qualitatively different representation of board positions than novice players, in terms of the aspects that they can immediately recognize and respond to (Chase & Chi, 1981). A similar phenomenon has been observed in more traditional school learning domains, such as physics, where highly competent performers also excel in developing an appropriate initial representation of a problem posed to them (Larkin, McDermott, Simon, & Simon, 1980; Simon & Simon, 1978). This representational skill allows the knowledgeable physicist to solve routine problems rapidly and without much conscious deliberation. An expert's representation of a physics problem tends to be organized around central principles of physics, whereas the knowledge of the novice is organized around more peripheral information such as the physical entities or objects described in the problem (Chi, Feltovich & Glaser, 1981).

The knowledge of experts and the mental representations they construct also include information regarding the application of what they know. In contrast, the novice's knowledge structure may be more loosely organized, containing the most centrally relevant information regarding the problem as stated but lacking the knowledge of related principles and their conditions of application. For this reason, novices may have more difficulty making inferences from the given problem statement. Their difficulties may be attributed to inadequacies of their knowledge bases as opposed to limitations on their capacities for carrying out problem solving processes.

In general, the competent individual can be described as having knowledge that is organized in a way that facilitates fast-access pattern recognition or encoding, greatly reducing mental processing load. These acquired knowledge patterns enable individuals to form an appropriate representation of the problem situation. The adequacy of the initial problem representation seems to be an index of developing competence, since the quality, completeness, and coherence of internal representations determine the efficiency and accuracy of further thinking. It seems appropriate then to consider the development of tests that will assess the learner's initial problem representations and level of knowledge organization.

Mental Models

Another research area with implications for a cognitive instructional theory of measurement deals both empirically and theoretically with the mental models that people construct in the course of solving problems. There are different kinds of mental models that are involved, and the implications for a theory of measurement may differ from one to the next. The "runnable" device or *qualitative process* model is perhaps the most important form. This type of model is a qualitative internal representation of a physical device along with a set of mental procedures for "running" that device, for simulating how the device changes as it operates. The *appearance* model is a related type, in which the person's procedural knowledge includes the ability to envision the appearance of a complex structure under various transformations. We discuss each of these below. In each case, we are concerned both with what is known about human capability and also with formal work attempting to specify what kind of modeling capability is needed to carry out various intelligent acts.

Qualitative Process Models. Qualitative physics is the effort to develop formalisms for representing the knowledge one can have about how things work (cf. de Kleer & Brown, 1984, and the entire issue of *Artificial Intelligence* in which it appears, "Qualitative Reasoning," 1984). One approach that has been taken is to represent each device in a system as a set of qualitative constraints (de Kleer & Brown, 1984). A device such as a resistor has qualitative constraints on it that are similar to Kirchhoff's current and voltage laws and Ohm's law. For example, the direction of change of current at one end of the resistor must match the direction of change in current at the other end, and the direction of change in resistance will be in the same direction as the change in voltage drop across the resistor. When devices are assembled into a system, the overall operation of the system can be envisioned by propagating the qualitative constraints of its components through the system. In a sense, then, running a device model is like solving a system of simultaneous quantitative equations.

It is very difficult to carry out this propagation mentally in real time. Experts tend to have highly practiced mental procedures for modeling a variety of common subassemblies of such systems. This makes them much faster, and at the limit more likely to succeed, in their mental modeling efforts. Further, because their modeling capability for routine situations is more efficient, they are more able to deal with novel variations from the routine. It should be possible to build tests of mental modeling capability by looking at relative speed and accuracy in an empirical progression of tasks such as (a) being able to state some of the constraints verbally but not being able to work with them, (b) having access to the most common, or classic, models in worked-out form, and (c) being able to modify these models to fit them to novel situations.

We have just begun in cognitive psychology to assess people's mental models, but this has been done in a few cases. For example, we can gather some of this information by asking people to predict the next state of objects in simple physics mechanics paradigms (McCloskey, Caramazza, & Green, 1980) or by asking them to describe simple electrical circuits (Gentner & Gentner, 1983, Riley, 1985). At LRDC, Jeffrey Bonar and his students have begun to develop environments in which subjects can make qualitative predictions of the effects of changes in a resistor network on various measurements in the network. We hope soon to be able to use such a capability to study possibilities for reliable mental model assessment.

Appearance Models. Another form of mental model is the *appearance model,* which represents how something looks or how it might look from various viewpoints. In studies we carried out on radiologists at differing levels of training, we realized that subjects varied in their ability to envision a patient's anatomy while looking at an x-ray picture. To assess their modeling ability, we asked them to draw, on the x-ray pictures, the contours of specific body structures (Lesgold, 1984a, Lesgold et al., in press). It was then possible to quantify performance by comparing the areas marked by the subjects with standard templates generated from expert protocols and other medical data. Measures such as proportion of template area covered by the subject's trace and proportion of the subject's trace that fell within the standard template region were computed. In this study, these measures were correlated with overall level of training and could be interpreted quite readily. Further, the subject's response (i.e., the tracing) could be input directly to a computer via various two-dimensional input devices, and the scoring done automatically.

Research on Acquisition of Subject Matters

It is in traditional school subject matters, of course, that achievement testing has had its widest application and most detailed development. Yet, perhaps it is school subject matters that most obviously demand a testing methodology that goes beyond normative scaling to become more relevant information for tailoring a student's instruction. As has been the case in testing methodology so far, different subject matters are likely to require different test item forms and perhaps even different overall testing approaches. We consider some of these in the sections that follow.

Reading. Progress has been made in understanding the nature of competence in reading, and there is beginning to be theory that might guide reading achievement test design. We can distinguish four reading processes that measurement should attend to. These four processes are: (a) word recognition; (b) accessing semantic word information; (c) sentence processing, and; (d) discourse analysis (see Curtis & Glaser, 1983).

A particularly important question is how the execution of one set of processes affects the efficiency of other reading processes. One component of the reading process that requires attention can affect reading comprehension by decreasing the amount of information maintained in memory and the amount of attention allocated to other processes. If, during reading, part of the thinking capacity is given over to word recognition, less capacity may remain for joining concepts that need to be interrelated in the reader's mind (Lesgold & Perfetti, 1978; Perfetti & Lesgold, 1977, 1979). That is, when word recognition is slow, comprehension processes become resource-limited (Norman & Bobrow, 1975), whereas faster recognition allows more effort to be directed to understanding what is read. In fact, poorer readers are generally slower at word recognition (Curtis, 1980; Lesgold & Curtis, 1981; Perfetti & Hogaboam, 1975).

Longitudinal research in the classroom, although difficult to implement, is a strong method for investigating the role of particular components (such as word recognition) over the course of learning a skill like reading. Rather than defining the development of learning in terms of grade level or age, the order in which subskills of reading are acquired can be specified directly if the same children are tested at different points in the course of their learning to read. This approach was used to observe the development of word recognition efficiency and its relation to comprehension skill development (Lesgold & Curtis, 1981; Lesgold, Resnick, & Hammond, 1985). Students were observed over a 4-year-period. Lesgold et al. (1985) examined student's reading efficiency in two reading curricula, one with an emphasis on word recognition training (phonics), and the other following a popular basal reading instruction program. Although no clear advantage was found for either curriculum, word processing speed measures did predict later reading comprehension in both groups. These results suggest that there are multiple approaches to developing reading comprehension but that automated word recognition is an important requirement for progress.

An interesting complication is that even though word recognition speed is the best predictor of reading achievement in the primary grades, as noted in the Lesgold study, listening comprehension becomes a better predictor thereafter (Curtis, 1980). This suggests that we do not yet have theories of the reading acquisition process adequate to support diagnostic testing. An adequate theory would have to account for the apparent fact that while word recognition ought to be the primary goal at the beginning of the curriculum, if a student is not doing well after several years, the focus needs to shift to comprehension skills. It will not suffice to use a checklist mastery approach, in which we have a schedule of subskills to be acquired, check off which ones the student has mastered, and diagnose that he should do the first thing on the list that is not yet checked.

A deeper understanding of how individuals retrieve word information can be used to guide assessment and instruction. There is a strong interdependency between ability to access the knowledge associated with words and overall comprehension skills. Three aspects of semantic retrieval capability seem to influence higher level processes: accuracy, flexibility, and fluency. (Beck, Perfetti, & McKeown, 1982). Understanding is not an all or none phenomenon; being accurate on one vocabulary item that uses a word does not necessarily mean that an individual fully understands that word. Items that reflect an individual's deeper knowledge of an item in terms of flexibility of usage in different contexts may be a more meaningful form of measurement. Qualitative differences in the levels of word knowledge can be assessed by presenting items that require specific and precise semantic discriminations (Curtis & Glaser, 1983). For instance, instead of a single word meaning question, a sequence of questions that reflect more detailed levels of understanding might be used, such as (a) *Which of the following synonyms best defines the word in question?* and (b) *Which of the following sentences uses the item correctly?* Contingent diagnostic testing sequences can be developed for individuals who vary in skill level. For example, if a student gets the simplest word meaning item incorrect, a subsequent question can be presented that gives the word in a context-providing sentence.

Thus, work to date suggests that diagnostic tests can be individualized to efficiently measure qualitative and quantitative differences in lexical/verbal knowledge. Efficient testing, in turn, might help make instruction more highly individualized. However, given the long history of difficulty in isolating multiple factors in tests of reading facility, it is clear that a sound theory of reading facility and its acquisition is needed before significant progress can be made. Recent efforts (e.g., Perfetti, 1985) seem a step toward such a theory.

Measuring comprehension skill raises a different set of issues. Understanding the sentences in a text requires prior knowledge. Knowledge of the topic or situation to which a passage refers, and knowledge of schemata, which are abstracted representations for situations and for discourse forms, can facilitate the understanding of passage content and its integration into existing memory organizations. Relevant schemata provide an interpretive framework for organizing the information mentioned in a text and for reading between the lines (inferring propositions which the author assumed did not have to be overtly stated, R. Anderson, 1978).

Hoepfner (1978) suggested that 10–20% of the items on reading comprehension tests assess schema-based knowledge. However, so long as these items are not recognized as dealing with a specific issue, their presence, through the natural selection processes involved in test construction and validation, does not provide any specialized diagnostic capability. If knowledge of specific schemata and prior knowledge of certain domains is a prerequisite to text comprehension and is not always sufficient, then comprehension items should be developed specifically to test for such knowledge. Another class of potentially useful items would test for inferential ability. Such comprehension tests would go beyond fact recall and test the subject's inferences based on the content of the passage. Presumably, these would be developed for discourse forms and topic domains for which the subject had previously demonstrated competence.

Another factor to consider when assessing discourse analysis is whether the examinee is having difficulty with comprehension in general or with reading in particular. This distinction generally is made by testing both reading and listening comprehension. However, it is important to note that comprehension in general is not wholly separable from reading comprehension; some argument forms simply cannot be presented orally, since they require too much temporary memory and therefore rely on the text itself as an external temporary memory.

To summarize, reading involves word recognition, lexical knowledge, knowledge of the forms in which discourses present information, and background knowledge for the domain about which any given text is written. Disciplined sequential testing strategies appear to have the potential for helping to isolate a student's reading problems to one or more of these areas. However, the current state, in which test items are developed without regard to a verified componential theory of reading acquisition and proficiency, and in which we lack the knowledge that would tell us that a specific item was measuring an identifiable skill component, does not permit tests to be used for detailed diagnosis.

Arithmetic.   Arithmetic, like reading, is a basic skill that involves considerable procedural facility. It differs from reading in being dependent only upon a fixed domain of schematic knowledge (reading skill depends on schematic knowledge of the text topic). Because the schemata needed for arithmetic performances are less numerous, more refined theoretical analysis has been possible. A major program of research began when Brown and Burton (1978) developed computer models of children's substraction performance. They decomposed subtraction into very small procedural steps. Then they constructed degraded models, each of which contained all but one, or a small number, of the components of the full model. Since each degraded model made different performance errors, it was possible to assess a student's knowledge by trying to match the pattern of his answers to a set of subtraction problems with the pattern produced by one of the degraded or "buggy" models.

However, representing arithmetic errors as "bugs," deficiencies of a needed program step, was not sufficient to account for students' performance (Brown & Van Lehn, 1980, 1982; Van Lehn, 1983a,b,c). It became apparent that, while the bug analyses could account for the performance of students with systematic errors on any one test, a given student's bug patterns did not remain constant from day to day. The theory, which evolved from cross-sectional comparisons, did not transfer well to providing longitudinal accounts. Working with Brown, Van Lehn worked out a more complex theory which he called "repair theory." Its essence is that "bugs" do underlie failure of arithmetic performance but that students realize that they have reached impasses in their performance and make attempts to repair their incomplete procedures. When their knowledge of the basic conceptual underpinnings of arithmetic is solid, these repairs produce correct performance, and they manifest no stable error pattern. When their conceptual knowledge is inadequate, they are forced to invent ways of accommodating what they do know. For example, a student who doesn't know how to do regrouping (borrowing), when faced with a problem like

$$\begin{array}{r} 100 \\ -33 \\ \hline \end{array}$$

may answer "133," reasoning that there has to be a number in each column of the answer. If he can't compute $0-3$, then he computes what he can, $3-0$, instead. However, he knows he is likely to be wrong, so he doesn't stick with the specific strategy of always subtracting smaller digit from larger but rather tries other approaches from time to time.

The important thing to learn from this body of work is that some diagnosis may require longitudinal data, that the current knowledge of a person cannot always be determined in sufficient detail to suggest a specific approach to remediation or further instruction from looking only at current performance. A secondary lesson is that formal modeling approaches and the comparison of student performance to that of alternative models can be very useful strategies in designing new approaches to diagnostic assessment.

Word Problems.   Quite a bit of work has been done on the kinds of problem solving that students are asked to do in school, such as the solving of arithmetic word problems. The general approach taken has been to attempt to specify the generic knowledge structures, or schemata, that subsume the knowledge needed to understand different categories of problem situations. As indicated above, schemata can be thought of as personal theories that we can test and revise. Learning can be thought of as being largely schema revision.

Riley, Greeno, & Heller (1983) have demonstrated that a small number of schemata can account for virtually all the arithmetic word problems that students are given in elementary school. Specifically, there are the following problem types, each of which requires different knowledge, i.e., a different schema:

- *Change.* Mary has i marbles and John gives her j more, so she has k in all. Any two of the three values would be given in the problem, and the student would have to find the third.

- *Combine.* Mary has i marbles and John has j. How many do they have altogether?

- *Compare.* Mary has i marbles and John has j. How many more does John have than Mary?

Further, Riley et al. suggested a developmental sequence for acquisition of these schemata. They found that problem schema type, rather than which arithmetic operations were required to solve a problem, was the best predictor of how early solution capability is acquired.

If solving a word problem requires knowing more than the arithmetic operations required to solve it, then the ability to diagnose student learning problems in arithmetic requires the ability to measure schematic knowledge, or to estimate it from the pattern of word problem types that a student can solve. Rather than simply looking at the total number of word problems a child solves, assessment procedures could examine or infer how students are representing the problem information. This form of measurement would indicate whether the student is having difficulty with the operations or with the semantic representation of the problem.

Writing. Recent work on the study of error in writing and composition has emphasized the identification of systematic misconceptions (see Bartholomae, 1980; Hayes & Flower, 1980; Hull, Ball, Fox, Levin, & McCutchen, 1985; Shaughnessy, 1977). While the same precision of error analysis that is seen in the mathematics work cannot be achieved in the writing domain, it is now clear that even students who write very poorly are following crude personal theories that they have formed for written communication. Systematic misconceptions or incomplete conceptions lead to errors, and can be detected from students' writing samples (Bartholomae, 1980). For example, poor writers may systematically mishandle verb endings, noun plurals, syntax, and sentence structure. If the current composition rules and schemata of a student can be determined, then presumably instruction can focus on specific efforts to move the student toward more appropriate understanding.

Like reading difficulty, poor written composition might, in principle, be due either to errors in general linguistic competence or to incomplete procedural rules for the specific medium, in this case writing. In order to rule out general linguistic competence as the problem in poor writers, Bartholomae had students read their writing samples out loud. In doing so he found that students, often unconsciously, corrected errors as they went along. This suggests that they have the general linguistic knowledge but do not have it, or cannot use it, in the specialized form needed to produce written products. As we refine our understanding of these procedural errors, we can better assess written composition and better develop individualized instruction aimed at repairing certain misconceptions and strengthening correct schemata.

Hull et al. (1985) used an extensive study of composition errors to develop computerized instruction in editing. Their software uses pattern matching techniques to assess systematic errors in writing and then helps students correct their own errors. Although this approach is still limited due to the complexity of error pattern detection in natural language texts, it has proven useful. By identifying errors, feedback can be provided to the learner regarding both the presence of errors and how to correct them. Highlighting of error regions in text-editor displays is used to help students learn to recognize and repair grammatical errors. Furthermore, instruction can be sequenced so that students can move from one level of skill to another, finding and correcting certain categories of errors and refining their own mental models. The integration of error identification with instructional remediation seems more promising as a diagnostic approach than are current tests of composition skill, although it remains unclear whether the breakthroughs are in diagnosis and individualized instruction or from increased understanding of the levels of competence in writing skills and of how learners can be assisted to acquire new knowledge given their current knowledge structures.

Scientific Concepts. An area in which much of instruction involves inducing change in students' schemata is science. There is now ample evidence that in certain cases where our environment provides a biased view of underlying natural processes, students tend to develop naive misconceptions that are extremely resistant to change (McCloskey, Caramazza & Green, 1980). For example, our everyday world, because of the friction effects of air and surfaces on which objects move, provides many experiences in which objects change velocity without being obviously affected by new forces. Thus, it is easy to conclude that force is required to sustain velocity, that velocity is proportional to force. After all, to go a constant speed in a car, you have to maintain constant pressure on the gas pedal. When students holding such misconceptions are exposed to formal physics instruction, they learn to solve physics problems that involve knowing that forces are proportional to accelerations, not velocities, but they do not generalize this knowledge to everyday life; they do not easily abandon their prior misconceptions. It seems unlikely that simply applying algorithms learned by rote will produce the needed learning. Thus, science instruction, like writing and arithmetic instruction, can be seen as involving diagnosis of a student's current schemata followed by efforts to move those schemata toward more expert form.

A methodology developed by Siegler (1976, 1978) is another promising approach to diagnostic measurement that is relevant here. Siegler assessed the underlying rule structure of certain cognitive performances and the progressive development of performance complexity in children. His "rule assessment" approach is based on two assumptions. The first is that human reasoning is rule governed, with the rules progressing from less sophisticated to more sophisticated as a function of age and learning. The second is that a way to assess these rule progressions is to develop diagnostic sets of problems that yield distinct performance patterns as a function of the rules a child knows. Just as with the arithmetic and writing research, this approach can determine what rules an individual uses in performing the task as well as what rules are common to various groups of individuals and age groups.

The first step in Siegler's procedure is to analyze the concept being studied. Through task analysis, one develops a first approximation of the condition-action pairing rules or specific rule knowledge that reflect competent performance on a task. Then, one attempts to characterize each known developmental stage as the presence of some subset of the final-stage rules or of rules with imperfect conditions or actions. The final analysis must be verified against actual children's performance. An acceptable set of rule stages has the property that each stage consists of only a small change, such as the acquisition of a rule or the elaboration of the conditions of a rule.

Siegler developed his rule assessment approach analyzing the performance of children on Inhelder and Piaget's (1958) balance beam task. The rules he identified involve understanding how balance is affected by the amount of weight applied, the distance of the weight from the fulcrum, the coordination of weight and distance, and finally how to compute the torques when necessary in order to choose the side of the scale with the greater value. These rules reflect a developmental progression in understanding the concept of balance. At this point, the methodology has not only provided a theoretical account of the capability being studied; it has also provided the basis for an instructionally diagnostic test. That is, one could identify a student's current stage and then proceed to teach him the rule or rule elaboration that enables performance at the next known stage.

Rule assessment approaches assume that conceptual development can be thought of as an ordered sequence of learned, partial understandings. If individuals learn concepts to various degrees of understanding and they develop understanding in a reasonably predictable fashion, the assessment of knowledge can be linked to appropriate instructional decisions. Rule assessment procedures, such as procedural analysis of arithmetic, error analysis in writing, and performance rules in scientific understanding, lead to diagnostic procedures that can provide deeper understanding of a subject matter that an individual brings to test performance. The concept of diagnosing test performance regularities at different levels of learning suggests a point of contact and possible integration of test theory, teaching practice, and the psychology of human cognition.

Technical Skill Development.   Cognitive research on the assessment of technical skills is just beginning. During the past 2 years, the Learning Research and Development Center has been conducting a study of the feasibility of cognitive task analysis procedures for use in determining who should be placed in particular Air Force job specialties, how they should be trained, and how their performance should be measured. Our results have important implications for assessment and instruction. In addition to the traditional procedure of using aptitude tests for selection and using achievement tests at most for correlational evaluation of selection and adaptive instruction, we expect to assess achievement throughout the learning process. An important characteristic of our work is to compare the trainees who are most competent on the job with those least competent. When done at several stages in the progression from beginning apprentice to master, this provides a developmental view of the characteristics associated with success at different stages in the course of training.

To develop a cognitive task analysis of an area as broadly defined as an Air Force specialty, we took a job component sampling approach. We generated a representative sample of the tasks involved and examined their perceived trouble spots extensively. We were able to compare better to worse performers and to develop preliminary hypotheses about the different stages of performance in the course of the airmen's on-the-job experience. Our goals were to identify the procedural and conceptual knowledge required for job proficiency in using specialized test stations to isolate parts failures in aircraft navigation equipment. In these components, what flows through wires can be thought of as a simple signal with a small number of defining parameters, such as voltage.

We paid particular attention to how high and low performers differed in both conceptual and procedural knowledge. We also identified skills that should be automated in order for airmen to concentrate on higher order troubleshooting issues, and we developed tests of their automaticity. In addition, we tested for depth and organization of fundamental concepts and for understanding, in terms of functional systems on the aircraft, of the units that they were required to test. Through extensive protocol collection we observed the airmen's initial problem representation and the constraints used to arrive at solutions. Each of these assessment devices was guided by cognitive theory. Much of the remainder of this chapter, especially the following section, is shaped by our experiences in this project.

COGNITIVE RESEARCH APPLIED TO TESTING METHODOLOGY

So far, we have tried to highlight cognitive research on learning and expertise that is potentially relevant to building a richer theory of educational measurement. Such a theory, though, must have methods as well as principles. In this next section, we describe several methods that seem promising.

The Assessment of Flexible Problem Solving Skill

Assessing relatively general problem solving skills is quite a different task from assessing specific, algorithmic performance capabilities that are part of the domain being taught. We have only begun to work on this problem, but a few possibilities already present themselves, particularly with respect to the more strategic, or metacognitive, skills of problem solving. To give a sense of our work, we trace the history of our efforts to analyze the performance of electronics technicians when they attempt to troubleshoot complex electronic circuitry. The complex cases are of particular interest because they are the ones where metacognitive skills are needed to organize processes which, in simple cases, might automatically lead to problem solution.

In our first attack on this problem, Drew Gitomer[4] developed a troubleshooting task that involved detection of complex faults in the test station used by our subjects. As a first formative approach, he simply videotaped subjects attempting to solve such fault detection problems. He then examined the protocols (transcriptions of the tapes) and attempted to count a variety of activities that seemed relevant to metacognitive as well as more tactical aspects of problem solving in this domain. While the results, published in his thesis (Gitomer, 1984), were of great interest, we wanted to move toward a testing approach that was less

---

[4]At the time a graduate student at LRDC.

dependent upon skilled cognitive psychological training. That, after all, is one aspect of what test development is largely about—rendering explicit the procedures that insightful researchers first apply in their laboratories to study learning and thinking.

Our breakthrough came not so much from our psychological expertise but rather from our interactions with an electronics expert[5] who had extensive experience watching novice troubleshooting performances. He pointed out that it was not a big chore to specify all of the steps that an expert would take as well as all of the steps that any novice was at all likely to take in solving even very complex troubleshooting problems. That is, even when the task was to find the source of a failure in a test station that contained perhaps 40 cubic feet of printed circuit boards, cables, and connectors, various specific aspects of the job situation constrained the task sufficiently so that the effective problem space could be mapped out. This then created the possibility that we could specify in advance a set of probe questions that would get us the information we wanted about subjects' planning and other metacognitive activity in the troubleshooting task. For what is probably the most complex troubleshooting task we have ever seen, there are perhaps 55 to 60 different nodes in the problem space, and we have specific metacognitive probe questions for perhaps 45.[6] Figure 3.1 provides an example of a small piece of the problem space and the questions we have developed for it.

An examination of the questions in the Figure reveals that some are aimed at very specific knowledge (e.g., *How would you do this?*), while others help elaborate the subject's plan for troubleshooting (consider *Why would you do this?* or *What do you plan to do next?*). Combined with information about the order in which the subject worked in different parts of the problem space, this probe information permits reconstruction of the subject's plan for finding the fault in the circuit and even provides some information about the points along the way at which different aspects of the planning occurred. In fact, we went a step further and also asked a number of specific questions about how critical components work and what their purpose is.

After reviewing the protocol, we developed six scales on which we scored each airman. Each of these scales could be further subdivided into subscales to permit more detailed and task-specific issues to be addressed. The six scales were titled *plans, hypotheses, device and system understanding, errors, methods and skills,* and *systematicity.* Table 3.1 gives two examples for each scale of the items for which points could be earned (in the error scale, more points means more errors and thus is a lower score).

---

[5]We are grateful to Mr. Gary Eggan for his many insights in this work.

[6]Debra Logan and Richard Eastman have been refining this technology in our laboratories (Logan & Eastman, 1986), and we expect that a more detailed account will be published by them at a later date.

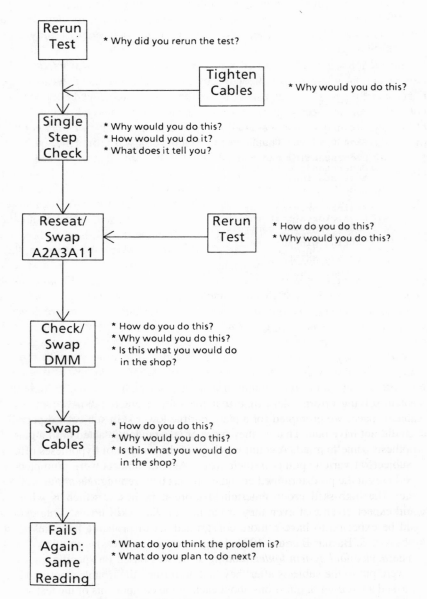

FIG. 3.1. Problem space map to guide probed protocol gathering.

TABLE 3.1
Examples of Criterion Questions Used to Score Protocols for Each
of the Six Problem-Solving Scales

● PLANS

   o Extend and test a card.
   o Trace through the schematic of an individual card

● HYPOTHESES

   o There is a short caused by a broken wire or a bad
     connection.
   o The ground is missing from the relay.

● DEVICE AND SYSTEM UNDERSTANDING

   o Understanding and use of the external control panel.
   o Understanding of grounds and voltage levels in the
     test station.

● ERRORS

   o Misinterpreting/misreading the program code, called
     FAPA, for a test that the test station carries out
     under computer control.
   o Getting pin numbers for a test wrong.

● METHODS AND SKILLS

   o Schematic understanding: Ability to interpret diagrams
     of relays, contacts, coils.
   o Ability to run confidence check programs.

● SYSTEMATICITY

   o The subject returns to a point where he knew what
     was going on when a dead end is encountered.
   o The path from the power source is checked.

Plans was a count of the number of plans mentioned by the subject during his problem-solving efforts. Any time that the subject entered a new part of the problem space, we prompted for a plan, but the lower skill subjects, especially, often did not have one. That is, they more or less randomly acted until a plan or hypothesis came to mind. A count was kept of the number of hypotheses offered by subjects at various points in their work. Again, subjects were prompted for hypotheses at the predetermined boundary points between regions of the problem space. The high-skill group entertained more hypotheses, which is what we would expect given that even they are at intermediate skill levels. True experts could be expected to have a more constrained set of probable hypotheses (cf. Benbassett & Bachar-Bassan, 1984; Lesgold et al., in press).

The *device and system understanding* scale was based on specific questions that were put to the subjects after they had performed the troubleshooting tasks. We asked a fixed set of questions about each of the components of the test station that played a role in the problems we had posed. These questions probed for knowledge about how the component worked, what role it played in the test station, what its general purpose in electronic system was, and what it looked like. The *errors* scale was simply a count of the number of incorrect steps taken by the airman in trying to troubleshoot the system. The *methods and skills* measure tallied which of the procedures needed to carry out the troubleshooting of the test station were successfully demonstrated by the subject. Finally, the *systematicity* measure consisted of a set of relatively broad criteria gauging the extent to which troubleshooting proceeded in a systematic manner rather than haphazardly or without a sense of goal structure.

With these scales, it is possible to provide a reasonable account of the components of performance. That is, there were no statements or behavior sequences of the airmen that could not be counted on one of our scales. This demonstrates that it is feasible to measure directly such complex cognitive performances as fault isolation in massive circuitry. By careful planning and the use of expert consultants with on-the-job supervisory and training experience, it is possible to develop measurement approaches that can help pinpoint a technician's stage of acquisition and, consequently, the level of further training needed. The approach is still rather expensive, but we feel that it is rapidly reaching the level of rigor associated with good experimental technique. Given its potential for more direct ties to theory by sharpening the criteria for the various scales used, it compares quite favorably with traditional approaches, which involve multiple-choice questions about somewhat simpler and less job-linked knowledge.

Gaining Objectivity and Simplicity

While cognitive psychology provides much guidance on what tests should be measuring, it has not so far contributed much to the technology of low-cost measurement. This optimization of cognitive measurement methods is critical to bringing cognitive science to bear on testing. If cognitive measurements cost two or three orders of magnitude more, they will not be used, even if they are the best alternative. We need to start searching for a middle ground between the overly-constraining 5-foil multiple-choice item and expensive verbal protocol procedures such as that just described. The multiple-choice formats currently used present two problems for us. On the one hand, they do not allow all of the responses subjects are likely to make to be included as alternatives, so great care is needed to understand how the range of possible student approaches will map onto a restricted set of possible answers. On the other hand, they tend to "give away" some aspects of the solutions to problems. That is, they can only be used where recognizing that one has a correct solution is sufficient performance. Below, we discuss some new ways to extend simple forced choice methods into the realm of complex cognitive activity. These approaches come closer to being "direct readouts" of knowledge and thus are more useful in building a representation of a person's cognitive capabilities.

Hierarchical Menus Methodology[7]

Computer-based menu systems offer the opportunity for extending the multiple-choice technology almost infinitely. Traditional multiple-choice tests require selection from a small set of alternatives. More elaborate alternatives have not generally worked well, probably because they impose a greater verbal processing load on the subject, who must keep in mind too much information at once in order to use them well. What the computer offers is the possibility of complex, choice-specific follow-up to individual items without placing any new test-taking skills demands on the subject.

In a sense, all computerized adaptive testing involves contingent sequencing of multiple-choice items. However, in existing adaptive procedures, the sequencing is not based on the content of the items, but rather on their classification into pools of different difficulty levels and different subscales. The same basic idea can be used to develop a cognitively oriented adaptive questioning procedure that is driven by propositional inferences rather than by statistical inference. The approach can best be understood through an example.

Suppose we wanted to know whether a student knew how to compute the mean of a set of numbers. If we simply want to determine whether he has this skill completely or not, we could make up simple multiple-choice items, such as the following:

The mean of the numbers 1, 3, 4, 10, and 15 is (a) 6.6; (b) 33; (c) 5; (d) 4; or (e) 15.

If the student chooses *a*, then he is correct. However, we can learn from the errors, since *b* is the answer one would get if every step but the final division were carried out, *c* is the count of the numbers, *d* is the median value, and *e* is the maximum. However, we cannot actually see how the student tried to represent and solve this problem, so we don't have any ability to separate correct knowledge that is not sufficiently practiced from incorrect knowledge. It would be useful to be able to give a test that objectively and replicably recovered the actual content of the student's performance on this problem. From that, we could construct remediation, additional practice activity, or additional new instruction that might serve the student better.

Jeffrey Bonar in our laboratories has developed an approach to computer-based programming instruction (called BRIDGE) that can do this. The approach is based on a hierarchical menu scheme. The subject is asked a broad question

---

[7]This section is very much inspired by an approach Jeffrey Bonar has taken to the development of menu alternatives to natural-language input for computer-based instructional systems.

that can be answered by choosing one of several alternatives. The choice of alternative also determines the nature of followup questioning. Finally, the whole process can be repeated several times to allow specification of a multistep solution to a problem. The methodology rests upon a combination of a full analysis of the task to be performed by the subject and a set of protocols of people trying to do the task.

In fact, one of the tasks that Bonar has worked with is writing a computer program to compute the mean of a set of numbers. In most current computer languages, this is done more or less as follows:

```
Set a counter to zero
Set a sum register to zero
Read the first number to be included in the average
While the current number is not the termination code do
     Increase the counter by 1
     Add the current number into the sum register
     Read the next number
If the counter is not equal to zero
     Divide the sum register value by the counter value and
     Place the quotient in the sum register
Print the sum register value
```

Unfortunately, no questioning scheme based on the correct algorithm will work. This is because there is a very different way that students think about this problem before learning computer programming. A student asked to describe what he would do will say something like this:

> Get the first number and write it down unless it is the stop code. Then do this over again for each new number. When you reach the stop code, count the numbers and add them up. Divide the sum by the count, and that's your answer.

What Bonar has done is to give problems like this to a large sample and then analyze the procedures they wrote down. After completing these analyses, he was able to create a hierarchical menu system that allows students to specify their algorithms in ways that do not make it appear that they understand more than they really do. For example, it distinguishes between formally specifying an iterative process and simply stating that some steps must be repeated without being explicit about which steps or about the condition for ending the iterative loop. Recently, the same problems were given to a set of enlisted military personnel. Their performance could be fully accommodated by the set of options originally generated in response to protocols from college students, so the method seems robust.

Figure 3.2 shows the computer screen at a point where this interrogation is underway. Bonar's hierarchical menus allow specification even of very complex algorithms because of the followup questioning capability, and because each step already specified is displayed on the computer screen. For example, if the subject picks the REPEAT option from the menu, he is then prompted to indicate which items should be repeated. He is also asked to specify how to decide when to stop the repetition. The options for stopping the repetition can include simple tests, tests based on the result of procedures, and implicit tests (do it for every member of a defined set). We see this approach as an important step toward the building of cognitively oriented diagnostic tests. To some extent, Bonar's work bears out our beliefs. He is using this type of menu capability in a programming tutor as the basis for coaching the student toward the specification of precise algorithms and finally the specification of an actual computer program.

To summarize the last sections, we see great promise in such computer-based approaches to testing. These approaches will go beyond and build upon many of the best intuitions of current test item writers and computerized adaptive testing researchers. One new aspect of the work will be deeper, more interactive interrogation via menu-based systems supported by graphics and other verbal-load-reducing aids. A second will be processing of the test responses that is driven by logical inference from knowledge of the domain and knowledge of how students learn in the domain rather than only by statistical inference based on normative item difficulty and internal consistency data.

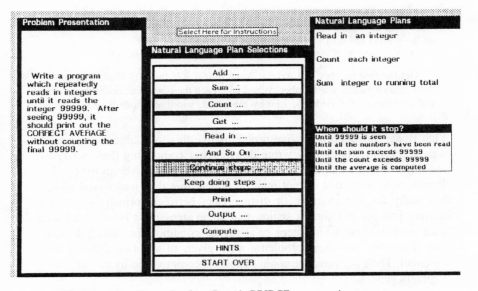

FIG. 3.2.   Menu illustration from Bonar's BRIDGE programming tutor.

The Procedural Ordering Task:[8] Measuring Sensitivity to Constraints

In a number of areas of skilled performance, the range of acceptable responses to a situation is often quite wide and the constraints often are rather abstract. This makes the measurement of competence quite difficult. Consider a case recently encountered by Richard Eastman, one of the research assistants in our group. We were attempting to measure how well airmen could carry out the task of reassembling a complex part of a jet engine after overhaul. The procedure we thought likely to work well was an ordering task. We would take the actual steps of the reassembly task directly out of the manufacturer's manual, print each step on a card that also included a picture of that step, and see if the airmen could sort the cards. This seemed very straightforward until we found that there was no correlation between performance in this task and our other indices of expertise.

This led Eastman to interview several known experts. When he asked them why they had not used the ordering indicated in the documentation, they pointed out the underlying constraints on successful performance and also clarified how the procedures specifically listed in the manufacturer's documentation were inefficient ways to satisfy those constraints. The constraints all involved preserving the calibration of an information pathway between the engine and a gauge in the cockpit of the plane. The manufacturers, wanting to get foolproof instructions written quickly, had never included the constraints in the documentation. Rather, they had chosen to write a set of instructions that, while inefficient, would keep them out of trouble, since they happened to preserve the constraints.

Making up test items based only on the documentation would have failed to capture the full range of knowledge that is included in this particular brand of expertise.[9] Further, it was necessary to have deeper understanding ourselves than could be gleaned from the printed materials that would have driven most standard test-writing exercises in this area. Finally, we should note that a particular expert's favorite alternative to the textbook method could still have two forms: rote knowledge and conceptually-deep knowledge. That is, a mechanic might simply be following someone else's approach rather than the book's but still understand neither.

To get around this problem, Eastman cleverly designed a family of sorting tasks that varied in which devices were already fitted to the engine and which still had to be attached. Knowing the constraints, an expert would sometimes be able to leave a piece of the system attached rather than having to remove everything and start from scratch. However, to preserve calibration, it is also sometimes

---

[8]This task was developed by Richard Eastman as part of the cognitive task analysis project we conducted for the Air Force Human Resources Laboratory.

[9]We take no position on whether such instructions should be followed in every case simply to preserve a disciplined approach to maintenance—that is an Air Force issue.

necessary to remove an already-installed component which cannot be finally calibrated until some other device has been attached. Thus, unless the airman has learned dozens of rote variations of the assembly procedure, he will not be able to give optimal and still safe performances in these varying situations. Further, it is possible to model the sorting performance for such a family of tasks.

When Eastman looked at the pattern of errors for a small sample, he found evidence consistent with two hypotheses. First, the errors made by rank beginners tended to involve orderings of activity that are physically impossible (e.g., one can't get device A attached if device B is already attached and in the way). Later in the course of acquisition, the errors were more deeply conceptual (you could get all the parts together that way, but the information pathways would not be calibrated). We have experimented with computerized presentation of this kind of ordering task, and it seems quite straightforward.

In our preliminary efforts, we present the steps of a procedure as a menu on a workstation equipped with a pointer device called a mouse. When the subject points to an entry in the menu, the step is illustrated on a high-resolution screen, minimizing unnecessary verbal load. Pressing a button on the mouse causes the item to which the subject is pointing to be added to an ordered list of steps. A simple arrangement allows the subject to rearrange that ordering until he is satisfied with it. He then points to a box labeled "Done" and presses the mouse button. By having a list of constraints of each type, the computer can then report scores for physical adequacy as well as functional adequacy of the proposed orderings. The testing can be repeated with different starting scenarios to establish the character of the subject's knowledge.

The ability to produce or alter graphical displays is an important new capability. We see many possibilities for new test forms that involve pointing to locations or tracing regions in graphic displays. This approach, and others that provide more direct expressions of subjects' knowledge (as opposed to the ability to verbalize about knowledge), will be helpful to the development of a cognitively based testing technology for technical training.

INTELLIGENT TUTORING SYSTEMS: LABORATORIES FOR INTEGRATING TESTING AND INSTRUCTION

At the Learning Research and Development Center, we have embarked on a substantial program developing intelligent computer-assisted instructional systems—expert systems for teaching and training. We have done this for at least two reasons. First, we feel that sufficiently facile tutoring systems can help teachers improve their teaching skills as well as directly tutor students. Second, we see the expert instructional system as a primary laboratory for testing emerging principles for measurement and instruction. Since expert systems are driven by explicitly specified knowledge, they are direct empirical tests of the hypotheses embodied by that knowledge. In this section, we concentrate on possibilities for testing hypotheses that involve the measurement of performance.

Tutor Architectures and Adaptive Instruction

Intelligent tutoring systems are the ideal laboratory for investigating new assessment techniques, because the fundamental activity of such tutors is driven by assessment of individual student knowledge. Further, because such tutors embody explicit representations of theoretical assertions about learning, they are perhaps the least confounded forms of experimental treatment for empirical investigations of new ideas about assessment and instruction. An explicit set of roles must be programmed into any intelligent tutor. At times the tutor plays the role of diagnostician, trying to decide what the student does and does not know. At times, it plays the role of strategist, trying to decide how to respond to the student's weaknesses by tailoring instruction. At times it plays the role of colleague or foil, interacting with the student as coach or advisor, or even as game opponent.

In some intelligent tutors, such as WEST,[10] separate major segments of the program correspond to these separate roles. There is an expert modeler, a student modeler, a set of issue analyzers that determine differences between the student's performance and the ideal and blame those differences on particular student shortcomings (see Fig. 3.3). There is also a module that plays the game with the student, and a module that uses a prioritized set of pending issues (things the student should be taught) to decide how and what to coach.

While the roles to be filled by the WEST tutor are very explicit, the curriculum structure is much more implicit. There is no explicit statement embodied in the program that makes it clear what any given student will be taught by the tutor. Rather, a variety of considerations interact to determine what the student is taught. This can pose two types of problems. First, different schools may have different emphases. For example, one school might favor arithmetic instruction over refinement of gaming strategy, while another may emphasize the metacognitive skills involved in successful play. Second, we want to include knowledge about the course of learning that is not reflected in a model of expert performance alone, nor even in the sorts of tutoring principles currently found in programs such as WEST. The first problem is not very severe; one could change the

---

[10]WEST is an intelligent tutor developed by Richard Burton and John Seely Brown (1982). It is based on an instructional game developed by Bonnie Seiler. The game is a variation of Chutes and Ladders (a children's game) in which the student must develop an arithmetic expression instead of rolling the dice to generate a move. Three randomly generated numbers are presented to the student, who can then move his game piece as many squares as are represented by the value of any one arithmetic expression he can specify that uses only the three numbers. WEST provides advice, or coaching, to the player, on arithmetic issues, game strategy, and the manipulation of arithmetic expressions.

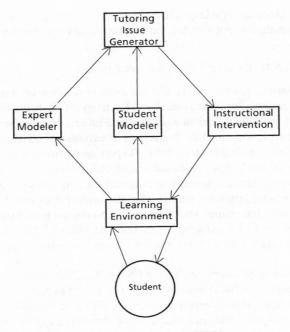

FIG. 3.3.   Major components of a tutor such as WEST.

prioritizing rules used by WEST to choose which of several potential tutoring issues is given priority. The second issue, the need to reflect knowledge about the course of acquisition for a specific domain of expertise, is more serious and will be discussed below.

Representing Curriculum Knowledge As Well As Domain Knowledge

In order to separate knowledge about how and what to teach from the expert knowledge that represents the goals of instruction, a group of us[11] at LRDC have been experimenting with a new architecture for tutors. In it, the sections of the program correspond explicitly to the lessons in a curriculum, and the roles that the tutor must fill are defined in a distributed manner, as part of the content of each lesson's program. This curriculum knowledge "layer" is separate from an expert domain knowledge layer. This basic intelligent systems design approach has been proven in the speech understanding research of the past decade or more,

---

[11]The original ideas came from Jeffrey Bonar (1985), who continues to paly a central role with us in developing this new approach. Other important contributors have been Paul Resnick, William Weil, Cindy Cosic, and Mary Ann Quayle.

and we are adapting it to the task of building an intelligent tutor. It permits direct expression of hypotheses about instruction and diagnosis in the knowledge base from which an intelligent system develops specific lessons. Thus, we think it has promise for a technology and science of instruction.

The approach that we have been taking is to specify the knowledge relevant to tutoring as consisting of three types. First, there is domain knowledge, the content to be taught. Second, there is curricular knowledge, the division of the domain to be taught into a hierarchy of instructional subgoals. Finally, there is aptitude-related or metacognitive knowledge, the tailoring of the course of instruction to suit individual student needs. The three knowledge types are shown in Fig. 3.4, and we shall discuss each in turn.

Whatever it is that we want the student to know after he has been taught, we can represent it as a network of concepts connected by predicates. Certain groupings within such a network are organized into schemata, which contain the

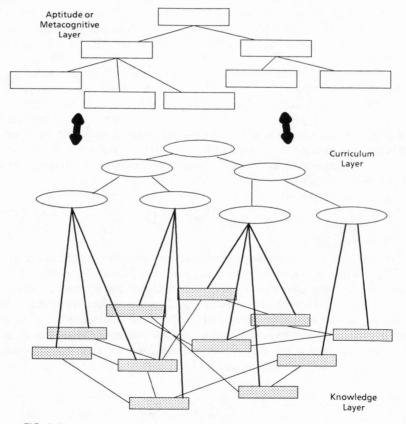

FIG. 3.4.   Layers of a tutor's knowledge base.

knowledge, both procedural and declarative, needed to deal with particular broad generic problems. While this higher level organization is central to expert performance, the knowledge one must acquire to become an expert is not neatly separable into clusters that can be taught or measured independently. Expert knowledge has the character that each part one might want to teach or measure is somewhat depedent on other parts which may well not have been taught yet. Thus, any plan for building expertise must include attention not only to the skills an expert has but also to the sequencing and forms of instruction used to build those skills.

An important source of the needed structure is an understanding of how the expertise being taught is learned. That is, particular pieces of knowledge are propaedeutic and thus should be taught first. Other pieces of knowledge seem to be acquired more readily if they are taught only after some particular prerequisite has been taught first. While many people believe that prerequisite structuring is a property of the domain knowledge alone, a central assertion of the cognitive psychology of learning is that prerequisite structuring depends also upon what sorts of knowledge bundles lead to what sorts of learning and what sorts of capability for further learning. Two examples may help clarify what has just been stated.

The first of these examples has to do with acquisition of substantial understanding about the physical world, including scientific understanding. As noted above, Susan Carey (in press) has noted that the course of development for certain kinds of scientific knowledge recapitulates the sequences of theories that have developed in various sciences. We can imagine that some personal theories are better scaffolding for one kind of later learning than for another just as has been the case for scientific theories. For example, the alchemy theories were a very poor foundation for a quantitative chemistry that could be related to an emerging physics. On the other hand, they may have been better suited to the fostering of a materials science. Indeed, much relevant descriptive knowledge of the properties of different materials was temporarily lost when modern chemistry overthrew alchemy.

The moral in this discussion is that an understanding of the particular aspects of expertise that are most important, along with understanding of the course of acquisition for that knowledge, is the basis for splitting the knowledge domain up into bundles or lessons to be separately taught and separately tested. Those lessons, or curriculum subgoals, can be thought of as constituting a separate layer of process and control in an intelligent tutor with connections downward to the knowledge layer. The particular bundlings that are most optimal will be determined by analysis of the course of learning.

A second example may help clarify this viewpoint. Consider the learning of arithmetic. We want children to be able to carry out all four arithmetic operations on numbers of any size. How do we decide whether to teach addition first, proceeding only with addition until even the largest numbers can be added easily, or to teach two or more operations on small numbers and then recycle through the operations again with progressively larger quantities? Currently, schools do the latter, because it turns out that certain parts of each operation reinforce parts of other operations. However, some have argued that a modest movement toward providing large-number problems earlier, which might mean working with fewer operations initially, would clarify certain matters that now seem to cause trouble (for example, you can't understand how to borrow across zero, as in $403-224$, unless you have had enough experience with 3 and 4-digit numbers to really establish your understanding of place value). Only when we know enough to specify the order of instruction can we be sure we understand how to handle the measurement problem with respect to diagnosis.

We propose that yet a third layer is needed in the knowledge base for a tutor. We call this the aptitude or metacognitive layer. Basically, this layer is concerned with individualizing the course of instruction to suit different students' capabilities. We presume that this layer sits on top of the curriculum layer, observing the student's progress and tuning the system's performance to optimize that progress. Thus, this layer is concerned with capability that is needed in order to become expert in a domain but is not actually part of the domain.

The optimization of student progress can occur in two ways. The system can either adapt to aptitude differences, or it can teach the skills that constitute aptitude. Adapting to aptitude might involve no more than changing the level of risk taking for the instruction. For example, if we have a student who learns with great facility, perhaps we should be less concerned if he misses a few problems in an early lesson, since he will probably pick up what he needs implicitly even if we give parts of the knowledge minimal explicit treatment. On the other hand, when we have a slow student, we may not want to take too many risks. Rather, we may not advance to a new lesson until the prerequisite lessons have been very well learned. A related form of aptitude optimization involves variation in the amount of support provided to a student in learning environments which foster discovery learning. For example, one might have a simulation program for a physics course that allows a variety of mechanics experiments to be simulated on the computer screen. For some students, very slight prompting might work very well, e.g., *See what you can figure out about the relationship between force and acceleration.* Other students with less-well-developed skills for exploratory learning might be led much more carefully through a specific set of experiments and prompted to specify what they had learned from particular experiences.

A different approach to aptitude is to diagnose the specific skill weaknesses that make some people learn better or faster than others. Under this approach, metacognitive skills are taken to be part of every domain of instruction, though they may be adapted specifically to each knowledge domain. The notion that we have in mind is one of observing the course of a student's progress in learning, inducing that certain aspects of metacognitive skill might be weak, and then establishing the teaching of those metacognitive skill components as high priority instructional subgoals. For example, the tutoring system might observe that the student never takes advantage of opportunities to conduct his own experiments in a simulation environment and respond by suggesting occasions when some experimentation would allow the student to test his understanding. Systems that begin to do this are being developed in our laboratories. With this approach, the metacognitive layer modifies the content of the curriculum layer by inserting additional curriculum subgoals. This can be of particular importance in instructional systems that attempt to foster discovery learning, since the student whose skills are insufficient for making discoveries is not well served otherwise.

Diagnosis With Curriculum Object Structuring

The tutor architectures we have been producing are based on an object-oriented programming approach. In such an approach, programs consist of independent modules (or objects). Each module contains a set of variables, the module's knowledge base, and a set of methods for responding to input messages. Control in such a system involves sending a message to one object which then carries out the method signaled by the message. Some of the actions of an object may involve sending messages to other objects. Variables and methods are defined via an inheritance hierarchy; they may be local to that object, defined for every object of a class, or even inherited from more abstract objects.

In our tutors, each subgoal of the curriculum is represented by an object, and higher-level objects act, in part, by asking their prerequisite objects to teach the needed prerequisite skills. We call the curriculum layer in such a system a curriculum-object lattice structure. The objects for a proposed tutor have the following content:

Declarative Knowledge

- Variables that identify how a given object's goals relate to the goals of other objects (i.e., which goals are prerequisite to the current one, and for which goals the current one is a prerequisite).

- Variables that identify how the knowledge an object is trying to teach relates to the knowledge other objects are trying to teach (pointers to the knowledge layer).

- Variables that represent the student's knowledge of the object's goal knowledge and functions that update those variables.

Procedural Knowledge

- Functions (methods) that generate instructional interventions based upon the student model held by the given object, including both manipulations of the microworld and various forms of coaching or advising.

- Functions that decide if the given object is to blame for problems that arise while objects for which it is prerequisite are in control (that is, if a student has trouble later on, the prerequisite objects can be asked if they see a reason for reviewing their lesson contents with the student).

A critical aspect of the diagnostic approach we are taking involves the notion of blame taking. The idea is to localize diagnosis. Existing approaches used in intelligent tutors use an *overlay* (Goldstein & Carr, 1977) approach. That is, they tend to take a sample of the student's performance and attempt to determine what sorts of deletions from the knowledge base would produce a system that behaved as the student does. This is very computationally intensive, and it depends on the assumption that the student's failings are all due to omissions in his knowledge; the student may also have misconceptions which cannot as easily be detected. To reduce the complexity of diagnostic processing in computer-based instructional systems, we have been developing a more localized view. At any given instant, a particular lesson is controlling the tutor; if the student has difficulties with that lesson, then control is transferred to the prerequisites for that lesson. If any of the prerequisite lesson objects finds reason to believe that what they taught was not adequately learned, it reteaches. This approach will be much more efficient than exhaustive, context-free diagnosis if most problems arise because an immediate prerequisite has not been learned adequately. However, it is likely to be more efficient any time that the prerequisite structure is adequate, i.e., that it captures the range of knowledge that could be missing. This is because the alternative is simply to search all of the knowledge space for an appropriate gap rather than to follow an optimizing search strategy.

We have described three layers for the intelligence that constitutes our proposed tutor: the aptitude layer, the curriculum layer, and the knowledge layer. The curriculum layer will be the driving layer of the system. At any given instant, a particular lesson object will control the course of processing. It will contain pointers to portions of the knowledge base and will report on its successes and failures to the appropriate object in the aptitude layer. In the course of responding to a report message from a lesson, the aptitude layer may take steps, such as adjusting risk-taking parameters, that involve changing the variables in various lesson objects. However, the basic controlling sequence will be driven by lessons that take control, ask for prerequisite lessons to be taught, integrate the prerequisite knowledge by presenting composite problems that involve multiple knowledge aspects all at once, and then notify the object that called them (for which they are prerequisite) that they are done. This lesson-driven approach sets the stage for eventual specification of a design approach that can be a replacement for the frame-oriented approach that has driven earlier generations of computer-assisted instruction.

SUMMARY: GENERAL DIMENSIONS FOR A COGNITIVE APPROACH TO THE MEASUREMENT OF ACHIEVEMENT

In what follows, we attempt to summarize ideas that could comprise a theoretical basis for the design of tests and assessment instruments to determine levels of knowledge and skill that are attained in the course of instruction. These ideas should be considered as a basis for test item construction coordinate with or prior to psychometric considerations.

Fundamentally, achievement measurement should be driven by the emerging cognitive theory of knowledge acquisition. We now realize that people who have learned the concepts and skills in a subject-matter domain have acquired a large collection of schematic knowledge structures. These structures enable understanding of the relationships inherent in their knowledge. We also know that someone who has learned to solve problems, to make inferences, and to be skillful in a subject-matter domain has acquired a set of cognitive procedures attached to knowledge structures that enable actions that influence learning, goal setting and planning.

At various stages of learning, there exist different integrations of knowledge, different degrees of procedural skill, differences in rapid access to memory and in representations of the tasks one is to perform. The fundamental character, then, of achievement measurement is based upon the assessment of growing knowledge structures and related cognitive processes and procedural skills that develop as a domain of proficiency is acquired. These different levels signal advancing expertise or passable blockages in the course of learning.

Achievement measurement theory, as we envision it, is at an early stage. Many of the ideas needed are yet to be worked out, but stimulating work has been done that gives indication of the shape of a guiding framework. Relatively speaking, we have most knowledge of differences between beginners and experts, but less knowledge of the intermediate stages and the nature of the transitions from level to level.

We can, however, on the basis of the work reported in this paper propose a tentative set of "dimensions" that comprise components of developing proficiency that might underlie the assessment of achievement. These dimensions are certainly covered to some extent in traditional forms of achievement assessment, but also may require new forms and methods of measurement. In any case, whether or not items take on new characteristics, they will be informed by a theoretical base which will drive more systematic rationales for interpretations of the meaning of test scores, particularly for diagnostic aspects necessary for instruction. We consider the following dimensions:

1. *Knowledge organization and structure.* As efficiency is attained in a domain, elements of knowledge and components become increasingly interconnected so that proficient individuals access coherent chunks of information rather than disconnected fragments. Beginners' knowledge is fragmentary, consisting of isolated definitions, and superficial understandings of the meanings of appropriate vocabulary. As proficiency develops, these items of information become structured, integrated with past organizations of knowledge so that they are retrieved from memory rapidly in larger units. The degree of fragmentation and structuredness and the degree of accessibility to interrelated chunks of knowledge becomes a dimension of assessment.

2. *Depth of problem representation.* It is now well known that novices recognize the surface features of a problem or task situation and more proficient individuals go beyond surface features and identify inferences or principles that subsume the surface structure. This growing ability for fast recognition of underlying principles is an indication of developing achievement and could be assessed by appropriate pattern recognition tasks in verbal and graphic situations. Certain forms of representation may be highly correlated wiht details of the ability to carry out a task or solve a problem. If this is the case, then test items might concentrate on assessing initial understanding and depth of representation and spend less time on the details of arriving at the correct answer.

3. *Quality of mental models.* People develop mental models of phenomena and situations with which they work. The nature of these representations is determined by what is useful for the tasks that need to be performed and the level of achievement that is required. One's mental model of a computer or a television set, of a mathematical proof, of an electric circuit, or the structure of DNA is dependent upon levels of knowledge and the processing requirements attached to performance. As tasks become more complex, these models are amended appropriately. There is a difference in the kind of knowledge required by the user, repairman, and designer of a television set. The nature of these models is an important dimension of achievement assessment; they indicate not only levels of task complexity that a person is capable of handling, but also the level at which the school requirements (and job demand) force people to think. The demands of school problem-solving tasks may require mental models less sophisticated than the curriculum implies. This discrepancy poses an interesting dilemma because when proficiency is assessed it is the model required by actual performance that is acquired and retained.

4. *Efficiency of procedures.* Carrying out procedures is an important aspect of many skills and is important also for effectiveness in higher level forms of problem solving and comprehension. Well-practiced procedures are significant for understanding and comprehension—for example, rephrasing or summarizing what one is reading is a performance characteristic of good comprehension; defining an audience and planning a structure are characteristic of good writing.

Such procedures need to be carefully assessed, but they cannot be measured in rote fashion. They must be assessed in terms of the effective goals that are guiding them. It is not enough to assess summarization and paraphrasing unless their effects on comprehension are considered. It is not enough to give an exercise in planning a composition, unless its effect on the writing process is engaged. The relationship between task understanding and efficient procedures is an important aspect of cognitive proficiency, and effective achievement measurement should exclude rote and piecemeal assessment of procedural skills that does not focus on performance goals.

5. *Automaticity to reduce attentional demands.* In investigations of competence, it has become evident that human ability to perform competing attention-demanding tasks is rather limited. When subtasks of a complex activity require simultaneous demands for attention, the efficiency of the overall task is affected. This fact has particular implications in the diagnostic assessment of the interaction between basic skills and advanced components of cognitive performance. As has been indicated, an example of this interaction has been of special interest in the investigation of reading and text comprehension, where attention may alternate between basic decoding skills of recognizing words and higher level skills of comprehension that integrate sentence ideas into memory. Although these component processes may work well when tested separately, they may not be efficient enough to work together. A slow, or inefficient, component process in interaction with other processes can lead to breakdowns in overall proficiency. If a task, such as reading, consists of an orchestration of basic skills and higher level strategic comprehension processes, then measurement procedures should be able to diagnose the inefficiencies in this complex performance.

The instructional implication is that in the development of higher levels of proficiency, basic skills should receive enough practice so that they become automatized and can be performed with little conscious attention. This leaves conscious processing capacity that can be devoted to higher level processes as necessary. A criterion for assessment then, is the level of efficiency or automaticity required for subprocesses to have minimal interference effects, i.e., whether the automaticity of a basic process has progressed to a point where it can facilitate and be integrated into the total performance of which it is a part. Has it reached a point so that further, more advanced learning and higher level performance can occur? Specific procedures for assessing automaticity might involve the measurement of response latency and of susceptibility to disrupting influences by simultaneous attention-demanding tasks.

6. *Proceduralized knowledge.* Modern learning theory has suggested that the course of acquisition of components of knowledge proceeds from an initial declarative form to compiled procedural form. In the early stage, we can know a principle or a rule or an item of specialized vocabulary without knowing the conditions under which that item of knowledge is applicable and is to be used the

most effectively. Studies of the difference between experts and novices indicate that beginners may have requisite knowledge but this knowledge is not bound to the conditions of its applicability. When knowledge is accessed by experts, it is always associated with indications of how and when it is to be used appropriately. The implication for measurement is that the progression from declarative to tuned procedural information is an indication of the development of achievement in an area of knowledge. Task analysis in various technical skills has shown that this progression can be assessed by qualitative differences in people's descriptions and definitions of their knowledge. Concepts, principles, and procedures can be measured in a way to determine the level of knowledge that is available to a learner. Test items can be comprised of two elements—information that needs to be known and conditions under which use of this information is appropriate. Our hypothesis is that advancing achievement will show changes in the level of knowledge from initial declarative knowledge to more complex combinations of actions and their conditions of use.

7. *Procedures for theory change.* As individuals learn, they solve problems and comprehend materials that foster further learning. This learning takes place on the basis of existing knowledge structures or theories held by students that can enhance or retard learning. With appropriate instruction, students can test, evaluate, and modify their current theories of knowledge on the basis of new information, and develop new schemata that facilitate more advanced thinking and problem solving.

While theories of knowledge held by students are a basis for new learning, current research has also emphasized that individuals hold naive theories, for example, at the beginning of a course in physics or economics, that make learning difficult. Even after a course of instruction, these naive theories persist, although students have learned, in some mechanical fashion, to solve problems in the course, but with little understanding. With this in mind, theories of knowledge become a target for assessment. The characteristics of a theory held by a student might indicate whether it is a tractable theory, amenable to change under certain instructional conditions, or whether the theory held is one that teachers find more intractable, that results in learning difficulties, and that requires additional instruction.

8. *Metacognitive skills for learning.* Metacognition is defined in a number of ways in the literature, but we consider here that aspect of it which refers to self-regulatory and self-management skills. Regulatory skills refer to generalized skills for approaching problems and for monitoring one's performance. These skills are called metacognitive because they are not specific performances or strategies involved in solving a particular problem or carrying out a particular procedure. Rather, they refer to the kind of knowledge that enables one to usefully reflect upon and control one's own performance. Representative kinds of regulatory performance include: knowing when or what one knows or does not know, predicting the correctness or outcome of one's performance, planning

ahead and efficiently apportioning one's time, and checking and monitoring the outcomes of one's solution or attempts to learn.

Research has indicated that these regulatory skills develop with maturity and that they may be less developed in students with learning disabilities or performance difficulties. It is likely that these skills appear in various forms and levels of competence over a wide range of individuals. An especially interesting characteristic of these skills is that they may be the particular aspect of performance that facilitates transfer to new situations. Individuals can be taught a rule or procedure that improves their task performance, but it is also important to learn how that rule is to be used and how to monitor its use. Self-regulatory activities of this kind are important candidates for assessment. Tests of an individual's competence in these metacognitive skills might be important predictors of success of the kind of problem-solving ability that results in learning.

Achievement testing as we have defined it is a method of indexing stages of competence through indicators of the level of development of knowledge, skill and cognitive process. These indicators display stages of performance that have been attained and on which further learning can proceed. They also show forms of error and misconceptions in knowledge that result in inefficient and incomplete knowledge and skill and that need instructional attention.

Achievement measurement defined in this way needs to be informed by theories of the acquisiton of subject-matter knowledge, by the development of knowledge and skill, and by various dimensions of performance such as degree of structure, automaticity, forms of representation and procedural efficiencies that indicate the growing and developing competence. We have speculated on possible indicators, but anticipate that theories of subject-matter acquisition will suggest both general indicators of competent performance, and also specific indicators dependent upon the nature of the knowledge and skill being assessed.

These theories require investigation and research, but work is proceeding rapidly. We anticipate that increasing sophistication in theory will be brought to achievement measurement, just as increasing sophistication in psychometric analyses has been brought to the design of tests after test items have been constructed. In essence, our paper is a signal for new orientations in achievement testing that will need to rely on the interrelationships between knowledge of learning and development, assessment of the indicators of growing competence, and their relevance to methods of instruction.

Finally, achievement measurement, as we have defined it, is an integral part of an instructional system. Teaching and testing are not separable events. Perhaps the term "learning assessment" better conveys our meaning than "achievement test," because the forms of measurement we envision provide information about the performance characteristics of levels of competence attained and about steps that can be taken to facilitate further learning.

ACKNOWLEDGMENT

Arlene Weiner provided substantial editorial assistance in preparing this chapter. Work we report was supported by the Office of Naval Research, the Air Force Human Resources Laboratory, and the National Institute of Education. None of these agencies has read or approved this document, and no endorsement of it by any of them should be inferred.

REFERENCES

Anderson, J. R. (1983). *The architecture of cognition.* Cambridge, MA: Harvard University Press.
Anderson, R. (1978). Schema-directed processes in language comprehension. In A. M. Lesgold, J. W. Pellegrino, S. D. Fokkema, & R. Glaser (Eds.), *Cognitive psychology and instruction* (pp. 67–82). New York: Plenum.
Bartholomae, D. (1980). The study of error. *College Composition and Communication, 31*(3), 253–269.
Benbassett, J., & Bachar-Bassan, E. (1984). A comparison of initial diagnostic hypotheses of medical students and internists. *Journal of Medical Education, 59,* 951–956.
Beck, I. L., Perfetti, C. A., & McKeown, M. G. (1982). An instructional redesign of reading lessons: Effects on comprehension. *Reading Research Quarterly, 17,* 462–481.
Belmont, J. M., & Butterfield, E. C. (1977). The instructional approach to developmental cognitive research. In R. V. Kail, Jr., & J. W. Hagen (Eds.), *Perspectives on the development of memory and cognition* (pp. 437–481). New York: Wiley.
Bonar, J. (1985, June). *Bite-Sized Intelligent Tutoring* (Technical Report) Pittsburgh: Learning Research and Development Center, University of Pittsburgh.
Borkowski, J. G., Cavanaugh, J. C., & Reichart, G. J. (1978). Maintenance of children's rehearsal strategies: Effect of training and strategy form. *Journal of Experimental Child Psychology, 26,* 288–298.
Bransford, J. D., Delclos, V. R., Vye, N. J., Burns, M. S., & Hasselbring, T. S. (1986, February). *Improving the quality of assessment and instruction: Roles for dynamic assessment* (Working Paper 1). Nashville, TN: John F. Kennedy Center for Research on Education and Human Development, Peabody College, Vanderbilt University.
Brown, A. L. (1978). Knowing when, where and how to remember: A problem of metacognition. In R. Glaser (Ed.), *Advances in instructional psychology,* (Vol. 1, pp. 77–165). Hillsdale, NJ: Lawrence Erlbaum Associates.
Brown, A. L., Bransford, J. D., Ferrara, R. A., & Campione, J. C. (1983). Learning, remembering, and understanding. In J. H. Flavell & E. M. Markman (Eds.), *Cognitive development* (Vol. 3 of P. H. Mussen (Ed.), *Handbook of child psychology* (pp. 77–166). New York: Wiley.
Brown, J. S., & Burton, R. R. (1978). Diagnostic models for procedural bugs in basic mathematical skills. *Cognitive Science, 2,* 155–192.
Brown, A. L., & French, L. A. (1979). *The zone of potential development: Implications for intelligence testing in the year 2000* (Technical Report No. 128). Champaign-Urbana, IL: Center for the Study of Reading.
Brown, J. S., & Van Lehn, K. (1980). Repair theory: A generative theory of bugs in procedural skills. *Cognitive Science, 4,* 379–426.
Brown, J. S., & Van Lehn, K. (1982). Towards a generative theory of "bugs." In T. P. Carpenter, J. M. Moser, & T. A. Romberg (Eds.), *Addition and subtraction: A cognitive perspective* (pp. 117–135). Hillsdale, NJ: Lawrence Erlbaum Associates.
Burton, R. R., & Brown, J. S. (1982). An investigation of computer coaching for informal learning

activities, in D. Sleeman & J. S. Brown (Eds.), *Intelligent tutoring systems* (pp. 79–98). Orlando, FL: Academic Press.

Carey, S. (1985). Are children fundamentally different kinds of thinkers and learners than adults? In S. F. Chipman, J. W. Segal, & R. Glaser (Eds.), *Thinking and learning skills: Vol. 2. Research and open questions*. Hillsdale, NJ: Lawrence Erlbaum Associates.

Cattell, R. B. (1963). Theory of fluid and crystallized intelligence: A critical experiment. *Journal of Educational Psychology, 54,* 1–22.

Champagne, A., Klopfer, L., & Anderson, J. H. (1980). Factors affecting the learning of classical mechanics. *American Journal of Physics, 48,* 1074–1079.

Chase, W. G., & Chi, M. T. H. (1981). Cognitive skill: Implications for spatial skill in large-scale environments. In J. Harvey (Ed.), *Cognition, social behavior, and the environment*. Hillsdale, NJ: Lawrence Erlbaum Associates.

Chase, W. G., & Simon, H. A. (1973). Perception in chess. *Cognitive Psychology, 4,* 55–81.

Chi, M. T. H., Feltovich, P., & Glaser, R. (1981). Categorization and representation of physics problems by experts and novices. *Cognitive Science, 5,* 121–152.

Curtis, M. E. (1980). Development of components of reading skill. *Journal of Educational Psychology, 72,* 656–669.

Curtis, M. E., & Glaser, R. (1983). Reading theory and the assessment of reading achievement. *Journal of Educational Measurement, 20,* 133–147.

deGroot, A. D. (1965). *Thought and choice in chess*. The Hague: Mouton.

deGroot, A. D. (1966). Perception and memory versus thought: Some old ideas and recent findings. In B. Kleinmuntz (Ed.), *Problem solving: Research, method, and theory*. New York: Wiley.

deKleer, J., & Brown, J. S. (1985). A qualitative physics based on confluences. *Artificial Intelligence, 24,* 7–84. Journal issue reprinted as D. G. Bobrow (Ed.). (1985). *Qualitative reasoning about physical systems* (pp. 205–280). Cambridge, MA: MIT press.

Fitts, P. M. (1964). Perceptual-motor skill learning. In A. W. Melton (Ed.), *Categories of human learning*. Orlando: FL: Academic Press.

Gentner, D., & Gentner, D. (1983). Flowing waters or teeming crowds: Mental models of electricity. In D. Gentner & A. L. Stevens (Eds.), *Mental models*. Hillsdale, NJ: Lawrence Erlbaum Associates.

Gitomer, D. (1984). *A cognitive analysis of a complex troubleshooting task*. Unpublished dissertation, University of Pittsburgh.

Glaser, R. (1984). Education and thinking: The role of knowledge. *American Psychologist, 39,* 93–104.

Goldstein, I., & Carr, B. (1977, October). The computer as coach: An athletic paradigm for intellectual education. *Proceedings of 1977 Annual Conference, Association for Computing Machinery,* Seattle, pp. 227–233.

Hayes, J. R., & Flower, L. (1980). Identifying the organization of writing processes. In L. N. Gregg & E. R. Steinberg (Eds.), *Cognitive processes in writing* (pp. 3–30). Hillsdale, NJ: Lawrence Erlbaum Associates.

Hoepfner, R. (1978). Achievement test selection for program evaluation. In M. J. Wargo & D. R. Green (Eds.), *Achievement testing of disadvantaged and minority students for educational program evaluation*. Monterey, CA: CTB/McGraw-Hill.

Hull, C. L. (1943). *Principles of behavior*. New York: Appleton-Century-Crofts.

Hull, G., Ball, C., Fox, J., Levin, L., & McCutchen, D. (1985). *Computer detection of errors in natural language texts: Some research on pattern matching*. Paper presented to the American Educational Research Association, Chicago.

Inhelder, B., & Piaget, J. (1958). *The growth of logical thinking from childhood to adolescence*. New York: Basic Books.

Kuhn, T. S. (1962). *The structure of scientific revolutions*. Chicago, IL: University of Chicago Press.

Larkin, J. H. (1983). Teaching problem solving in physics: The psychological laboratory and the practical classroom. In D. T. Tuma & F. Reif (Eds.), *Problem solving and education: Issues in teaching and research*. Hillsdale, NJ: Lawrence Erlbaum Associates.

Larkin, J. H., McDermott, J., Simon, D. P., & Simon, H. A. (1980). Expert and novice performance in solving physics problems. *Science, 208*, 1335–1342.

Lesgold, A. M. (1984a). Acquiring expertise. In J. R. Anderson & S. M. Kosslyn (Eds.), *Tutorials in learning and memory: Essays in honor of Gordon Bower*. San Francisco: W. H. Freeman.

Lesgold, A. M. (1984b). Human skill in a computerized society: Complex skills and their acquisition [Presidential address to the Society for Computers in Psychology]. *Behavioral Research Methods, Instruments & Computers, 16*, 79–87.

Lesgold, A. M., & Curtis, M. E. (1981). Learning to read words efficiently. In A. M. Lesgold & C. A. Perfetti (Eds.), *Interactive processes in reading*. Hillsdale, NJ: Lawrence Erlbaum Associates.

Lesgold, A. M., & Perfetti, C. A. (1978). Interactive processes in reading comprehension. *Discourse Processes, 1*, 323–336.

Lesgold, A. M., Resnick, L. B., & Hammond, K. (1985). Learning to read: A longitudinal study of word skill development in two curricula. In T. G. Waller & G. E. MacKinnon (Eds.), *Reading research: Advances in theory and practice* (Vol. 4, pp. 107–138). Orlando, FL: Academic Press.

Lesgold, A. M., Rubinson, H., Feltovich, P., Glaser, R., Klopfer, D., & Wang, Y. (in press). Expertise in a complex skill: Diagnosing X-ray pictures. In M. T. H. Chi, R. Glaser, and M. Farr (Eds.), *The nature of expertise*. Hillsdale, NJ: Lawrence Erlbaum Associates.

Lidz, C. S. (Ed.). (in press). *Dynamic assessment: Foundations and fundamentals*. New York: Guilford Press.

Logan, D., & Eastman, R. (1986). *Mental models of electronics troubleshooting*. Paper presented to the annual meeting of the American Educational Research Association, San Francisco.

McCloskey, M., Caramazza, A., & Green, B. (1980). Curvilinear motion in the absence of external forces: Naive beliefs about the motion of objects. *Science, 210*, 1139–1141.

Murphy, G. L., & Medin, D. L. (1985). The role of theories in conceptual coherence. *Psychological Review, 92*, 289–316.

Norman, D. A., & Bobrow, D. G. (1975). On data-limited and resource-limited processes. *Cognitive Psychology, 7*, 44–64.

Perfetti, C. A. (1985). *Reading ability*. New York: Oxford University Press.

Perfetti, C. A., & Hogaboam, T. W. (1975). The relationship between single word decoding and reading comprehension skill. *Journal of Educational Psychology, 67*, 461–469.

Perfetti, C. A., & Lesgold, A. M. (1977). Discourse processing and sources of individual differences. In P. Carpenter & M. Just (Eds.), *Cognitive processes in comprehension*. Hillsdale, NJ: Lawrence Erlbaum Associates.

Perfetti, C. A., & Lesgold, A. M. (1979). Coding and comprehension in skilled reading. In L. B. Resnick & P. Weaver (Eds.), *Theory and practice of early reading*. Hillsdale, NJ: Lawrence Erlbaum Associates.

Qualitative Reasoning about Physical Systems. (1984). [Special issue]. *Artificial Intelligence, 24* (1–3). [Also published as D. G. Bobrow (Ed.). (1985). *Qualitative Reasoning about Physical Systems*. Cambridge, MA: MIT Press.]

Riley, M. S. (1985). *Structural understanding in performance and learning*. Unpublished doctoral dissertation. Pittsburgh, PA: University of Pittsburgh.

Riley, M. S., Greeno, J. G., & Heller, J. I. (1983). Development of children's problem-solving ability in arithmetic. In H. P. Ginsburg (Ed.), *The development of mathematical thinking* (pp. 153–196). Orlando, FL: Academic Press.

Rumelhart, D. E. (1975). Notes on a schema for stories. In D. G. Brown & A. Collins (Eds.), *Representation and understanding: Studies in cognitive science*. Orlando, FL: Academic Press.

Rumelhart, D. E. (1981). *Understanding understanding*. La Jolla: University of California, Center for Human Information Processing.

Schneider, W. (1984). Practice, attention, and the processing system. *Behavioral and Brain Science, 7,* 80–81.

Shaughnessy, M. (1977). *Errors and expectations.* New York: Oxford University Press.

Siegler, R. S. (1976). Three aspects of cognitive development. *Cognitive Psychology, 4,* 481–520.

Siegler, R. S. (1978). The origins of scientific reasoning. In R. S. Siegler (Ed.), *Children's thinking: What develops?* Hillsdale, NJ: Lawrence Erlbaum Associates.

Simon, D. P., & Simon, H. A. (1978). Individual differences in solving physics problems. In R. S. Siegler (Ed.), Children's thinking: What develops? Hillsdale, NJ: Lawrence Erlbaum Associates.

Simon, H. A., & Chase, W. G. (1973). Skill in chess. *American Scientist, 61,* 394–403.

Spence, K. W. (1956). *Behavior theory and conditioning.* New Haven, CT: Yale University Press.

Van Lehn, K. (1983a). Human procedural skill acquisition: Theory model and psychological validation. *Proceedings of the National Conference on Artificial Intelligence,* Washington, DC.

Van Lehn, K. (1983b). On the representation of procedures in repair theory. In H. P. Ginsburg (Ed.), *The development of mathematical thinking* (pp. 201–252). Orlando, FL: Academic Press.

Van Lehn, K. (1983c). *Felicity conditions for human skill acquisition: Validating an AI-based theory* (Report CIS-21). Cognitive and Instructional Sciences Series, Xerox Palo Alto Research Center: Palo Alto, CA.

Vygotsky, L. S. (1978). *Mind in society: The development of higher psychological processes.* (M. Cole, V. John-Steiner, & E. Soubermen, Eds. & Trans.). Cambridge, MA: Harvard University Press.

4 The g Beyond Factor Analysis

Arthur R. Jensen
University of California, Berkeley

The problem of *g*, essentially, concerns two very fundamental questions: (1) Why are scores on various mental ability tests positively correlated? and (2) Why do people differ in performance on such tests?

SOME DEFINITIONS

To insure that we are talking the same language, we must review a few definitions. Clarity, explicitness, and avoidance of excess meaning or connotative overtones are virtues of a definition. Aside from these properties, a definition per se affords nothing to argue about. It has nothing to do with truth or reality; it is a formality needed for communication.

A *mental ability test* consists of a number of *items*. An *item* is a task on which a person's performance can be *objectively* scored, that is, classified (e.g., "right" or "wrong," 1 or 0), or graded on a scale (e.g., "poor," "fair," "good," "excellent," or 0, 1, 2, 3), or counted (e.g., number of digits recalled, number of puzzle pieces fitted together within a time limit), or measured on a ratio scale (e.g., reaction time to a stimulus or the time interval between the presentation of a task and its completion). *Objectively* scored means that there is a high degree of agreement between observers or scorers or pointer readings in assigning a score to a person's performance on an item.

An item measures an *ability* if performance on the item can be objectively scored such that a higher score represents better performance in the sense of being more accurate, more correct, quicker, more efficient, or in closer conformance to some standard—regardless of any value judgment concerning the aesthetic, moral, social, or practical worth of the optimum performance on the particular task. An item measures a *mental* (or cognitive) ability if very little or none of the individual differences variance in task performance is associated with individual differences in physical capacity, such as sensory acuity or muscular strength, and if differences in item difficulty (percent passing) are uncorrelated with differences in physical capacities per se.

In order for items to show individual differences in a given group of people, the items must vary in difficulty; that is, items without variance (0% or 100% passing) are obviously nonfunctional in a test intended to show individual differences. A test, like any scientific measurement, requires a standard procedure. This includes the condition that the *requirements* of the tasks composing the test must be understood by the testee through suitable instructions by the tester; and the *fundaments* of the task (i.e., the elements that it comprises) must already be familiar to the testee. Also, the testee must be motivated to perform the task. These conditions can usually be assured by the testee's demonstrating satisfactory performance on easy exemplaries of the same item types as those in the test proper.

Mental ability tests (henceforth called simply *tests*) that meet all these conditions can be made up in great variety, involving different sensory and response modalities, different media (e.g., words, numbers, symbols, pictures of familiar things, and objects), different types of task requirements (e.g., discrimination, generalization, recall, naming, comparison, decision, inference), and a wide range of task complexity. The variety of possible items and even item types seems limited only by the ingenuity of the inventors of test items.

SOME FACTS OF NATURE

When a collection of such items is given to a large representative sample of the general population under the specified standard conditions, it is found that there is an abundance of positive correlations between the items; negative correlations are very scarce and are never as large as the positive correlations, assuming, of course, that all the items are scored in such a way that what is deemed as the desirable performance on every item receives a higher score than undesirable performance. The negative correlations are not only scarce and small, they become scarcer and smaller as the number of persons increases, suggesting that the existence of negative item intercorrelations in the abilities domain is largely or entirely due to error. There is no corresponding shrinkage of the positive inter-item correlations with an increase in sample size. If a fair number of items having authentically and reliably negative correlations with the majority of items could be found, it should be possible to combine a number of such negative items to create a test that would have the usual properties of a good psychometric test in terms of internal consistency reliability and test-retest reliability. Such a test then should show large negative correlations with tests composed by sampling only from the majority of items that are positively intercorrelated. No such "negative" test has ever been created, to my knowledge. The creation of such a test is a challenge to those who doubt the phenomenon of *positive manifold,* that is, ubiquitous positive correlations among items or tests in the ability domain.

But a correlation matrix will also tend to be predominantly positive by pure mathematical necessity. While it is entirely possible (and usual) for all of the correlations among n tests to have positive values ranging between 0 and $+1$, the negative counterpart to this condition is a mathematical impossibility. In a matrix of zero-order intercorrelations, negative values are constrained. If variables A and B are negatively correlated -1, it is impossible that both can be negatively correlated with variable C, or D, or any other variable. While the average size of all the correlations in a matrix can have any positive value between 0 and $+1$, the largest possible average negative value of all the correlations in any matrix of n variables is $-1/(n - 1)$; hence, if the negative correlations are large, they must be few, and if they are not few, they must be small. Although there is a mathematical limitation on negative correlations, the proportion and size of the positive interitem correlations actually found in the ability domain far exceeds the amount of positive intercorrelations that would be expected by chance.

Yet the generally positive correlations between items, as a rule, are rather surprisingly small. Given the internal consistency reliability (K-R 20), r_{xx}, of a test of n items, the average item intercorrelation, $\bar{r}_{ij}$, is $\bar{r}_{ij} = r_{xx}/[n - r_{xx}(n - 1)]$. In the case of even such a homogeneous test as the Raven Progressive Matrices, the value of $\bar{r}_{ij}$ is only about $+.12$ or $+.13$. The small correlations are partly due to an artifact, namely, the restriction of variance as the item difficulty of dichotomously scored items departs from .50. Even after correcting for the effect of this restriction of variance on the correlations, however, it is apparent that single test items have relatively little of their variance in common. In fact, typically less than a quarter of the variance of single items overlaps the total variance of any collection of n such items, even when the items are homogeneous in type. The collection of items may be a random sample from a large pool of diverse items, in which case the average interitem correlation would be relatively low, or it may be a selection of highly similar, or homogeneous, items, in which case the average item intercorrelation will be relatively high. But even the high interitem correlations will average only something between about $+.10$ and $+.15$.

Nevertheless, interitem correlations greater than 0 and less than .15 are large enough to create a test with a very substantial proportion of reliable or true-score variance, provided the number, n, of items composing the test is large enough. This is inevitable, because the reliable variance of total scores on a test is equal to the sum of all the interitem covariances in the square matrix of interitem covariances. A test of n items with an average interitem correlation of $\bar{r}_{ij}$ will have an internal consistency (K-R 20) reliability of $r_{xx} = n\bar{r}_{ij}/[1 + (n - 1)\bar{r}_{ij}]$. Consequently, by increasing the number of items sampled from the ability domain, as previously defined, one can create a test of any desired reliability (less than 1). Most standard tests have reliabilities greater than .90 when used on samples of the general population. When a number of such highly reliable ability tests, comprising diverse contents and item types, are administered to a representative sample of the general population, the intercorrelations of the tests are all positive and generally substantial. In other words, the various tests have a lot of variance in common.

This seems to be an unavoidable fact of nature. It has proven impossible to create a number of different mental tests, each of highly homogeneous items, and with high reliability, that do not show significant correlations with one another. The "positive manifold" of test intercorrelations is indeed a reality, a fundamental fact, that calls for scientific explanation.

A hypothesized explanation of the correlation between any particular pair of different, but singly homogeneous, tests will often point to certain common surface features of the two tests that may seem to plausibly account for their correlation. But hypotheses of this kind run into greater and greater difficulty as they try to explain intercorrelations among diverse tests. The surface features of tests soon prove inadequate to the explanatory burden when the number and diversity of tests increases but still displays positive manifold. It is well-nigh impossible, for example, to account for the correlations between vocabulary, block designs, and backward digit span in terms of common features of the tests. Explanations of correlations in terms of the surface features of tests would turn out to require nearly as many explanations as there are pairs of different, but correlated, tests. From the viewpoint of scientific theory, such a multiplicity and specificity of explanations is quite unsatisfactory, if not entirely unacceptable, and, in fact, no one systematically even attempts it.

Psychometricians since Spearman have preferred to describe the intercorrelations among a number of tests in terms of a smaller number of hypothetical factors (i.e., sources of variance) that certain tests have in common. The burden of explanation, therefore, shifts from explanations of single correlations between particular pairs of tests to a much more limited number of hypothetical factors that a number of tests measure in common.

FACTOR ANALYSIS AND THE HIGHEST ORDER FACTOR

Spearman (1904, 1927) hypothesized that the positive correlation among all cognitive tests is due to a general factor that is measured by every test. His invention of factor analysis permitted estimation of the proportion of the total variance in a collection of tests that is attributable to the *general factor, g,* as well as the correlation (termed a *factor loading*) of each test with the g factor that is common to all of the tests. Variance that is not attributable to the *g* factor (call it the non-*g* variance), is assignable to (1) other factors, called *group factors,* because they account for the non-*g* correlations among only certain groups of tests, (2) *specificity,* or that portion of a test's true score (i.e., reliable) variance that is not shared in common with any other tests in the collection of tests subjected to factor analysis, and (3) *error* variance.

Aside from error variance, *specificity* is the least interesting from a psychological and psychometric standpoint, because specificity can dwindle as more tests of similar types are added to the collection; then some of the specific variance turns into additional group factors (also termed *primary,* or *first-order,* factors).

The general factor, *g,* is the highest common factor in the correlation matrix, accounting for more of the total common factor variance than any other factor, and often even more than all of the other factors combined.

A *g* factor can be extracted by any one of three methods in current use. It can be represented by (1) the first principal component of a principal components analysis, or (2) the first factor of a common factor (or principal factor) analysis, or (3) a hierarchical factor analysis, in which all of the first-order factors are rotated to an oblique "simple structure" and the correlation among the first-order factors are then factor analyzed to yield a second-order factor. The *g* factor, the apex of the hierarchy, most typically emerges as the only second-order factor, although in large and highly diverse collections of tests, *g* appears as a third-order factor at the apex of the hierarchy.

It is desirable to "residualize" the factor loadings at each level in the hierarchy, i.e., the variance that is common to the oblique (i.e., correlated) first-order factors is partialled out and transferred up to the second-order oblique factors, and their common variance also is partialled out and transferred to the third-order factor. This procedure orthogonalizes the entire hierarchy; that is, all the factors are uncorrelated with one another, within and between levels of the hierarchy. This hierarchical analysis can be accomplished by means of the Schmid-Leiman (1957) procedure, which yields the factor loadings of all the tests on each of the orthogonal factors at every level of the hierarchy. A schematic factor hierarchy is shown in Fig. 4.1.

Is there a preference among these methods of extracting a *g* factor? Yes, although each method has certain advantages and disadvantages. The first principal component is the least affected by sampling error, and the hierarchical analysis is the most affected, and therefore should be used with samples that are very much larger than the number of tests. The first principal component will always yield the largest *g* in terms of its eigenvalue or the proportion of total variance accounted for, but this is not a real advantage, because some small part of that variance consists of *uniqueness* (i.e., the specific and error variance), which is more or less evenly spread over all the components in a principal components analysis. Thus we often find that the various tests' loadings on the

General Factor

Second-Order Factors

Primary Factors

Tests

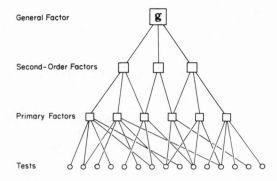

FIG. 4.1.   Example of a hierarchical factor analysis with three levels.

first principal component, although they are slightly larger overall than the corresponding loadings on the first principal factor, are somewhat less clear-cut. Despite this, the first principal component and first principal factor are nearly always extremely alike. I have yet to find a correlation matrix of real tests for which the congruence coefficient between the first principal component and the first principal factor is lower than +0.99, which means that for most purposes they can be regarded as virtually identical. (This is not true of the subsequent unrotated components or factors extracted after the first; the congruence between the corresponding components and factors decreases with each successive component extracted.)

The hierarchical g is always smaller than the g represented by either the first principal component or first principal factor. This is because the process of extracting a hierarchical g (using the Schmid-Leiman orthogonalization transformation) does not result in any significant negative correlations in the residual matrix after the g factor is removed, so that positive manifold of the residual matrix is preserved when factors are partialled out at every level of the hierarchy, and virtually all of the statistically reliable factor loadings are positive on all factors. This condition is theoretically desirable in terms of thinking of all abilities as positive vectors and as always facilitating, and never hindering, performance on any cognitive task that is at all affected by the ability. (The preservation of all positive loadings on all factors was originally advocated by Thurstone (1938, 1947), as one of the aims of factor rotation to approximate simple structure.)

In extracting g by principal factor analysis and hierarchical factor analysis from the same set of data, I have found that the hierarchical g usually contains some 10% to 20% less variance than the g represented by the first principal factor. Yet the relative sizes of tests' loadings on the first principal factor and on the Schmid-Leiman hierarchical g are usually highly similar, with coefficients of congruence of +0.99 or greater. When both the first principal factor and the hierarchical g are extracted from the intercorrelations (based on the national standardization data) of the 13 subtests of the Wechsler Intelligence Scale for Children, for example, the coefficient of congruence between them is +0.999 (Jensen & Reynolds, 1982). I have compared both types of g factors in many collections of tests and have never found the relative magnitudes of the factor loadings to differ appreciably. However, an advantage of the hierarchical g is that it is less affected by variations in the sampling of tests entering into the analysis. For example, if we included a half-dozen or so more different types of memory span tests in the Wechsler battery, the first principal factor would be pushed somewhat in the direction of the memory factor, that is, its loadings on the memory span tests would be enlarged. The hierarchical g, however, would remain relatively unaffected by the number of tests of different types in the battery. In short, the hierarchical g is more stable than the first principal factor across variations in psychometric sampling.

When the first-order factors are rotated, the first factor loses its status as the highest common factor; its variance is scattered among the rotated primary factors, and what could properly be called a g factor disappears. The most popular rotational criterion is Thurstone's concept of *simple structure,* which aims for a factor pattern that contains no negative loadings and a maximum of zero loadings. An idealized simple structure is shown in Table 4.1. (If the factors were all orthogonal, there would be no g.) If the rotated factors are forced to be orthogonal (i.e., uncorrelated), achievement of a clean simple structure has proved to be impossible in the abilities domain. The basic assumption underlying orthogonal simple structure is that test scores are simple in factorial composition. Simple structure implies the hope that a number of tests could be devised, each of which measures only one ability, so-called primary mental abilities. But despite

TABLE 4.1
A Rotated Factor Matrix Showing Factor Loadings
of an Idealized Simple Structure

Variable	A	B	C	D	h^2
		Rotated Factors			
1	1	0	0	0	1
2	1	0	0	0	1
3	1	0	0	0	1
4	0	1	0	0	1
5	0	1	0	0	1
6	0	1	0	0	1
7	0	0	1	0	1
8	0	0	1	0	1
9	0	0	0	1	1
10	0	0	0	1	1
Eigenvalue	3	3	2	2	
% Variance	30	30	20	20	

h^2 = communality

concerted efforts, this goal has never been attained. No matter how homogeneous each of a number of tests is, or how "factor pure" their constructors have striven to make them, they are always found to be substantially correlated with one another in any sizeable representative sample of the general population. When the correlations among such tests are factor analyzed and rotated to orthogonal simple structure, which is now most commonly done analytically, using Kaiser's (1958) varimax, the desired "simple structure" is never "clean," that is, instead of many near-zero factor loadings there are many low but significant loadings scattered throughout the matrix, representing the dispersal of the general factor throughout all the primary factors. Although varimax or other simple structure rotation aids in the identification and interpretation of the group factors because of the fairly sharp contrast between large and small factor loadings that serves to highlight the various primary factors, it has the disadvantage of scattering and submerging the g factor beyond recognition.

To overcome this problem, Thurstone suggested oblique rotation yielding correlated primary factors; this achieves a much closer approximation to simple structure. But the g variance then resides in the correlations among the primary factors, which, when factor analyzed, yield the g factor at the top of the hierarchy. Hence, in the abilities domain, it is an incomplete and unacceptable practice to stop factor extraction with orthogonal rotation of the primary factors. So, too, are oblique primary factors an incomplete analysis, unless one goes on to extract g (and any other higher-order factors). To pretend that g does not exist because it can be "rotated away" is merely deceptive. The purely mathematical argument that any position of the factor axes is as good as any other, is theoretically unacceptable. The argument rests simply on the fact that the same amount of common factor variance is accounted for regardless of the position to which the factor axes are rotated, and any factor structure (given the same number of factors) can reproduce the original zero-order correlations among the tests equally well. While it is indeed true that an unlimited number of different positions of the factor axes is possible, and that all of them are mathematically equivalent in reproducing the original correlations, some factor structures make much more sense, theoretically, than others. Some possible factor structures may even create quite misleading impressions. When we "hide" the g factor in the orthogonal simple-structure primary factors, for example, we create the expectation that some of the mental tests are uncorrelated, when in fact this is contradicted by the all-positive matrix of actual test of intercorrelations. Orthogonal simple structure also does not reflect the fact that the average differences *between* individuals on a number of tests are larger than the average differences between tests *within* individuals. The g factor, along with the smaller group factors in a hierarchical analysis, best represents all these salient facts far better than any orthogonal rotation of multiple first-order factors that dissipates g.

The g factor of a large and heterogeneous battery of mental ability tests differs in one important way from all the other rotated or unrotated factors that can be extracted, besides the fact that *g* is the single largest factor. The *g* factor cannot easily be characterized, if indeed it can be described at all, in terms of the features of the tests on which it has its most salient loadings, while all the primary factors can be characterized in terms of test content, such as verbal, numerical, spatial, and memory. When such diverse tests as Wechsler Vocabulary and Raven Matrices both have almost equally high *g* loadings when factor analyzed among a battery of diverse tests, psychological interpretations of *g* are difficult and certainly not obvious. The apparent features of the tests and the overt behavioral skills evinced by successful performance on the tests afford scant clues as to the basis for their high correlations with each other and with *g*. In attempting to characterize *g*, one is forced to seek a level of generality that transcends the "phenotypic" features of particular tests and to invoke theoretical concepts involving deeper levels of analysis. In confronting *g*, we are dealing with a highly abstract theoretical construct.

Factors, including *g*, are not themselves explanatory constructs. They are constructs which themselves require explanation. The *g* factor, above all, is a phenomenon worthy of scientific analysis and explanation. At present, we are still not very far ahead of the position noted by Spearman in 1927, when he stated that

> This general factor *g*, like all measurements anywhere, is primarily not any concrete thing but only a value or magnitude. Further, that which this magnitude measures has not been defined by declaring what it is like, but only by pointing out where it can be found. It consists in just that constituent—whatever it may be—which is common to all the abilities inter-connected by the tetrad equation. This way of indicating what *g* means is just as definite as when one indicates a card by staking on the back of it without looking at its face. Such a defining of *g* by site rather than by nature is what was meant originally when its determination was said to be only "objective." Eventually, we may or may not find reason to conclude that *g* measures something that can appropriately be called "intelligence." Such a conclusion, however, would still never be a definition of *g*, but only a "statement about it." (pp. 75–76)

I believe Spearman was quite correct in tentatively identifying intelligence only with *g* rather than with *all* of mental ability. There is no theoretical limit to the possible number of ability factors, so long as we can go on making slight variations in numerous mental tests such that their intercorrelations are less than 1 when corrected for attenuation. Hence, to equate intelligence with all of mental ability would surely render this concept scientifically undefinable and unmeasurable. If we reject this alternative, and *g* as well, as definitions of intelligence, we are left either with the problem of deciding which other factor should be included in our definition or of resorting to pure operationalism, declaring that one particular test is *the* measure of intelligence.

FLUID AND CRYSTALLIZED ABILITY

Cattell (1963, 1971) discovered that, when various tests with contents reflecting past learning experiences, cultural acquisition, and scholastic knowledge and verbal and numerical skills are factor analyzed along with tests involving novel problem solving and forms of reasoning based on analogies, series, and matrices all consisting of abstract or nonrepresentational figures, there emerges at the second level of a hierarchical analysis two factors which Cattell has labeled fluid and crystallized G, or G_f and G_c. Fluid ability, G_f, can be described as relation eduction, abstraction, and reasoning in novel problems. Crystallized ability, G_c, reflects the acquisition of specific and transferrable skills and knowledge made available by the individual's culture, education, and experience. The G_f much more nearly corresponds to Spearman's concept of g than does G_c. Since Cattell's hierarchical model does not go beyond the second level, Humphreys (1979) has described it as an "incomplete hierarchical model" (p. 108). Because G_f and G_c are correlated, and usually highly correlated, in an oblique solution, a substantial g should emerge as a third-order factor—a g which is essentially the same as Spearman's g. The degree of correlation between G_f and G_c seems to be related to a number of conditions:

1. When the persons are of similar cultural background and have had fairly equal amounts of school experience, G_f and G_c are highly correlated. In our university undergraduates, for example, the correlations between various typical tests of fluid and crystallized abilities are just about as high as the correlations between tests of the same type. And Raven's Advanced Progressive Matrices, a classical marker test for G_f, is more highly loaded ($+0.80$) on the overall g factor (first principal factor) of the Wechsler Adult Intelligence Scale than are any of the WAIS subtests themselves, even though the WAIS is generally viewed as being predominantly a test of crystallized abilities.

2. A random or representative sample of the general population shows higher correlations between G_f and G_c tests than samples with a more restricted range of ability.

3. As the collection of tests becomes larger and more varied in contents and item types, G_f and G_c become less clearly distinguishable. The total unweighted composite score on a sufficiently large and broadly representative sample of cognitive tasks is almost perfectly correlated with Spearman's g, that is, the highest-order g. Although I have not seen a definitive empirical demonstration, I venture the hypothesis that collections of tests that are considered typical measures of G_c would yield a g that comes increasingly closer to the g of a collection of tests that are considered typical measures of G_f as the number and variety of G_c-type tests increases. In other words, an increasing amount of G_f can be "distilled" out of typical G_c tests as they are sampled more broadly, because the only factor common to all the highly varied measures of crystallized abilities will

be fluid ability, G_f. The fluid aspect of G_c is increasingly siphoned into G_f, and the crystallized residue recedes into the residualized primary factors, or becomes at best merely a minor second-order factor.

Something very much like this picture is seen in two recent factor analyses of large batteries of highly varied psychometric tests selected to represent a number of the second-order factors previously identified in factor analyses by other investigators and which include G_f and G_c. When a Schmid-Leiman hierarchical factor analysis is applied to these data, G_f and G_c clearly appear as second-order factors. But when the hierarchical analysis is continued to the third level, yielding g, the residualized second-order G_f simply disappears; it is completely absorbed into g. In Gustafsson's (1984) analysis, the correlation between G_f and g is +1.00, and Gustafsson concludes that "the second-order factor of fluid intelligence is identical with a third-order g-factor" (p. 179). In this analysis, much of G_c is also "absorbed" by g, the correlation between them being +.76. Undheim (1981a, 198ab, 1981c) re-analyzed the correlations among the 20 tests of the Horn and Cattell (1966) study which identified G_f, G_c, and three other second-order factors (G_v—spatial visualization, G_r—fluency, and G_s—"speediness"). But Undheim carried the hierarchical analysis to the third level, yielding g. The residualized G_f turns out to be very small, accounting for less than half as much variance as G_c and less than one fifth as much variance as g. Undheim, with Gustafsson, concludes that Cattell's second-order G_f is equivalent to g, as defined in an orthogonalized hierarchical model—a g referred to by Undheim as a neo-Spearmanian g, because it is arrived at by a method of factor analysis quite different from Spearman's outmoded tetrad method. And the residualized G_c should not really be considered a general factor at all, but a minor second-order factor correlated with primary factors arising from tests of verbal, educational, and general cultural knowledge. G_c is practically equivalent to a residualized V:ed (verbal-educational) factor in Vernon's (1950) hierarchical model.

SIZE AND INVARIANCE OF g

As the first (unrotated) principal factor, g inevitably comprises more variance than any other factor that could be extracted from the matrix of test intercorrelations. But how large a percentage of the total variance does g actually account for? The answer depends on the number and diversity of the tests and the range of ability in the subject sample. To get a rough idea of the size of g, I have examined 20 independent correlation matrices comprising a total of more than 70 tests, such as the Wechsler battery, all the tests used in the National Longitudinal Study, the Kaufman Assessment Battery for Children, the Armed Services Vocational Aptitude Battery, the General Aptitude Test Battery, and other miscellaneous collections of tests. The tests have been administered to large and fairly representative samples of children and adults. (As all scores are age-standardized, the effects of age do not enter into the correlations.) The average percentage of variance accounted for by g in the 20 data sets is 42.7% (with a range from 33.4% to 61.4%). The average percentage of variance attributable to all other factors that have eigenvalues greater than 1, and thus can be said to constitute other common factors, is 15.3% (with a range from 9.6% to 22.8%)—call this the non-g common factor variance. The ratio of g variance to non-g common factor variance was determined for each of the 20 analyses; the mean ratio over the 20 studies is exactly 3:1; that is, g accounts for three times as much variance as the non-g common factor variance. (The g/non-g ratios ranged from 1.6 to 5.2.)

Spearman originally believed that g is invariant across different collections of tests, but this belief depended on the truth of his two-factor theory, namely, that the true-score variance of every test comprises only g variance and specific variance. But the overly simple two-factor theory had to be discarded. With the acknowledgment of group factors, the invariance of g across different collections of tests is no longer logically assured, but is an open empirical question. It is certainly true that the particular composition of the test battery will affect its g. A collection of tests in which all of them are verbal will yield a g which is some amalgam of both general and verbal ability and will therefore be a somewhat different g from a test composed of both verbal and nonverbal tests in roughly equal proportions. The degree of invariance of g is a function of the *number, diversity,* and cognitive *complexity* of the tests in the collection that is factor analyzed. Increasing any one or a combination of these conditions increases the similarity of the g factor extracted in different collections of tests.

The robustness of g in maintaining its identity when extracted from different test batteries, however, actually seems quite impressive. Tests with larger g loadings in one battery generally have large g loadings in most other batteries. It is a rare finding, for example, when a high-g test such as the Raven Matrices has a g loading below the median g in any collection of psychometric tests. When this nonverbal test is factor analyzed among just the six verbal subtests of the WAIS, for example, the size of its g loading is second only to that of Vocabulary. When the Raven Matrices and all 11 of the WAIS subtests, which includes five nonverbal performance tests, are factor analyzed, the Raven has the highest g loading among all of the tests.

Another example of the robustness of g: The g loadings of the 12 scales of the Wechsler Intelligence Scale for Children-Revised (WISC-R) were obtained for the 1868 white children in the national standardization sample. In an independent sample of 86 white children, the same 12 WISC-R subtests were factor analyzed along with the 13 subtests of the Kaufman Assessment Battery for Children (K-ABC), a mental ability test designed with the hope of being quite different from the WISC-R.[1] How similar are the WISC-R g loadings across two independent

---

[1] I am indebted to Dr. J. A. Naglieri for providing these data.

samples and when the 12 WISC-R subtests are factor analyzed as a 12 × 12 correlation matrix (the standardization sample) and as part of a 25 × 25 matrix including the 13 K-ABC subtests? The average *g* loadings of the WISC-R subtests in these two conditions are +0.57 and +0.58, respectively, and the rank-order correlation between the two sets of *g* loadings is +0.97. In short, the two *g* factors are practically identical, even across different samples and different collections of tests.

The robustness of *g* across diverse test batteries was shown long ago in a study by Garrett, Bryan, and Perl (1935), who factor analyzed a battery of six varied memory tests (meaningful prose, paired-associates, free recall of words, digit span, memory for forms, memory for objects) and extracted the *g* factor. This battery of tests then was factor analyzed along with four other diverse tests not especially involving memory (motor speed, vocabulary, arithmetic, form board). The *g* loadings of the memory tests in the two analyses were correlated .80. The overall correlation between *g* factor scores based on just the memory tests and *g* factor scores based on just the nonmemory tests was .87. This is evidence that the *g* of the six memory tests is very close to the *g* of the nonmemory tests. To be sure, the memory tests were not as highly loaded on *g* (average *g* loading = .42) as the vocabulary and arithmetic tests (average *g* loading = .65), but what little *g* the memory tests have is much the same *g* as found in the nonmemory tests. One would like to see larger-scale studies of this type based on many diverse psychometric tests, to determine the range of correlations between *g* factor scores extracted from different nonoverlapping sets of tests, controlling for reliability. My hunch is that all the *g* factors would be found to be highly similar.

We now have considerable evidence that *g* is highly consistent across different racial populations when they share the same language and general cultural background. In nine independent studies in which test batteries comprising anywhere from six to thirteen tests were administered to large representative samples of black and white Americans and a *g* factor was extracted separately from the correlation matrices in the black and white samples, the coefficients of congruence between the *g* factors obtained in the black and white samples of the nine studies ranged between +0.993 and +0.999, with a mean of +0.996. Such congruence coefficients indicate virtual identity of the *g* factor in the black and white populations (Jensen, 1985). (From the same data, the mean group difference in *g* is estimated at about 1.2 σ, where σ is the average within-group standard deviation.)

PRACTICAL EXTERNAL VALIDITY OF *g*

The practical predictive validity of intelligence and aptitude tests is mainly dependent on *g*. This has been so frequently demonstrated with respect to the prediction of scholastic achievement as to not bear further reiteration. Other factors, such as verbal and numerical factors, may enhance prediction of perfor-

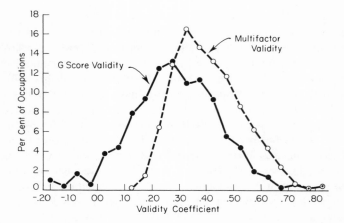

FIG. 4.2. Frequency distribution of 537 validity coefficients of the General Aptitude Test Battery for 446 different occupations. G score is general intelligence; multifactor validity is based on an optimally weighted composite of nine GATB aptitudes (including G) for each job category. The median validities are +0.27 for G and +0.36 for the multifactor composite.

mance in school and college and in the various armed forces training programs, because the predicted criterion is factorially complex, but the increases in the validity coefficient that result from adding other factors after g in the prediction equation are surprisingly small. The same is true for the prediction of occupational performance, although a clerical speed and accuracy factor and a spatial-visualization factor contribute significantly to the predictive validity for certain occupations. The g factor has predictive validity for job performance in nearly all jobs, and the validity of g increases with job complexity. I have found that the average predictive validities of each of the GATB aptitude tests, for 300 occupations, are substantially correlated (+.65) with the g loadings of these aptitude tests (Jensen, 1984). The frequency distribution of 537 GATB validity coefficients for predicting performance in 446 different jobs is shown in Fig. 4.2. The G score validity is a simple r, whereas the multifactor validity is a multiple R, which by its nature can never be less than zero and is always biased upwards. Hence, the small average difference between the two sets of validity coefficients is noteworthy. It seems very likely that no other mental ability factor or combination of factors, independent of g, has as many educationally, occupationally, and socially significant correlates as g.

THE "REALITY" OF g

We are frequently warned of the danger of reifying g, but it is never made very clear just what this might mean. Is there a danger of reifying the physicist's concept of energy, which is also an abstract theoretical construct? One and the same energy is assumed to be manifested in various forms, such as "kinetic," "chemical," and "potential" energy. Is the physicist guilty of reification when the concept of gravitation enters into his explanation of certain physical events? For nearly a century the gene was a hypothetical construct; quantitative genetics and population genetics were developed entirely in terms of this construct.

Factor analysts and intelligence theorists have always viewed *g* as a theoretical construct. The status of factors as theoretical constructs has been so thoroughly discussed by Burt (1940) in the chapter on "The Metaphysical Status of Factors" in his famous book *The Factors of the Mind* as to leave hardly anything more that could reasonably be said on this topic. Anyone who feels inclined to argue about this matter, I would insist, should first study Burt's masterful chapter. If it is thought that there is really anything left to argue about concerning the legitimacy of *g* as a bona fide theoretical construct, we should not be deprived of this enlightenment, explicated, one would hope, with the same philosophic thoroughness and scientific erudition that characterize Burt's chapter.

Recognition of *g* as a hypothetical construct is not to say that *g* represents nothing more than a mathematical artifact or a fiction entirely created by the algebraic operations of factor analysis applied to an arbitrary collection of tests. If this were proven true, *g* would indeed be of little scientific interest. The *g* factor gains interest to the extent that it is found to be significantly related to variables outside the realm of psychometric tests, from which the *g* construct originated. It has already been noted that a *g* factor dependably appears as a major hypothetical source of individual differences when we factor analyze any collection of diverse cognitive tasks on which a person's performance must meet some objectively quantifiable standard and on which task difficulty is not a function of sensory or motor skills, that is, the easy and hard tasks do not make different demands on sensorimotor abilities per se. And the *g* factors extracted from different collections of diverse cognitive tasks are much more highly correlated with one another than are the tasks themselves, or than are a simple unweighted sum of the scores on the tasks in each collection. Even though *g* is not absolutely invariant, the considerable congruence of the *g* factors extracted even from quite dissimilar collections of tests is consistent with the interpretation of the observed variability in *g* as a form of measurement error due to psychometric sampling. Variability in *g* arises from the fact that tests differ in their *g* loadings relative to other non-*g* factors, and most collections of tests that are submitted to factor analysis are quite limited in size. Hence there is psychometric sampling error in the *g* measured by any particular limited collection of tests. The resulting variability of *g* merely attenuates its potential correlation with external variables that might enhance its interest as a theoretical construct. In spite of such sampling variability, *g* is found to be related to a number of theoretically important variables which themselves have no connection whatsoever with psychometrics or factor analysis. Psychometric tests were never devised with the express purpose of predicting these variables. Here are some noteworthy examples.

Heritability of WAIS Subtests.   A simple method for inferring whether there is a statistically significant proportion of genetic variance in a metric trait is Fisher's variance ratio, F, based on the within-pair variances obtained in groups of monozygotic (MZ) and dizygotic (DZ) twins; that is, $F = s^2_{WDZ}/s^2_{WMZ}$. The rationale for this ratio is that the difference between the members of a pair of DZ twins (who have, on average, only about half of their segregating genes in common) is attributable to both genetic and environmental factors, while the difference between members of a pair of MZ twins (who have identical genotypes) can be attributable only to nongenetic factors. For the genetic traits, therefore, the within-pair variance of DZ twins is necessarily greater than that of MZ twins; the F ratio reflects this difference between DZ and MZ twins, and can be used as a statistical test of its significance. An F not greater than 1 is interpreted theoretically as indicating the absence of genetic variance in the trait in question, and the more that F exceeds 1, the larger is the contribution of genetic factors to the total variance in the trait. (The precise value of $F > 1$ required for statistical significance, of course, depends on the level of significance, α, and the degrees of freedom of the numerator and denominator of the variance ratio.)

There are two independent studies in which the 11 subtests of the Wechsler Adult Intelligence Scale (WAIS) were given to samples of MZ and DZ twins and the F ratios were determined for each of the WAIS subtests (Block, 1968; Tambs, Sundet, & Magnus, 1984). (The study by Block had 60 pairs each of MZ and DZ twins; Tambs et al. had 40 pairs each of MZ and DZ twins.) The F ratios in the two studies range from 1.36 to 4.51, with a mean of 2.26; 18 out of the 22 F ratios are significant beyond the 5% level. In each study I have calculated the rank-order correlation between the profile of F ratios on the 11 WAIS subtests with the profile of g loadings of the subtests obtained from the WAIS standardization sample for ages 19 to 24 years. Thus the F ratios and g loadings are based on independent samples. The rank-order correlation between the profiles of F ratios and g loadings is $+.62$ ($p < .05$) for the Block data and $+.55$ ($p < .05$) for the Tambs et al. data. These correlations should be compared with the rank correlation of $+.62$ between the profiles of F ratios obtained in the two studies. If that correlation can be regarded as an estimate of the reliability of the F profiles, the correlation between the F and g profiles corrected for attenuation becomes $+.79$ and $+.70$, respectively. (It should be noted that test reliability itself does not enter into the F ratios, since measurement error contributes the same proportion of error variance to the within-pair differences for MZ and DZ twins alike, and the proportionality factor cancels out in the F ratio, i.e., s^2_{WDZ}/s^2_{WMZ}.) In brief, these studies show that there is a relationship between the size of g loadings of the WAIS subtests and the degree to which the subtests reflect genetic variance.

Family Correlations.   Nagoshi and Johnson (1966) correlated the g loadings of 15 highly varied cognitive tests with the degree to which the tests are correlated between different pairs of family members in a large sample (927 families) of Americans of European ancestry. The correlations of the 15 tests' profile of *g* loadings with the profile of family correlations (disattenuated) on each of the 15 tests are as follows:

Between spouses	+.90, $p < .001$
Father-son	+.55, $p < .05$
Mother-son	+.69, $p < .01$
Father-daughter	+.59, $p < .05$
Mother-daughter	+.76, $p < .001$
Brother-brother	+.33
Sister-sister	+.42
Brother-sister	+.26

Nagoshi and Johnson note that the heritability of *g* (to the extent that heritability can be assessed through family correlations) appears to be higher than that of non-*g*, possibly because of greater assortative mating for *g* than for non-*g*; *g* appears to have greater influence on educational and occupational attainment than does non-*g*.

Inbreeding Depression.   If the genetic factors (alleles) that enhance the phenotypic expression of a trait are dominant, the effect of inbreeding is to lower the mean of the trait in the inbred group relative to the mean of a noninbred but otherwise comparable population—a phenomenon known as "inbreeding depression." The effect depends on the presence of genetic dominance, and the presence of dominance indicates that the trait has undergone directional selection in the course of its evolution. Hence the presence of inbreeding depression, signifying dominance, in the case of psychometric tests of ability suggests that variance on such tests reflects in part a trait of biological relevance as a fitness character for which there has been positive selection in the course of human evolution.

There are now at least 12 independent studies that have reported the genetically predictable effects of inbreeding on mental test scores (reviewed by Jensen, 1983; Agrawal, Sinha, & Jensen, 1984). The effect of inbreeding depression on the IQs of the children of first-cousins, as compared with children of unrelated parents, is about one third of a standard deviation for the Wechsler IQ (Jensen, 1983) and about one half of a standard deviation on the Raven Matrices, a more purely *g*-loaded test (Agrawal et al., 1984).

The degree of inbreeding depression on the various subtests of the Wechsler Intelligence Scale for Children (WISC) is directly related to the subtests' *g* loadings. The rank-order correlation between the profile of the index of inbreeding depression on 11 WISC subtests and the profile of the subtests' *g* loadings is about +0.8 (Jensen, 1983). Varimax rotated factor loadings show markedly smaller correlations with the index of inbreeding depression than do the *g* factor loadings. These results are consistent with the hypothesis that psychometric *g* reflects to some extent a biological aspect of intelligence that acts as a fitness character which has been subjected to natural selection in the course of human evolution.

Speed of Mental Processing.   A variety of reaction time (RT) tasks, or elementary cognitive tasks (ECT), have been found to be correlated with psychometric tests of intelligence and scholastic achievement (Carlson & Jensen, 1982; Carlson, Jensen, & Widaman, 1983; Carroll, 1980; Cohn, Carlson, & Jensen, 1985; Jensen, 1982a, 1982b; Jensen & Munro, 1979; Vernon, 1983; Vernon & Jensen, 1984). Not only are subjects' median RTs (measured over a number of trials) correlated with psychometric tests, but intraindividual variability (measured as the standard deviation of the subject's RTs over a number of trials) shows comparable correlations. The correlation of RT and ECTs with psychometric tests of ability seems to depend mostly, perhaps even entirely, on g. The remarkable thing about these simple tasks designed to measure speed of mental processing is that the tasks usually involve nothing that would ordinarily be regarded as intellectual content. The tasks are so simple and the error rates are so low that individual differences in performance usually cannot be reliably scored in terms of the number of right or wrong responses. RTs measured in milliseconds, however, when averaged over a number of test trials for each subject, yield measures with satisfactory reliability. The easiness of the tasks is suggested by median RTs that are generally less than one second.

With a sample of university students, Vernon (1983) used scores on the eleven subtests of the WAIS in a multiple regression to predict a composite RT score created by summing subjects' median reaction times and intraindividual variability after these were converted to z scores. The shrunken multiple R was substantial (.44), even in this restricted university sample (Full Scale IQ = 122, $SD = 8$). However, the correlation of only the g factor of the WAIS is $-.41$; that is, all the non-g variance in the 11 WAIS subtests increases the multiple R by only .03. The profile of g loadings of each of the WAIS subtests shows a rank-order correlation of $-.73$ with the profile of each of the subtests' correlations with the composite RT score, but this correlation is attenuated in this university sample which has a restricted range on g, as the lowest Full Scale IQ of any subject in the study was at the 75th percentile of the WAIS standardization sample. (The data for this analysis were provided by P. A. Vernon.)

A similar effect is seen in a study by Hemmelgarn and Kehle (1984), who used a RT apparatus like that described by Jensen and Munro (1979), in which the subject's RT to either 1, 2, 4, or 8 light-button alternatives is measured. (See Appendix for a description of this paradigm.) In this arrangement, RT is an increasing linear function of the number of bits of information in the stimulus array (i.e., bit = $\log_2 n$, where n is the number of light-button alternatives), an effect known as Hick's law. The slope of this function is regarded as a measure (inverse) of the speed of information processing, in milliseconds per bit. Hemmelgarn and Kehle correlated individual differences in the RT slope measure with scores on each of the 12 subtests of the WISC-R in a group of 59 elementary school pupils. (Chronological age was partialled out.) The profile of 12 correlations showed a rank-order correlation of $-.83$ ($p < .01$) with the profile of the subtests' *g* loadings. That is, the degree to which a WISC-R subtest is correlated with a RT index of information processing speed is related to the size of its *g* loading. The overall correlation between RT slope and Full Scale IQ was only $-.32$, but a larger correlation would hardly be expected, considering the generally low test-retest reliability of the slope measure. RT measures, and particularly the slope, are quite sensitive to physiological state, which fluctuates for individuals from day to day.

Evoked Cortical Potentials.   Various parameters of the electrical potentials of the cerebral cortex evoked by visual or auditory stimuli have been found to be correlated with IQ. Haier, Robinson, Braden, and Williams (1983) conclude:

> Perhaps, the most startling conclusion suggested by this body of work is not just that there is a relationship between brain potentials and intelligence, but that the relationship is quite strong. This supports the proposition that the variance of intelligence, with all its complex manifestations, may result primarily from relatively simple differences in fundamental properties of central brain processes. (p. 598)

Eysenck and Barrett (1985) derived a measure from the average evoked potential (AEP) that reflects the *complexity* of the waveform as indicated by the contour perimeter of the AEP wave in a given time-locked epoch. Higher IQ is associated with greater complexity of the AEP waveform; correlations in excess of $+.60$ have been found between IQ and AEP. Eysenck and Barrett factor analyzed the correlations among the 11 subscales of the WAIS obtained on 219 subjects on whom there were also obtained a composite measure of AEP complexity, which subtracts the complexity measure from the variability of the AEP, as variability is negatively correlated with IQ. When the composite AEP measure was included in the factor analysis along with the 11 WAIS subtests, the AEP had a loading of $+.77$ on the *g* factor. Moreover, the profile of *g* loadings of the WAIS subtests showed a rank-order correlation of $+.95$ ($p < .01$) with the profile of correlations of each of the WAIS subtests with the AEP. (When all the correlations in each profile were corrected for attenuation, the rank-order correlation dropped to $+.93$ [$p < .01$].) In short, the *g* factor of the WAIS is shown to be highly reflected in an electrophysiological measurement of cortical activity in response to simple stimuli (auditory "clicks") that cannot be regarded as cognitive or intellectual by any conventional definition of these terms.

Following a lead from Eysenck, Schafer (1985) independently has discovered a highly similar effect based on the AEP. In a sample of 52 adults of average or superior intelligence (WAIS Full Scale IQs of 98 to 142), Schafer measured the amplitudes of AEPs to two blocks each of 25 stimuli (auditory clicks). The percentage difference between the averages of the first and second blocks was a measure of EP habituation. (Subjects show a decrease in EP amplitude over repeated trials.) This measure of EP habituation correlated +.59 ($p < .01$) with WAIS Full Scale IQ. (When corrected for the restricted range of IQ in this sample, the correlation is +.73.) A range-corrected multiple R of .80 was obtained when another index derived from the AEP was used along with the habituation measure. Schafer correlated the profile of WAIS subtest loadings on the first principal component in his sample with the profile of correlations between each of the subtests and the EP habituation index; the rank-order correlation is +.91. When the same analysis is done using the first principal factor (instead of the first principal component) to represent the g of the WAIS, the results are as shown in Fig. 4.3. The rank-order correlation is +.77 ($p < .01$). The g loadings of the WAIS subtests in Schafer's sample show a congruence coefficient of +.98 with the loadings of the same subtests in the WAIS national standardization sample and therefore can be regarded as representing the same g.

The idea that g is really no more than merely an artifact peculiar solely to conventional psychometric tests and the mathematical manipulations of factor analysis applied to the intercorrelations among tests is utterly inconsistent with these findings showing that the g factor, rather than other components of variance in psychometric tests, is the most highly correlated with such variables

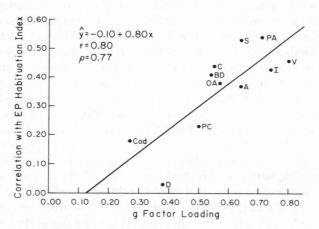

FIG. 4.3.   Correlation of the habituation index of the evoked potential (EP) with Wechsler Adult Intelligence Scale (WAIS) subtests plotted as a function of the subtests' g loadings (i.e., first principal factor) in Schafer's study. WAIS subtests: 1—Information, 2—Comprehension, 3—Arithmetic, 4—Similarities, 5—Digit Span, 6—Vocabulary, 7—Digit Symbol, 8—Picture Completion, 9—Block Design, 10—Picture Arrangement, 11—Object Assembly.

outside the realm of psychometrics as heritability, inbreeding depression, reaction times in elementary cognitive tasks, and certain parameters of cortical evoked potentials. The alotted space does not permit a proper summary and evaluation of a number of other physical correlates of *g*, such as stature, brain size, myopia, blood types, and body chemistry. (I am presently preparing a detailed critical review of all the evidence on the physical correlates of *g*.)

The evidence reviewed here also seems to contradict the notion expressed by a modern factor analyst, Undheim (1981c), who, in criticizing the Spearman and Cattell interpretation of *g* as a "free-floating capacity" states that ". . . there is no difference between intelligence and intellectual achievements. There is no measure of 'capacity,' only different measures of achievement" (p. 257). It is hard to understand in what sense *g*-correlated reaction times and evoked potentials can be described as "achievements" by any generally accepted meaning of that word.

One can make various statements about *g* while not fully understanding its nature. In light of our present understanding, it would seem safe to say that *g* reflects some property or processes of the human brain that is manifested in many forms of adaptive behavior, and in which people differ, and that increases from birth to maturity, and declines in old age, and shows physiological as well as psychological or behavioral correlates, and has a hereditary component, and has been subject to natural selection as a fitness character in the course of human evolution, and has important educational, occupational, economic, and social correlates in all industrialized societies. The behavioral correlates of *g* bear a close resemblance to popular or commonsense notions of intelligence. But whether the word "intelligence" is attached to *g* is unimportant, scientifically. An advantage of pursuing *g* is that we have a specified set of operations on a specified class of empirical data that dependably yields a phenomenon that we can study in generally the same analytic manner that science approaches any other natural phenomenon.

REFINING *g*

The notion that *g* comes about because test constructors intentionally make up tests so that they will all be positively correlated with one another, and that they discard all tests (or test items) that are not positively correlated with all the rest, is simply false. In fact, psychometricians have often striven to devise mental tests that would *not* be correlated with one another. Thurstone (1935), for example, devoted years to trying to produce a number of tests that would yield uncorrelated measures of what he then regarded as independent factors of ability, termed primary mental abilities (PMA). No amount of psychometric refinement of the various PMA tests could eliminate their substantial intercorrelations, and, in a review of Thurstone's work, Eysenck (1939) factor analyzed all of the

Thurstone tests and found that a large g factor could be extracted from their intercorrelations. All but a very few of the tests had larger factor loadings on g than on the particular primary mental ability factors that they were specially devised to measure as purely as possible.

However, it can be argued that a correlation between two tests is not necessarily evidence that the tests measure an ability that is common to both, except in a trivial sense. That is, the common factor implied by a correlation need not be anything we could legitimately regard as an ability or a cognitive process. Common factors can arise from different causes, some more profound or intrinsic than others. If psychometric g could be shown to be the result of some relatively superficial common factor, it would drastically change the complexion of g theory. Factor analysis per se makes no assumptions about the causes of correlation and is totally indifferent to the fact that two variables may covary without sharing any common process. It could be hypothesized, for example, that g merely reflects cultural differences that affect a broad spectrum of cognitive skills acquisition, or nutritional differences that affect motivation and performance of all kinds. To illustrate the point in the simplest way, I can make up an analogies test on which all of my relatives will obtain much higher scores than can be obtained by any other group of people on earth. The analogies would consist entirely of items like this:

Linda is to Lydia as Leo is to: Art, Bob, Eddie, Lou. All of the names in such items are of relatives who are related as spouses, siblings, parent-child, cousins, etc. If such a test, based on the names of my relatives, were given to all my relatives and to all of yours, there would be plenty of variance, very high item intercorrelations, and a big g factor. This g, however, would have arisen entirely from the *between* families component of the correlations, and the g would diminish drastically, or even disappear entirely, if the correlations were obtained *within* families.

The methodology for obtaining *between*-family and *within*-family correlations among tests and for contrasting the factors extracted from the two types of correlation matrices is a way of assessing the relative proportions of wheat and chaff that we have in our g factor and in the g loadings of any given variable in the analysis. (The same can also be said in regards to any other factors.) I have explicated this methodology elsewhere (Jensen, 1980).

Does the existence of g depend on those sources of test score variance that differ *between* families, such as cultural and social class influences on intellectual development? If so, a g factor should show up only in a *between*-families factor analysis; the g of a *within*-families analysis should be negligible, or at least quite different. Cultural and social class sources of variance exist only *between* families. By far the larger part of what most psychologists and sociologists mean by "environment," when they speak of environmental differences that affect performance on IQ tests, refers to the between-families aspect of environmental variance. Siblings reared within the same family share the same cultural and social class influences. By factor analyzing correlations among tests between and within families, we can determine the degree to which the extracted factors are a function of between-families variance. If a factor is essentially the same both between and within families, it can be said to reflect a more intrinsic or basic source of individual differences than if it exists only between families.

Between-families (BF) and within-families (WF) correlations require a sample of *N* families, each with two or more full siblings, to each of whom are administered two or more tests on which scores are age-standardized. A BF correlation between tests X and Y, for example, is obtained by correlating the *N* family means of each set of siblings on text X with the corresponding means on test Y. A WF correlation is obtained by correlating the signed difference between siblings on test X with their difference on test Y. The WF correlation, therefore, can reflect none of the BF variance. When BF and WF correlations are obtained on a number of different tests, we can extract a *g* from each correlation matrix and compare the BF and WF *g* factors by means of the coefficient of congruence, an index of factor similarity on a scale from 0 to ± 1.

So far we have no really ideal study of this type in terms of a sufficiently broad sample of tests. But three independent large sets of sibling data that I have analyzed give such consistent results as to suggest that other collections of cognitive ability tests would probably lead to the same conclusion. In one study (Jensen, 1980), children in 1,495 white families and 901 black families in grades 2 to 6 were given seven tests: memory, figure copying, pictorial IQ, nonverbal reasoning (figure analogies, matrices), verbal IQ, vocabulary, and reading comprehension. Only the two siblings most similar in age in each family were used. BF and WF intercorrelations of the tests were factor analyzed separately for black and white samples. The coefficients of congruence between the BF *g* and the WF *g* were +.985 and +.987 for the black and white samples, respectively. In other words, the *g* factors extracted from the BF and WF correlations are practically identical in this collection of tests, for both black and white children. (The average congruence coefficient between the black and white *g* factors is +.991.)

In an independent study, being prepared for publication, four of Thurstone's Primary Mental Ability tests (Verbal, Numerical, Spatial, and Reasoning) and Cattell's Test of *g* (from Cattell's 16 P.F. battery) were obtained on 313 siblings in 135 white families. The coefficient of congruence between the BF *g* and WF *g* is +.98.

It has been hypothesized that the intercorrelation of otherwise uncorrelated abilities, thereby giving rise to *g*, comes about as a result of cross-assortative mating for various abilities (Price, 1936). If each of two abilities is influenced by entirely separate sets of genes, and if both abilities are socially perceived as desirable, there will tend to be cross-assortative mating for the abilities. That is, not only will like attract like for either ability alone, but the separate abilities will be perceived with some degree of equivalence in terms of desirability, and there will be a marital correlation between the two abilities. This common assortment of the genes that affect two traits results in a genetic correlation between the traits in the offspring—but it is only a *between*-families genetic correlation. Because the separate genes segregate in the process of gametogenesis and each offspring of a given pair of parents receives a random half of each parent's genes, there will be no *within*-family genetic correlation between the traits that are genetically correlated in the population.

Hence a test of the hypothesis that g arises from genetic correlations due to cross-assortative mating for otherwise genetically independent abilities consists of a comparison of the BF and WF correlations between measures of different abilities.

The correlation of about $+.2$ between height and IQ appears to be this type of adventitious genetic correlation due to cross-assortative mating for stature and intelligence. Although the population correlation between height and IQ is a quite reliable phenomenon, no correlation has been found *within* families. Gifted children, for example, are taller than their nongifted age peers in the population, but they are not taller than their nongifted siblings.

A within-family genetic correlation between traits is usually attributable to *pleiotropy*, that is, the same gene affects two or more phenotypically distinct traits.

So far there have been too few studies of the genetic basis of correlated traits to permit any compelling conclusions. The results of the two BF and WF factor analyses previously mentioned, however, suggest that the correlations between abilities are probably not explainable in terms of cross-assortative mating for different abilities. But a satisfactory answer must await more detailed and systematic BF and WF correlational studies that are specifically designed to answer this question. The outcome of studies based on WF factor analysis has extremely important implications not only for the theory of g, but for the structural representation of all the abilities identified by factor analysis. The same method can be applied to chronometric measurements of processing components.

If there is any hope at all for identifying independent or uncorrelated elementary cognitive processes, it will be realized in the study of WF correlations. The study of abilities, throughout most of its history, has shown an obsession with independence. Many theorists have pursued it, hoping to discover components of ability that are truly independent in a more real sense than part of the uncorrelated residual variance of two (or more) ability tests after their common factor is partialled out. The desire for real components that are uncorrelated has been the philosopher's stone of psychometrics; it seems to be a philosophic position, not one dictated by scientific necessity. Since psychologists have not succeeded in devising psychometric tests that are uncorrelated, the search for this presumably desirable condition has moved on to the measurement of elementary cognitive processes. By measuring smaller and smaller components of performance on cognitive tasks, presumably, correlations between them, and hence g, will vanish. But it might well turn out that positive correlations between any measurable components of ability will vanish only at the point where correlation becomes impossible, that is, where there is no true variance in one (or both) of the correlated components. Just where in a reductionist analysis that point will be found we cannot say at present, but it is not impossible that variance and intercorrelations could be found all the way down to the level of neural structure and biochemical activity, just short of the molecules, or even atoms, that compose the brain. The well established substantial heritability of individual differences in *g* indicates that there is some biological substrate of individual difference in *g*, presumably in the neural structure and physiology of the cerebral cortex.

TASK COMPLEXITY AND *g*

Probably the most undisputed fact about *g* is that the *g* loadings of cognitive tasks are an increasing monotonic function of the perceived complexity of the tasks. Subjective judgments of task complexity are a fairly accurate predictor of the rank order of the tasks' *g* loadings. In general, *g* loadings decrease monotonically for tasks classified as relational, associative, perceptual, and sensorimotor. An especially clear demonstration of this is a factor analytic study by Maxwell (1972), who regards the relationship between *g* and task complexity as highly consistent with Thomson's (1948) sampling theory of *g*, which posits overlapping neural elements or bonds sampled by different tests. More complex tests presumably sample a larger proportion of the total available elements and therefore would have a greater amount of overlap than relatively simple tasks. But Spearman's theory of *g* as a general mental energy that is available for any cognitive task is equally consistent with Maxwell's results. Successful performance on the more complex tasks simply requires more mental energy. Spearman characterized *g* as ''the eduction of relations and correlates'' on the basis of his finding that tests involving relation eduction consistently had the largest *g* loadings of any of the many types of tests that he included in his factor analyses.

The fact that much simpler tasks than those involving relation eduction, even tasks that do not require any kind of reasoning at all, are also *g* loaded, albeit to a lesser degree, indicates that Spearman's own characterization of *g* is much too limited.

The apparent failure of the Galton and Cattell attempts to measure intelligence with quite simple ''brass instrument'' laboratory tests, such as various types of sensory discrimination and reaction time, and Binet's success, using much more complex tasks, led to the strongly entrenched belief among psychologists that complex tasks are an essential condition for the measurement of intelligence. Yet if intelligence tests are distinguished by very high *g* loadings, it is then also true that they differ from the much simpler tasks of the Galton-Cattell variety only in degree, for tests' *g* loadings vary in a perfectly continuous manner, ranging from values close to 1.00 on down to near 0.

A high level of task complexity, therefore, appears to be a sufficient but not necessary condition for the emergence of *g*. Some significant, positive, nonzero *g* loading is evident even in simple sensory discrimination tasks and simple reaction time (RT). As these simple tasks are made slightly more complex, their *g* loadings increase. Choice RT is more *g* loaded than simple RT, dual sensory discrimination tasks are more *g* loaded than single discrimination, and backward digit span is more *g* loaded than forward digit span. Various elementary cognitive tasks (ECTs) can be rank ordered in degree of complexity on the basis of the mean response latencies in performing the tasks. The rank order is highly correlated with the rank order of the tasks' correlations with psychometric *g* derived from unspeeded complex tests of reasoning and general knowledge. The ECTs here referred to are so simple that their mean response latencies are less than 1.5 seconds for average adults. Yet even these simple tasks are *g* loaded, and the loadings increase with task complexity as indexed by mean latency. Figure 4.4 shows the correlation of each of eight very simple ECTs with *g* factor scores derived from the ten subtests of the Armed Services Vocational Aptitude Battery (ASVAB). (The tasks are described in Jensen, 1985, p. 209.)

It will be noticed in Fig. 4.4 that the correlations of the single ECTs with the ASVAB *g* scores are all quite low, ranging from less than +.10 to about +.35.

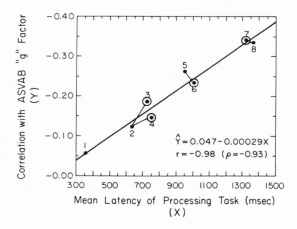

$$\hat{Y} = 0.047 - 0.00029X$$
$$r = -0.98 \ (\rho = -0.93)$$

FIG. 4.4.   Correlation of ECTs with ASVAB *g* factor scores as a function of task complexity as indexed by mean response latency (RT in msec.) on each task in a vocational college sample ($N = 106$). The dual tasks (#3, 4, 6, 7) are shown as circled dots and are connected to their single-task counterparts (#2, 5, 8) by straight lines. The tasks are described in the Appendix. (The numbers beside the data points indicate the specific processing tasks: 1—RT, 2—DIGIT, 3—DT2 Digits, 4—DT3 Digits, 5—SD2, 6—DT2 Words, 7—DT3 Words, 8—SA2.)

The shrunken multiple R between all eight of the ECTs and the ASVAB g, however, is .47, which can be compared with the average of the correlations among the ten ASVAB subtests: $\bar{r} = +.36$, $SD = .19$.

Findings such as this raise the interesting question of whether all of the g variance derived from very complex psychometric tests of reasoning, problem solving, and the like, can possibly be predicted by a composite score on a sufficient number of elementary cognitive tasks, none of which involves more than a very simple level of complexity. Another way of asking the same question: Is there nothing in g that depends upon the higher mental processes, or the so-called *metaprocesses?*

This is one of the key questions in this field, and it has not yet been adequately investigated. It is not enough to use just a few simple tasks, however reliable the scores may be made by repeated measurements. By *simple* tasks I mean ECTs that provide chronometric data such as choice RT in the Hick paradigm, speed of scanning short-term memory in the S. Sternberg paradigm, and speed of access to overlearned verbal codes in long-term memory as in the Posner paradigm. (I have described these paradigms elsewhere [Jensen, 1982a].) Each such task is much like a very homogeneous psychometric test in which all the items are of the same type. Most such homogeneous tests have a great deal of specificity (i.e., task-specific variance) and consequently not much g or other common-factor variance. Yet these ECTs are positively correlated with one another, and each is also correlated with the g factor of psychometric tests. But these single-task correlations are generally quite low, mostly falling between .3 and .4 in unrestricted samples, and even with proper corrections for attenuation, the upper limit of correlation is not greater than .50. A composite score derived from several different ECTs, however, can show larger correlations with psychometric g, because the total variance of a composite reflects the covariances among the components more than the variances that are specific to each component, and the covariances contain the g of the ECTs, some part of which is the same as the g of psychometric tests. It seems a likely possibility that if response latencies on as many as a dozen or so simple but distinctly different chronometric ECT paradigms were optimally combined, the composite score would correlate about as highly with psychometric g as do, say, the Raven Matrices, or Cattell's Culture-Fair Test of g, or the Wechsler, or the Stanford-Binet. Yet none of the ECTs entering into the composite score would involve anything that would ordinarily be regarded as intellectual content or as requiring reasoning or problem solving in the generally accepted sense of these terms.

Although correlations of the magnitudes being found between single ECTs and single psychometric tests may seem rather small, they should not be cause for despair. Remember that chronometric ECTs have virtually no method variance in common with unspeeded psychometric tests. It is instructive to compare the typical .3 to .4 correlations between ECTs and psychometric tests with the correlations between various psychometric tests in terms of each of their com-

TABLE 4.2

Components of Correlations[a] Among Subtests of the WISC-R Derived from Factor Loadings in a Schmid-Leiman Orthogonal Hierarchical Factor Analysis, with g Correlations Below the Diagonal, and Correlations Based on the Group Factors (Verbal, Memory, and Performance) Above the Diagonal

WISC-R Subtest	I	S	V	C	A	DS	TS	Cod	PC	PA	BD	OA	M
Information		13	16	13									
Similarities	45		17	13									
Vocabulary	48	48		17									
Comprehension	40	40	43										
Arithmetic	38	38	41	34		16	14	08					
Digit span	29	29	32	26	25		21	12					
Tapping span	23	23	25	21	20	15		11					
Coding	25	25	27	22	21	16	13						
Picture completion	34	34	37	31	29	22	18	19		08	15	15	09
Picture arrangement	33	33	35	29	28	21	17	18	25		12	12	07
Block design	43	43	47	39	37	29	23	24	33	32		22	14
Object assembly	33	33	36	30	29	22	17	19	25	25	33		14
Mazes	25	25	27	22	21	16	13	14	19	18	24	19	

(Group factor brackets above the diagonal: verbal over C, A; memory over DS, TS, Cod; performance over PA, BD, OA, M.)

[a] Decimals omitted.

mon factors. Table 4.2 shows the factor-generated correlations among the WISC-R subtests in the white standardization sample, representing the full range of ability in the white population. Below the diagonal are the correlations due to the g factor, in a Schmid-Leiman hierarchical analysis. Above the diagonal are the correlations among tests due to the group factors, Verbal, Memory, and Performance, orthogonal to g and to one another. (Correlations not significantly greater than zero at the .05 level, with $N = 1868$, are not included.) If ECTs are correlated only with the g factor of psychometric tests, we should expect the correlations to fall in the same ballpark as the correlations among psychometric tests that are due entirely to g. Such correlations, shown below the diagonal in Table 4.2, range from $+.13$ to $+.48$, with a mean of $+.28$.

Experimental Manipulation of Complexity. The g loadings of tests may be related to their complexity because responses to test items are scored as pass or fail (i.e., "right" or "wrong") and individuals' scores are determined by the threshold on the continuum of item difficulty at which the information processing system is inadequate to the task. The efficiency or capacity of the processing system may be revealed most clearly when the system is pushed or strained. Individual differences in the threshold of breakdown of the system may provide the most efficient measure of g

The processing difficulty of an item can be measured in terms of percent failing the item, if it is difficult enough to allow failure, or in terms of mean response latency when the item is easy enough for subjects to pass it. This hypothesis was tested in an extreme fashion by one of my graduate students (Paul, 1984). The Semantic Verification Test (SVT) consists of 14 item types, or conditions, each presented six times with different permutations of the three letters ABC. The 14 conditions are shown in Table 4.3. Following each item is

TABLE 4.3
The Fourteen Conditions of the Semantic
Verification Test

SVT Variable	Semantic Condition
1	___before___
2	___not before___
3	___after___
4	___not after___
5	___first___
6	___not first___
7	___last___
8	___not last___
9	___between___ & ___
10	___not between___ & ___
11	___before___ & ___
12	___not before___ & ___
13	___after___ & ___
14	___not after___ & ___

some permutation of ABC which either agrees ("true") with the preceding statement or disagrees with it ("false"). The subject responds True or False to each item. When the SVT is given as a chronometric task to university students, the correlation between their median RTs and scores on the untimed Advanced Raven Matrices test is about −.50. Considering the great simplicity and lack of intellectual content of the SVT, and the restricted range of ability in the university group, this is a remarkably high correlation. A high level test of verbal knowledge and reasoning, Terman's Concept Mastery Test, is correlated about +.50 with the Advanced Raven Matrices in the university population, and WAIS Vocabulary, the most highly g loaded of the 12 WAIS subtests, is correlated only +.44 with the Raven.

The SVT was given as an untimed paper-and-pencil test to 77 third-grade pupils to determine the percent failing each item. The SVT test was also given as a chronometric task to 50 university students. The mean median RTs to the 14 conditions of the SVT ranged from about 650 msec to 1200 msec, and the overall error rate was 7%. The task was obviously of trivial difficulty for university students. The interesting point, however, is that the difficulty levels (percent failure) of the 14 conditions for the third graders shows a rank-order correlation of +.79 (disattenuated = +.83) with the mean median RTs of the 14 SVT conditions in the university sample. In university students taking the SVT as a chronometric test, the correlation of mean error rates on the 14 SVT conditions with the corresponding mean median RTs was +.82. Twenty-five university students were also asked to rank the 14 SVT conditions in the order of their complexity, according to the students' subjective judgments of complexity. The average correlation between subjects' rankings was +.80 and the reliability of the composite rank order of the 25 complexity rankings was +.99. This judged complexity of each of the 14 SVT conditions was correlated +.86 with the difficulty levels of the 14 conditions in the third graders and +.82 with the mean median RTs of the university sample. Hence there is a close relationship between judged item complexity, item difficulty (measured as percent failing), and item processing times.

These SVT RT data, however, present a seeming paradox with respect to psychometric g as measured by the Advanced Raven Matrices. Although the correlations between Raven scores and the median RTs of the 14 SVT conditions range between −.30 and −.50, the degree of correlation is *inversely* related to task complexity as indicated by median RT or judged complexity. The correlation between tasks' median RT and their correlation with the Raven is −.67, that is, the *less* complex SVT conditions show the *higher* correlation with Raven scores. Another paradox: although the *positive* SVT conditions (e.g., A before B) are less complex and have RTs that average 210 msec less than the *negative* SVT conditions (e.g., A not before B), the mean correlation of the RT for positive SVT items with the Raven is −.42, as compared with −.39 for the negative items (disattenuated, these are −.45 and −.43, respectively). And when the RTs of the 14 SVT items are factor analyzed, the positive items have the higher mean loading on the first principal factor (.91 vs. .88; disattenuated, .99 vs. .96). It had been hypothesized that the negative condition would necessitate an extra mental manipulation in the processing to produce a correct response and that this increased complexity would increase the item's *g* and its correlation with the Raven. Although the negative items are clearly judged as being more complex and have longer RTs (by 210 msec, on average), they are not more highly correlated with a marker test of psychometric *g*. It is surprising and puzzling. We plan to repeat the study to see if this paradoxical result is replicated.

Another experimental manipulation of complexity is by means of comparing RTs to *single* and *dual* tasks. If tasks A and B are performed separately in such a way that performance on one does not affect performance on the other, they are termed *single* tasks. If they are presented simultaneously or in close temporal proximity in such a way that performance on either A or B is significantly affected by their proximity, then the task on which performance is measured (usually chronometrically) is termed a *dual* task. (Dual tasks are also referred to as *competing* tasks.) The effect of dual tasks is commonly interpreted as dividing attention and straining processing capacity. The effect of this generally is to increase the *g* loading of the dual task relative to its *g* loading as a single task. In a dichotic listening task, for example, the subject simultaneously hears a different pattern of three notes in each ear (e.g., left ear: high, low, high; right ear: low, high, low) and is then randomly postcued to report the pattern presented to one ear. Using such paradigms, Stankov (1983; also see Fogarty & Stankov, 1982) discovered that performances are more highly intercorrelated and therefore more *g* loaded when presented as dual than as single tasks. Dual tasks were also more highly correlated with subjects' educational level than their single-task counterparts. In the most thorough study of a wide variety of dual tasks that I have come across in the literature, Fogarty (1984) found that dual tasks have higher *g* loadings than their single-task counterparts only when the latter have relatively low *g* loadings. Tasks that have high *g* loadings when presented as single tasks, however, have somewhat lower *g* loadings when they are presented as a dual task. Presumably, when a task is already high *g* as a single task, making it a dual task strains processing capacity to the point of breakdown, which lowers the reliability of the performance by increasing the rate of chance successes and consequently attenuates the task's *g* loading. Fogarty's factor analysis of single and dual tasks also suggests, although not very strongly, that dual tasks are factorially more complex than the single component tasks and that dual tasks may involve cognitive processes that are not operative in single tasks. But the evidence for this is weak and ambiguous, and in a study explicitly addressed to this question, Lansman, Poltrock, and Hunt (1983) found no evidence for any distinct abilities to divide or focus attention.

The importance of the relationship between single vs. dual tasks and *g* is that the increase in *g* loading must be purely a process phenomenon arising from the greater strain placed on cognitive capacity by dual tasks. There is no increase in the informational content of the dual task.

In our own lab we have worked with four single and dual tasks (Jensen, 1985; Vernon, 1983; Vernon & Jensen, 1984). Our various ECTs, in which performance is always measured in terms of median RT, are described in the Appendix (taken from Jensen, 1985, p. 209). Returning to Fig. 4.4, which shows the relationship between task complexity (as indicated by the mean latency, or RT, on the task) and the task's correlation with the *g* factor scores derived from the Armed Services Vocational Aptitude Battery (ASVAB) in a sample of 106 vocational college students, we see that the correlation between these variables is quite large, $r = -.98$, $\rho = -.93$. It appears anomalous, however, that one of the four dual tasks (#6) has a slightly lesser correlation with *g* than its single-task counterpart. These correlations are so similar, however, that this reversal might be due to sampling or measurement error. Another way of looking at this relationship is in terms of mean differences in median RTs between two groups that differ in general ability, or *g*. The mean differences between two contrasting groups should be less attenuated by measurement error. Figure 4.5 shows the correlation between the complexity of the processing tasks, as indicated by their mean latency (RT), and the mean difference between vocational college students and university students; both groups are normal youths of comparable age, and both groups are of above-average intelligence, although they differ about one standard deviation in psychometric *g*. As seen in Fig. 4.5, there is a high correlation ($r = +.97$, $\rho = +.98$) between task complexity and the degree to which the tests discriminate between the vocational and university groups. Also, in every case, the dual tasks show greater discrimination than their single-task counterparts. These data are highly consistent with the hypothesis that dual tasks, or task competition, increases *g* loading.

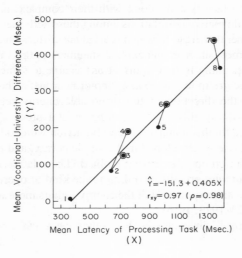

FIG. 4.5. Mean difference (in msec.) between vocational college students ($N = 106$) and university students ($N = 100$) on various elementary cognitive tasks as a function of task complexity as indicated by mean response latency (RT) on each of the tasks in the vocational college group. The same task, when presented as part of a dual task, is shown as a circled dot connected to its single-task counterpart by a straight line. Note that in every case, the dual tasks are more discriminating between the vocational and university groups than the single tasks. The tasks are the same as those in Fig. 4.4.

THEORIES OF *g*

Ever since Galton originally propounded the notion of intelligence as a general ability which could be channelled into any kind of intellectual activity, and Binet advanced the idea of intelligence as the average level of a number of different abilities and skills, various theories of intelligence, and of *g*, have been classifiable into two broad categories: *unitary* theories and *multiple* theories. The same divisions might also be labeled *power* theories and *sampling* theories, respectively. This division of theoretical conceptions has continued down to the present day. One of the major challenges to the field at present is to achieve a satisfactory theoretical resolution and consensus on the problem of the unitary or multiple nature of *g* based on empirical evidence. The answer may depend on the level of analysis we choose for our study of cognitive abilities. In formulating laws of mechanics, matter can be regarded as unitary—the solid, seeable, touchable, solid objects in our surroundings. For most of the laws of chemistry, matter is seen as multiple at the level of mixtures, compounds, and molecules, but as unitary at the level of atoms. In subatomic physics, atoms are no longer unitary but are seen as composed of multiple particles—protons, neutrons, etc., which are also analyzable into more elemental components, the quarks, and there is still no assurance that even the quarks are the ultimate units of matter that defy further analysis.

Unitary Theories of *g*

Spearman's "Mental Energy". Spearman suggested that *g* is a "mental energy" of which there is a limited amount for each individual and in which individuals differ. The brain's "energy" can be directed to any kind of mental activity executed by different "neural machines." Individual differences in the "machines" show up as group factors and, along with their complex interactions, as specificity. The overall positive correlations among these activities is all being powered by the same general energy, in which individuals differ. To quote Spearman's (1923/1973) own most succinct and explicit statement of this theory: "The brain may be regarded (pending further information) as able to switch the bulk of its energy from any one group to any other group of neurons; as before, accordingly, the amount and the direction of the disposable energy regulate respectively the intensity and the quality of the ensuing mental process" (p. 346). Elsewhere he elaborates: "In this manner, successful action would always depend, partly on the potential energy developed in the whole cortex, and partly on the efficiency of the specific group of neurons involved. The relative influences of these two factors could vary greatly according to the kind of operation; some kinds would depend more on the potential of the energy, others more on the efficiency of the engine" (1923/1973, p. 6).

I have used the word "energy" in quotes in this context, because it is not always clear whether Spearman endows the term with the meaning it has in the physical sciences, which is its only scientifically legitimate meaning, or whether he intends it merely as an analogy or metaphor. If g is equated with energy in the accepted physical sense of the term, then, as Thomson (1948, p. 58) pointed out, Spearman's theory can be rejected in its literal form, because the brain (or the cerebral cortex) does not act as a reservoir of free-floating energy that can be consolidated and shifted around from one group of neurons to another. Whatever energy exists in the brain resides within the individual nerve cells as an electrochemical reaction propogated along the neural membrane. If, on the other hand, Spearman's use of "energy" is merely metaphorical, it contributes little, if anything, to the scientific understanding of g. It merely underscores Spearman's belief in the unitary nature of the cause of g but does not suggest what this unitary cause is in empirically testable terms. Spearman's "mental energy" theory of g has always been regarded metaphorically by most psychologists, and consequently has not been taken very seriously. As metaphor, it has been peculiarly unfruitful in generating empirical investigation, and today Spearman's "energy" theory has only the status of an historical relic.

Burt's Neurophysiological Theory.   Burt (1940, p. 217; 1961) proposed a unitary theory of g that is not metaphoric, but anatomical and physiological. He held that g reflects the general character of the individual's brain tissue, such as the degree of systematic complexity and organization in the neural architecture, and he cites histological evidence that the cerebral cortex of some mentally deficient persons shows less density and branching of neurons than is seen in the brains of normal persons. To account for the ubiquity of g, Burt hypothesizes that the general quality of an individual's cerebral cortex is more or less homogeneous throughout; hence every intellectual function would reflect this homogeneous quality of the nervous system. As with Spearman's theory, specialized areas or neural structures, in addition to particular classes of acquired knowledge and skills, give rise to group factors and specificity. Burt's theory, being non-metaphoric, has the virtue of being testable, at least in principle, but I am not aware that, so far, there have been any systematic histological investigations of individual differences in the brain's architectonics in relation to psychometric g among normal persons. There is little that psychologists as such can do to confirm or substantiate Burt's theory, and so it has attracted little attention.

Motivation or Drive Theories of g.   A number of Spearman's contemporaries, such as Maxwell Garnett, suggested that g results from individual differences in will, motivation, or drive level, which affects performance on all cognitive tasks (see Spearman, 1927, pp. 88–89). Essentially the same notion has been recently revived by Macphail (1985), who equates g with Hull's D (for *d*rive). This theory runs into difficulty on at least three grounds.

First, no independent evidence has been brought forth to show that high-g persons are more highly motivated in test-taking situations than low-g persons.

Differences in range and intensity of intellectual interests are more likely a result than a cause of differences in *g*.

Second, a theory of *g* as *D* runs into trouble with the Yerkes-Dodson law, the empirical generalization that the optimal drive level for error-free or efficient performance of a task is lower for simple than for complex tasks. Yet cognitively complex tasks are generally more *g* loaded than simple tasks, and high- and low-*g* individuals differ more on complex than on simple tasks. We should predict just the opposite if *g* were equated with *D*. (No one has yet proposed an inverse equation of *g* with *D*.)

Third, there is direct empirical evidence showing that higher levels of ability in a cognitive task are not associated with higher motivation or arousal during task performance, as measured independently by pupillary dilation, a sensitive indicator of motivational arousal and effort. Ahern and Beatty (1979) measured the degree of pupillary dilation as an indicator of effort and autonomic arousal when subjects are presented with test problems. They found that (1) pupillary dilation is directly related to level of problem difficulty (as indexed both by the objective complexity of the problem and the percentage of subjects giving the correct answer), and (2) subjects with higher psychometrically measured intelligence show less pupillary dilation to problems at any given level of difficulty. (All subjects were university students.) Ahern and Beatty concluded:

> These results help to clarify the biological basis of psychometrically-defined intelligence. They suggest that more intelligent individuals do not solve a tractable cognitive problem by bringing increased activation, "mental energy" or "mental effort" to bear. On the contrary, these individuals show less task-induced activation in solving a problem of a given level of difficulty. This suggests that individuals differing in intelligence must also differ in the efficiency of those brain processes which mediate the particular cognitive task. (p. 1292)

Speed of Processing and Neuronal Errors in Transmission as the Basis of g.   Unitary theories of *g* necessarily hypothesize individual differences in some extremely basic attribute that plausibly could affect every kind of cognitive performance. Galton originally hypothesized mental speed, and proposed using RT to visual and auditory stimuli as a measure of general ability.

Galton's own efforts and those of his leading American disciple, James McKeen Cattell, were notably unsuccessful in establishing any substantial relationship between RT and independent criteria of intellectual ability, and the pursuit of intellectual correlates of RT was virtually abandoned for more than half a century.

In the past decade, however, with the development of relatively sophisticated chronometric techniques in experimental cognitive psychology (e.g., Posner, 1978), this line of research has been vigorously pursued by many investigators. As a result, many different *g*-loaded psychometric tests have been found to show significant correlations with RT measurements derived from a considerable variety of cognitive tasks ranging in complexity from simple RT (response to the onset of a single stimulus) to response latencies in verbal and figural analogies. I have reviewed the research on many of these RT tasks and their relationship to psychometric g elsewhere (Jensen, 1982a, 1982b).

Correlations between RTs measured in different paradigms are highly positive, indicating a large general speed factor that loads in a wide variety of ECTs. This general speed factor is correlated with the psychometric g derived from nonspeeded traditional tests of intelligence, both verbal and nonverbal.

The correlation between psychometric g and speed on ECTs increases with the complexity of the ECT only up to a point; beyond it the correlation diminishes with increasing task complexity. The reason is probably that the more complex tasks invite different strategies for attaining the preferred response and these tend to confound individual differences in sheer speed of mental processing with individual differences in choice of strategy. In the great variety of psychometric test items, on the other hand, strategy effects become relegated to specificity or narrow group factors, and the g factor reflects the more fundamental attribute of mental speed. Hence psychometric g is more highly correlated with relatively simple ECTs that do not invite a variety of solution strategies.

Not only speed is correlated with g, but also the consistency of RTs to the same task over repeated trials. We measure intraindividual variability in RT in terms of the standard deviation of RT over n trials, signified as σ_i. This measure is often more highly correlated (negatively) with psychometric g than is the median RT, despite the usually higher reliability of the median RT.

Mean differences in these parameters between criterion groups selected from different regions of the IQ distribution have shown more consistent and clear-cut results than correlations between these parameters and psychometric test scores within groups. The reason for this seems to be that correlations are always attenuated by unreliability of measurement and restriction of the range of ability, whereas a mean group difference is little affected by these factors. Differences between clearly separated criterion groups are more capable than correlations of detecting the more subtle effects in various RT paradigms.

One of our recent studies (Cohn, Carlson, & Jensen, 1985) illustrates the contrasts in mental speed between academically gifted and nongifted youths (ages 12 to 14 years) on a variety of ECTs (described in the Appendix) ranging in complexity from simple and choice RTs, to S. Sternberg's short-term memory scan for digits, to discriminating physically same vs. different word pairs, and discriminating simple synonyms vs. antonyms. All but the simple and choice RT tasks were presented both as single and as dual tasks (DT). The gifted (G) group ($N = 60$), with an average age of 13.5 years, consisted of manifestly talented youths whose scores on the SAT were on a par with university students five to six years older. The G subjects were enrolled in university courses, competing successfully in a predominantly math and science curriculum. The nongifted

(NG) group consisted of 70 white junior high school students averaging about 1 *SD* above statewide norms on the California Test of Basic Abilities. The G and NG groups differed 1.9 *SD* on the Raven Standard Progressive Matrices. For both the G and NG groups, the chronometric tasks were of trivial difficulty, with mean response latencies never as long as 2 seconds, even in the NG group.

Figure 4.6 shows the mean latencies on the eight mental processing tasks for the G and NG groups and a group of 50 U.C., Berkeley undergraduates (Un). The rank-order correlations between the shapes of the profiles are all +.98 or above. Groups G and NG differ significantly (*p* < .01 to .001) on all of the tasks, but G and Un show no significant differences. (G and Un differ only a nonsignificant 2 points on the Raven Matrices.) The within-group multiple correlation of the eight processing tasks with Raven Matrices is .60 and .50 for groups G and NG, respectively.

Most remarkable is the difference between the G and NG groups on the Hick paradigm, since it has the least intellectual content of any of the tasks, requiring only that the subject release a pushbutton when a light goes on among an array of either 1, 2, 4, or 8 lights (corresponding to 0, 1, 2, and 3 bits of information). Figure 4.7 shows the results. The groups differ beyond the .001 level at every level of task complexity from 0 to 3 bits, for both RT and MT (the interval between releasing the home button and pressing the button adjacent to the light). Also, the slopes of RT for the G and NG groups differ by .70 *SD*s, which is highly significant (*p* < .001), and intraindividual variability in RT differs significantly at every level of bits.

Such findings show that psychometric *g* can be measured by means of tests that have little or no knowledge content and that require no complex problem-solving strategies. In these respects, they are very unlike ordinary IQ tests, yet

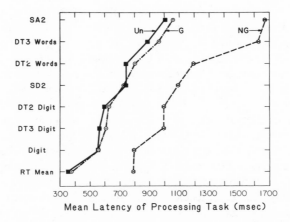

FIG. 4.6.   Mean latency of various processing tasks in three groups: university students (Un), gifted (G), and nongifted (NG).

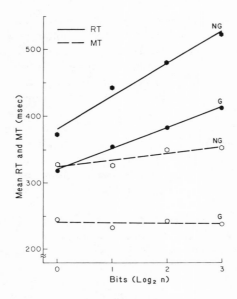

FIG. 4.7. Reaction time (RT) and movement time (MT) in NG and G groups as a function of bits of information corresponding to 1, 2, 4, and 8 light/button alternatives.

they are clearly correlated with IQ and discriminate between groups that differ in terms of generally accepted criteria of intelligence. These findings also suggest that the processes underlying g may be essentially simpler than their manifestations in complex problem solving and other "real-life" behavior, just as the cause of a disease may be simpler than its multifarious symptoms.

The speed factor that we are measuring with these tasks should not be thought of as intentional, overt speed at the level of gross behavior. It is not the kind of speed that suggests hurrying and rushing through the performance of a task. Speed can be thought of in two senses: cognitive and conative. Cognitive speed is speed of information processing. Conative speed is speed due to conscious effort, minimizing rest pauses, and the like. Conative speed as it affects performance on psychometric tests cannot begin to explain the correlation between RT and test scores. Complete abandonment of this overly simple and superficial explanation is long overdue. In our own work, we have taken pains to minimize the speed factor in test taking. All psychometric tests are given without time limit; subjects are urged to take their time and to attempt every item. We have also found that when tests were given with a time limit and scored and then subjects were given as much additional time as they felt they needed to earn a maximal score, subjects remained in approximately the same rank order under both methods of scoring, so that the correlation of the scores with another variable would be scarcely affected whether the test was timed or untimed. Also, we have found that speeded tests show no higher correlations with RT tasks than untimed tests. Clerical checking tests, which are the most dependent on speed, have the lowest g loadings and the poorest correlations with RT measures. For example, the Coding test, the most speed-dependent test of the ten tests in the ASVAB battery, has the lowest *g* loading in this battery and the lowest correlation with the general speed factor extracted from a battery of eight RT tests (Vernon & Jensen, 1984). The same thing is true of the speeded Coding (or Digit Symbol) subtest of the WAIS (Vernon, 1983). The clincher is that we have found a correlation close to zero between individual differences in total test-taking time (under untimed conditions) and total scores on the test.

How then can we explain the correlation between RTs in ECTs and psychometric *g?*

Several well-established concepts and principles of cognitive psychology provide a rationale for the importance of a time element in mental efficiency. The first such concept is that the conscious brain acts as a one-channel or *limited-capacity* information-processing system. It can deal simultaneously with only a very limited amount of information; the limited capacity also restricts the number of operations that can be performed simultaneously on the information that enters the system from external stimuli or from retrieval of information stored in short-term or long-term memory (STM or LTM). Speediness of mental operations is advantageous in that more operations per unit of time can be executed without overloading the system. Second, there is *rapid decay* of stimulus traces and information, so that there is an advantage to speediness of any operations that must be performed on the information while it is still available. Third, to compensate for limited capacity and rapid decay of incoming information, the individual resorts to *rehearsal and storage* of the information into intermediate or long-term memory, which has relatively unlimited capacity. But the process of storing information in LTM itself takes time and therefore uses up channel space, so there is a "trade-off" between the storage and the processing of incoming information. The more complex the information and the operations required on it, the more time that is necessary, and consequently the greater the advantage of speediness in all the elemental processes involved. Loss of information due to overload interference and decay of traces that were inadequately encoded or rehearsed for storage or retrieval from LTM results in "breakdown" and failure to grasp all the essential relationships among the elements of a complex problem needed for its solution. Speediness of information processing should therefore be increasingly related to success in dealing with cognitive tasks to the extent that their information load strains the individual's limited channel capacity. The most discriminating test items would thus be those that "threaten" the information-processing system at the threshold of "breakdown." In a series of items of graded complexity, this "breakdown" would occur at different points for various individuals. If individual differences in the speed of the elemental components of information processing could be measured in tasks that are so simple as to rule out "breakdown" failure, as in the various RT paradigms we have used, it should be possible to predict individual differences in the point of "breakdown" for more complex tasks. This is the likely basis for the observed correlations between RT variables measured in relatively simple tasks and total scores on complex g-loaded tests.

The speed of elemental information processing may not be the most basic source of individual differences in intelligence but may be only a secondary phenomenon, derived from a still more basic source of individual differences—a hypothetical construct I have termed "neural oscillation," which would account for individual differences in intertrial variation in RT as well as in individual differences in RT averaged over a given number of trials (Jensen, 1982a, pp. 6–10). Eysenck (1982a) also regards differences in mental speed and RT as derivative, in the sense that a person's average RT is not directly attributable to the speed of neural conduction or synaptic transmission. He hypothesizes that speed differences arise from individual differences in the rate at which errors occur in the transmission of neural impulses in the cortex. The stimulus message must persist until the "pulse train" of neural impulses exceeds a certain fidelity threshold. The more random "noise" or error tendency in the neural system, the more time this takes, and hence speed of reaction is a derivative phenomenon.

So far, there has been no way empirically to decide between the hypotheses of processing speed and errors, or "noise," in the neural transmission of errors as basic to g. Whether these concepts will be able to account for all or only some fraction of the true-score variance in the g derived from a large and diverse sample of psychometric tests has yet to be determined. It will be necessary, first of all, to determine how large a correlation with g can be obtained from a battery of various simple chronometric tasks of sufficient number and diversity to minimize the proportion of task-specific variance in the composite score. The best composite correlations we have obtained thus far would account for at most only about half of the variance in g.

Multiprocess Theories

Thomson's Sampling Theory of g.   E. L. Thorndike (1927) was the first systematic proponent of the theory that g is explainable in terms of the hypothesis that human abilities consist of independent multiple bonds or neural connections acquired through experience, and that successful performance on various tests enlists somewhat different but overlapping "samples" of all the myriad bonds that constitute ability. Thorndike believed that individuals differ innately in the potential number of bonds they can acquire, the total number being limited by the number and degree of branching of the neural elements. As this theory proposes no inherent structure or organization of the bonds themselves, Spearman (1927, Ch. V) termed all theories of this type "anarchic."

Sir Godfrey Thomson, who spent a year's postdoctoral followship working with Thorndike, developed Thorndike's bond-sampling theory further, formalizing it mathematically in his now famous book *The Factorial Analysis of Human Ability* (1948, Ch. XX). Essentially, he showed that the correlation between two tests, X and Y, could be represented as $r_{xy} = (p_x p_y)^{1/2}$, where p is the proportion of the total pool of elements or ''bonds of the mind'' ''sampled'' by a given test. From this formulation, Thomson was able to demonstrate mathematically how both *g* and specificity could come out of the factor analysis of a number of tests that call upon different but overlapping samples of elements. Thomson's sampling theory, as it has come to be known, is illustrated in Fig. 4.8. It can be seen that in this model the factors yielded by factor analysis do not represent anything in the mind, which consists only of innumerable disparate bonds or elements of some kind. The organization or structure represented by factors is seen as an artifact of the tests, which can be devised to sample large or small numbers of elements. Complex tests would sample more elements than simple tests, and complex tests would therefore be apt to be more highly correlated with other tests, and consequently would be more *g* loaded. To simulate the typical results of Spearman's factor analyses, the sampling model only requires, in Thomson's (1948) words,

> that it be possible to take our tests with equal ease from any part of the causal background; that there be no linkages among the bonds which will disturb the random frequency of the various possible combinations; in other words, that there be no ''faculties'' in the mind. . . . The sampling theory assumes that each ability is composed of *some but not all* of the bonds, and that abilities can differ very markedly in their ''richness,'' some needing very many ''bonds,'' some only a few. (p. 324).

Thomson left the number and nature of the hypothetical bonds, or elements, of the sampling theory completely unspecified. This deficiency is the core of the theory's weakness in terms of its testability as empirical science. It can be proved mathematically that any number of composite aggregates of whatever degree of correlation with each other can always be expressed as functions of elements that are themselves uncorrelated (Spearman, 1927, p. 59). Despite its superficial plausibility, Thomson's sampling theory does not qualify as a scientific theory. Although it has enjoyed much greater uncritical popularity in recent years than

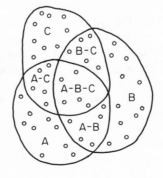

FIG. 4.8.   Illustration of Thomson's sampling theory of abilities, in which the small circles represent elements or bonds and the large circles represent tests that sample different sets of elements (labeled A, B, and C). Correlation between tests is due to the number of elements sampled in common, represented by the areas of overlap.

Spearman's theory of "mental energy," it has been no more fruitful in advancing empirical research on the nature of g or intelligence. Loevinger's (1951) verdict seems inescapable:

> The sampling theory hardly qualifies as a true theory, for it does not make any assertion to which evidence is relevant. Perhaps the large number of adherents to this view is due to the fact that no one has offered evidence against it. But until the view is defined more sharply, one cannot even conceive of the possibility of contrary evidence, nor, for that matter, confirmatory evidence. A statement about the human mind which can be neither supported nor refuted by any facts, known or conceivable, is certainly useless. Bridgman and other philosophers of science would probably declare the sampling theory to be meaningless. (pp. 594–95)

Along with Spearman's theory of "mental energy," Thomson's rival sampling theory can be consigned to the museum of psychology's past history, but unlike phlogiston, without ever having enjoyed the scientific virtue of being empirically disproved.

Modern descendants of the sampling theory are scarcely more definite as to the number and nature of the sampled elements. A number of modern theorists conceive of intelligence, or g, as the entire repertoire of an individual's knowledge, skills, and problem-solving strategies available at a given point in time (e.g., Humphreys, 1984; Tyler, 1976, pp. 24–25; Undheim, 1981c). In the same key, the g factor has also been attributed to individual differences in the number of well-learned cognitive skills that generalize across a broad spectrum of problem-solving situations.

All theories of this type run into difficulty with the empirical finding that a relatively small variety of tests, which can in no way be construed as a representative sample of the entire repertoire of knowledge, skills, and strategies, are capable of measuring g. One obviously does not require a sample of the entire repertoire of knowledge, skills, and strategies to measure g. A few relatively content-free tests of the "fluid g" variety are even more g loaded than are tests that aim to sample individuals' entire cognitive repertoire. It is also hard to see how these theories can accommodate the substantial correlations between RT measures derived from quite simple ECTs and psychometric g. What repertoire is sampled by these ECTs, most of which seem entirely too elementary to be described in terms of "knowledge, skills, and strategies"? If most of the g variance could be predicted by chronometric measures on a number of ECTs, or by a physiological measure such as the evoked potential, which involves no conscious behavioral aspects at all, these neo-Thomsonian sampling theories (perhaps better termed "repertoire" theories) would be empirically falsified in terms of any of their meaningful implications.

Component Process Theories of g.   Process theories of g are essentially sampling theories, but with an important difference from Thomson's bond-sampling theory and from theories that identify g with the entire repertoire of knowledge, skills, and strategies. The essential difference is that process theories posit some limited number of basic information-processing components, each of which can be described in terms of the particular functions it performs—functions that, when viewed in isolation, are usually too elemental to be thought of as skills or strategies at the level of overt behavior. An *information-processing component* is itself a hypothetical construct, defined as a process that operates on sensory inputs or internal representations of objects or symbols. These elementary cognitive processes have been described by terms such as stimulus apprehension, sensory encoding, iconic memory, short-term memory (STM), memory scanning, retrieval of information from long-term memory (LTM), transformation of encoded information, transfer, discrimination, generalization, eduction and mapping of relations, visualization and mental rotation of figures in 2- or 3-dimensional space, and response execution. A less elemental class of operations are *metaprocesses,* which are acquired strategies for selecting, combining and using the elementary processes, problem recognition, rule application, planning, organization of information, time allocation, and monitoring of one's own performance.

Processing theory explains psychometric g in terms of a small number of components or metacomponents that are required for performance in an extremely broad variety of tests. Individual differences in the presence or absence or efficiency of operation of these general or common components and metacomponents are what account for the positive intercorrelations among practically all complex mental tests and the consequent emergence of g when all the intercorrelations are factor analyzed. The interpretation of g in terms of componential theory has been quite thoroughly explicated by Sternberg and Gardner (1982).

Figure 4.9 depicts the hypothesized relationship between the processing variables and psychometric variables. The horizontal dashed line in Fig. 4.9 separates the behaviorally measurable or inferred psychological variables (above the line) from those that are measurable only physiologically, such as evoked brain potentials, or inferred physiological processes, such as cortical conductivity (Klein & Krech, 1952), synaptic errors (Hendrickson, 1982), neural oscillation (Jensen, 1982a), and the like. The physiological level is represented as one general factor, g_B (B for "biological"), although, given our present state of knowledge, this level could just as well be represented as several distinct physiological processes or as correlated processes, due to their sharing one common process, i.e., g_B. The nature of this physiologic underpinning of human abilities is a major focus of Eysenck's (1982b) theorizing about the findings of correlations between features of the average evoked potential and psychometric g, or g_P, which is depicted in the hexagon at the top of the hierarchy in Fig. 4.9. All of the solid lines in the figure represent correlations. (Correlations could also be shown between elements at every level and every other level of the hierarchy, but these have been omitted for the sake of graphic simplicity.)

The various elementary cognitive processes (P) are correlated through their sharing of common physiological processes. Different parts of the brain or differ-

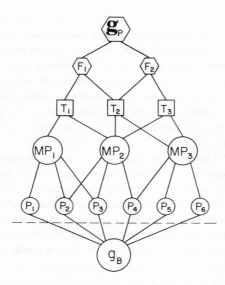

FIG. 4.9. Simplified representation of hypothesized relationships among processing components and psychometric variables: g_P—psychometric g, F—group factor, T—test, MP—metaprocesses, P—elementary cognitive process, g_B—a general biologic substrate, as reflected in physiological indices such as evoked potentials.

ent neural assemblies are presumably specialized for various aspects of information processing. The processes in this model, depicted here as being closely connected with some biological substrate, can all be measured by means of chronometric tasks, either directly or through derived scores. By subtraction of response latencies of simple tasks from the latencies of more complex tasks, one can measure individual differences in the additional processes involved in the latter.

Different sets of elementary processes, *P*, can be utilized by a given *metaprocess (MP)*. Because metaprocesses are further removed from the biologic substrate and are probably mainly products of learning and practice, their connection to the biologic substrate is via the elementary processes which enter into the metaprocesses. Different metaprocesses are intercorrelated because they share certain elementary processes in common and also because the experiential factors which inculcate metaprocesses are correlated in the educational and cultural environment. It is probably at the level of metaprocesses that cultural differences have their primary impact.

Both processes and metaprocesses enter into performance on complex *psychometric tests (T)*. Even a single complex test item may well depend on a number of *P*s and *MP*s for successful performance. Various tests are intercorrelated, moreover, not only because they share certain common *P*s and *MP*s, but also because they may share common information stored in long-term memory. Note that at each level in this hierarchy, something new is added in terms of environmental inputs. The cumulative impact of these acquired elements is at its maximum at the level of single items in psychometric tests. Item variance is largely *specificity*, which may arise from individuals' idiosyncratic experiences, making for unique and uncorrelated bits of information, or from complex and unique interactions among the P and MP demands and the informational content of a particular test item. In fact, all primary psychological measurements are saturated with task-specific variance. Chronometric measurements of elementary processes in specially contrived laboratory tasks are no exception. Specificity, which is the bane of individual differences research, can be reduced only by using composite scores or factor scores (which are a particular weighted composite of the component scores) derived from a number of varied tasks or tests, thereby "averaging out" the specificity of the individual tasks.

The top part of the hierarchy in Fig. 4.9, including T, F, and g_P, encompasses the realm of traditional psychometrics, including various test scores and hierarchical factors extracted by factor analysis. Here, for the sake of simplicity, are represented only two first-order factors (F_1 and F_2) and one second-order factor, psychometric g, or g_P. (The most general factor, of course, may emerge as a third-order or other higher-order factor.) Each successively higher factor level excludes some sources of variance. The primary factors, for example, exclude the test-specific variance, and the second-order factors exclude the variance that is peculiar to each primary factor, and so on. The most general factor, g_P, is the variance common to all the sources below it in the hierarchy.

Some homogeneous tests, such as Raven's Progressive Matrices, contain relatively little specificity and are therefore quite good measures of g_P. Other tests, like the Wechsler scales, although containing quite heterogeneous items and subtests with considerable specificity, yield composite scores from which, in effect, the specificity is "averaged out," providing a good measure of g_P.

Superficially very different tests, such as Verbal Analogies, Digit Span, and Block Designs, are intercorrelated presumably not because of common content or correlated educational experiences, but because they have a number of elementary processes and metaprocesses in common. Because the more superficial differences between tests contribute mainly to their specificities, these differences are not reflected in g_P. Hence it has been found that g factor scores are more highly correlated with chronometric measures of elementary processes than are any particular types of tests. Thus, although g_P and P_1, P_2, etc., appear widely separated in the schematic hierarchy, they actually seem to have greater variance overlap, as shown by the correlation, than do some of the more proximal variables. This picture may also help to elucidate the otherwise surprising finding that, although g_P is derived from factor analysis of psychometric tests which bear virtually no superficial resemblance in format, content, or method of administration to the RT techniques used in elementary cognitive tasks (ECTs), g_P shows correlations with ECTs almost as large as with the psychometric tests from which g_P is derived.

One of the crucial theoretical questions, with reference to Fig. 4.9, regarding which there is presently little consensus, is whether more of the variance in psychometric g (g_p) is attributable to the processes (P) or to the metaprocesses

(*MP*). The learned information content in the psychometric tests (*T*) can already be virtually ruled out as an important source of *g* variance, because tests that differ markedly in their information content, such as vocabulary and matrices, are nevertheless highly saturated with one and the same *g*. The multiple correlation of several simple ECTs with g_P has been so substantial in some studies as to suggest that perhaps as much as 50% of the g_P variance is accounted for by individual differences in elementary cognitive processes. If task specificity were further minimized in such studies, by using at least three or four different techniques for measuring each of the elementary processes that have already been shown to yield substantial correlations, it seems likely that even more than half of the *g* variance would be associated with the elementary processing variables. Also, the existing studies have not taken sufficient account of the reliability of these processing measures. Proper corrections for attenuation might appreciably raise the correlations between ECTs and g_P. Split-half or other internal consistency estimates of the reliability of ECTs usually overestimate the test-retest reliability, and it is the test-retest reliability which should be used in correcting correlations for attenuation when the correlated measurements have been obtained in different test sessions, on different days, for example, or even at different times of the same day, such as before and after lunch. Some of the ECT measurements are so highly sensitive to an individual's fluctuating physiological state from morning till night and from day to day as to have quite low test-retest reliability as compared with most psychometric tests. Theoretical interest, of course, focuses on the *true-score* multiple correlation between the elementary cognitive processes and g_P. Individual differences in metaprocesses, or strategies, might even obscure task correlations with *g*. Hughes (1983), for example, found that a measure of learning rate is more highly correlated ($r = -.59, p < .001$) with *g* (i.e., Raven Matrices) when all subjects are constrained by instructions to use the same strategy for learning than when they are not so instructed and can choose their own strategies ($r = +.16$, n.s.). This is just the opposite of what one should predict if metacomponents (strategies) were the chief sources of variance in learning rates or in *g*. One goal of componential research is to determine the proportions of variance in *g* accounted for by each of a number of clearly identifiable processes and metaprocesses. This has not yet been accomplished.

There is a crucial difference between *factors* and *processes* that is often overlooked. Factors arise completely out of individual differences, and factors, including *g*, reflect only individual differences in whatever causal mechanisms are involved in the factors. Because of their exclusive dependence on variance, therefore, factors do not necessarily represent the operating principles of the mind. Processes that were so essential to individual survival in the course of human evolution as to be left with little or no genetic variance would not show up as factors. As far as I know, it has not been determined if there are any cognitive processes of this nature, that is, processes that might show age differences but not reliable individual differences among biologically normal, healthy persons. It is at least a safe assumption that various processes may differ in the extent of their individual differences variance, and this can be assessed when individual differences are measured chronometrically, since such measures are on a ratio scale, which permits comparisons of variability based on the coefficient of variation ($V = \sigma/\mu$). The point is that *processes* will be reflected in *factors* in proportion to their coefficients of variation. (For example, the *g* factor is always smaller, relative to other factors, in college students than in the general population, because students are selected essentially on *g*.) Unlike a factor, a process can be identified and its importance in the mental economy assessed without need to take account of individual differences. RT is measured on a task (e.g., simple RT) which it is hypothesized requires processes A and B, and RT is measured on a task (e.g., choice RT) which requires processes A, B, and C. The difference in milliseconds beween the mean RTs on the two tasks is taken as evidence for process C and indicates its magnitude in relation to other processes assessed by the same type of experimental paradigm, known as the *subtraction* method, originated by Donders (1868–69/1969) in the early years of mental chronometry. The processes that best account for *g* will not necessarily be those that experimental cognitive research determines are the most important in terms of their mean effects, but those on which there is the largest variance. These two features of processes may or may not be related.

Although Sternberg believes that the bulk of *g* is attributable to variance in metaprocesses, this view is not an essential feature of componential theories in general. Moreover, its truth has not yet been demonstrated. A proper test would logically require that an adequate number of measures of elementary cognitive processes be entered first into the stepwise multiple regression, followed by the metaprocess measures, for predicting *g* factor scores, thereby determining the independent contribution of metaprocess to the variance in *g*. The outcome of such a study would be of great theoretical importance. My guess at this point is that Sternberg's belief is wrong, and that most of the *g* variance will be accountable in terms of elementary cognitive processes, with little if any variance left for the residualized metaprocesses. I conjecture that the opposite would be found for many narrow group factors or, in particular, certain types of tasks that lend themselves to various strategies. A lack of some clear demarcation between processes and metaprocesses would invite further debate. Studies permitting ''strong inference'' are most needed.

If processes (or metaprocesses) are uncorrelated, then, of course, we must explain *g* in terms of a number of common processes that enter into performance on a wide variety of tests. This seems to be the gist of Sternberg's componential theory of *g* (Sternberg & Gardner, 1982). But if the processes themselves are correlated with each other and yield a *g* much like psychometric *g*, then the theoretical picture is quite different. How do we explain the correlations between the process measures? In terms of still other, even more elemental, processes?

And what if they too are correlated? How far down the reductionist hierarchy will this "infinite regress" extend?

There is every indication that elementary cognitive processes are, in fact, quite highly correlated. This fact has frustrated some of Sternberg's componential analyses, the clarity of which depends on there not being very high correlations between measures of putatively different processes. For example, Sternberg and Gardner (1982, p. 249), using chronometric techniques, measured individual differences in three different tasks which were intended to yield parameter estimates of three distinct components. But the three tasks (analogies [A], classification [C], and series completion [S]) were all so highly correlated $(r_{AC} = .86, r_{AS} = .85, r_{CS} = .88)$ that when the common factor was partialled out, the little remaining variance attributed to the residualized components was unreliable. The loadings of the three tasks on their common factor are A = .91, C = .94, S = .93, without correction for attenuation. It leaves one to wonder if there are individual differences in components independent of the common factor, which may be the ubiquitous g. Sternberg himself has specifically noted that when the time taken for each of the component processes in his chronometric analogies tasks are factor analyzed with psychometric reference tests of g, individual differences in the average time for all the components (what Sternberg calls the regression constant) show a higher correlation with g than any of the single component latencies. Sternberg (1979a) writes:

Information-processing analyses of a variety of tasks have revealed that the "regression constant" is often the individual differences parameter most highly correlated with scores on general intelligence tests. This constant measures variation that is constant across all of the item or task manipulations that are analyzed via multiple regression. The regression constant seems to bear at least some parallels to the general factor. (p. 24)

Referring to the same point elsewhere, Sternberg (1979b) says this about the "regression constant": ". . . we can feel pleased to be rediscovering Spearman's g in information processing terms." This is not an admission of failure for the componential theory of g, but an important discovery for which Sternberg deserves credit. But it also suggests that the search for g has to be pushed below the level of metaprocesses and elementary cognitive processes. Look again at where that leads us in terms of Fig. 4.9. *Any* kind of sampling theory, at least at the level of cognitive processes, may prove wholly unnecessary for explaining g. Do people differ in psychometric g because they are strong or weak on different components? Or is the g of the processing components essentially the same as psychometric g? Although there are distinctly different information processes, as demonstrated in experimental mental chronometry (e.g., Posner, 1978), individual differences in these processes may be very highly correlated because of some general property of the nervous system that acts in all of them.

One of the best known ECTs, the S. Sternberg short-term memory scanning paradigm (S. Sternberg, 1966, 1975), can be used to illustrate the problem of seeking the explanation of *g* in terms of tests sampling a number of elementary cognitive processes that are common to many tests, but which are themselves so saturated with some common source of variance, perhaps the same *g* they are intended to explain, as to force us to seek the explanation of *g* at a still more basic level of analysis. In the Sternberg memory-scan (M-scan) paradigm, the subject is shown (either simultaneously or sequentially) a set of digits, varying in set size (*s*) from 1 to 7 digits. After the subject has studied the series (termed the *positive set*) for a few seconds, the set disappears, and 1 or 2 seconds later a single target digit appears on the screen. The subject responds as quickly as possible by pressing buttons labeled either YES or NO in terms of whether the target digit was or was not a member of the positive set. The subject's RT is measured in milliseconds. Numerous studies have shown that it takes slightly longer to respond NO than YES, and RT increases as a linear function of set size. (The serial position of the target digit in the positive set has no effect on the RT.) Studies have also shown that the intercept and slope of this function, or the overall mean RT, are negatively correlated with psychometric *g* (e.g., Chiang & Atkinson, 1976; Keating & Bobbitt, 1978; McCauley, Dugas, Kellas, & DeVellis, 1976).

The *intercept* of the linear function relating RT to set size reflects *E*, the time required for encoding the target digit; *B*, the time for making a binary decision (Yes or No); and *R*, response production (releasing or pressing a button). The *slope* of the function reflects *S*, the speed of scanning short-term memory, specifically the time required per digit. A subject's mean RT for any given set size is hypothesized to comprise the time required for each of the information-processing components (i.e., *E, B, R, S*).

The reverse of this M-scan paradigm is called visual scan (V-scan). Everything is exactly the same except that the single target digit is presented *first*, followed by the positive set. The subject must visually scan the positive set and respond YES or NO as to the presence or absence of the target digit in the positive set. No scanning of STM is involved, just visual scanning of the physically displayed set of digits.

Visual scanning and STM memory scanning are obviously completely different processes. Yet in the four studies in which both the V-scan and M-scan paradigms have been used with the same group of subjects, there were no significant differences between V-scan and M-scan in intercepts, slopes, or overall mean RT (Ananda, 1985; Chiang & Atkinson, 1976; Gilford & Juola, 1976; Wade, 1984). But the really important point, in terms of implications for the componential sampling theory of *g*, is the finding that individual differences in the RT parameters are very highly correlated across the V-scan and M-scan tasks, so much so, in fact, as to swamp the possibility of demonstrating any independent abilities in the two types of task. Ananda (1985) found a correlation of +.69 between mean RTs on M-scan and V-scan; Wade (1984) found a correlation of +.85. There is no telling how much higher these correlations would be if they could be corrected for attenuation. (Neither study determined test-retest reliability.) Chiang and Atkinson (1976) gave their subjects more trials and therefore obtained considerably more reliable measurements of individual differences. Their correlation between V-scan and M-scan was +.97 for intercepts and +.83 for slopes. These very high correlations (not corrected for attenuation) were obtained despite the restricted range of ability in the Stanford University students who served as subjects. (Corrected for attenuation [using Day 2-Day 3 test-retest reliability], the above correlations are 1.20 and 1.13, respectively.) Chiang and Atkinson state, ''It might be argued that performance on these search tasks is related to a general factor, speed, and that it is not useful to break down performance into several component processes or to distinguish between parameters of these processes'' (p. 668). But this conclusion is a nonsequitur. Distinctly different processes may be involved in M-scan and V-scan, but the different processes may not be distinguishable in terms of individual differences because some more basic general factor that affects speed in all cognitive operations is common to both processes. In fact, we generally find such high correlations among the RTs to various ECTs that only one factor accounts for nearly all of the intercorrelation among the ECTs. Nonspeeded psychometric tests of *g* also have considerable loadings on the same general speed factor.

If the condition I have described with respect to the M-scan and V-scan tasks is found in future research to be generally typical of most other ECTs that presumably involve distinctly different processes, and if it is their largest common factor, rather than any subordinate factors, that is correlated with psychometric *g*, it would seem clear that an adequate theory of *g* will most probably have to invoke some even more basic level of analysis than is provided by the processing-component sampling theory. It seems likely that continuing effort to achieve a scientifically adequate theory of one of the most controversial psychological constructs will force it out of psychology altogether and arrive at an empirically testable formulation in genuinely physiological terms. But this may be the ultimate fate of any truly important construct of psychology. Is it not the ultimate ''psychologists' fallacy'' to be satisfied with a psychological explanation of a psychological phenomenon?

REFERENCES

Agrawal, N., Sinha, S. N., & Jensen, A. R. (1984). Effects of inbreeding on Raven Matrices. *Behavior Genetics, 14,* 579–585.

Ahern, S., & Beatty, J. (1979). Pupillary responses during information processing vary with Scholastic Aptitude Test scores. *Science, 205,* 1289–1292.

Ananda, S. M. (1985). *Speed of information processing and psychometric abilities in later adulthood.* Unpublished doctoral dissertation, University of California, Berkeley.

Block, J. B. (1968). Hereditary components in the performance of twins on the WAIS. In S. G. Vandenberg (Ed.), *Progress in human behavior genetics*. Baltimore, MD: Johns Hopkins.

Burt, C. (1940). *The factors of the mind: An introduction to factor analysis in psychology*. New York: Macmillan.

Burt, C. (1961). Factor analysis and its neurological basis. *British Journal of Statistical Psychology, 14*, 53–71.

Carlson, J. S., & Jensen, C. M. (1982). Reaction time, movement time, and intelligence: A replication and extension. *Intelligence, 6*, 265–274.

Carlson, J. S., Jensen, C. M., & Widaman, K. F. (1983). Reaction time, intelligence, and attention. *Intelligence, 7*, 329–344.

Carroll, J. B. (1980). *Individual difference relations in psychometric and experimental cognitive tasks*. Chapel Hill, NC: L. L. Thurstone Psychometric Laboratory, University of North Carolina.

Cattell, R. B. (1963). Theory of fluid and crystallized intelligence: A critical experiment. *Journal of Educational Psychology, 54*, 1–22.

Cattell, R. B. (1971). *Abilities: Their structure, growth and action*. Boston: Houghton-Mifflin.

Chiang, A., & Atkinson, R. C. (1976). Individual differences and interrelationships among a select set of cognitive skills. *Memory and Cognition, 4*, 661–672.

Cohn, S. J., Carlson, J. S., & Jensen, A. R. (1985). Speed of information processing in academically gifted youths. *Personality and Individual Differences, 6*, 621–629.

Donders, F. C. (1969). Over de snelheid van psychische processen. In W. G. Koster (Ed. and Trans.), *Attention and performance II, Acta Psychologia, 30*, 412–431. (Original work published 1868–69)

Eysenck, H. J. (1939). Primary mental abilities. *British Journal of Educational Psychology, 9*, 270–275.

Eysenck, H. J. (Ed.). (1982a). *A model for intelligence*. Heidelberg: Springer-Verlag.

Eysenck, H. J. (1982b). The psychophysiology of intelligence. In C. D. Spielberger & J. N. Butcher (Eds.), *Advances in personality assessment* (Vol. 1). Hillsdale, NJ: Lawrence Erlbaum Associates.

Eysenck, H. J., & Barrett, P. (1985). Psychophysiology and the measurement of intelligence. In C. R. Reynolds & V. Willson (Eds.), *Methodological and statistical advances in the study of individual differences*. New York: Plenum.

Fogarty, G. J. (1984). *The structure of abilities underlying performance on competing tasks*. Unpublished doctoral dissertation, University of Sydney.

Fogarty, G. J., & Stankov, L. (1982). Competing tasks as an index of intelligence. *Personality and Individual Differences, 3*, 407–422.

Garrett, H. E., Bryan, A. I., & Perl, R. E. (1935). The age factor in mental organization. *Archives of Psychology* (No. 176).

Gilford, R., & Juola, J. (1976). Familiarity effects on memory search and visual search. *Bulletin of the Psychonomic Society, 7*, 142–144.

Gustafsson, J.-E. (1984). A unifying model for the structure of intellectual abilities. *Intelligence, 8*, 179–203.

Haier, R. J., Robinson, D. L., Braden, W., & Williams, D. (1983). Electrical potentials of the cerebral cortex and psychometric intelligence. *Personality and Individual Differences, 4*, 591–599.

Hemmelgarn, T. E., & Kehle, T. J. (1984). The relationship between reaction time and intelligence in children. *School Psychology International, 5*, 77–84.

Hendrickson, A. E. (1982). The biological basis of intelligence. Part I: Theory. In H. J. Eysenck (Ed.), *A model for intelligence*. Heidelberg: Springer-Verlag.

Hughes, O. L. (1983). A comparison of error based and time based learning measures as predictors of general intelligence. *Intelligence, 7*, 9–26.

Humphreys, L. G. (1979). The construct of general intelligence. *Intelligence, 3,* 105–120.

Humphreys, L. G. (1984). General intelligence. In C. R. Reynolds & R. T. Brown (Eds.), *Perspectives on Bias in Mental Testing* (pp. 221–247). New York: Plenum.

Jensen, A. R. (1980). Uses of sibling data in educational and psychological research. *American Educational Research Journal, 17,* 153–170.

Jensen, A. R. (1982a). Reaction time and psychometric *g.* In H. J. Eysenck (Ed.), *A model for intelligence* (pp. 93–132). Heidelberg: Springer-Verlag.

Jensen, A. R. (1982b). The chronometry of intelligence. In R. J. Sternberg (Ed.), *Advances in the psychology of human intelligence* (Vol. 1). Hillsdale, NJ: Lawrence Erlbaum Associates.

Jensen, A. R. (1983). Effects of inbreeding on mental-ability factors. *Personality and Individual Differences, 4,* 71–87.

Jensen, A. R. (1984). Test validity: *g* versus the specificity doctrine. *Journal of Social and Biological Structures, 7,* 93–118.

Jensen, A. R. (1985). The nature of the black-white difference on various psychometric tests: Spearman's hypothesis. *Behavioral and Brain Sciences, 8,* 193–219.

Jensen, A. R., & Munro, E. (1979). Reaction time, movement time and intelligence. *Intelligence, 3,* 121–126.

Jensen, A. R., & Reynolds, C. R. (1982). Race, social class and ability differences on the WISC-R. *Personality and Individual Differences, 3,* 423–438.

Kaiser, H. F. (1958). The varimax criterion for analytic rotation in factor analysis. *Psychometrika, 23,* 187–200.

Keating, D. P., & Bobbitt, B. (1978). Individual and developmental differences in cognitive processing components of mental ability. *Child Development, 49,* 155–169.

Klein, G. S., & Krech, D. (1952). Cortical conductivity in the brain-injured. *Journal of Personality, 21,* 118–148.

Lansman, M., Poltrock, S. E., & Hunt, E. (1983). Individual differences in the ability to focus and divide attention. *Intelligence, 7,* 299–312.

Loevinger, J. (1951). Intelligence. In H. Helson (Ed.), *Theoretical foundations of psychology.* New York: Van Nostrand.

McCauley, C., Dugas, J., Kellas, G., & DeVellis, R. F. (1976). Effects of serial rehearsal training on memory search. *Journal of Educational Psychology, 68,* 474–481.

Macphail, E. M. (1985). Comparative studies of animal intelligence: Is Spearman's *g* really Hull's *D? Behavioral and Brain Sciences, 8,* 234–235.

Maxwell, A. E. (1972). Factor analysis: Thomson's sampling theory recalled. *British Journal of Mathematical and Statistical Psychology, 25,* 1–21.

Nagoshi, C. T., & Johnson, R. C. (1986). The ubiquity of *g. Personality and Individual Differences, 7,* 201–207.

Paul, S. M. (1984). *Speed of information processing: The Semantic Verification Test and general mental ability.* Unpublished doctoral dissertation, University of California, Berkeley.

Posner, M. I. (1978). *Chronometric exploration of mind.* Hillsdale, NJ: Lawrence Erlbaum Associates.

Price, B. (1936). Homogamy and the intercorrelation of capacity traits. *Annals of Eugenics, 7,* 22–27.

Schafer, E. W. P. (1985). Neural adaptability: A biological determinant of *g* factor intelligence. *Behavioral and Brain Sciences, 8,* 240–241.

Schmid, J., & Leiman, J. M. (1957). The development of hierarchical factor solutions. *Psychometrika, 22,* 53–61.

Spearman, C. E. (1904). "General intelligence" objectively determined and measured. *American Journal of Psychology, 15,* 201–293.

Spearman, C. E. (1927). *The abilities of man: Their nature and measurement.* London: Macmillan.

Spearman, C. E. (1927). *The abilities of man: Their nature and measurement.* London: Macmillan.

Spearman, C. E. (1973). *The nature of 'intelligence' and the principles of cognition.* New York: Arno Press. (Original work published 1923)

Stankov, L. (1983). The role of competition in human abilities revealed through auditory tests. *Multivariate Behavioral Research Monographs* (No. 83-1).

Sternberg, R. J. (1979a). *Components of human intelligence* (Tech. Rep. No. 19). Office of Naval Research.

Sternberg, R. J. (1979b). In R. J. Sternberg & D. K. Detterman (Eds.), *Human intelligence: Perspectives on its theory and measurement.* Norwood, NJ: Ablex.

Sternberg, R. J., & Gardner, M. K. (1982). A componential interpretation of the general factor in human intelligence. In H. J. Eysenck (Ed.), *A model for intelligence* (pp. 231–254). Heidelberg: Springer-Verlag.

Sternberg, S. (1966). High speed scanning in human memory. *Science, 153,* 652–654.

Sternberg, S. (1975). Memory scanning: New findings and current controversies. *Quarterly Journal of Experimental Psychology, 27,* 1–32.

Tambs, K., Sundet, J. M., & Magnus, P. (1984). Heritability analysis of the WAIS subtests. A study of twins. *Intelligence, 8,* 283–293.

Thomson, G. H. (1948). *The factorial analysis of human ability* (3rd ed.). Boston: Houghton-Mifflin.

Thorndike, E. L. (1927). *The measurement of intelligence.* New York: Teachers College, Columbia University.

Thurstone, L. L. (1935). *Vectors of mind.* Chicago: University of Chicago Press.

Thurstone, L. L. (1938). Primary mental abilities. *Psychometric Monographs* (No. 1). Chicago: University of Chicago Press.

Thurstone, L. L. (1947). *Multiple factor analysis.* Chicago: University of Chicago Press.

Tyler, L. E. (1976). The intelligence we test—an evolving concept. In L. B. Resnick (Ed.), *The nature of intelligence* (pp. 13–26). Hillsdale, NJ: Lawrence Erlbaum Associates.

Undheim, J. O. (1981a). On intelligence I: Broad ability factors in 15-year-old children and Cattell's theory of fluid and crystallized intelligence. *Scandanavian Journal of Psychology, 22,* 171–179.

Undheim, J. O. (1981b). On intelligence II: A neo-Spearman model to replace Cattell's theory of fluid and crystallized intelligence. *Scandanavian Journal of Psychology, 22,* 181–187.

Undheim, J. O. (1981c). On intelligence IV: Toward a restoration of general intelligence. *Scandanavian Journal of Psychology, 22,* 251–265.

Vernon, P. A. (1983). Speed of information processing and general intelligence. *Intelligence, 7,* 53–70.

Vernon, P. A., & Jensen, A. R. (1984). Individual and group differences in intelligence and speed of information processing. *Personality and Individual Differences, 5,* 411–423.

Vernon, P. E. (1950). *The structure of human abilities.* London: Methuen.

Wade, J. P. (1984). *The relationships among intelligence and six chronometric paradigms with academically able students.* Unpublished doctoral dissertation, Arizona State University.

APPENDIX

Two types of RT apparatus were used. The first is shown in Figure A. Templates are placed over the console, exposing either 1, 2, 4, or 8 of the light-button combinations. When one of the lights goes on, the subject removes his finger from the central home button and presses a button adjacent to the light, which puts out the light. Fifteen trials are given at each level of complexity—1, 2, 4, or

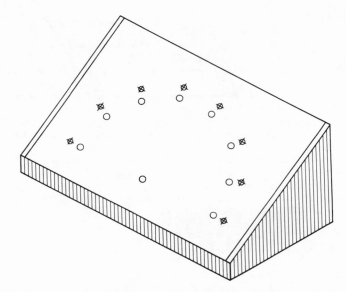

FIG. A.   Subject's console of the reaction time aparatus. Pushbuttons indicated
by circles, green jewelled lights by circled crosses. The "home" button is in the
lower center.

8 light-buttons. RT is the time taken to get off the home button after one of the
lights goes on. I shall refer to this task simply as the *RT task* (RT). The other
tasks all use a two-choice console pictured in Figure B. In the *Memory Scan* task
(DIGIT), a set of digits consisting of anywhere from 1 to 7 digits is simultaneously presented for 2 seconds on the display screen. After a 1-second interval, a single probe digit appears on the screen. The subject's task is to respond as
quickly as possible, indicating whether or not the probe was a member of the set
that had previously appeared by raising his index finger from the home button
and pushing one of the two choice buttons labeled "yes" and "no." The
subject's RT is the interval between the onset of the probe digit and the subject's
releasing the home button. The subject's score (the average of his RTs to 84 such
digit sets) provides a measure of the speed of short-term memory processing, that
is, the speed with which information held in short-term memory can be scanned
and retrieved.

The *Same–Different* tasks (SD2) measures the speed of visual discrimination
of pairs of simple words that are *physically* the same or different, for example,
DOG–DOG or DOG–LOG. The instant that each of 26 pairs of the same or
different words is presented, the subject raises his finger from the home button
and presses one of the two choice buttons labeled *S* (same) and *D* (different).

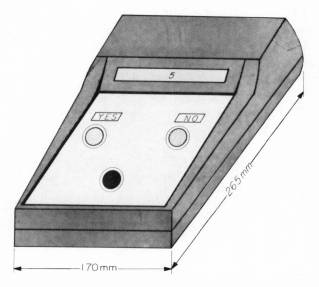

FIG. B.   Subject's console used for the digit memory scan, physically same-different words, and synonyms-antonyms test, showing display screen, the two-choice response buttons, and the "home" button (lower center).

Again, the subject's RT is the average interval between onset of the word pair and releasing the home button.

The *Synonym–Antonym* task (SA2) works much the same way, but in this test pairs of words are presented that are semantically either similar or opposite in meaning, for example, BIG–LARGE or BIG–LITTLE. All the synonyms and antonyms are composed of extremely common, high-frequency words, and all items can be answered correctly by virtually any third-grader under nonspeeded test conditions. The only reliable source of individual differences is the speed with which the decisions are made. This task measures the subject's speed of access to highly overlearned verbal codes stored in long-term memory.

In the *Dual Processing* tasks, the subject is required to do two things, thus creating some degree of cognitive trade-off, or processing efficiency loss, between storage of information in short-term memory and retrieval of semantic information from long-term memory. In this task, we sequentially combine the digit Memory Scan task and the Same–Different task, or the Memory Scan task and the Synonyms–Antonyms task. First, the subject is presented with a set of 1 to 7 digits for 2 seconds. This presentation is immediately followed by a Same–Different (or Synonym–Antonym) word pair, and the subject must respond "same" or different" (pressing buttons labeled *S* or *D*). Next, the probe digit appears, and he must respond "yes" or "no" to indicate whether or not the probe was a member of the digit set shown previously. The RT (release of home button) is measured for the Same–Different responses to the words (DT2 WORDS) and for the yes–no responses to the probe digits (DT2 DIGITS). The very same dual task procedure is also used with synonyms-antonyms (in place of physically same-different words) and digits (DT3 WORDS and DT3 DIGITS).

II COGNITIVE APPROACHES TO PSYCHOMETRIC ISSUES: APPLICATIONS

5 The Assessment of Cognitive Factors in Academic Abilities

Stephen L. Benton
Kansas State University

Kenneth A. Kiewra
Utah State University

Nearly 30 years ago, Lee Cronbach (1957) distinguished between the two disciplines of correlational psychology, which investigated naturally occurring individual variance in behavior, and experimental psychology, which examined the effectiveness of certain treatments on behavior. Essentially, correlational psychology examined individual differences using factor analytic techniques; whereas experimental psychology attempted to eliminate individual differences using appropriate interventions. Cronbach believed that these two disciplines should join together to promote aptitude-treatment interaction (ATI) research that would identify effective treatments for certain types of individuals. With this combined approach, different tratments could be prescribed for skilled and less skilled individuals.

The ATI research methodology had limited success, however, because of inconsistency in findings and because of difficulty in replicating some of the treatments (Tobias, 1985). In addition, results rarely revealed disordinal interactions (which indicate that treatments differentially affect those on the lower and the higher ends of the performance continuum). One explanation for the lack of disordinal interactions was that methods for identifying skilled and less skilled students on a given academic behavior were not far advanced (Tobias, 1985). What was needed were precise methods for measuring specific skills required for successful academic achievement.

Recent developments in cognitive psychology have provided more precise methods that may help to advance both ATI research and the field of measurement. Sternberg (1977), for example, has investigated the underlying cognitive processes in intellectual behavior using componential analysis. Essentially, componential analysis investigates the underlying componenets involved in task performance. By specifying these components and the various combination rules one might employ, differences can be observed among individuals in the number of components utilized, the combination rules employed, the order of the component operations, the mode of processing (e.g., serial vs. parallel), and the time required to execute a component. This approach is more precise than the previous factor analytic approaches of correlational psychologists, because the latter measured only the end products of behaviors and not the components of mental organization (Vernon, 1970, p. 100).

A more recent trend in cognitive psychology has been to examine differences in mental abilities between experts and novices in particular subject matter areas such as math and reading. Such cognitive curriculum analysis can not only specify cognitions that distinguish experts and novices, but can promote the construction of tests in particular subject-matter areas that can diagnose the cognitive difficulties underlying performance. By identifying the underlying components involved in academic performance, differences may then be observed that allow for more precise measurement and more effective treatments.

The cognitive approach to assessment suggests that there are several factors that contribute to successful or unsuccessful academic behaviors. These generally interactive factors are the learner's declarative knowledge, procedural knowledge, control processes, cognitive strategies, and metacognitive processes. Cognitive psychology has advanced to the point where it can offer tools for measuring these factors that may help to clarify the specific interventions that must be made. In many instances, however, the tools are still being developed and applied to specific academic areas so that subject-matter remediation can be more precise.

The purpose of the current chapter, then, is to investigate how these cognitive factors may be measured within the academic domains of reading, writing, mathematics, and science. What immediately follows is a brief overview of the cognitive factors and a description of how they may be assessed, in general. (A more detailed account can be found in Meyer, 1981.) Following that overview, methods for assessing these factors within the various academic domains are discussed.

DECLARATIVE KNOWLEDGE

Declarative knowledge refers to knowledge of facts and information. Several researchers stress the importance of having appropriate declarative knowledge for demonstrating expertise in problem solving or in higher-order thinking. This view is well supported by Resnick (1984), who purports that thinking can only be taught in knowledge-rich areas, and by proponents of artificial intelligence who now share the view that intelligent thinking is knowledge based (Minsky & Papert, 1974).

Experts and novices working in a particular area differ in both the quantity and the quality of their domain-specific knowledge. Expert chess players, for example, have more knowledge about chess positions than do chess novices (Chase & Simon, 1973). Not only do novices have less knowledge, but their knowledge is often not as hierarchically organized as is the knowledge of experts (e.g., Chi, Glaser & Reese, 1982). Novices also appear to have fewer links or pathways among their memory nodes, thereby decreasing the activation of related knowledge. This limits both encoding and retrieval processes, which, of course, are necessary for effective problem solving, memorization, and comprehension.

Experts not only have sufficient declarative knowledge about the particular domain of inquiry, they also have knowledge about the structure of knowledge that helps them to learn and to understand. Someone trying to comprehend a story about baseball, for example, not only needs baseball knowledge, but also knowledge about the structure of stories. As we hear or read a story, we expect the events of that story to correspond to our story schema that may include an introduction, a characterization, a resolution, and so forth. When we comprehend, we selectively modify the story's events to conform to our current schema. Therefore, stories presented in a manner inconsistent with our story schema are more difficult to comprehend (Thorndyke, 1977). Differences between good and poor readers (discussed later in greater detail) are, in fact, often due to the readers' immature story schemata. This is why Resnick (1985) maintains that meaning is as much within the learner as it is upon the printed page. Resnick therefore advocates that particular story schemata be taught, because adequate schemata have transfer value that will increase the likelihood of comprehension across content areas.

If content knowledge and knowledge about the structure of knowledge contribute to expertise, then researchers and educators need methods for assessing such declarative knowledge. Cognitive psychologists have recently provided the tools for such measurement. The cognitive approach to assessing declarative knowledge involves analyzing verbal knowledge into composite units and indicating the structure governing those units. A structure model of a person's knowledge is represented in the form of a network or a tree, both of which indicate symbolically the major elements of a person's knowledge and the relationships among those elements—much like a sentence grammar indicates the parts and relations within a sentence. One derives a story schema, for example, by first breaking a story down into simple sentences. Each sentence is then placed within one of the designated components of a story schema. Story schemata are thought to include information about setting, theme, plot, and resolution. Each of these structures can, in turn, be analyzed into component parts. A setting contains information about characters, location, and time; a plot contains various episodes further comprised of subgoals, attempts to reach subgoals, and outcomes. Thorndyke (1977) has suggested, for example, that the following parsing rules or categories capture most sentences contained within a narrative:

Rule 1: Story = Setting + Theme = Plot + Resolution
Rule 2   Setting = Character + Location + Time
Rule 3: Theme + Events + Goal
Rule 4: Plot = Episodes
Rule 4a: Episode = Subgoal + Attempts + Outcome
Rule 5: Resolution = Event or State

The structural model developed for a particular story can then be compared to the actual recall performance of individuals who have read the story. Because individuals generally use story schemata when comprehending stories (Thorndyke, 1977), such a comparison can identify specific gaps in an individual's knowledge about the topic and, perhaps more importantly, about the structure of that knowledge.

It appears that cognitive structures are formed and used in various areas. As examples, Kintsch (1974) has identified a schema structure for scientific reports, and Spilich, Vesonder, Chiesi, and Voss (1979) have developed schema structures for understanding radio broadcasts of baseball games. The task, then, is for cognitive psychologists and psychometricians to develop these sorts of schematic structures in other areas. Doing so can permit instructors to teach the particular story schemata relevant to a particular area, and can help instructional designers design instructional materials consistent with the organizational structure of a content area.

PROCEDURAL KNOWLEDGE

Effective learners not only have adequate declarative knowledge, but also procedural knowledge that assists them in using declarative knowledge (Resnick, 1976; Woods, Resnick, & Groen, 1975). Skilled math students, for example, do not simply learn or memorize countless solutions to math problems; they are able to solve novel problems such as 638 divided by 19 because they have learned higher-order procedures or rules for doing so.

Cognitive psychologists, interested in the procedures incorporated by the expert and the procedural errors made by the novice in a given field, have developed two similar methods for representing and assessing procedural knowledge. One method is called a program, which is a step-by-step list of actions to be taken; the other is a flowchart, which is a set of boxes and arrows used to represent the processes and decisions one makes when solving a problem. A process model for solving a particular type of problem is derived by observing several individuals solve problems of that nature, and by interviewing them about their procedures. A program or flowchart that corresponds to apparent procedures is then generated. The validity of the process model is then tested by comparing the processes and performance of other individuals solving similar problems to the processes and performance designated by the model. This sort of analysis can successfully pinpoint the specific procedural error(s) that a student is making.

An important example of the use of a process model for determining procedural errors was offered by Brown and Burton (1978), who developed a computer program called BUGGY that identifies process bugs or errors in the solving of subtraction problems. This program can determine the precise procedural error a student makes when subtracting. For example, a learner may always subtract the smaller number from the larger regardless of which number is on top; or the student may have difficulty borrowing across zero. The BUGGY program, then, does not only specify the correctness of a student's response, but, more importantly, it identifies the particular procedural error(s) made by the student. With this type of information, teachers can become more effective in teaching specific procedures, rather than waiting and hoping that students discover them.

Cognitive tools like the BUGGY program certainly have implications for educational measurement as well. More programs specific to particular academic areas need to be constructed for developing tests that assess procedural errors and that determine the procedures used by resident experts. The stage has especially been set in the area of mathematics (Groen & Parkman, 1972; Resnick, 1976), which depends heavily on procedural knowledge. The importance of procedural knowledge in mathematics and other academic areas are discussed in later sections.

CONTROL PROCESSES

Recent research has indicated that individuals who differ on intelligence tests (e.g., Sternberg, 1977) and on ability tests (e.g., Hunt, 1978) also differ in their information-processing capabilities. Earl Hunt and his colleagues (Hunt, 1978; Hunt, Frost, & Lunneborg, 1973; Hunt, Lunneborg, & Lewis, 1975) have developed or modified several tasks that distinguish the particular information-processing components (sensory memory, short-term memory, working memory, and long-term memory) and/or control processes (attention, rehearsal, chunking, manipulating information in working memory, encoding, and searching long-term memory) associated with individual differences in verbal ability. In general, their work has indicated that differences between high- and low-verbal individuals can be more precisely interpreted as cognitive information-processing differences. In particular, they found that high- and low-verbal individuals differ on cognitive tasks involving search speed through long-term memory, the holding capacity of short-term memory, and the speed of manipulating information in working memory.

Developmental research on human information processing suggests that individual differences on cognitive tasks are due more to the effective use of control processes than to differences in the cognitive machinery or memory structures among individuals. Apparently, structure or hardware changes (e.g., number of holding slots in short-term memory) are negligible after early childhood (see Chi, 1978; Harris, 1978). Cognitive processes, like rehearsal and encoding, are, however, modifiable within certain limits. In fact, even learning disabled students (e.g., Torgesen, 1977), and retarded students (Campione & Brown, 1977), have shown significant improvement in memory performance following brief instruction in using rehearsal. (Research on the developmental aspects of control process training is reviewed by Chi, 1976; and by Hagen & Stanovich, 1977.)

Although substantial experimental memory research indicates that those who remember more are apt to use control processes more often or more effectively (see, for example, Bransford, 1979), it is, of course, impossible for researchers to directly assess these processes. Because these memory processes are not amenable to direct assessment, some researchers have corroborated the inferred processes through self-report techniques or through observation. Torgesen (1977), for example, observed the mouthing of words to infer rehearsal, and has observed picture rearrangements to infer organization processes in working memory.

Although cognitive psychologists have largely determined that differences in intelligence and verbal ability are due to cognitive processes, there remain questions about exactly what those processes are and how to more objectively measure them. As the pioneering work of Hunt and Sternberg continues to be applied to specific academic areas, perhaps these issues can be more successfully addressed. Furthermore, only by looking at control processes in specific areas can we be sure of their relative effectiveness for determining expertise when other cognitive factors, such as subject matter knowledge, are also considered.

COGNITIVE STRATEGIES

Another factor involved in solving general ability or specific academic problems is the cognitive strategies incorporated by the learner. Cognitive strategies are thoughts that influence how learners select, acquire, organize, or integrate new knowledge. These strategies represent a plan of attack for achieving a designated goal. In determining the types of strategies people use in solving problems, cognitive psychologists have presented people with problems and have asked them to think aloud as they solved them. From these self-reports, psychologists have identified the strategies that humans use—often programming them into a computer—and have, then, tested the programmed strategies against actual human performance. Through this method, psychologists have identified the strategic behaviors that distinguish experts from novices with regard to solving general ability problems or problems associated with particular content areas.

Although there are several documented general strategies for problem solving (e.g., means-end analysis, working forward, reasoning by analogy, and brainstorming), cognitive psychologists have focused investigations on means-ends analysis. Ernst and Newell (1969) and Newell and Simon (1972), for example, constructed a computer program called General Problem Solver (GPS), using the self-report procedures described earlier, that uses means-ends analysis. GPS solves problems, as do many humans, by first determining a problem space consisting of one's goal state, starting state, and all possible solution paths. (It should be apparent that appropriately structured declarative knowledge is critical for constructing the problem space.) Second, a goal-directed search is made by searching planfully through the problem space. This planful search is executed through the cognitive strategy of means-ends analysis, which entails generating and solving subgoals necessary for achieving the terminal goal. (A more complete description of GPS and means-ends analysis can be found in Ernst and Newell, 1969.)

The investigation of problem solving in particular content areas seems critical, because problem solving appears to depend substantially on the declarative knowledge one brings to the situation. Expert chess players, for example, actually behave less strategically, in some cases, than do novices. Expert players often do not use means-ends analysis to reduce the gap between their current state and the goal state, as novices are apt to do. Instead, experts respond almost automatically to the problem situation; namely, the current positioning of the chess pieces (e.g., Feltovich, 1981; Newell & Simon, 1972). Perhaps this is because of the expert's superior knowledge and experience with a variety of possible chess positions. Thus, it is believed that the major differences beween experts' and novices' problem-solving abilities in a particular area are due to the following knowledge-derived factors: (a) Experts represent the problem more effectively than do novices; (b) experts have more subject-matter knowledge that is usually organized hierarchically; and (c) experts, because of their more rich and coherently structured knowledge, are able to hold more information in memory and therby entertain several hypotheses at a time. Novices, however, operate in a piecemeal fashion, reacting to the latest cue and forgetting to consider previous information. (See Gagné, 1985, pp. 136-161 for a description of problem-solving factors that distinguish novices and experts.)

Although the literature has reported modest success in teaching general problem-solving strategies like means-ends analysis (e.g., Covington, Crutchfield, & Davies, 1966), it seems that knowledge in an area is critical for applying effective strategies. Therefore, cognitive psychologists should not only continue to advance the technology of systems like GPS to more closely simulate human problem representation and solution search, but should especially focus these efforts in particular areas where the amount and the structure of knowledge affects strategic behaviors. Subsequent sections describe the use of cognitiive strategies in knowledge-rich domains.

METACOGNITION

Metacognition refers to what a person knows about his or her cognitive processes and the ability to control these processes by planning, choosing, and monitoring. A learner with good metacognition engaged in problem solving would likely be aware of his or her procedural and declarative knowledge relative to the problem, and would call upon appropriate control processes and cognitive strategies when necessary. Furthermore, he or she would periodically monitor the current state relative to the goal state. Thus, metacognition allows the learner to orchestrate or to control the cognitive factors previously discussed.

There is abundant research indicating developmental differences in metacognition between children of different ages. (See Brown, 1978, for a review.) Younger children, for example, are often unaware of their own knowledge relative to older children. Young children, given deliberately incomplete instructions for a card game, do not realize that instructions are inadequate until they play the game (Markman, 1979). Older children more readily realize the inconsistencies. Another metacognitive ability that often distinguishes developmentally different individuals, is the ability to assess the demands of the task. Older children relative to younger children realize that more study time for learning pictures results in better recall, and that paired associates that are opposites (good, bad) are easier to learn than are random pairs (ball, cigar) (as in Kreutzer, Leonard, & Flavell, 1975). Furthermore, older children relative to younger children know that active strategies of learning are more likely to result in superior learning than less active strategies (Kreutzer et al., 1975). Other areas identified by Brown (1978), in which children's metacognitive deficiencies have caused problems, include predicting the outcome of strategy employment both before and after the use of strategies (Brown & Lawton, 1977), and monitoring the success of their attempts to learn (Brown & Barclay, 1976; Brown, Campione, & Barclay, 1978). Many of these metacognitive factors are also responsible for performance differences between learners who are classified as "normal" and those who are considered cognitively disadvantaged (e.g., learning disabled and mentally retarded). In fact, Brown and Barclay (1976) point out that the greatest problem with retardates may be their inability to use what they know.

Although research consistently indicates that metacognitive abilities distinguish cognitively disadvantaged learners and normal learners, as well as younger and older learners, the critical point is that metacognitive deficiencies are among the problems of most novices regardless of age. Novice chess players, for example (Chi, 1978), have metacognitive problems similar to those of young card players (Markman, 1979). Similarly, novice x-ray technicians show inept scanning patterns (Thomas, 1968) like those of young children first learning to search a visual array (Mackworth & Bruner, 1970). It seems, then, that metacognitive abilities are related, at least in part, to the knowledge one brings to a situation. Therefore, it is not surprising that experts in particular academic areas, such as reading and mathematics, not only have more knowledge, but also display more effective metacognitive behaviors that permit them to apply their knowledge and cognitions.

Each of the cognitive factors discussed thus far contributes to successful or unsuccessful performance across a variety of academic domains. Because of this contribution, educators are interested in measuring these factors so that appropriate remediations can be made. Psychometricians must, therefore, draw upon the plethora of research in knowledge-rich areas that has been conducted by cognitive psychologists. In the following sections, research investigating the cognitive factors of knowledge, control processes, cognitive strategies, and metacognition within the academic domains of reading, writing, mathematics, and science are discussed. In addition, the implications of this research for measuring academic abilities are considered.

READING

The cognitive processes involved in reading have generally been divided into the two main components of decoding and comprehending (LaBerge, 1980; LaBerge & Samuels, 1974). In decoding, the reader matches the printed code to a known memory pattern and recodes the pattern into a string of sounds. In comprehending the reader imposes meaning upon the text. Automaticity in decoding is necessary for good reading ability because readers have a limited amount of processing resources they can allocate, and automatization of decoding frees up resources for comprehension. The relationship between decoding and comprehension has, in fact, been supported, because children instructed in decoding skills have subsequently improved their reading comprehension (Pflaum, Walberg, Karegianes, & Rasher, 1980).

The comprehension component of reading involves both literal and inferential comprehension. Literal comprehension requires the dual processes of lexical access and parsing. Put simply, lexical access is the process by which words are assigned meaning, and parsing is the process by which words are connected to form ideas. In inferential comprehension, the reader goes beyond the literal meaning of the text to integrate ideas, to summarize, and to elaborate upon the text with inferences and extrapolations.

Although it is sometimes useful to speak of decoding and comprehension as being separate components, they are actually interrelated and do not necessarily follow a "bottom-up" sequence going from the decoding of letters up through literal and inferential comprehension. For example, Bartlett's (1932) early work with story schemata, in which he observed reconstructive aspects of text recall, suggests that a "top-down" sequence is more parsimonious. Specifically, Bartlett believed that the reader's declarative knowledge of the subject matter and of text structure guided the processes of decoding, lexical access, and parsing, such that meaning was constructed and not merely extracted by the reader. Further consideration is, therefore, given to the role that declarative knowledge plays in reading ability and to how such knowledge can be assessed.

Assessing Readers' Declarative Knowledge

Several reading specialists have suggested that two sources of variance in reading ability are the degree of organization and elaboration of information in memory (Anderson & Reder, 1979; Frase, 1973; Meyer, 1977). Organization refers to the quality of hierarchical structures among categories and subsets of information in memory, whereas elaboration refers to the amount of links or pathways among memory nodes through which the activation of information can spread. Such characteristics of memory may be used to explain why, for example, skilled readers outperform less skilled readers on simple word matching tasks. For example, Ehri and Wilce (1983) compared young readers' speed at reading familiar printed words such as "hat," "boy," or "car" with their speed at reading one digit numbers. Their results indicated that less skilled readers were slower at reading words than they were at reading digits; whereas, no such differences were observed among skilled readers. These findings suggest that differences in word matching ability may have more to do with semantic knowledge than processing speed. Other investigators have also found that, at younger ages, less skilled readers are slower at labeling letters and words (Frederiksen, 1981; Jackson & MClelland, 1979; Perfetti, Finger, & Hogaboam, 1978; Perfetti & Hogaboam, 1975; Vellutino, 1979). Notably, such differences between skilled and less skilled readers have not been observed beyond the fourth grade, however, which suggests that less skilled readers' decoding processes may be slower because they have not developed well-organized and elaborate semantic knowledge structures.

Lack of well-organized and elaborate declarative knowledge may also help explain comprehension deficiencies. Bower, Black, and Turner (1979), for example, investigated how having knowledge about a topic facilitates inferential comprehension. Specifically, Bower et al. asked students to read a story about visiting the doctor and then had them recall what they had read. Because visiting the doctor was a familiar experience to most of the students, 20% of their recalls included information not found in the original story. They had filled in the details with information obtained from prior experience with visiting a doctor. The extent to which the readers' recalls included such elaborations beyond the text may presumably reflect the amount of prior knowledge they had about visiting the doctor. Such a technique could be used as a prereading test for measuring a student's prior knowledge about a topic. Typically, teachers pretest students on their semantic knowledge of vocabulary that will be included in a reading assignment. Perhaps it is just as important that teachers pretest students on their experience with and knowledge about events that will be described within a passage. By having students read and recall short passages similar in content to the main reading assignment, teachers can then identify the extent to which readers' recalls include elaborations beyond the text. Although this process might be tedious from a pedagogical standpoint, less skilled readers should nevertheless be pretested and be given additional declarative knowledge about a topic prior to reading.

Good readers not only have sufficient declarative knowledge about a particular topic, they also have knowledge about the structure of the specific discourse grammar (e.g., narrative, expository, or argumentative). Comprehension is, in fact, enhanced if readers have well-organized and elaborate discourse schemata in memory that serve to facilitate encoding and retrieval processes. Research has shown, for example, that skilled readers rely more upon the structure of a passage in developing a summary then do less skilled readers (Bartlett, 1978; Meyer, Brandt, & Bluth, 1980; Taylor, 1980). Specifically, Meyer et al. (1980) found that about three-fourths of good readers, one-half of average readers, and less than one-fourth of poor readers used text structure in their recall summaries. Those readers who did not use the text structure tended to simply list ideas from the text in a random fashion. These results suggest that good readers use text structure in recall because it is adaptable to their own schematic representation of text in memory. Essentially, then, meaningful interpretation of text requires well-structured and elaborate declarative knowledge about various discourse schemata.

Psychologists and educators are, of course, interested in how such discourse schemata may be assessed. The cognitive approach to assessing such schemata involves comparing a reader's recall of a passage with a structural model that indicates the major elements of a text and the relationships among those elements. The structural model of the passage serves as a scoring template used to examine both the amount and the type of information recalled by the reader, thereby revealing differences between the text structure and the reader's organization in recall. From this analysis, psychologists then infer the amount of discrepancy between the structural model and the reader's schematic structure for a given discourse in memory.

Cognitive psychologists have developed different approaches for analyzing text structure (e.g., Frederiksen, 1975; Kintsch & van Dijk, 1978; Meyer, 1981), but have, as yet, failed to converge on a simple, widely accepted method. Meyer (1981) cites several reasons for this lack of agreement. First, interest in describing text structures has historically come from disciplines as diverse as rhetoric, folklore, linguistics, education, psychology, and artificial intelligence. Such plurality in backgrounds makes it difficult for academicians to reach consensus. Second, because of these diverse disciplines, the purpose for which structural analyses were developed has varied from that of assessing recall of main ideas to that of assessing the integration of logical relationships. Finally, since reading is a "top-down" process, the structure of a text will be described differently by readers who possess different prior knowledge and experience. This will be particularly problematic when the inherent structure of a text is more implicitly than explicitly stated.

Despite these confounding variables that affect how text structure is analyzed, psychometrians should attempt to establish a standard analytical method not open to the subjective affects of prior knowledge. Perhaps computer programs would be beneficial for building objective structural models of various discourse types. The programmer could specify the type of discourse to be analyzed and the intent (e.g., to identify main ideas or to identify logical relationships), and then enter the specific passage into the system so that an objective structural analysis could be conducted. Subsequently, each reader's recall could be entered into the system so that a "goodness of fit" comparison could be made between the computer-generated model and the reader's recall protocol. Upon making the comparison, the computer could then specifically identify, for the reader, what discrepancies might exist between the organization of the structural model and the organization of the readers' discourse schema in memory.

The importance of assessing declarative knowledge among readers has been well-established. An equally important cognitive factor that must be assessed is the control processes that operate within the information-processing system during reading. A discussion of these processes and how they may be measured is addressed in the following section.

Assessing Readers' Control Processes

Individual differences in control processes may account for differences observed between skilled and less skilled readers in recoding ability. Recoding, which involves connecting a string of sounds, requires holding small bits of information in temporary storage until sufficient amounts have been received in order to apprehend meaning (Baddely, 1970; Conrad, 1972). Presumably, then, recoding might involve the control processes of attention, rehearsal, chunking, and the manipulation of information in working memory.

Research investigating speed of recoding reveals that less skilled readers are slower at starting to say pseudowords than are skilled readers (Frederiksen, 1981). Such deficits in recoding speed would be expected among less skilled readers, because their decoding processes have not yet become automatized. It is important to note, however, that differences in recoding ability have been observed to disappear by the third grade (Venezky & Johnson, 1973) and, consequently, one must again consider the role knowledge plays in performance of these tasks.

Additional research by Perfetti and Roth (1981) illustrates differences among skilled and less skilled readers in their ability to integrate sentences. Sentence integration requires the holding and the manipulating of information in working memory, because the reader must combine successive sentences in order to integrate ideas. Specifically, Perfetti and Roth (1981) asked students to listen to pairs of related sentences in which the last word in the second sentence was missing, and to then predict the last word in the second sentence. An auditory presentation was used in order to focus on the comprehension process and not on the decoding process. The results indicated that skilled readers, relative to less skilled readers, produced a greater number of appropriate sentence-ending words on moderate-constraint sentences. (These are sentences that can be ended with a moderate selection of possible words.) Apparently, then, less skilled readers were more likely to produce inappropriate words to complete the sentence because they were unable to hold the relevant information from the first sentence in working memory.

Related findings by Frederiksen (1981) indicate that less skilled readers' reading speed is slowed down when the second sentence in a pair contains a pronoun reference or an implicit reference to a noun phrase in the previous sentence. Presumably, the slower reading rate occurs because readers cannot hold an adequate amount of information in working memory and must, consequently, look back to the prior sentence to identify the noun. One explanation for why less skilled readers perform poorly on this task is that they have limited working-memory capacity. Findings that support this view include those that reveal deficits in short-term memory recall of digits (Corkin, 1974; Bakker, 1972; Jorm, 1977) and of word strings (Bauer, 1977; Torgeson & Goldman, 1977) among less skilled readers.

Despite the abundance of research supporting a capacity hypothesis, alternative hypotheses must be noted. One hypothesis is that individual differences in readers' working memory capacities are due more to differences in control processes than to differences in hardware. Such control processes as rehearsal and chunking are limited in their simultaneous application and, therefore, compete for the readers' attention. Most memory-span tasks require readers to simultaneously attend to incoming data while rehearsing information already temporarily stored in working memory. Therefore, it is the competition between these control processes, and not the capacity of working memory, that hinders performance on such tasks. A second hypothesis, tested by Daneman and Carpenter (1980), posits that less skilled readers do poorly on memory-span tasks because they do not perform some of the simpler literal comprehension processes (i.e., lexical access and parsing) as automatically as do skilled readers. Specifically, the authors devised a reading-span task whereby subjects read sentences aloud at their own pace and then attempted to recall the last item from each sentence. Results found the reading-span task to be a better predictor of verbal ability and of reading comprehension than was a conventional digit-span task. Daneman and Carpenter (1980) concluded, therefore, that less skilled readers performed poorly on the reading-span task not because they have a limited working-memory capacity, but because they have difficulty assigning meaning to words or putting words together.

Research investigating differences in control processes among readers has implications for the field of measurement. First, based on Daneman and Carpenter's (1980) findings, it would be unwise to draw conclusions about the nature of a reader's working memory capacity unless he or she does poorly across a wide variety of memory-span tasks. Second, performance deficits on memory-span tasks do not necessarily indicate a fixed capacity limitation in working memory. Developmental research suggests that individual differences observed on these tasks are due more to the use of control processes than to differences in architecture. Besides, the prospect of a fixed capacity limitation leaves little hope for the possibility of appropriate remediation. It is perhaps more reasonable for psychometrians to investigate methods for assessing the underlying deficiencies in control processes that characterize poor readers.

Assessing Readers' Cognitive Strategies

Another factor to consider in assessing reading ability is the reader's cognitive strategies. Cognitive strategies are methods for reaching some goal in an optimal way (van Dijk & Kintsch, 1983). They require conscious, controlled, cognitive representations that dominate the moves of an action sequence. The fact that cognitive strategies are conscious makes them amenable to measurement through verbal reports of individuals as they solve problems. Examples of what might be discovered from such reports are that individuals may break a problem down into subproblems, they may attempt to obtain more information to solve the problem, or they may return to previously solved states of a problem if an error is made.

Language strategies, which operate during reading, are unlike typical cognitive strategies because they are not consciously controlled. They occur almost automatically, particularly with continued practice. A number of actions are involved, for example, in reading that occur rather unconsciously, such as identifying letters, constructing words, analyzing syntactic structures, and understanding sentential and textual meanings. In spite of the effortless nature of these processes, van Dijk and Kintsch (1983) believe it is appropriate to speak of strategies that operate in discourse comprehension for the following reasons: (a) The language user is confronted with the task of understanding an action; (b) such an action has a well-defined goal (comprehension); (c) the solution occurs step-by-step, and may be broken down into subtasks; and (d) the solution is not always obvious, and therefore alternative routes may need to be taken (pp. 71-73). Essentially, the authors suggest that discourse comprehension is an instance of human problem solving and, therefore, necessarily requires the use of language strategies.

Language strategies are different from language rules (which more generally specify correct structures for phonology, morphology, or syntax) because they are context-dependent. That is, rules describe proper structure for clauses, sentences, and paragraphs; strategies describe how these rules are employed within the context of the semantic analysis of a passage. Rules, then, have to do with syntax, whereas strategies have to do with semantics. The importance of language strategies for reading is that they efficiently apply abstract language rules in such a way that several levels of discourse can be processed simultaneously. The specific nature of these strategies, as described by van Dijk and Kintsch (1983), is now discussed.

Propositional Strategies. A proposition is a composite unit that includes a predicate and one or more arguments, where a predicate is defined as being a property or a relation, and an argument is defined as being a thing or a person. The unit "a boy" would not be considered a proposition, because it only contains an argument. The unit "a boy ran home" would be considered a proposition, however, because it contains both an argument and a predicate. Propositions are constructed by the reader based on the context of the passage and word meanings activated from semantic memory. Propositional strategies guide the reader in placing predicates and arguments into configurations, and in helping the reader make best guesses about the likely structure or meaning of incoming data. An example of a propositional strategy is assigning a noun or a pronoun as the subject of a proposition even before the rest of the clause has been analyzed. If such an assignment turns out to be wrong, then a second strategy would be to go back over the clause applying the rules of syntactic structure. These kinds of propositional strategies operate continually and facilitate automaticity in reading.

Research indicates that skilled readers are more proficient at using propositional strategies. Specifically, Frederiksen (1981) asked high school students to read sentences that had the last word missing and, after they had read each sentence, to press a stimulus that released the missing word. Students were then to pronounce the word as fast as they could. Frederiksen (1981) reasoned that if they were expecting the word, the students would pronounce it faster than if they were not expecting it. Two types of sentences were provided: those providing "weak context" and those providing "strong context." Again, the author reasoned that if good readers were more proficient at propositional strategies, they would benefit more from having the strong context than would the poor readers. Results, in fact, found that good readers did show a greater difference in reaction time between weak and strong context sentences than did poor readers. Frederiksen concluded, therefore, that skilled readers used propositional strategies to make several best guesses about word meaning possibilities, and were therefore prepared to pronounce any one of them.

Local Coherence Strategies. Local coherence strategies help to establish meaning among successive sentences. The assumption underlying local coherence strategies is that language users attempt to establish some coherent relation before they have fully processed a pair of sentences. They will do so by relating fragments of the new sentence to the sentence previously processed. More specifically, local coherence will be established among sentences by searching for propositions that contain related facts or potential links, or by recognizing argument repetition that may be both explicitly and implicitly stated. Essentially, then, local coherence is strategic because relatedness among sentences must be established by the reader.

Research indicates that skilled readers are more proficient than less skilled readers at establishing local coherence. As has been previously described, Perfetti and Roth (1981) asked 8 to 10 year old students to listen to pairs of related sentences and to predict the last word in the second sentence. To perform well on this task, one must establish commonalities among the two sentences in order to make an accurate prediction. Again, Perfetti and Roth's results indicated that skilled readers were more accurate than were less skilled readers with sentences that contain moderate-constraint sentences. These findings suggest that skilled readers are better able to integrate sentences efficiently because they employ strategies for integrating common propositions between sentences.

Macrostrategies.   Macrostrategies operate at the level of macrostructures that describe the overall meaning or gist of a passage. Macrostructures are different from schema structures because the latter represent the form of a discourse grammar (e.g., a story schema contains information about plot, setting, resolution, and so forth). A macrostructure, on the other hand, is the global meaning inferred from a passage. In order to establish this global meaning, the reader must continually form best guesses about the main idea, even before he or she is finished reading. Macrostrategies, consequently, use propositions to form best guesses about a macrostructure that can, in turn, be used to understand subsequent sentences. This type of macrostrategy is described by van Dijk and Kintsch (1983) as semantic inference. Semantic inference is influenced by prior knowledge, by redundancy of propositions, and by macropropositions that are topical or thematic expressions that signal what the main idea is about. Such expressions often appear at the beginning or at the end of paragraphs, or may be signaled by larger print or by italics. Macropropositions that appear at the beginning of a section help the reader form hypotheses about the meaning of sentences to come; whereas those that appear at the end of a section serve to evaluate already established macrostructures.

The notion of discourse comprehension strategies seems useful if comprehension is considered to be a problem solving activity. The reader continually makes best guesses about how to solve the problem that concerns what the discourse is about. If, as van Dijk and Kintsch suggest, these strategies are not consciously controlled, how, then, can psychometricians devise tests to measure them? The traditional method of assessing cognitive strategies through verbal reports seems hardly valid in this case. The previously described tasks employed by Frederiksen (1981) and Perfetti and Roth (1981), however, seem useful for assessing propositional and local coherence strategies, respectively. Such tasks are amenable to computer administration and scoring, and seem to come from a theoretical base closely aligned with the notion of language strategies. Steps should be taken to make these kinds of tasks readily available to those interested in assessing propositional and local coherence strategies. At the level of macrostrategies, cognitive psychologists have for years analyzed the free recalls of readers in order to assess the proportion of macropropositions they can remember. Educators should continue this type of testing so as to monitor whether readers can infer the main idea from a passage.

To validly and reliably assess discourse comprehension strategies, tests must require the examinee to actually connect propositions such that local and global coherence is established. The tasks cited above are a beginning, but innovative assessment devices must still be created. Recent research in the assessment of discourse production strategies (Benton & Kiewra, 1985), to be discussed within the writing section of this chapter, may provide insight into how comprehension strategies may be assessed.

Assessing Readers' Metacognitive Processes

Investigations into the metcognitive processes of reading reveal differences between good and poor readers in their comprehension monitoring. Comprehension monitoring is a two-stage process of goal checking and remediating. In goal checking, the reader checks to see if he or she is achieving the goal of comprehension. Goals may vary according to whether one is reading for the purpose of skimming or for the purpose of obtaining a thorough understanding of a passage. During remediation, the reader looks back to previously processed discourse in order to pick up relevant information that was missed.

Differences have been observed between mature and less mature readers in their goal-checking strategies (Harris, Kruithos, Terwogt, & Visser, 1981). Specifically, Harris et al. (1981) asked third and sixth grade students to read stories, some of which contained an anomalous sentence relative to the title of the story (e.g., the sentence "He sees his hair getting shorter" within a story titled "John at the Dentist."). Other stories containing the same sentence were more aptly titled "John at the Hairdresser's." Results found that reading speed was slower in the inappropriately titled stories for both grade levels, which suggests all students were cuing themselves that something was wrong with the anomalous sentence. Interestingly, however, 30% of the third graders could not identify the anomalous sentence, compared to only 11% of the sixth graders who could not. Apparently, then, students in both grade levels produced signals that their comprehension was faltering (because of a slower reading speed), but sixth graders were able to check the source of that signal. The authors contend, therefore, that mature readers are more adept at goal checking.

In order to investigate remediation skills, Garner and Reis (1981) examined a "lookback" strategy among students in the fourth through tenth grades. Specifically, students read passages containing successive paragraphs, each followed by three questions that required looking back to preceding paragraphs. Skilled readers, across all grade levels, looked back on an average of 30% of the questions as compared to less skilled readers who did so on only 9% of the questions. In addition, the six oldest readers looked back on 80% of the questions. Such findings suggest that mature readers employ remediation strategies in monitoring their comprehension.

The techniques used by Harris et al. (1981) and by Garner and Reis (1981) may prove useful as assessment devices for determining which students employ goal checking and remediation strategies during reading. Students should also be questioned individually about their use of metacognitive strategies in order to precisely identify the source of their deficiencies. Weinstein (1978), for example, has developed a questionnaire to assess readers' strategies for elaborating upon a text. The questionnaire directs students to think about the purpose for their reading and to relate the passage to their own knowledge and experience. Similar questionnaires could be developed that assess the degree to which readers monitor their comprehension through goal checking and remediation strategies. Such questionnaires would presumably query readers about whether they understand the meaning of a passage and about their use of lookback strategies.

Summary

Research in cognitive psychology suggests that readers should be assessed with regard to their declarative knowledge, control processes, discourse comprehension strategies, and metacognitive processes. In assessing readers' declarative knowledge, teachers must be encouraged to provide prereading assignments that test the reader's knowledge about a given topic. In addition, in assessing the organization of declarative knowledge, psychologists need to establish a standard method for the structural analysis of text amenable to computer scoring. Second, before drawing conclusions about a reader's working memory capacity limitations, he or she should be tested on a variety of memory-span tasks. Such limitations may actually have more to do with deficient control processes, however, than with deficient information-processing hardware. Third, discourse comprehension is established at the levels of propositional strategies, local coherence strategies, and macrostrategies. Propositional and local coherence strategies can be assessed with tests that require readers to integrate propositions both within and between sentences. Macrostrategies can be conveniently measured with free recalls of the main ideas contained within a passage. Finally, metacognitive processes, such as comprehension monitoring, can be assessed using tests that determine readers' goal checking and remediation strategies. By focusing on these specific cognitive factors that operate during reading, educators can hopefully define specific skill deficits and provide precise interventions.

WRITING

Within the academic domain of writing, John Hayes and Linda Flower (1980) of Carnegie-Mellon University have developed a model of writing formulated through direct analysis of writing processes. Their model proposes three interacting components within writing: (a) the task environment, (b) long-term memory, and (c) the writing processes. The task environment refers to the conditions surrounding the writing behaviors; that is, the writing assignment itself and the text generated thus far. The long-term memory component includes the writer's declarative knowledge about the topic, the informational needs of the intended audience, and the overall plans that guide the writing processes. Within the third component of the model, Hayes and Flower (1980) describe three processes: *planning, translating,* and *reviewing.* Within the planning process, there are three subprocesses: *goal setting, generating,* and *organizing.* Goal setting refers to the purpose for writing and to the goals writers set for themselves. Generating involves accessing relevant information from long-term memory and the task environment to generate ideas for writing. Finally, in the organizing subprocess, the writer attempts to establish both cohesion and coherence in writing. Cohesion refers to the use of linguistic devices (e.g., pronouns, conjunctions, and implicit linguistic ties) that integrate related ideas. Coherence, on the other hand, refers to how well an entire passage fits together.

In translating, ideas (semantics) are transformed into external symbols (syntax). This is actually the direct opposite of decoding in the reading process, in which symbols are translated into ideas. Finally, in reviewing, the writer evaluates what has been written and makes revisions where needed. This process, therefore, involves the two subprocesses of evaluating and revising.

The components of the Hayes and Flower (1980) model are both iterative and interactive, because the writer continuously passes back and forth across these components during writing. Although the Hayes and Flower (1980) model is useful for identifying the various writing processes, it is, nonetheless, inadequate for investigating individual differences, because it fails to specify the cognitive factors that influence such processes. For this reason, a discussion of those cognitive factors follows, with particular attention given to how each may be assessed.

Assessing Writer's Declarative Knowledge

Writing is perceived as an instance of information processing, because information must be retrieved from long-term memory to impose meaning on the specific writing task and to generate ideas for writing (Hayes & Flower, 1980). In order to write effectively then, writers must possess appropriate declarative knowledge in long-term memory. What kinds of knowledge contribute to expertise in writing ability? According to Perfetti and McCutchen (in press), relevant knowledge for writing includes a) discourse schema knowledge, b) lexical knowledge, and c) syntactic knowledge. Other authors (Benton & Blohm, 1986; Moore, Moore, Cunningham, & Cunningham, 1986) also include topic-specific knowledge as essential for effective writing.

Discourse schema knowledge refers to knowledge of discourse forms (Meyer, 1975; Stein & Glenn, 1979; Stein & Trabasso, 1981). More specifically, discourse schemata "include knowledge of the general structure and ordering of information within a given discourse, the typical qualitative nature of that information, and the kinds of linguistic ties that link that information into a coherent discourse" (Perfetti & McCutchen, in press, p. 42). Discourse schema knowledge would, for example, be important for someone trying to write a story. As we write a story, we construct the events of that story to correspond to our story schema which may include an introduction, a characterization, a resolution, and so forth. We do this because stories that are presented in a manner consistent with story schema structure are more comprehensible (Thorndyke, 1977). Knowledge of discourse structure seems essential, then, for expertise in writing, because such knowledge influences how prose is structured.

With regard to the Hayes and Flower (1980) writing model, the organizing and reviewing processes would seem to be most affected by such knowledge. Individual differences have been observed among writers, for example, in their ability to produce well organized text. Specifically, McCutchen and Perfetti (1982) compared text structures written by fourth and sixth graders. Students were asked to consider several constraints about a topic (e.g., the topic had to be about something both fun and dangerous), because the authors believed that the ability to simultaneously satisfy several constraints at once produces well-organized prose. Fourth graders tended to produce text with a listlike structure, considering one constraint at a time, whereas many sixth graders produced text with a zigzag structure that weaved back and forth across constraints. McCutchen and Perfetti also compared the students' writing with an ideally coherent text produced by the authors. They found that 60% of the sixth grade texts resembled the ideal structure, whereas only 44% of the fourth grade texts were so structured. Older students' essays were apparently better structured because of their more mature discourse schema structures. It seems, then, that skilled writers have acquired well-organized schema structures that assist them in organizing prose.

Similarly, discourse schema knowledge influences the reviewing process in writing. In fact, individual differences in the reviewing process are considered largely developmental in nature (Scardamalia & Bereiter, 1983), which underscores the importance of having adequate knowledge of discourse. Writers cannot, for example, effectively evaluate prose unless they have adequate schematic representations in memory with which to compare it. Writers with better organized and elaborate schemata for different discourse types will likely be more adept at establishing a goodness-of-fit between their prose and an ideal structure within memory. Consequently, they will be more proficient at both evaluating and revising their writing.

Stallard (1974) found that students differ in both the quality and the quantity of their revisions. Educators may want to use this diversity by employing cooperative writing methods that pair skilled with less skilled writers. Research has consistently demonstrated that cooperative learning facilitates academic achievement (Dansereau et al., 1979; Sharan, 1980; Slavin, 1980) as well as transfer to individual learning (McDonald, Larson, Dansereau, & Spurlin, in press). Cooperative learning has, in fact, been proposed as a useful instructional device in teaching writing (Gebhardt, 1980; Jacko, 1978). Educators have used this technique by creating *peer response teams* comprised of from two to five students who evaluate what each has written (Moore et al., 1986). In using peer response teams, however, teachers should encourage students to a) focus initially on what is done well, b) state negative reactions as questions, c) use either oral or written responses, and d) initially listen to all feedback before responding to criticism.

Cooperative learning is effective because it presumably provides the opportunity for observational learning and for immediate peer evaluation. Students who pair off and then write, exchange, and revise may assist each other in evaluating the quality of their schematic structures necessary for organizing and revising prose. This method seems more effective than the traditional pedagogical techniques of correcting errors and writing comments that require no academic response by the learner. Educators must realize, however, that additional findings suggest that teachers should still be involved in the evaluation of writing, because many students apply evaluative criteria significantly different from those of their instructors (Newkirk, 1984). Teachers who urge students to write solely for their peers may, therefore, reinforce writing that fails to meet the expectations of academic audiences.

Besides discourse schema knowledge, writers must possess lexical knowledge—knowledge of words and their meanings—as well as syntactic knowledge, along with procedures for coordinating that knowledge. Lexical and syntactic knowledge assist in the manipulation of ideas into their correct ordering within a sentence. The process in writing influenced by such knowledge would most likely be translating.

Writing blocks, which hinder automaticity in the translating process, may presumably occur if the writer lacks adequate lexical and syntactic knowledge. If the writer continually struggles to access a word or agonizes over concerns with grammatical structure, then the fluent translation of ideas will be blocked.

Effective writers apparently have methods for acquiring additional information so that translating is more automatic. They may read texts on writing style, or perhaps flip through a thesaurus if searching for the correct word. Whatever the method, one would expect that good writers have acquired the lexical and syntactic knowledge needed for facilitating automaticity in translating. Again, educators may assist writers in assessing their lexical and syntactic knowledge through cooperative learning methods. *Peer editing teams* can help the writer monitor features of writing mechanics by providing feedback about spelling, punctuation, and word usage (Moore et al., 1986). Whereas peer response reacts to the writing as a whole, peer editing reacts to the specific structure of sentences.

In assessing lexical knowledge, educators may also want to pretest their students on vocabulary that would be relevant to a given topic. It may be of even greater value to test whether students can then generate sentences that contain certain vocabulary, because practice in using the words in writing may facilitate automaticity. In addition, tests that assess basic grammar, such as the Test of Standard Written English (TSWE) of the College Board (1983), should continue to be used for the purpose of assessing students' knowledge of syntax, punctuation, and word usage.

In addition to knowledge of discourse and mechanics, expert writers must also have sufficient knowledge of specific topics. The extent of one's knowledge about a particular topic would presumably influence the generating process in writing, because such knowledge contributes to the elaborateness and the relevance of ideas produced in writing (Voss, Vesonder, & Spilich, 1980). Voss et al., for example, asked college writers with equal verbal ability, but with varying degrees of knowledge about baseball, to write an account of one-half inning of baseball. Students' written texts were then analyzed by categorizing propositions according to those dealing with game actions, auxiliary game actions, relevant nongame actions, and irrelevant nongame actions. Results indicated that writers with greater baseball knowledge generated a higher proportion of auxiliary game action propositions (e.g., elaborations about where a ball went when hit) than did those with limited baseball knowledge, whereas those with limited baseball knowledge generated a higher proportion of irrelevant nongame actions (e.g., propositions concerning the fans' behaviors).

Recent advances have been made in measuring the influence of knowledge on the generating process based on structural analyses of students' writing (Benton & Blohm, 1986). Specifically, Benton and Blohm contend that the generating process in writing can be measured by considering the extent to which writers elaborate upon their ideas with explanations and examples. Because ideas should be well organized, methods for measuring such elaborations in writing must be sensitive to the relationships between superordinate and subordinate ideas contained within a passage. This relationship can be broken down into three basic concepts that reflect both elaboration and hierarchical relationships: top-level, mid-level, and base-level ideas (Meyer, 1977). Specifically, ideas are top-level when they are related to an idea of central importance that relates several concepts together. Mid-level ideas are explanations, definitions, or descriptions that clarify the relationship directly stated or inferred in a top-level idea. Finally, base-level ideas provide specific details that exemplify a mid-level explanation or a top-level relationship. Consider the following example from a text generated by a student who wrote on the topic "Wastefulness is a necessary part of the American way of life":

> We, as Americans, are very wasteful (top-level idea). Each day millions of us get up out of bed and immediately begin being wasteful (mid-level idea). Soaps, powders, lotions, cosmetics, tissues, and other elements are consumed (five base-level ideas).

This type of structural analysis is useful for assessing generating in writing because it provides both a quantitative and a qualitative measure of elaboration. Within the preceding passage, for example, one can count a total of seven ideas. More importantly, however, there are five base-level ideas for each mid-level idea, and one mid-level idea for the single top-level idea. These types of measures indicate to what depth the writer elaborates upon mid- and top-level ideas.

Appropriate prior knowledge is an important prerequisite for good writing, and must therefore be assessed within the context of the various processing components of the writing model. Other aspects of the writer that should be considered are the control processes that operate within the translating component.

Assessing Writers' Control Processes

Recent investigations within the domain of writing have identified individual differences in the information-processing system (Benton, Kraft, Glover, & Plake, 1984). These differences between good and poor writers (as defined from holistic impressions of writing samples) are reflected in the holding capacity of short-term memory, and the manipulation of information in working memory.

Holding Capacity of Short-Term Memory.   In writing, as verbal information is transferred from long-term to short-term memory, it must be held there while translating processes are carried out. One must be able to hold letters together so that they may be put together to make a word, and words must be held together to make a clause. If the holding capacity of short-term memory is small, then presumably the process of language production will require more time and be less automatic.

In order to measure the holding capacity of short-term memory among good and poor writers, Benton et al. (1984) used a modified version of a task developed by Peterson and Peterson (1959). Subjects were presented with four consonants on a screen, one at a time, for .50 s followed by a distractor task of reading numbers from the screen for a variable amount of seconds. They were then asked to recall the four letters in their correct order. This task assessed holding capacity, because it required a person to hold information in short-term memory while concentrating on something else. Similarly, writing involves holding information in memory while deciding how to connect it to other information.

In a high school sample, good writers recalled significantly more letters in their correct order on this task than did poor writers, controlling for reading comprehension, reading speed, and scholastic achievement. These results suggest that the holding capacity of short-term memory is one factor that discriminates good from poor writers.

Manipulation of Information in Working Memory.   Another important control process that is crucial for language production is the ability to perform rapid operations on information held in working memory. In order to write, a person needs to combine letters into words, words into clauses, and clauses into sentences.

When Benton et al. (1984) sought to assess writers' abilities to manipulate information in working memory, they developed a letter reordering task. Good and poor writers were exposed to a sequence of five randomly selected consonants displayed for .50 s on a microcomputer display screen. They were instructed to hold the letters in working memory and to recall them in alphabetical order. Results found that good writers recalled significantly more letters in correct alphabetical order than did poor writers. These differences were observed in both high school and college samples when reading speed, reading comprehension and achievement were controlled.

The methods devised by Benton et al. (1984) are amenable to simple administration and scoring, particularly when using a microcomputer. As has been suggested with regard to working memory capacity among readers, however, writers should also be tested with several tests before conclusions are reached about any translating deficits. In addition, it would be wise to obtain post-hoc verbal protocols of writers that describe the cognitive strategies they may use while performing these tasks.

Assessing Writers' Cognitive Strategies

As mentioned previously, Kintsch and van Dijk's (1978) model of strategic discourse processing posits that comprehension strategies operate at several levels of discourse. Specifically, their model describes propositional strategies, which integrate words and clauses; local coherence strategies, which integrate successive sentences; and macrostrategies, which integrate macropropositions of the overall text. Although their model was originally developed for discourse comprehension analysis, van Dijk and Kintsch (1983) contend that the basic mappings between surface structure expressions and semantic representations are the same for both comprehension and production of prose, even though the reader and the writer are concerned with different aspects of strategic discourse. The model, therefore, seems appropriate for analyzing strategies employed during the writing process.

Recently, methods for assessing discourse strategies among good and poor writers have emerged. Specifically, good writers have been observed to perform more effectively on tests involving word reordering within scrambled sentences, sentence reordering within scrambled paragraphs, and paragraph assembly, which requires the ordering of sentences into multiple paragraphs (Benton & Kiewra, in press; Benton et al., 1984). Notably, good writers outperformed poor writers on these tests, in both high school and college samples, when reading comprehension, reading speed, general knowledge, verbal ability, and achievement were controlled. Each of these specific tests and their intended level of measurement is now discussed in greater detail.

Word Reordering Test.   This test was designed to assess propositional strategies used in writing that integrate propositions within a sentence. Specifically, students are presented items that contain a scrambled sentence and are directed to unscramble each sentence as rapidly as possible and to write in the correct version of the sentence. Although there may be more than one correct ordering, students are told to provide only one response. An example of a scrambled sentence and its correct form appear below:

> *Scrambled version*: Fight feels him with teases anyone must he boy who the.
> *Correct version*: The boy feels he must fight with anyone who teases him.

The word reordering test presumably measures the writer's abilities to detect clause boundaries and to integrate propositions. Specific propositional strategies that might be employed in this kind of test item include the following sentence parsing strategies.

1. Whenever you find a determiner, begin a new noun phrase (Clark & Clark, 1977). In the previous example, the writer who employs this strategy would begin a phrase with "The boy," because that is the only logical noun-determiner combination.
2. Whenever you find a relative pronoun (that, which, who, whom), begin a new clause (Clark & Clark, 1977). Again, drawing upon the example given, the writer who uses this strategy would attempt to begin clauses with "who must," "who feels," or "who teases."

It seems reasonable to assume, then, that such strategies for discourse production would be employed in the word reordering test, which requires writers to integrate scrambled propositions. Differences observed between good and poor writers on this test might, then, be attributed to differential use of propositional strategies.

Sentence Reordering Test.   This test was devised in order to assess local coherence strategies. In this test, students are presented with a series of items, each containing a chronological paragraph whose order of sentences has been scrambled. Students are directed to order the sentences chronologically by placing the correct order number for events in the blank alongside each sentence. Although there may be more than one correct ordering, students are told only to provide one solution. An example of a scrambled paragraph with one possible solution appears below.

 8 Subsequently, each day that Hugh did a better job of putting the food in his mouth instead of elsewhere, I rewarded him with peaches.

 7 Hugh received no peaches.

 1 Hugh had a great fondness for peaches.

 3 I showed him the peaches he could expect and pointed out that he should put the food in his mouth, not on the floor.

 5 I gave him the peaches.

 2 I told him that he could have peaches for dessert if he did not mess his food up so much.

 4 He did better, although liberal amounts of food still fell on the floor.

 6 The next day Hugh was in an exuberant mood and scattered his vegetables far and wide.

 9 He improved rapidly and was eventually willing to substitute other fruits for his reward.

The sentence reordering test measures local coherence strategies, because writers must connect successive sentences in a chronological fashion by searching for related propositions and potential links. In order to perform well on this test, writers must consider both previous sentences as well as the present sentence being processed. Using this logic, one can strategically determine that the sentence "Hugh had a great fondness for peaches" is the only one not dependent upon a previous idea. Consequently, this sentence is ordered first. Upon further investigation, the writer infers that the sentences number 2 and 3 above must necessarily be successive, because they contain the common ideas of "told him he could have peaches . . ." and ". . . showed him the peaches he could expect . . . ;" as well as ". . . not mess up his food so much . . ." and ". . . not on the floor." One would expect, then, that writers who perform well on this test also efficiently employ local coherence strategies during writing.

Paragraph Assembly Test.   The paragraph assembly test was designed to assess macrostrategies employed during writing. Specifically, students are presented with items containing one set of three scrambled paragraphs taken from an essay originally generated by Bruning (1968). (In that original essay, each paragraph contained one topic sentence and three subordinate sentences.) Students are directed to correctly group the sentences into three, four-sentence paragraphs by placing a letter (A, B, or C) in the blank before each sentence. An example of a three paragraph set is presented below with the letters in the blanks representing an ordering into the three correct paragraphs.

<u> B </u>   There are only 450 miles of paved roads in Mala.

<u> C </u>   The only non-military high official in Mala is the premier.

<u> A </u>   Aluminum mining has been especially productive for the northern region.

<u> A </u>   The economy of Northern Mala is based on mining.

<u> B </u>   There is only one telephone for every 15,000 inhabitants of Mala.

<u> C </u>   The cabinet of the premier must be approved by a panel of military officers.

<u> A </u>   About two-thirds of the work force in the north are involved in mining.

<u> C </u>   The government of Mala can be classified as a military dictatorship.

<u> B </u>   There are only 300 miles of railways in the entire country.

<u> A </u>   Mining of all types provides about 80% of the income in the northern region.

<u> B </u>   Mala's communication system would probably rank as the worst of all African nations.

<u> C </u>   Whoever controls the Malan army controls the country of Mala.

The paragraph assembly test presumably draws upon the macrostrategy of semantic inference, because writers must infer three basic topics from twelve sentences. Specifically, the writer must make subtle differentiations among the sentences because all twelve sentences deal with the same basic topic—the mythical nation of Mala. Because semantic inference is influenced by prior knowledge, different readers will derive different inferences from the same text. Knowing this, writers must attempt to constrain this kind of personal variation in interpretation through textual signaling of the main theme or topic throughout the passage, such that the sentences within the text share similar ideas. It is imperative, then, that good writers be able to differentiate between closely related concepts, so that only similar ideas are grouped together in a paragraph. The paragraph assembly test attempts to assess this ability, because writers must impose meaning upon groups of sentences that do share similar ideas. Macrostrategies thus come into play because the writer forms best guesses about the theme that connects a group of sentences, and then reads further to evaluate whether such hypothesized macropropositions are correct.

    Recent research by Benton and Kiewra (in press) has investigated the concurrent validity of the word reordering, sentence reordering, and paragraph assembly tests with measures of writing ability. Results have indicated that these tests are significantly correlated with holistic impressions of writing samples.

Admittedly, however, it is difficult to actually construct tests that uniquely assess these strategies. Within the sentence reordering test, for example, propositional strategies are involved in reading each sentence. Similarly, within the paragraph assembly test, both propositional and local coherence strategies are involved in finding common propositions between sentences. According to the Kintsch and van Dijk model, however, one can not devise a test that uniquely measures macrostrategies or local coherence strategies, because such strategies are interrelated.

These language strategies are apparently involved in the organizing component of the planning process. Speculatively, writers use propositional strategies to organize words and clauses, local coherence strategies to organize sentences, and macrostrategies to organize paragraphs. Psychometricians should, perhaps, use measures such as the word reordering, sentence reordering, and paragraph assembly tests to assess these strategies that facilitate well-organized prose. Such measures can be easily administered and scored, and may have more validity than verbal reports, because language strategies are not consciously controlled. Processes that are more consciously controlled, referred to as metacognitive processes, are discussed in the next section.

Assessing Writers' Metacognitive Processes

Although research investigating metacognitive processes involved in writing is still in its infancy, methods for assessing such processes, as they influence the translating and reviewing components of the writing model, have emerged.

One writing process influenced by metacognition is translating. As has been previously mentioned, automaticity in translating may be hindered by blocking, a common psychological phenomenon that hinders effective communication in any setting. Cognitive therapists (e.g., Arnkoff & Glass, 1982; Beck, Rush, Shaw, & Emery, 1979) have identified cognitive components of blocking (e.g., distorted thinking, automatic thoughts, inferences, and assumptions that appear in "self-talk" of patients) that inhibit effective therapeutic intervention. Generally, these therapists help patients recognize and record faulty cognitions and teach them new "self-talk" statements that are more adaptive.

Similar progress has been made in the investigation of self-talk during writing (Boice, 1985). Boice has identified seven components of faulty metacognitive processing that impede effective translating (1985, pp. 97-98): (a) self-talk about the aversiveness of writing; (b) self-talk that justifies avoiding or delaying writing; (c) self-talk that reflects burnout, anxiety, panic, or groundless worries; (d) self-talk concerned with achieving more in less time or of unnecessary deadlines;

(e) self-talk indicating internal criticism that allows no mistakes or imperfections; (f) self-talk about fears of rejection; and (g) self-talk about maladaptive strategies for writing (e.g., favoring a single draft over revisions).

It seems apparent that these kinds of maladaptive thoughts will prevent effective communication in writing. Perhaps effective writers are characterized not just by specific writing skills, but also by "healthy" metacognition. Educators may do well, then, to interview students who find writing aversive in order to identify faulty cognitions that impede the translating process.

Metacognitive strategies also influence the reviewing process in writing. During the early elementary school years, writers first learn to evaluate whether something is wrong with their prose, but they may not be capable of revising it until the later elementary school years (Scardamalia & Bereiter, 1983). Scardamalia and Bereiter, for example, asked elementary students to evaluate and revise each sentence as they wrote an essay. The quality of both the evaluating and the revising was then judged by expert adult writers. Results found that 85% of the time fourth grade students could recognize that something was wrong with their writing, but 70% of the time they could not remediate problems they had identified. Older students, on the other hand, were consistently successful at revising a problem they had recognized. These findings suggest that less skilled writers have the necessary knowledge for evaluating their writing, but often fail to take the required steps to revise. What can educators do to facilitate those steps? Again, the peer editing and peer response teams described earlier may be useful, because students learn to edit and revise errors they would not normally identify themselves.

Research into the metacognitive strategies employed during writing have implications for the field of measurement. Most multiple-choice tests of writing ability assess the writer's skills at recognizing errors in sentence structure, punctuation, and syntax. If, as the previously cited findings indicate, most writers can recognize problems in their writing, but may fail to remediate them, then the key variable in the reviewing process—revising—is not actually being tested. Multiple-choice tests may, then, be of questionable validity. In fact, the Conference on College Composition and Communication, declared in the 1970s that multiple-choice measures of writing were narrowly focused and provided gross distortions of writing competence (Troyka, 1982). These kinds of tests, nonetheless, continue to be widely used.

Recently, however, writing samples have also been used with greater frequency for the purpose of measuring writing ability. Although writing samples appear to be more valid measures, they are too frequently first drafts, because the writer is only allowed a set time period in which to write. Consequently, the essay is then handed in, with no opportunity for revisions. Both multiple-choice tests and writing samples, then, fail to assess the writer's ability to revise, which is an essential component of writing. In fact, Stallard (1974) has observed that one important distinction between skilled and less skilled writers, which is often overlooked, is that skilled writers make more revisions.

Psychometricians must direct their efforts, therefore, toward assessing how writers make revisions in their writing. One method for doing so would be to employ short-answer items that require writers to rewrite sentences or even paragraphs that contain flaws. The drawbacks of such items are many in terms of scoring; but unless writing assessment moves in this direction, tests of writing ability will remain of questionable validity.

Summary

Research into the cognitive factors that influence writing has several implications for the field of measurement. First, educators must be encouraged to assess prior knowledge as it affects the generating, translating, organizing, and reviewing components of the writing model. Specifically, students should be tested concerning their prior knowledge of the writing topic, their vocabulary, and their knowledge of basic grammar before writing actually begins. In this way, instructional interventions can be made that will facilitate the generating and the translating processes in writing. In addition, teachers should be encouraged to write an ideally coherent essay with which to evaluate the structure of students' essays. Structural models of both the teacher's and the students' essays can then be made in order to compare the organizational structure within each. Students' essays can also be assessed using an analysis by Benton and Blohm (1986) that counts the number of top-, mid-, and base-, level ideas within an essay. This type of scoring system indicates both the quantity and the quality of elaboration in writing. Finally, students can assess their own knowledge of discourse structure by exchanging their essays with one another and by receiving immediate feedback about their own skills at evaluating and revising their prose.

With regard to control processes, writers should be assessed on several kinds of memory-span tests before being diagnosed as having a limited working memory capacity. In addition diagnosticians who use such tests should be cautioned against interpreting results as being indicative of a fixed capacity limitation. Finally, post-hoc verbal reports might be employed to ascertain the control processes writers use on these tests.

Strategies for discourse comprehension have been successfully measured by tests designed specifically to assess propositional strategies, local coherence strategies, and macrostrategies. Specifically, the word reordering, sentence reordering, and paragraph assembly tests might be used along with writing samples or multiple-choice tests to measure local and global coherence in writing ability.

Finally, research into the metacognitive processes involved in writing suggests that tests must be designed to assess writers' revising skills, because most students can recognize errors in their writing, but may fail to revise them.

Unfortunately, most multiple-choice tests of writing ability assess evaluating but not revising.

The study of cognitive factors in academic abilities has been quite extensive with regard to reading and writing. Although less work has been done in the areas of mathematics and science, individual differences in cognitive factors are, nonetheless, apparent in those domains as well. The exact nature of those differences and how they can be measured is now discussed.

MATHEMATICS

Generally, educators separate mathematical ability into two broad components: (a) computation, which involves the application of algorithms and rules for carrying out mathematical operations; and (b) conceptualization, which requires problem representation and the application of heuristics and problem solving strategies. Although Briars (1983) has suggested that cognitive factors, especially prior math achievement, are the best predictors of math computation and conceptualization, the literature is sparse with regard to how such factors may be measured. A discussion follows, nonetheless, of how prior knowledge, control processes, cognitive strategies, and metcognitive processes in mathematics performance can be assessed.

Assessing Math Students' Prior Knowledge

Several investigators have observed that skilled math students organize their declarative knowledge differently than do less skilled math students (Chartoff, 1977; Hinsley, Hayes, & Simon, 1977; Krutetskii, 1976; Silver, 1979). Silver (1979), for example, found that skilled math students organize knowledge according to categories of solution methods, whereas less skilled math students organize knowledge according to categories of problem contents. Specifically, Silver asked seventh-grade students to categorize 16 word problems that varied in both their content and in their solution methods. Students subsequently solved the same 16 problems and, based on their performance, were categorized into good, average, and poor math problem solvers. The author found that good math problem solvers grouped problems together on the basis of solution methods. Poor math problem solvers, on the other hand, had grouped problems together on the basis of the problem content. In addition, Silver found that the ability to categorize problems on the basis of solution similarities was strongly correlated with standardized measures of mathematics ability.

Chartoff (1977) employed a similar procedure with secondary and postsecondary level students. The students in that study were asked to rate the similarity of algebra word problems. The results again showed that the most important dimension for categorizing algebra problems was how they were solved.

These findings suggest that proficient math students are able to grasp the formal structure of math problems, and that they possess schemata for various types of problem solutions. What this implies is that good math students perceive a problem structure prior to its solution. Apparently, they establish a goodness of fit between their schemata for solution methods and a given math problem before solving it.

The knowledge discussed thus far has most to do with problem representation, an aspect of the conceptualization component of mathematics. Besides possessing well-organized structures in memory for problem representation, however, skilled math students likely possess adequate procedural knowledge for various mathematical computations. R. M. Gagné and Paradise (1961), for example, advocated the importance of assessing prerequisite procedural knowledge (intellectual skills) required for solving linear equations. Such preassessment, obtained by employing rational task analysis, can uncover lower-order skills that must be mastered prior to performing higher-order skills. By specifying which prerequisite skills must be mastered, psychologists have discovered that low achieving math students commit errors because they lack prerequisite procedural knowledge (e.g., knowledge of how to find a common denominator or of how to simplify fractions). Brown and Burton (1978), who refer to lack of procedural knowledge as "bugs," developed the BUGGY program specifically to assess errors made in subtraction. They translated subtraction procedures into a computer program capable of 100% accuracy in computation. Changes were then made in the program to mimic students' errors in order to see if the same patterns of errors emerged from the computer. These kinds of analyses are valuable because they provide a map for more specific diagnosis of students' errors. In using the methods of rational task analysis and computer programming, then, educators can diagnose specific deficient skills by testing less skilled math students at each prerequisite step. In this way, specific remediations can be made and the student can advance to the next skill level.

Essentially, then, educators must assess two types of knowledge in mathematics performance: declarative knowledge of problem representation, and procedural knowledge of mathematical computation. These two types of knowledge presumably require different kinds of tests. Specifically, knowledge of problem representation requires discriminatory tests such that students "may progress almost without limit in such functions as understanding, critical thinking, appreciation, and originality" (Anastasi, 1982, pp. 97–98). Tests assessing conceptual knowledge of mathematics need to allow for individual differences among students' achievement, because complete mastery of this domain is not possible.

Tests that assess procedural knowledge of mathematical computation, however, require mastery tests in order to determine whether or not the examinee has acquired the prerequisite skills. Ultimately, the purpose of such tests is to determine whether or not more instructional time is needed for each student, and not to determine individual differences (Hanna, 1981).

Assessing Math Students' Control Processes

Another cognitive factor that affects mathematical computational ability that must be considered is that of control processes. Several researchers have studied the relationship between mathematical computational ability and performance on memory-span tasks. Speigel and Bryant (1978), for example, examined the relationship between speed of information processing, intelligence, and math achievement in 94 sixth grade students. They used a sentence-picture comparison task, a pictorial similarities-and-differences task, and a matrix analysis task, similar to the Raven's Progressive Matrices. They found processing speed to be correlated -.40 with math computation scores. With intelligence controlled, however, the relationship between these measures was almost neglible. Such findings suggest, then, that processing speed does not contribute uniquely to math achievement, and is probably more related to general intelligence.

Webster (1979) examined differences in memory-span between mathematically proficient students (those performing at or above grade level on the WRAT arithmetic subtest) and a group of "mathematically disabled" students (those performing 2 or more years below grade level). Subjects were tested using memory span for seven digits and for strings of seven nonrhyming consonants that were presented both aurally and visually at one second exposure and one second intervals. Results indicated that the mathematically disabled group had significantly lower memory-span scores than did the mathematically proficient.

Overall, these findings suggest that memory-span performance is related to mathematical computation skills, but that speed of information processing is not. As has already been suggested within the domains of reading and writing, multiple assessments of memory-span performance should be made before conclusions are reached about deficits in a student's control processes or information-processing machinery. Again, differences in memory span do not necessarily imply that proficient math students have larger working memory capacities. It is more likely that they are able to allocate attentional capacity economically such that they can simultaneously hold and manipulate information in working memory. It has been suggested that such attentional capacity develops concommittantly with proficiency in mathematics achievement, and is not necessarily a precursor to good computational skills (Briars, 1983).

Another promising area of test development may be that of assessing cognitive strategies related to mathematics achievement. Because of the limited amount of studies in this area, however, the assessment of cognitive strategies and metacognitive processes in mathematics are addressed in one section.

Assessing Math Students' Cognitive Strategies and Metacognitive Processes

The strategies used by proficient math students generally may be broken down into three types: (a) heuristics, (b) awareness of problem-solving processes, and (c) belief systems (Briars, 1983). Heuristics would fall into the general category of cognitive strategies as described in this chapter, whereas awareness of problem-solving processes and belief systems would be considered metacognitive processes.

Heuristics are more or less rigid operating routines that serve to narrow the potential behavioral alternatives considered by a student when confronted with a problem. These types of strategies are independent of content, because they may be applied within the context of any problem. Examples of heuristics used in solving math problems include drawing a diagram or thinking of a similar problem solved previously. These types of heuristics enable math students to impose a more meaningful representation upon a problem.

Awareness of one's problem-solving processes, a metacognitive skill in mathematics, can help math students recall and execute appropriate routines. This awareness is beneficial in making two types of decisions: (a) tactical decisions about selecting the appropriate method, and (b) strategic decisions, which involve decisions about how one allocates time (Schoenfeld, 1979). Poor strategic decisions may be the most costly among less skilled math students. Schoenfeld (1979) has observed, for example, that less skilled math students do not make good strategic decisions, because they do not monitor their progress toward a solution (e.g., they spend 10 minutes calculating the area of a triangle without considering what that will contribute to the final solution.)

Finally, belief systems and expectations about math can affect math performance. Examples of faulty beliefs that impede math performance include the following (Lester & Garofalo, 1982; Silver, 1981):

1. The difficulty of a problem depends on the size of the numbers.
2. Problems require the application of only one math principle for their solution.
3. Key words appear only in the last sentence of a problem.
4. There is only one correct way to solve a problem.
5. Problems should take only a few minutes to solve.

It is easy to understand how beliefs such as these can impede success in mathematics.

Cognitive strategies and metacognitive processes in mathematics performance have been neglected by psychometricians, even though they appear to be important factors in such performance. Some heuristics could be easily assessed by having students hand in their worksheets, which show how they solved the problems, along with their test. Other types of heuristics will presumably have to be measured through verbal reports of math students as they solve problems. Students should also be asked to keep a time log of their solution steps, so that the strategic decision making of time allocation can be assessed. Finally, beliefs about mathematics can be assessed with questionnaires that ask students to evaluate the truth or falsity of statements such as those listed above.

Summary

It seems that psychometricians have done a good job of designing mastery tests to measure procedural knowledge in mathematics computation. They may need to do more, however, in developing discriminatory tests that measure other cognitive factors related to math achievement (e.g., organization of declarative knowledge, heuristics, and metacognitive processes). The methods used by Silver (1979) and Chartoff (1977) for assessing students' declarative knowledge, for example, should be adapted for testing students' organizational structure for math concepts in memory. Asking students to record their solution strategies on paper, along with an approximate time log, may also go far in identifying those students who make poor strategical decisions in solving math problems. Again, the need for assessing these kinds of cognitive factors in mathematics may encourage psychometricians to move away from the mastery model and toward the realm of discriminatory tests.

SCIENCE

As in mathematics, the domain of science is sparse with regard to studies investigating individual differences in cognitive factors. Two factors that seem most relevant to studying individual differences within science, however, are prior knowledge and cognitive strategies.

Assessing Science Students' Prior Knowledge

The assessment of prior knowledge in science must access both procedural and declarative knowledge. In measuring procedural knowledge, rational task analysis and the mastery model have been applied in science as they have in mathematics. Okey and Gagné (1970), for example, performed a task analysis of the prerequisites needed to solve solubility-product problems in chemistry. (The solubility problem, common in chemistry classes, concerns the question of whether or not a solid matter will form when two chemicals are mixed together.) Based on a hierarchy of prerequisite skills needed for solving solubility problems, the authors instructed and tested the students at each level of those skills. They then tested the students on solubility type problems and found that performance increased as knowledge of prerequisite procedures increased. The authors concluded, therefore, that success in science problem solving is associated with knowledge of prerequisite procedures.

In addition to knowledge of prerequisite procedures, the organization and the content of one's declarative knowledge influence science problem solving. Specifically, Chi, Feltovich, and Glaser (1981) gave Ph.D. physicists and students, who had had one course in physics, twenty category labels for describing physics problems. In response to these labels, the subjects were to tell all they could about problems subsumed within the label and how they might be solved. Based on these responses, the authors constructed a network of declarative knowledge to reflect each subject's organizational structure for scientific declarative knowledge in memory. Results found that the experts' memory structures contained more physics principles and a more hierarchical organization than did the novices'. As in the previously discussed domains of reading, writing, and mathematics, then, expert science problem solvers have more elaborate and better organized memory structures than do novices.

The observed differences between experts' and novices' prior knowledge have implications for the measurement of scientific abilities similar to those in mathematics assessment. As in mathematics, educators should test their students on prerequisite procedural knowledge required for solving science problems. In so doing, they will be able to diagnose specific skill deficits that, with proper instruction, can be remediated. In addition, structural models of students' declarative knowledge can be constructed and compared to well-organized structures of scientific principles (e.g., as in the structure contained within science textbooks). Analyses of students' memory structures could presumably reveal the "missing links" that need to be learned for better understanding of specific scientific principles.

Assessing Science Students' Cognitive Strategies

Of equal importance to prior knowledge are cognitive strategies, which aid in both understanding and in solving science problems. Specifically, individual differences have been observed in the strategies used for understanding a problem, and in the types of problem-solution paths generated.

Within the realm of the social sciences, for example, Voss, Tyler, and Yengo (1983) discovered differences between novices and experts in how they represented a problem. These authors focused on one type of social science problem: an undesirable state of affairs that requires improvement. Specifically, they compared the thinking-aloud protocols of political scientists, whose specialty was Soviet politics, with those of college students taking a Soviet political science course. Each subject was asked to assume the role of the Soviet Ministry of Agriculture and to consider the problem of how to improve productivity after experiencing low agricultural productivity during the previous 5 years. Voss et al. found that 24% of the experts' protocol statements were devoted to defining the problem, whereas almost none of the novices' statements were so devoted. More specifically, experts began by defining the constraints of the problem (e.g., Soviet ideology, soil conditions, and so forth), whereas novices simply began by listing possible solutions. What these findings suggest is that experts seek a deeper understanding of a problem before attempting to generate solutions.

Further findings suggest that individuals differ not only in how they represent a problem, but also in their problem-solution paths. It has been observed, for example, that novices engage in solution searching by attempting several paths toward reaching the goal of the correct solution; experts, on the other hand, follow one solution path (Larkin, McDermott, Simon, & Simon, 1980). These authors asked novices and expert physicists to think aloud while solving a problem for determining velocity. The experts used a "working forward" solution path, because they began with that which was known and proceeded step-by-step to the solution. Novices, on the other hand, used a "working backward" approach, because they began with the goal (solving for velocity) and tried to solve for it immediately before completing prerequisites steps. Based on this kind of finding, Gagné (1985) has drawn an analogy between being lost in a forest and solving science problems that captures the essence of the expert-novice distinction:

> If one is lost in a forest, one is better off determining the direction (N,S,E,W) of one's goal and limiting one's search for a path to this direction than wandering around at random. The difference between novices and experts is that experts are not lost; they know a path that leads to the goal and follow it. (p. 282)

Even with regard to problem-solving strategies in science, then, one cannot underestimate the importance of prior knowledge, because one must have some knowledge of the constraints involved before representing a problem adequately. Similarly, in order to select the appropriate solution path, one must also have prior knowledge of what will or will not work. An important distinction between the novice and the expert, however, may be that novices do not bother to acquire the needed prior knowledge before generating possible solutions.

Summary

As in mathematics, psychometricians have probably been successful at assessing procedural knowledge in science problem solving using rational task analysis and mastery tests. More can be done, however, in constructing discriminatory tests that measure the organization of declarative knowledge and the application of problem solving strategies. Tests that require students to categorize scientific problems (as in Chi et al., 1981) may be useful for assessing the organization of structures for science concepts in memory. In addition, verbal protocols could help to reveal the cognitive strategies employed by students as they solve science problems. Such protocols would presumably vary within as well as between students, however, depending upon their prior knowledge of the content area.

CONCLUSION

Research in cognitive psychology has identified underlying cognitive factors that contribute to intellectual performance across academic domains. If psychometricians are to follow the lead of cognitive psychologists, they must devise tests that measure domain-specific prior knowledge, control processes, cognitive strategies, and metacognitive processes. In so doing, measurement will become more valid and precise, and instructional treatments will presumably become more effective.

A major goal of measurement should be to assess the declarative knowledge structures that influence performance in various academic tasks, as "the nature and power of students' organized structure of knowledge is a key aspect of educational achievement, because it either facilitates or hinders what he or she can do in a subject area" (Messick, 1984, p. 217). In fact, Glaser (1984) criticizes much of the research favoring the importance of control processes, because it was conducted in "knowledge-lean" domains (p. 94). Glaser further argues that it is the interaction of control processes with domain-specific knowledge that produces expertise. Psychometricians should, therefore, develop tests that assess students' knowledge structures within each academic domain, using the structural model approach of cognitive psychologists. In this way, network or tree structures can be constructed that indicate symbolically the elements of a person's knowledge and the relationships among those elements. These structures can then be compared to ideally organized knowledge structures so that teachers can identify students' schemata that need to be restructured or elaborated.

In addition to declarative knowledge, learners should be assessed with regard to their procedural knowledge. Educators have actually been quite proficient in measuring procedural knowledge, as in the domains of mathematics, and science by using rational task analysis. They must, however, make greater use of computer programs (e.g., BUGGY), which list step-by-step actions to be taken, and of flowcharts, which present processes and decisions to be made, in order to specifically pinpoint students' procedural errors. Ultimately, then, teachers will become more successful in identifying and in remediating specific procedural deficits.

In assessing control processes, memory-span tests, similar to those described in previous sections of this chapter, should be used to measure attentional capacity, rehearsal, chunking, and manipulation of information in working memory.

Hopefully, then, students who lack automaticity in decoding or in translating, which are affected by such processes, can be identified for remedial instruction.

Cognitive strategies should also be assessed across all academic areas. Such strategies, which are means for achieving a designated goal, may or may not be consciously controlled. Consciously controlled strategies (e.g., representing the problem, means-ends analysis, and so forth), which operate particularly within math and science, can be assessed through verbal reports of students as they solve problems. These kinds of data should continue to be collected and analyzed, and then programmed into computers to simulate human problem solving. Strategies that are not consciously controlled (e.g., language strategies within reading and writing), however, require alternative methods of assessment. They may be assessed with tests that tap such strategies, as in the word reordering, sentence reordering, and paragraph assembly tests used to measure discourse production strategies in writing.

Finally, more emphasis should be placed on the measurement of metacognitive processes. These processes are important because they facilitate the self-checking and the remediating processes involved in all academic areas, and because they orchestrate and control the previously discussed cognitive factors. Innovative assessment methods, which have been described within this chapter, should be employed to develop tests that measure metacognition within each academic domain.

The notion of developing tests, based on known cognitive factors that differentiate between experts and novices, seems in contrast to the more traditional approach of testing in which items are based on vague curriculum objectives, which may or may not be related to expertise (Messick, 1984). Tests that assess domain-specific cognitive skills seemed reasonable even to Cronbach (1957), however, nearly 30 years ago, when he wrote:

> In dividing pupils between college preparatory and non-college studies. . . a general intelligence test is probably the wrong thing to use. This test, being general, predicts success in all subjects, therefore tends to have little interaction with treatment, and if so is not the best guide to differential treatment. We require a measure of aptitude which predicts who will learn better from one curriculum than from the other. (pp. 680–681)

Essentially, then, the cognitive approach to the assessment of academic abilities is closely related to the long-standing specificity doctrine first proposed by correlational psychologists. Those who hold this view, and those who adhere to the current cognitive approach, contend that individual differences consist of nothing more than differences in specific knowledge and skills acquired through learning. Cognitive psychology's greatest contribution to the assessment of academic abilities will, therefore, probably be the notion that academic deficits have more to do with lack of domain-specific knowledge and skills than with lack of general intelligence.

REFERENCES

American College Testing Assessment Program. Research and Development Division. (1973). *Assessing students on the way to college* (Technical report for the ACT assessment program). Iowa City, IA: Author.

Anastasi, A. (1982). *Psychological testing*. Fifth Edition. New York: Macmillan.

Anderson, J. R., & Reder, L. M. (1979). An elaborative processing explanation of depth of processing. In L. S. Cermak & F. I. M. Craik (Eds.), *Levels of processing in human memory* (pp. 385–403). Hillsdale, NJ: Lawrence Erlbaum Associates.

Applebee, A. N., Durst, R., & Newell, G. (1984). The demands of school writing. In A. N. Applebee (Ed.), *Contexts for learning to write* (pp. 55–77. Norwood, NJ: Ablex.

Arnkoff, D. B., & Glass, C. R. (1982). Clinical cognitive constructs. In P. C. Kendall (Ed.), *Advances in cognitive behavioral research*. Orlando, FL: Academic Press.

Baddeley, A. D. (1970). Effects of acoustic and semantic similarity on short-term paired associate learning. *British Journal of Psychology, 61*, 335–343.

Bakker, D. J. (1972). *Temporal order in disturbed reading*. Rotterdam: Rotterdam University Press.

Bartlett, B. J. (1978). *Top-level structure as an organizational strategy for recall of classroom text*. Unpublished doctoral dissertation, Arizona State University, Tempe.

Bartlett, F. C. (1932). *Remembering: A study in experimental and social psychology*. London: Cambridge University Press.

Bauer, R. (1977). Short-term memory in learning disabled and non-disabled children. *Bulletin of the Psychonomic Society, 10*, 128–130.

Beck, A. T., Rush, J. A., Shaw, B. F., & Emery, G. (1979). *Cognitive therapy of depression*. New York: Guilford.

Benton, S. L., & Blohm, P. J. (1986). Effect of question type and position on measures of conceptual elaboration in writing. *Research in the Teaching of English, 20*, 98–108.

Benton, S. L., Glover, J. A., & Plake, B. S. (1984). Employing adjunct aids to facilitate elaboration in writing. *Research in the Teaching of English, 18*, 189–200.

Benton, S. L., & Kiewra, K. A. (in press). Measuring the organizational aspects of writing ability. *Journal of Educational Measurement*.

Benton, S. L., Kraft, R. G., Glover, J. A., & Plake, B. S. (1984). Cognitive capacity differences among writers. *Journal of Educational Psychology, 76*, 820–834.

Birnbaum, J. C. (1982). The reading and composing behaviors of selected fourth-and seventh-grade students. *Research in the Teaching of English, 16*, 241–260.

Boice, R. (1982). Increasing the writing productivity of blocked academicians. *Behavior Research and Therapy, 20*, 197–207.

Bower, G. H., Black, J. B., & Turner, T. J. (1979). Scripts in memory for text. *Cognitive Psychology, 11*, 177–220.

Bransford, J. D. (1979). *Human cognition: Learning, understanding, and remembering*. Belmont, CA: Wadsworth.

Briars, D. J. (1983). An information-processing analysis of mathematical ability. In R. F. Dillon & R. R. Schmeck (Eds.), *Individual differences in cognition* (pp. 181–204). New York: Academic Press.

Brown, A. L. (1978). Knowing when, where, and how to remember: A problem of metacognition. In R. Glaser (Ed.), *Advances in instructional psychology*. Hillsdale, NJ: Lawrence Erlbaum Associates.

Brown, A. L., & Barclay, C. R. (1976). The effects of training specific mnemonics of the meta-mnemonic efficiency of retarded children. *Child Development, 47*, 71–80.

Brown, A. L., Campione, C. D., & Barclay, C. R. (1978). Training self-checking routines for estimating test readiness: Generalization from list learning to prose recall. Unpublished manuscript, University of Illinois.

Brown, A. L., & Lawton, S. C. (1977). The feeling of knowing experience on educable mentally retarded children. *Developmental Psychology, 4,* 364–370.

Brown, J. S., & Burton, R. R. (1978). Diagnostic models for procedural bugs in basic mathematical skills. *Cognitive Science, 2,* 155–192.

Bruning, R. H. (1968). Effects of review and test-like events within the learning of prose materials. *Journal of Educational Psychology, 59,* 16–19.

Campione, J. C., & Brown, A. L. (1977). Memory and metamemory development in educable retarded children. In R. V. Kail, Jr., & J. W. Hagen (Eds.), *Perspectives on the development of memory and cognition.* Hillsdale, NJ: Lawrence Erlbaum Associates.

Chartoff, B. T. (1977). An exploratory investigation utilizing a multidimensional scaling procedure to discover classification criteria for algebra word problems used by students in grades 7-13. *Dissertation Abstracts International, 37,* 7006A.

Chase, W. G., & Simon, H. A. (1973). The mind's eye in chess. In W. G. Chase (Ed.), *Visual information processing* (pp. 215–281). New York: Academic Press.

Chi, M. T. H. (1976). Short-term memory limitations in children: Capacity of processing deficits? *Memory and Cognition, 4,* 559–572.

Chi, M. T. H. (1978). Knowledge structures and memory development. In R. Siegler (Ed.), *Children's thinking: What develops?.* Hillsdale, NJ: Lawrence Erlbaum Associates.

Chi, M. T. H., Feltovich, P. J., & Glaser, R. (1981). Categorization and representation of physics problems by experts and novices. *Cognitive Science, 5,* 121–152.

Chi, M. T. H., Glaser, R., & Reese, E. (1982).Expertise in problem solving. In R. Sternberg (Ed.), *Advances in the psychology of human intelligence* (Vol. 1, pp. 7–75). Hillsdale, NJ: Lawrence Erlbaum Associates.

Clark, H. H., & Clark, E. V. (1977). *Psychology and language.* New York: Harcourt Brace Jovanovich.

The College Board. (1983). *The test of standard written English.* Princeton, NJ: The College Board.

Conrad, R. (1972). Speech and reading. In J. F. Kavanagh & Mattingly (Eds.), *Language by ear and by eye: The relationships between speech and reading.* Cambridge, MA: MIT Press.

Corkin, S. (1974). Serial-ordering deficits in inferior readers. *Neuropsychology, 12,* 347–354.

Covington, M. V., Crutchfield, R. S., & Davies, L. B. (1966). *The productive thinking program.* Berkeley, CA: Brazelton.

Cronbach, L. J. (1957). The two disciplines of scientific psychology. *American Psychologist, 12,* 671–684.

Daneman, M., & Carpenter, P. A. (1980). Individual differences in working memory and reading. *Journal of Verbal Learning and Verbal Behavior, 19,* 450–466.

Dansereau, D. F., Collins, K. W., McDonald, B. A., Holley, C. D., Garland, J., Diekhoff, G., & Evans, S. H. (1979). Development and evaluation of a learning strategies training program. *Journal of Educational Psychology, 71,* 64–73.

van Dijk, T. A., & Kintsch, W. (1983). *Strategies of discourse comprehension.* Orlando, FL: Academic Press.

Ehri, L. C., & Wilce, L. C. (1983). Development of word identification speed in skilled and less skilled beginning readers. *Journal of Educational Psychology, 75,* 3–18.

Ernst, G. W., & Newell, A. (1969). *GPS: A case study in generality and problem solving.* New York: Academic Press.

Feltovich, P. J. (1981). *Knowledge-based components of expertise in medical diagnosis* (Tech. Rep. No. PDS-2). Pittsburgh, PA: University of Pittsburgh Learning Research and Development Center.

Frase, L. T. (1973). Integration of written text. *Journal of Educational Psychology, 65*, 252–261.
Frederiksen, C. H. (1975). Acquisition of semantic information from discourse: Effects of repeated exposures. *Journal of Verbal Learning and Verbal Behavior, 14*, 158–169.
Frederiksen, J. R. (1981). Sources of process interactions in reading. In A. M. Lesgold & C. A. Perfetti (Eds.), *Interactive processes in reading*. Hillsdale, NJ: Lawrence Erlbaum Associates.
Gagné, E. D. (1985). *The cognitive psychology of school learning*. Boston, MA: Little, Brown.
Gagné, R. M., & Paradise, N. E. (1961). Abilities and learning sets in knowledge acquisition. *Psychological monographs: General and applied* (No. 518).
Garner, R., & Reis, R. (1981). Monitoring and resolving comprehension obstacles: An investigation of spontaneous text lookbacks among upper-grade good and poor comprehenders. *Reading Research Quarterly, 16*, 569–582.
Gehardt, R. (1980). Teamwork and feedback: Broadening the base of collaborative writing. *College English, 42*, 69–74.
Glaser, R. (1984). Education and thinking: The role of knowledge. *American Psychologist, 39*, 93–104.
Glynn, S. M., & Britton, B. K., Muth, K. D., & Dogan, N. (1982). Writing and revising persuasive documents. *Journal of Educational Psychology, 74*, 557–567.
Groen, G. J., & Parkman, J. M. (1972). A chronometric analysis of simple addition. *Psychological Review, 79*, 329–343.
Hagen, J. W., & Stanovich, K. G. (1977). Memory: Strategies of acquisition. In R. V. Kail & J. W. Hagen (Eds.), *Perspectives on the development of memory and cognition*. Hillsdale, NJ: Lawrence Erlbaum Associates.
Hanna, G. S. (1981, April). *What can/should be criterion referenced?*. Paper presented at Symposium 55 at the Annual Convention of the International Reading Association, New Orleans.
Harris, P. (1978). Developmental aspects of children's memory. In M. M. Gruenberg & P. E. Morris (Eds.), *Aspects of memory*. London: Methuen.
Harris, P. L., Kruithos, A., Terwogt, M. M., Visser, T. (1981). Children's detection and awareness of textual anomaly. *Journal of Experimental Child Psychology, 31*, 212–230.
Hayes, J. R., & Flower, L. S. (1980). Identifying the organization of writing processes. In W. Gregg & E. R. Steinberg (Eds.), *Cognitive processes in writing* (pp. 3–30). Hillsdale, NJ: Lawrence Erlbaum Associates.
Hinsley, D. A., Hayes, J. R., & Simon, H. A. (1977). From words to equations—meaning and representation in algebra word problems. In M. Just & P. Carpenter (Eds.), *Cognitive processes in comprehension*. Hillsdale, NJ: Lawrence Erlbaum Associates.
Hunt, E. (1978). Mechanics of verbal ability. *Psychological Review, 85*, 109–130.
Hunt, E., Frost, H., & Lunneborg, C. E. (1973). Individual differences in cognition: A New approach to intelligence. In G. Bower (Ed.), *Advances in learning and motivation* (Vol. 7, pp. 87–122). New York: Academic Press.
Hunt, E., Lunneborg, C. E., & Lewis, J. (1975). What does it mean to be high verbal? *Cognitive Psychology, 7*, 194–227.
Jacko, C. M. (1978). Small group triad: An instructional mode for the teaching of writing. *College composition and communication, 29*, 290–292.
Jackson, M. D., & McClelland, J. L. (1979). Processing determinants of reading speed. *Journal of Experimental Psychology: General, 108*, 151–181.
Jorm, A. F. (1977). Effect of word imagery on reading performance as a function of reader ability. *Journal of Educational Psychology, 69*, 45–54.
Kintsch, W. (1974). *The representation of meaning in memory*. Hillsdale, NJ: Lawrence Erlbaum Associates.
Kintsch, W., & van Dijk, T. A. (1978). Toward a model of text comprehension and production. *Psychological Review, 85*, 363–394.

Kreutzer, M. A., Leonard, C., & Flavell, J. H. (1975). An interview study of children's knowledge about memory. *Monographs of the society for research in child development, 40,* (1, serial No. 159).

Krutetskii, V. A. (1976). *The psychology of mathematical abilities in school children.* Chicago: University of Chicago Press.

LaBerge, D. (1980). Unitization and automaticity in perception. In J. Flowers (Ed.), *Nebraska symposium on motivation.* Lincoln: University of Nebraska Press.

LaBerge, D., & Samuels, S. J. (1974). Toward a theory of automatic information processing reading. *Cognitive Psychology, 6,* 293–323.

Larkin, J. H., McDermott, J., Simon, D. P., & Simon, H. A. (1980). Expert and novice performance in solving physics problems. *Science, 208,* 1335–1342.

Lester, F. K., & Garofalo, J. (1982, March). *Metacognitive aspects of elementary school students' performance on arithmetic tasks.* Paper presented at the annual meeting of the American Educational Research Association, New York.

Mackworth, N. H., & Bruner, J. S. (1970). How adults and children search and recognize pictures. *Human Development, 13,* 149–177.

Markman, E. M. (1979). Realizing that you don't understand. *Child Development, 50,* 643–655.

Mayer, R. E. (1981). *The promise of cognitive psychology.* San Francisco: W. H. Freeman.

McCutchen, D., & Perfetti, C. (1982). Coherence and connectedness in the development of discourse production. *Text, 2,* 113–139.

McDonald, B. A., Larson, C. O., Dansereau, D. F., & Spurlin, J. E. (in press). Cooperative dyads: Impact on text learning and transfer. *Contemporary Educational Psychology.*

Messick, S. (1984). The psychology of educational measurement. *Journal of Educational Measurement, 21,* 215–237.

Meyer, B. J. F. (1975). *The organization of prose and its effect on memory.* Amsterdam: North Holland.

Meyer, B. J. F. (1977). The structure of prose: Effects on learning and memory and implications for educational practice. In R. C. Anderson, R. J. Spiro, & W. E. Montague (Eds.), *Schooling and the acquisition of knowledge* (pp. 179–200). Hillsdale, NJ: Lawrence Erlbaum Associates.

Meyer, B. J. F. (1981, April). *Prose analysis: Procedures, purposes, and problems.* Paper presented at the meeting of the American Educational Research Association, Los Angeles.

Meyer, B. J. F., Brandt, D. M., & Bluth, G. J. (1980). Use of top-level structure in text: Key for reading comprehension of ninth grade students. *Reading Research Quarterly, 16,* 72–103.

Moore, D. W., Moore, S. A., Cunningham, P. M., & Cunningham, J. W. (1986).*Developing readers and writers in the content areas.* New York: Longman.

Minsky, M., & Papert, S. (1974). *Artificial intelligence.* Eugene, OR: Oregon State System of Higher Education.

Newell, A., & Simon, H. A. (1972). *Human problem solving.* Englewood Cliffs, NJ: Prentice-Hall.

Newkirk, T. (1984). How students read student papers: An exploratory study. *Written Communication, 1,* 283–306.

Okey, J. R., & Gagné, R. M. (1970). Revision of a science topic using evidence of performance on subordinate skills. *Journal of Research in Science Teaching, 7,* 321–325.

Perfetti, C. A., Finger, E., & Hogaboam, T. (1978). Sources of vocalization latency differences between skilled and less skilled young readers. *Journal of Educational Psychology, 70,* 730–739.

Perfetti, C. A., & Hogaboam, T. (1975). Relationship between single word decoding and reading comprehension skill. *Journal of Educational Psychology, 67,* 461–469.

Perfetti, C. A., & McCutchen, D. (in press). Schooled language competence: Linguistic abilities in reading and writing. In Sheldon & Rosenberg (Eds.), *Advances in applied psycholinguistics.* New York: Cambridge University Press.

Perfetti, C. A., & Roth, S. F. (1981). Some of the interactive processes in reading and their role in reading skill. In A. M. Lesgold & C. A. Perfetti (Eds.), *Interactive processes in reading* (pp. 269–297). Hillsdale, NJ: Lawrence Erlbaum Associates.

Perl, S. (1979). The composing processes of unskilled college writers. *Research in the Teaching of English, 13,* 317–336.

Pflaum, S. W., Walberg, H. J., Karegianes, J. L., & Rasher, S. P. (1980). Reading instruction: A quantitative analysis. *Educational Researcher, 9,* 12–18.

Resnick, L. B. (1976). Task analysis in instructional design: Some cases from mathematics. In D. Klahr (Ed.), *Cognition and instruction.* Hillsdale, NJ: Lawrence Erlbaum Associates.

Resnick, L. B. (1984). Cognitive science as educational research: Why we need it now. In *Improving education: Perspectives on educational research.* Pittsburgh: National Academy of Education.

Resnick, L. B. (1985, April). *Cognition and curriculum.* Paper presented at the meeting of the American Educational Research Association, Chicago.

Scardamalia, M., & Bereiter, C. (1983). The development of evaluative, diagnostic, and remedial capabilities in children's composing. In M. Martten (Ed.), *The psychology of written language: A developmental approach* (pp. 67–95). London: Wiley.

Scardamalia, M., Bereiter, C., & Goelman, H. (1982). The role of productive factors in writing ability. In M. Nystrand (Ed.), *What writers know: The language, process, and structure of written discourse,* (pp. 173–210). New York: Academic Press.

Schoenfeld, A. H. (1979). Explicit heuristic training as a variable in problem-solving performance. *Journal for Research in Mathematics Education, 10,* 173–187.

Sharan, S. (1980). Cooperative learning in small groups: Recent methods and effects on achievement, attitudes, and ethnic relations. *Review of Educational Research, 50,* 247–271.

Silver, E. A. (1979). Student perceptions of relatedness among mathematical verbal problems. *Journal for Research in Mathematics Education, 10,* 195–210.

Silver, E. A. (1981). Recall of mathematical problem information: Solving related problems. *Journal for Research in Mathematics Education, 12,* 54–64.

Slavin, R. E. (1980). Cooperative learning. *Review of Educational Research, 50,* 315–342.

Spiegel, M. R., & Bryant, N. D. (1978). Is speed of processing information related to intelligence and achievement? *Journal of Educational Psychology, 70,* 904–910.

Spilich, G. J., Vesonder, G. T., Chiesi, H. L., & Voss, J. F. (1979). Text processing of domain-related information for individuals with high and low domain knowledge. *Journal of Verbal Learning and Verbal Behavior, 18,* 275–290.

Stallard, C. K. (1974). An analysis of the writing behavior of good student writers. *Research in the Teaching of English, 8,* 206–218.

Stein, N. L., & Glenn, C. G. (1979). An analysis of story comprehension in elementary school children. In R. Freedle (Ed.), *Advances in discourse processing 2: New directions in discourse processing.* Norwood, NJ: Ablex.

Stein, N. L. & Trabasso, T. (1981). What's in a story: An approach to comprehension and instruction. In R. Glaser (Ed.), *Advances in instructional psychology* (Vol. 2). Hillsdale, NJ: Lawrence Erlbaum Associates.

Sternberg, R. J. (1977). *Intelligence, information processing, and analogical reasoning: The componential analysis of human abilities.* Hillsdale, NJ: Lawrence Erlbaum Associates.

Taylor, B. M. (1980). Children's memory for expository text after reading. *Reading Research Quarterly, 15,* 399–411.

Thomas, E. L. (1968). Movements of the eye. *Scientific American, 219,* 88–95.

Thorndyke, P. W. (1977). Cognitive structures in comprehension and memory of narrative discourse. *Cognitive Psychology, 9,* 77–110.

Tobias, S. (1985, August). *Whatever happened to aptitude-treatment interaction research?* Paper presented to the meeting of the American Psychological Association, Los Angeles.

Torgesen, J. K. (1977). Memorization processes in reading-disabled children. *Journal of Educational Psychology, 5,* 571–578.

Torgeson, J. K., & Goldman, T. (1977). Verbal rehearsal and short-term memory in reading-disabled children. *Child Development, 48* 56–60.

Troyka, L. A. (1982, October). Looking back and moving forward. In K. L. Greenberg, H. S. Wiener, & R. A. Donovan (Eds.), *Notes from the National Testing Network in Writing.* New York: City University of New York, Instructional Resource Center.

Vellutino, F. R. (1979). *Dyslexia: Theory and research.* Cambridge, MA: The MIT Press.

Venezky, R. L., & Johnson, D. (1973). Development of two letter-sound patterns in grades one through three. *Journal of Educational Psychology, 64,* 109–115.

Vernon, P. E. (1970). Intelligence. In W. B. Dockrell (Ed.), *On intelligence.* Toronto: The Ontario Institute for Studies in Education, pp. 99–117.

Voss, J. F., Vesonder, G. T., & Spilich, G. J. (1980). Text generation and recall by high-knowledge and low-knowledge individuals. *Journal of Verbal Learning and Verbal Behavior, 19,* 651–657.

Voss, J. F., Tyler, W., & Yengo, L. A. (1983). Individual differences in the solving of social science problems. In R. F. Dillon & R. R. Schmeck (Eds.), *Individual differences in cognition* (pp. 205–232). New York: Academic Press.

Webster, R. E. (1979). Visual and aural short-term memory capacity deficits in mathematics disabled students. *Journal of Educational Research, 72,* 277–283.

Weinstein, C. E. (1978). Elaboration skills as a learning strategy. In H. F. O'Neil, Jr. (Ed.), *Learning strategies.* New York: Academic Press.

Woods, S. S., Resnick, L. B., & Groen, G. J. (1975). An experimental test of five process models for subtraction. *Journal of Educational Psychology, 67,* 17–21.

6 Theoretical Implications from Protocol Analysis on Testing and Measurement

K. Anders Ericsson
University of Colorado at Boulder

One of the goals of psychology has always been to describe, understand, and measure individual differences. The diversity of human behavior makes it particularly challenging to seek to identify general and stable underlying elements that correspond to systematic individual differences. A major problem in the efforts to identify such elements is that the elements cannot be observed directly. The primary method has been to use the current psychological theory to develop procedures to measure such hypothetical elements. In this chapter I present a new theoretic framework, based on verbal reports from subjects, for identifying and measuring individual differences. I argue that this framework is superior to the previous ones; hence, I briefly review some of the earlier approaches to measurement of individual differences.

When scientific psychology was first established over 100 years ago, the predominant method of investigation consisted of eliciting introspective verbal reports from trained observers. During the introspective era, the research was directed toward uncovering the basic sensations and cognitive processes that provided the building blocks of the varied and complex human experiences. Within this theoretical perspective, it was assumed that observable individual differences in normal cognitive functioning were a consequence of differences in basic cognitive processes. It was furthermore assumed that individual differences in performance on simple tasks, like simple reaction time, letter cancellation, and sensory discrimination, would directly reflect individual differences in the corresponding basic processes. However, the first studies of individual differences on simple tasks showed disappointingly low correlations among tasks as well as to grades in school and other indices of ability (Guilford, 1967).

Particularly damaging for this view of simple tasks reflecting basic processes was the finding that substantial improvement in performance was observed with practice (Binet cited in Varon, 1935). Although subsequent successful attempts to measure intelligence reliably relied almost exclusively on *complex* tasks involving comprehension, the view that individual differences are due to differences in basic processes was never completely discarded. Exceptional ability (exceptional memory) was consistently interpreted as a result of differences in such basic processes.

The behavioristic era had interesting implications for measurement, in that a theory of cognitive structures was explicitly rejected. Among extreme behaviorists, all individual differences were attributed to differences in learning, or exposure to relevant experiences. Hence, measurement of basic cognitive functions would be meaningless. The measurement of individual differences in complex tasks had to be conducted in an inductive mode, where stable patterns of individual differences were discovered empirically rather than deduced theoretically. Lacking a cognitive theory, a general theory of measurement was developed and refined through the years. This theory of measurement was incorporated as an integral part of the methodology of experimental psychology. A central problem with the behavioristic approach was to understand what the observed performance on a test actually measures.

Using the computer as a metaphor, theories of human information processing were proposed in which the focus was placed on the intermediate processing stages necessary to produce observable behavior. Many of the old concepts of attention and different types of memory stores were reintroduced in these theories with more explicit definitions and characteristics. The emphasis of these models on process rather than final responses led to a concern for observations providing information about the process, like latencies, eye-fixations, and verbal reports. It became important to use converging evidence from many different types of observations to identify the ongoing cognitive processes.

For the purpose of this chapter one could divide contemporary cognitive research into the mainstream of cognitive psychology, which only uses traditional performance measures, like accuracy and latency, and other research emphasizing supplementary data on the cognitive processes, like eye-fixations and verbal reports. The aim of the first category of research has been to provide a finer grain analysis of what the psychometric test measures. Some of this research has measured individual differences on tasks assumed to provide pure measures of critical capacities according to current cognitive theory. These pure measures were then related to compound abilities like verbal IQ (Hunt, 1978). Other researchers, notably Sternberg (1977), have analyzed the latencies and errors for performing tasks similar to test-items on psychometric tests, to identify measurements of critical information processes. In both the above approaches the composite performance (reaction time and accuracy) is factored into components using theoretical assumptions, which cannot be directly tested and evaluated within this framework. At least one of the reasons for the remarkable impact of these theoretical efforts on research on individual differences and testing is the methodological compatibility between test theory and these theories of cognition.

Another research approach within cognitive psychology has been directed toward understanding the detailed structure of cognitive processes. The aim has been to develop models of cognitive processes at a level where one can simulate the observable behavior of subjects by a computer program. The pioneering work of Newell and Simon (1972) showed that building such models required very detailed information about subjects' cognitive processes. The method used by Newell and Simon (1972) to elicit such detailed knowledge about subjects' cognitive processes was to instruct subjects to "think aloud," i.e., verbalize their thoughts, as they solved the presented problems. In a recent review of research using verbal reports, Ericsson and Simon (1984) showed that this methodology has been successfully applied to research problems in all major areas of psychology—memory, decision-making, educational psychology, instruction, and clinical psychology. Although much of that research has implications for measurement of individual differences, I know of only a limited number of studies using verbal reports of cognitive processes to directly address issues of measurement and assessment of individual differences.

AN OUTLINE OF THE CHAPTER

The goal of this chapter is to argue for the importance of verbal report data in understanding what current psychometric tests actually measure and for the usefulness of verbal report data in the design of future test instruments. The argument has three parts. First, I need to present a convincing case that particular kinds of verbal reports provide valid data and that a rigorous methodology for the analysis of verbal reports is available. Then, I present a theoretic framework that relates verbal report data to other, more traditional kinds of data, like correctness of response and latency. Finally, I show that studies using verbal reports have significantly altered our understanding of the processes measured by prevailing tests.

The chapter has three major sections that roughly correspond to the different parts of the argument. The first section provides an introduction to how verbal reports on cognitive processes can be used as valid data. This section summarizes my work with Herbert Simon (Ericsson & Simon, 1980, 1984) and describes a model of how some types of verbal reports yield reliable data on the sequence of thought in tasks. I briefly show how these forms of verbal reports differ from other disreputable forms of verbal reports, like introspection and rationalization.

The second section presents a theoretical framework for identifying and encoding sequences of cognitive processes from verbal reports. Hence, protocol analysis provides a tool for gaining empirical data on the sequence of cognitive processes elicited in a given task for a certain subject. Such data is shown to give us an empirical method for determining what process or sequence of processes are mediating performance in a test. Theoretical assumptions of mediating processes can therefore be empirically evaluated in a more direct manner. This section also describes inductive approaches, where important cognitive processes are abstracted from the verbal protocols to give generalizable accounts of cognitive mechanisms in different domains.

In the final section, I illustrate how verbal reports have extended our understanding of individual differences. For example, within the context of tests measuring spatial ability, I demonstrate differences in strategies used by subjects of high- and low-spatial ability and how verbal reports can improve our understanding of what available psychometric tests actually measure. In another example, I show how verbal reports can give insights into the structure of practice-effects and the structure of exceptional memory.

Let me first turn to an introduction to the analysis of verbal reports on cognitive processes.

PROTOCOL ANALYSIS AND VERBAL REPORTS

The use of verbal reports on cognitive processes has a long history filled with many methodological controversies. The early pioneers of psychology used introspective reports in an attempt to describe the sensory images underlying perception and thinking. Following several contradictory findings by different research laboratories, the introspective method was seriously criticized. Many moderate psychologists (for example, Woodworth, 1938) suggested that introspective analysis (which directed attention toward underlying sensations) was misguided, and said this method should be replaced by verbal reports that expressed thoughts. A careful historic review shows that the founder of behaviorism, Watson, rejected introspection, but accepted verbalization of thinking. In fact, Watson (1920) was the first investigator to publish an analysis of the verbalized thoughts of a subject while he was "thinking aloud." Even so, the rejection of introspection by behaviorists was so complete that it generalized to any use of verbal reports.

With the emergence of information-processing models of cognition, several researchers started to consider verbal reports as a means to get more direct and detailed access to the cognitive processes of subjects. In contrast with most early introspective studies, these investigators collected extensive performance data and hence were able to evaluate the veridicality and converging validity of verbal reports. With his newly developed blank-trial technique, Levine and his associates (Frankel, Levine, & Karpf, 1970; Karpf, & Levine, 1971) showed essentially perfect correspondence between verbally reported concepts and specific judgments about instances. In studies of memory, subjects' verbal reports on mediating associations were found to have remarkable effects on memory performance (for a review see Montague, 1972). Newell and Simon's (1972) analyses of verbal reports during problem solving was the most extensive and intensive use of such data. On the basis of verbal reports they were able to construct computer programs powerful enough to both solve problems and regenerate essential aspects of the reported thought processes. Newell and Simon (1972) instructed their subjects to verbalize their thoughts concurrently, i.e., "think aloud," whereas subjects in the memory studies often recalled their thoughts retrospectively. Other investigators using other kinds of instructions found that subjects giving verbal reports performed differently from subjects who were not required to give verbal reports—thus throwing some doubt on the validity and representativeness of verbalized thought.

The basic concern of Ericsson and Simon (1980) was to propose a model in which the cognitive processes responsible for verbalization of thoughts in attention(heeded thoughts) could be explicated. In its most general and abstract form, information processing theory (Anderson & Bower, 1973; Newell & Simon, 1972; Simon, 1979) postulates that a cognitive process can be seen as a sequence of internal states successively transformed by a series of information processes. Moreover, each of these successive states can be described in large part in terms of the small number of information structures, or chunks, attended to, or available in the limited-capacity short-term memory store (STM). Information in the vast long-term memory (LTM) and in the sensory memories (of brief duration) can be accessed, but the results of these access processes will be attended to (heeded) and available in STM. In Fig. 6.1 I have illustrated a sequence of successive states, showing how new thoughts are expressed verbally as they enter attention, and hence become observable as verbalization segments.

The general relation between heeded thoughts, i.e., thoughts in attention, and the observable verbalizations is much easier to understand in the context of specific examples. In Table 6.1, the thinking-aloud protocol of a subject mentally multiplying 36 times 24 is given. Most of the verbalized information consists of generated intermediate steps, like "4," "carry the 2," "144." There is no difference in principle between these intermediate steps and the final result, "864." Even when one asks students to answer questions like, "What is the number of windows in your parents house?," their thinking-aloud protocols are remarkably similar. A representative example of such a thinking-aloud protocol

FIG. 6.1.   A thought process represented as a sequence of states of heeded information. Each state is associated with verbalization of new information entering attention.

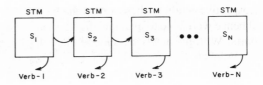

TABLE 6.1
A Transcript of a Thinking-Aloud Protocol From a Subject
Mentally Multiplying 36 Times 24

OK	36*
36 times 24	<u>24</u>
um	144
4 times 6 is 24	<u>720</u>
4	864
carry the 2	
4 times 3 is 12	
14	
144	
0	
2 times 6 is 12	
2	
carry the 1	
2 times 3 is 6	
7	
720	
720	
144 plus 72	
so it would be 6	
6	
864	

* On the right side, the same multiplication is performed
using the traditional paper and pencil method.

is given in Table 6.2. Notice that the subject verbally expresses intermediate steps (heeded thoughts) rather than explaining or describing her thought processes.

From this model of concurrent verbalization it is clear that the subject has to have time to complete the verbalization of the heeded information before new thoughts enter attention. For tasks where subjects have extensive experience, the

TABLE 6.2
A Transcript of a Thinking-Aloud Protocol From a Subject
Recalling the Number of Windows in Her Parent's House

Let's see, there's 3 windows in the living room,
3 windows in my room, 1 in the bathroom, 2 in the
sewing room, that's 5 and 3, 6, 7, 8, 13--4 in the
kitchen which would make 17; 3, 4 in the TV room
which would make 21, 2 in my brother's room, 23; and
1 in the upstairs bathroom, 24; and 3 in my parent's
room, 27; and then 1 in the attic, 28

Adapted from Ericsson and Simon (1984).

sequence of thoughts is so closely connected that a concurrent sequential verbalization of the spontaneously occurring thoughts is not possible. In such situations, the subjects can report their thoughts in retrospect by recalling the sequence of thoughts just after the completion of the task. When the time taken to complete the task is relatively short (about 5–30 seconds) our model predicts a rather complete retrospective report of all heeded thoughts. For tasks with longer duration, concurrent reports (thinking-aloud) will be more detailed than the corresponding retrospective reports.

One would not expect either retrospective reports or thinking-aloud protocols to change the cognitive processes under study. If the essence of the cognitive process is the sequence of heeded information, then thinking-aloud doesn't change that sequence. A large number of studies have compared subjects thinking aloud with silent subjects doing the same task (for a review see Ericsson & Simon, 1984). None of these studies has shown evidence for changes in structure of the process due to thinking aloud, as measured by ability to solve problems, type of solution, eye-movement pattern, etc. Several studies have shown that subjects thinking aloud take more time than silent control subjects. This follows from our model, because verbally expressing a thought takes additional time.

A recent analysis (Deffner & Ericsson, 1985) of the temporal structure of subjects thinking aloud showed that they verbalize their thoughts rapidly in speech bursts (at 100–150 words per minute), while most time is spent in silence. If the time spent actively verbalizing is measured and then subtracted, the mean solution time is no different for silent and think-aloud subjects. Hence, it appears that the effect on solution time can be accurately predicted by assuming a local slowing-down of cognitive processes during verbalization.

Ericsson and Simon's (1980, 1984) analysis of studies that do show effects of concurrent verbalizing demonstrates that these studies used quite different instructions to subjects. Typically, subjects are required to verbalize motives or reasons for their actions and thoughts. From subject's thinking-aloud protocols on the same or similar tasks we know that only a subset of the generated thoughts are based on deductions or retrievals with explicit premises verbalized. Forcing a subject to provide reasons for all reported thoughts would therefore clearly change the subject's thought processes. This means, of course, that the sequence of heeded thoughts is changed, which in turn influences performance and the structure of the solution process. For example, many students are accustomed to the situation of solving a mathematics problem at the blackboard in front of class. Some subjects confuse the instruction to think aloud with such a systematic generation of explanations, and investigators of mathematical problem solving explicitly tell subjects: "Do not try to explain anything to anyone else. Pretend there is no one here but yourself. Do not tell about the solution but solve it" (Krutetskii, 1976, p. 93). It is useful to give subjects "warm-up" tasks, where thinking aloud is particularly easy. Examples of such tasks are mental multiplication and anagram problem solving.

In a well-known paper criticizing the validity of verbal reports, Nisbett and Wilson (1977) showed that in many studies of social psychology, subjects report incorrect reasons in response to why-questions. For example, a subject selecting among a set of displayed stockings will argue, if asked, that the selected stocking is better in terms of some of its physical attributes. Such reasons are given by subjects even when the displayed stockings are identical, although they are not informed of that. Nisbett and Wilson (1977) argued that in responding to the why-question, subjects do not try to remember their thoughts while the associated behavior was generated, but theorize and try to infer reasons for their behavior. Our model of verbal report is consistent with Nisbett and Wilson's argument as long as the subjects generate the incorrect reasons without recalling their corresponding thoughts during the task.

In some situations, the why-question is asked after such a delay following the corresponding behavior that subjects cannot recall their thoughts or are not willing to spend the effort required for successful retrieval. In other situations, the behavior is elicited without mediating thoughts and hence there are no thoughts to be retrieved and used in answering the why-question. For example, when normal subjects generate a word starting with "a," a high proportion simply report that "apple" emerged. When you ask such subjects why they generated "apple" rather than any of the other words starting with "a," they may not be unwilling to speculate. Often they suggest that perhaps they learned the association between "a" and "apple" while learning the alphabet. Regardless of the truth of these subjects' hypothesis, I can agree with Nisbett and Wilson (1977) that the validity of these subjects' speculations about their own behavior would not be any greater than that of subjects speculating about the reasons for other people's selection behavior.

Our model of verbal report also provides considerable guidance for how verbal reports should be encoded and what inferences can legitimately be made. During the era of introspection, experienced and respected observers made observations on their own thought processes. These observations were assumed to represent facts—a subject reporting X would imply that X was true. Within our framework, we would argue that the fact is that *the subject reports X*. The rather uncontroversial inference we want to make is that the subject attends to X.

Let us clarify this by returning to the protocol on mental multiplication. A traditional psychologist might only accept the validity of the verbalization of the final answer. From the verbalization of the final answer we infer that the final answer was generated and heeded. In an analogous way we infer from the sequence of verbalized intermediate products a corresponding sequence of heeded information. The verbally reported thoughts are data, and a model is needed to account for how relevant thoughts are generated—hence a full model would regenerate the heeded information. In many cases, one will find that a simulation model able to regenerate the verbally reported intermediate steps will be powerful enough to generate the final solutions to the presented problems.

It may appear that I am unduly cautious in accepting inferences drawn from verbal reports. However, much of the poor reputation of verbal reports comes from the debatable validity of psychodynamic analysis of dreams and fantasy. Furthermore, all too often general statements like, "I always do X," are interpreted to be unconditionally true, and when inconsistent performance data are obtained, the inference is made that all verbally reported information is questionable. Herbert Simon and I interpret such verbalizations to simply indicate that the subject at that time believes (correctly or incorrectly) that he always does X.

Traditionally, subjects have been interviewed at the end of experiments and test-taking sessions about their strategies and thought processes *during* the experiment. At the end of the experiment subjects have poor memory for their actual sequences of thoughts leading to specific solutions. Furthermore, investigators often encourage subjects to describe a general strategy that encourages them to make inferences and speculate rather than attempt to recall specific memories for actual solutions. It is not surprising that strategies assessed through such postexperimental probing provide a poor fit to the subjects' performance during all phases of the experiment.

For most tasks it is easy to determine what constitutes a thought. In Table 6.3 I have reproduced a protocol from a subject solving an anagram problem, where

TABLE 6.3
A Transcript of a Thinking-Aloud Protocol From a
Subject Solving the Anagram 'NPEHPA' Recorded by Sargent (1940)

N-P, neph, neph	
Probably PH goes together	C:PH*
Phan	A:phan
Phanny	A:phanny
I get phen-ep	A:phan-ep
no. Nap-	A:nap
Phep-an, no	A:phep-an
E is at the end	C:E(end)
Phap-en	A:phap-en
People, I think of	A:people
Try PH after the other letters	C:PH(end)
Naph, no	A:naph
I thought of paper again	A:paper
E and A sound alike	
couldn't go together without a consonant	
Try double P	C:PP
happy	A:happy
Happen	A:happen

*On the right side encodings of the verbalized thoughts are given. Adapted by Ericsson and Simon (1985).

the object is to rearrange the letters to form a single English word. On the right-hand side of Table 6.3 I have given corresponding encodings of the verbalized thoughts. There are two types of task-relevant thoughts. First, the subject selects likely letter combinations and decides where in the solution word they are likely to occur. I denote these constraints or cues as C:### (position). Second, the subject generates alternative possible solution words (denoted by A:###). These encodings can then be used as data for further model-building and hypothesis-testing.

By necessity, this description of the model for verbal report generation and protocol analysis, developed by Simon and myself, is brief. The interested reader should consult the more extensive discussion of these issues in our recent book (Ericsson & Simon, 1984). In spite of its brevity, I hope I have conveyed to you that protocol analysis stands on sound methodological ground and that findings from analyses of verbal protocols can be accepted as facts in our attempts to understand the human mind.

IMPLICATIONS OF VERBAL REPORTS FOR
MEASUREMENT AND THEORETICAL ABSTRACTIONS

Verbal reports on cognitive processes provide a much more detailed description of the cognitive processes in a task than the traditional forms of data, i.e., response accuracy and latency. The stuation is structurally similar to the differences between observations made by the naked eye and the same observations made with a microscope or a telescope. Objects appearing to be similar or even identical to the naked eye are demonstrated to either remain identical or to appear very different with the availability of more information about their detailed structure and components. There are two rather different approaches to systematizing the newly acquired, detailed information. The first method is to focus on objects assumed to be similar or identical, and examine their detailed properties to validate or refute the assumption of similarity. This method examines theoretical assumptions in essentially a hypothesis-testing mode. The other method is primarily inductive and considers the detailed information directly. From the detailed information, critical entities are identified and attempts to form meaningful abstractions are made. In this section, I examine how these two methods can be and have been used to relate verbal reports on cognitive processes to compound measures, such as reaction time and response accuracy. I start by examining some theoretical assumptions about the similarity of cognitive processes elicited by a given task or collection of test items.

Traditionally, investigators select test items such that some or all elicit the same process or sequence of processes for all tested subjects. This selection is based on intuition or some considerations based on informal or formal theories. In Fig. 6.2 I have illustrated the data recorded for three individuals on two test

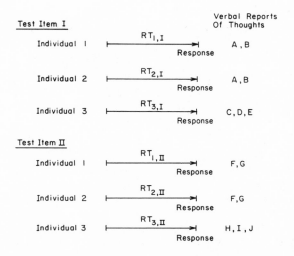

FIG. 6.2.   Traditional data (latency and response) and verbal report data from three subjects' solutions to two test-items.

items. For each subject and test item, both the correctness of the response and the reaction time to respond are recorded.

If the theory used for item selection is correct, then we would be entitled to aggregate the data over test items to attain a more accurate measure of accuracy and latency for the measured process. There are only limited techniques for testing the assumption that all test-items evoke the same process or sequence of processes. Only the lack of positive correlation between different subjects' performance on two items would provide evidence against the assumption. Even small positive correlations would be consistent with the theoretical claim.

The situation is quite different when verbal reports on the cognitive processes are available. According to our earlier-presented model, I assume that for every heeded thought there is a process responsible for its generation. Hence, when I talk about a sequence of heeded thoughts, the corresponding sequence of processes is implicit. In the lefthand panel of Fig. 6.2 I have abstractly represented sequences of verbally reported thoughts for each test item. For solutions to the same test item one can compare the sequence of heeded thoughts directly. Such a comparison for the two test items indicates that two of the subjects relied on the same sequence of thoughts, whereas the third subject relied on a different sequence. The fact that all the subjects' thought sequences differ across test items is to be expected as the content of the two test items are different.

By introducing the theoretical idea of processes one can argue that a different sequence of thoughts are the reflection of the same sequence of processes. It is necessary that the processes are explicitly defined prior to the empirical analysis. In Fig. 6.3 I have illustrated a number of processes, which would characterize

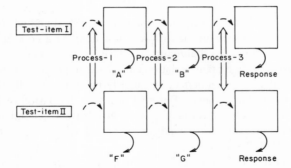

FIG. 6.3. Illustration of how two different sequences of verbally reported thoughts can be described as the realization of the same sequence of processes.

the relation between generated thoughts and different content in test items (input). Through the assumption of processes, I can now argue that the aggregation of test items provides a legitimate estimate of the speed of the component processes. However, for only two of the subjects the same sequence of processes are measured. It is important to note that processes are theoretical entities, which may or may not correspond to some unitary psychological process.

Out of the large number of possible relations between sequences of reported thoughts to two test items, we can identify two cases where one can legitimately argue that the protocol information is consistent with the claim that the same process or sequence of processes is measured by the two items.

The first case is the extreme case, where no mediating thoughts are verbalized for either of the two test items. Such a lack of mediating thoughts would be expected for highly automatic reactions, like naming familiar objects, reading, etc. It is commonly assumed that rapid reactions (faster than 2 seconds) assure no mediating states. However, I later present evidence showing that such a view is not correct.

The second case is the most interesting, where the sequences of reported thoughts for the two test items can be seen as the realization of the same sequence of processes. For example, a subject performing a mental addition of two 2-digit numbers can follow the same process sequence even though the specific numbers are different for the two test items. By assuming the existence of a general addition process for any two digits, one can see those two different mental additions as two realizations of the same general process sequence. Even in this uncontroversial example one can question the theoretical status of the general addition process. There is evidence showing that the simple addition of two digits takes different amounts of time depending on the digits involved (Miller, Perlmutter, & Keating, 1984). For adult subjects the differences are small enough to make the abstraction of general adding processes completely acceptable.

It is unlikely to find classes of test items for which the second case is absolutely true. It is reasonably likely that situations will be found where equivalence of the cognitive processes on the different test items is a good approximation. Through the collection of verbal reports on the cognitive processes on test items, it si possible to identify blatant violations of the assumptions of measurements of the same general process sequence, by identifying systematically different strategies among the tested subjects. Before I turn to a discussion of how different investigators have analyzed verbal protocols to abstract general processes, we briefly consider an example of analysis of verbal reports for a task with fast latencies (less than 2 seconds).

Ericsson and Simon (1984) reviewed the relatively extensive evidence showing that subjects' retrospective verbal reports provide reliable information to predict the latencies for a variety of task domains. The validity of retrospective verbal reports extended to tasks with average latencies of less than 2 seconds. Systematic attempts to derive a processing model to predict the observed reaction times on the basis of retrospective reports are much more rare. Two English investigators, Hamilton and Sanford (1978), studied subjects who made simple judgments of whether two presented letters, like "RP" or "MO," were in alphabetical order or not. In accord with previous investigators, they found that the reaction times were longer when the two presented letters occurred close together in the alphabet as opposed to when they were far apart. From the reaction-time data alone, one would infer a uniform retrieval process, where factors internal to the retrieval process required more time for order decisions for letters occurring close together in the alphabet. Retrospective verbal reports for subjects doing individual decisions indicated two types of cognitive processes. For some of the trials, subjects reported no mediation or direct access of their order judgment. For the other trials, subjects reported they ran through brief segments of the alphabet before making a decision of order. For example, when the letter-pair "MO" was presented, a subject reported retrieving "LMNO" before the subject reached the decision that the letters were in alphabetical order. In another case a subject reported retrieving "RSTUV" before rejecting the letter-pair "RP" as not being in alphabetical order. In a subsequent analysis of the reaction times, Hamilton and Sanford (1978) found very different relations with the separation of the two letters for trials with direct access, versus trials with retrieval of segments of the alphabet. For trials with retrieval, the observed reaction time was a linear function of the number of retrieved letters. The estimated rate of retrieval corresponded closely to rates obtained in studying simple recital of the alphabet. For trials with reports of direct access, no relation of reaction time to the amount of separation of the two letters was found. Hamilton and Sanford (1978) concluded that the original effect was due to a mixture of two quite different processes, and that closeness of the letters influenced the probability that recall of letters would be necessary before an order decision could be made.

Hence, even in simple tasks with rapid responses, one can see variability in cognitive processes or reported thought sequences leading to differences in observed reaction times. As the complexity of the task increases, the range of possible thought sequences giving the correct response increases dramatically. With practice on a task, the availability of short-cuts and emergence of different and more efficient representations and corresponding strategies makes the space of possible thought sequences mediating correct solutions intimidatingly large. In a later section I more directly address the issues of assessing the availability of strategies and representations for subjects. The conclusion I draw at this point is that protocol analysis provides a sensitive measure to help us define equivalent classes of processes for which proper measurement of the speed of component processes is valid. Consistent individual differences in mean reaction time cannot and should not be interpreted as evidence for stable characteristics of basic processes. For many types of test items, considerable diversity in frequency of use of short-cuts and strategies is possible.

On the detailed level of description provided by verbal reports, the variability between individuals appears so large that any attempt to search for general theories of cognitive activities might appear futile.

Before turning to the final section with applications of protocol analysis to tests and measurements, I briefly review research from three areas of general psychology where protocol analysis has been related to such general models. The three areas are problem solving, decision making, and memory. In each of these areas, I show how detailed descriptions of processes can be reconciled with abstract and general, sometimes mathematical, descriptions of processes.

It is appropriate to start with a discussion of problem solving, because it was the analyses of problem solving by Newell and Simon (1972) that led them to produce the first computer simulations of cognitive processes. In their pioneering work of subjects proving theorems in propositional logic they collected thinking-aloud protocols from subjects solving such tasks. The verbalized thoughts were identified as being results of induced general information processes, which could be explicated as routines in a computer program. Newell and Simon (1972) also induced a general organization of problem solving, which they called means-ends analysis. They found that a simulation model of human problem solving was sufficiently powerful to produce the solution, and at the same time the mediating steps of the program corresponded closely to the verbally reported thoughts of subjects. The correspondence of subjects' verbal reports and the theory or simulation model was on the level of types of intermediate steps rather than *exact* order of intermediate steps leading to the solution.

Subsequent evidence for means-ends analysis has been demonstrated for a wide range of problems (Ericsson & Simon, 1984). For example, I can illustrate the similarity of verbalized thought across different subjects for the 8-puzzle. In the 8-puzzle, subjects are presented with a 3x3 matrix of numbered tiles as shown in Fig. 6.4. By sliding one of the directly adjacent tiles into the empty

START

GOAL

FIG. 6.4. Example of a configuration for the 8-puzzle (left); this is to be transformed into a goal configuration (right).

space, the arrangement of tiles can be changed. Subjects are instructed to move tiles until they attain the goal configuration given on the right in Fig. 6.4.

According to means-ends analysis, subjects should solve this problem by finding differences between the goal configuration and the current arrangement of tiles. From an analysis of the task it is possible to a priori predict the space of possible thoughts (problem space) that subjects will generate in response to a problem like the 8-puzzle. The first difference they encounter is that the tile with number 1 is not in its correct location. In Table 6.4 I have illustrated a small sample of the times subjects verbalized their intention to put Tile 1 in its correct place.

The verbalizations in Table 6.4 differ in exact wording but the thought is the same. Once they placed Tile 1 they would proceed to place Tile 2, etc. A more complete account of subjects' problem solving in the 8-puzzle is given by Ericsson (1975).

Means-ends analysis appears to provide a general account of subjects' behavior on problems with which they are naive or unfamiliar. With expertise and considerable experience, the structure of the problem solving is quite different and becomes a function of the subject's extensive knowledge of the task domain (Chi, Feltovich, & Glaser, 1981; Larkin, McDermott, Simon, & Simon, 1980).

TABLE 6.4
Examples of Verbalizations to Attain Correct Placement of Tile 1

```
I'm going to try          to get 1
I must                        get 1 up there
I shall try               to get 1    here
              first           get 1    there instead of 4
    I shall               have 1 up
    I want to        have the 1 up there
                         move 1 up where it should be
thinking of moving            1 up at once
that I shall              get 1    here
                      to get 1 up (and get 2 there, first 1 up)
in any case               get 1    in place first and foremost
now I want to        have 1 up right from the beginning
try to get them in order
to start with                 1 upmost to the left and get it in
```

The demonstration of general problem-solving methods has received considerable attention from educators, who have explored the possibility of teaching students such methods. In the final section I discuss this attempt to describe individual differences among subjects in terms of the availability of such general methods to subjects. Training subjects to use means-ends analysis appears to be somewhat misguided, as virtually all subjects exhibit such a method spontaneously in unfamiliar tasks.

Another domain with consistent patterns of cognitive processes is decision making. In the paradigmatic decision-making situation, a subject is presented with a set of alternatives. Each alternative is characterized by different attributes on several common dimensions. The prevailing model of how decisions are made is that all attributes are combined using a mathematical weighting function to form a single evaluation score. Deciding which is the "best" alternative in the set would then correspond to selecting the one with the highest evaluation score. Few, if any, investigators have argued that such a mathematical formula mirrors the cognitive processes of human subjects making decisions.

Verbal protocols of subjects making decisions have shown cognitive processes quite different from a sequential full evaluation of each alternative (Payne, 1976; Svenson, 1979). Instead, subjects begin by rejecting alternatives because they have unacceptable values on important dimensions. When only a couple of viable alternatives remain, subjects switch to a more intensive analysis, where differences on some dimensions are traded off or compared to differences on other dimensions. Other data, recording what information subjects attend to, have provided converging support for the existence of these different processes. Analogous to the previously discussed work on problem solving, general processes sufficiently powerful to account for the observed behavior have been identified.

Research on how subjects evaluate alternatives (judgment) has found that verbally reported categorical decisions can describe a series of judgments equally as well as an empirically fitted linear regression model (Einhorn, Kleinmuntz, & Kleinmuntz, 1979). In one of their experiments, Einhorn et al. (1979) observed a subject thinking aloud while judging many cereals on a five-category scale. From the thinking-aloud protocols they identified a number of rules used by the subject. These rules predicted the subject's categorizations of a new set of cereals remarkably well, in fact as well as a regression model identified for the first set of judgments. Einhorn et al. (1979) established the correspondence between these different types of models by showing how a linear regression model can closely approximate categorical rules as reflected in a verbal report. This last result is particularly important as it demonstrates that prevailing mathematical models can be reconciled with the more detailed evidence from verbal protocols.

The research in both problem solving and decision making has shown the types of cognitive processes revealed through protocol analysis provide a sufficient and general account of subjects' performance. The consistency across subjects is intriguing, and many investigators have argued that general information processing constraints lead subjects toward adopting such processes and strategies. At least, these analyses show that the adopted processes are compatible with the well-known limits of attention and short-term memory.

Studies of memory and retention have always been one of the central areas in general psychology. Ever since Ebbinghaus (1964, 1885) invented the nonsense syllable, there has been explicit concern to study pure memory, that is, memory and retention uncontaminated by previous knowledge. During the behaviorist era, few investigators challenged the assumption that no intermediate processes were involved during memorization. In the 50s, it was demonstrated that nonsense syllables were differentially difficult to memorize and that this difficulty could be independently predicted from the meaningfulness of the nonsense syllable (Noble, 1952). In the 60s and early 70s, investigators asked subjects to verbally report their thoughts during study. These investigators found a remarkable diversity of different mediating thoughts reported by different subjects. I have extracted some examples of mediating thoughts in Table 6.5 from studies of Martin, Boersma, and Cox (1965), and Prytulak (1971).

The central issue concerned whether different reported mediators during study of items were related to subsequent recall performance on the corresponding items. Several different encoding schemes were developed to use explicit criteria for the goodness of the generated mediating responses, like those in Table 6.5. Although the biggest difference appeared between some mediating response versus no mediating response (rote rehearsal) these encoding schemes were also able to capture differences between types of mediating responses. This extensive research is fully reviewed by Montague (1972). Subsequent research in which subjects formed meaningful associations via visual images or constructing sentences have demonstrated very large effects compared to uninstructed subjects'

TABLE 6.5
Examples of Mediating Thoughts in Memorizing Individual
Nonsense Syllables and Paired Associates

Individual CVC[a]	Reported Mediator[a]
CAZ	case
CIB	sibling
BUH	bunch
JEK	jerk
Paired Associate[b]	Verbal Report[b]
Sagrole - Polef	Each word contains an OLE. Sagrole begins with S and Polef with F, thought of State Police
Rennet - Quipson	Changed Rennet to Bennet and saw Quips in Quipson--thought; Bennet Cerf Quips on TV

[a]From Prytulak, 1971.
[b]From Martin, Boersma, and Cox, 1965.

performance (Bellezza, 1981; Bower, 1972). From an individual difference perspective, it is interesting that some subjects report using such effective means for memorization without instruction (Bower, 1972).

Detailed descriptions of the associations making up the memory trace are by no means inconsistent with current mathematical theories of memory. These theories represent memory traces as associations of different strengths. Verbal reports allow us to assess the micro-structure of these associative bonds.

Summary

Verbal reports on cognitive processes in a task provide a series of intermediate steps (heeded thoughts), which are generated by corresponding cognitive processes. Hence, verbal report data can be used to confirm that subjects' responses to test items are generated by the same sequence of component processes. In the case that verbal reports show different sequences of processes for a set of test items as evidenced by short-cuts or different strategies, average reaction times and accuracies for items in a test will *not* measure differences in stable characteristics of assumed underlying processes, and thus these average results of the test reflect a composite of factors and cannot be interpreted as a pure measure of anything.

For the domains of problem solving, decision making, and memory, systematic analysis of verbal reports allows for the abstraction of postulated cognitive processes. These cognitive processes, like forming meaningful associations or interactive visual images (memory), or means-ends analysis (problem solving), were generally found for all individuals in the corresponding task domain and appeared to account for previous findings based on traditional performance data. These and other demonstrations (Ericsson & Simon, 1984) that generalizable aspects of cognitive processes can be induced from analyses of verbal reports give considerable confidence that similar analyses of cognitive processes elicited by tests will be successful.

Protocol Analysis in Assessment and Measurement

The purpose of this final section is to select a small number of important measurement issues and illustrate how protocol analysis has been applied to further our understanding. The first issue concerns how one can identify actual and valid cognitive processes. The fact that it is possible to verbally describe a hypothetical cognitive process does not assure its empirical validity. After a brief historical review of earlier attempts to identify processes and representations of general applicability, I concentrate on more recent efforts to specify such general processes in the analysis of mathematical ability.

The second issue regards the importance of differences in strategies for performance on psychometric tests. I focus on some recent research on tests measuring spatial ability. In the introduction I mentioned that one of the few individual differences consistently explained by differences in basic processes concerns exceptional abilities, especially exceptional memory (Wechsler, 1952). Drawing on my collaborative research with Bill Chase, I will examine whether such memory processes are basic and direct, as evidenced by a lack of mediating states in the verbal reports.

Use of Verbal Reports to Assess Individual Differences

Some of the earliest studies using verbal reports identified general differences between subjects' reported cognitive processes and representations. The importance of differences in cognitive processes was shown by Heidbreder (1924), who found consistent differences in concept formation between subjects actively generating and testing hypotheses and subjects more passively waiting until hypotheses occurred to them. The importance of differences in representation were demonstrated by several independent studies of human maze learning, which found striking differences in learning rate as a function of the mode of encoding (motor, spatial, or verbal) reported by subjects when they had to memorize solution paths. (For a review see Ericsson & Simon, 1984.)

Since the publication of Bloom and Broder's influential study of problem solving in 1950, research on individual differences using the verbal report methodology primarily has focused on identifying general and task-independent processes and strategies. Although the results of this research on general processes have been rather disappointing, it is worthwhile to describe some of these studies and discuss reasons for the lack of success of such approaches. Later I discuss other research focusing on more task-specific processes and knowledge.

Bloom and Broder (1950) were interested in processes of thought and reasoning rather than simple fact retrieval, as emphasized in many educational tests. By selecting test items requiring reasoning, they found intriguing differences between think-aloud protocols of subjects with high and low aptitude scores. Low aptitude subjects tended not to be able to represent the problem in such a way that their relevant knowledge could be retrieved or used for inferences in generating solutions. The weakness of low aptitude subjects was taken as a focus for a remedial program for training low aptitude subjects. The training program was successful, and Bloom and Broder (1950) attribute its success to training in general cognitive processes. However, the lack of methodological controls in their study makes their results only suggestive.

In the domain of mathematics, similar ideas have been explored with explicit concern for methodological issues. Many have the belief that mathematical ability is something more general than a composite of specific abilities to solve types of mathematical problems. Polya (1957) is one of the few theorists who has explicitly proposed general methods (heuristic questions) in mathematical problem solving. Examples of such heuristic questions are "What is the unknown?",

"Will a figure help?", "Have I solved a related problem before?", "Can I see that it is correct?" (Polya, 1957).

In his pioneering dissertation, Kilpatrick (1968) took these questions and attempted to describe cognitive acitivity that would provide evidence for the existence of such general problem-solving heuristics. After considerable exploratory work, he identified a revised set of heuristics relevant to the mathematical problems solved by 8th-grade subjects. From the thinking-aloud protocol of each subject, Kilpatrick (1968) would determine if evidence for the application of any one of the heuristics was available.

Kilpatrick's attempt to predict mathematical problem-solving performance (time, percent age correct) from the frequency with which heuristics were used failed. Ericsson and Simon (1984) have summarized similar negative results of several other studies using encoding schemes based on Polya's work (1957).

In examining the failure to identify heuristics, it is important to realize that the hypothesized processes were not induced or abstracted from the protocols, but derived theoretically. Even more important is the fact that these heuristics were not (and possibly could never be) explicated in such detail that one would know when and exactly how to apply them. It is implicitly assumed in Kilpatrick's (1968) aggregation procedure that application of any one of the heuristics will always be helpful in solving any problem. A subsequent study Gimmestad (1977) showed that application of various heuristics was differentially useful for

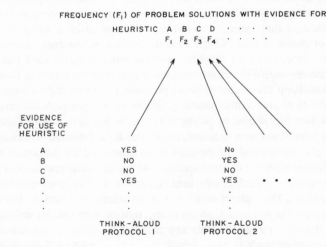

FIG. 6.5. The aggregation of information about judged use of specified heuristics for a given subject. Each thinking-aloud protocol is first scored with a dichotomous decision regarding use of a given heuristic. An aggregate measure is obtained for each subject by counting the number of problems where a given heuristic was used.

solving different problems. In fact, application of some heuristics was found to be *negatively* related with success on some problems.

The best evidence against the implicit generality of these heuristics comes from studies of training subjects in applying these heuristics. There appears to be little or no transfer of heuristics to problems different from practice problems (Lucas, 1972). However, some transfer in use of heuristics has been observed for problems similar (but not identical) to the problems used in training (Schoenfeld, 1979). It appears safe to conclude that application of general heuristics requires knowledge of when and how to apply them. This knowledge is necessarily relatively specific to types of problems.

Studies assessing the use of heuristics have provided important additional data on factors determining performance on mathematics tests. Webb (1975) found that basic tests of mathematical achievement accounted for 40% of the variance on mathematics tests, which was considerably more than any predictor related to the use of heuristics.

In their classic work on problem solving, Newell and Simon (1972) argued for the importance of knowledge on effective problem solving, and for the specificity of problem-solving methods. Lesgold (1984) reviewed evidence from a wide range of domains and demonstrates the importance of specific knowledge in the acquisition of skill for each domain.

In parallel with the studies relying on Polya's heuristics, other researchers have studied mathematical problem solving with much more emphasis on knowledge and domain-specific methods. Hinsley, Hayes, and Simon (1977), for example, showed that subjects would reliably sort algebra word problems in categories or problem types (e.g., mixture problems, distance/rate/time problems). From an analysis of thinking-aloud protocols they found that subjects appeared to categorize a given problem early during the solution of that problem and use knowledge about that type of problem to aid in the solution process. Subjects' ability to sort mathematical problems into types with the same mathematical structure was shown by Silver (1979) to be predictive of subjects' performance on a related mathematics test, even after IQ scores and scores on tests of mathematical concepts and computation were controlled for. Similarly Kennedy, Eliot, and Krulee (1970) analyzed students' thinking-aloud protocols while solving algebra problems in content-defined steps, which were determined separately for each problem. Their major result was that students of lower ability were less able to generate the necessary physical inferences from the information in the problem statement, rather than having any basic deficits in knowledge about algebra and mathematics.

The most successful attempts to identify individual differences come from rather complete analyses of very simple and specific tasks. Children in school are taught explicit procedures to solve different types of problems in arithmetic. By matching the target procedure against the observed sequence of processing steps it has been possible to identify school childrens' systematic errors and misconceptions. In some early work, Buswell and John (1928) identified around 150 types of errors from students solving arithmetic problems aloud.

The importance of verbal reports for assessing many types of errors becomes clear from the three types of errors in division shown in Table 6.6.

In more recent work, several investigators (Brown & Burton, 1978; Brown & VanLehn, 1980; Young & O'Shea, 1981) have developed simulation models that can account for and describe errors in the subdomain of subtraction problems, with reference to general rules for carrying out the subtraction procedure. These attempts do not rely on verbal reports, but induce the type of error from consistent patterns of incorrect results on several problems. This means that diagnosis of errors can be conducted automatically through a computer program, which also can serve as a tutor by explaining to the student the nature of his or her specific types of errors.

This brief review of studies on individual differences in mathematical ability shows essentially no evidence for the mediation of very generalizable cognitive processes. The protocol data suggest the importance of cognitive processes related to problem types as well as specific procedures and knowledge. However, protocol analysis can only provide a partial answer to the question of how general or specific the cognitive processes are that generated the thoughts given in the verbal reports. It can provide a lower bound for the generality, in that when subjects verbalize recognition of specific types of problems, like "distance-time-rate" problems in mathematics or "conservation of energy" problems in mechanics, the inferred processes need to be equally general. The inferences about the generality of processes generating intermediate steps/thoughts is an empirical issue that can only be clarified by observing subjects' solutions to a specified

TABLE 6.6
Three Examples of Verbal Reports From Students Thinking Aloud While
Dividing two Numbers (Shown to the Left)

Used Remainder Without New Dividend Figure

	306	Another pupil said, "16 into 57 goes 3 times [multiplied
16	576	and subtracted]; 16 into 9 won't go [wrote 0 in the quotient];
	48	16 into 96 goes 6 times."
	96	
	96	

Added Remainder to Quotient

	442	The pupil said, "2 into 9 is 4 times and 1 over; 2 into 6,
2	964	3 times and 1 is 4; 2 into 4, 2 times."

Began Dividing at Units' Digit of Dividend

	26	One boy said, "7 into 42, 6; 7 into 15, 2 and 1 over."
7	31542	He was puzzled because 7 would not go into 3 and 26
		did not look right but could think of no other method.

Each verbal report illustrates a common type of error.
From Buswell and John, 1928, pp. 184, 186.

class of problems and tasks. It is clear that verbal reports will be indispensable data in these empirical tests of generality.

Assessing Strategies in Tests of Spatial Ability

In a recent article in *Psychological Review,* Just and Carpenter (1985) present a very interesting analysis of cognitive processes involved in the performance measured by a psychometric test of spatial ability. Examples of a couple of test items from a cube comparison test are illustrated in Fig. 6.6.

The task is to decide if the two drawings *could* or *could not* be views of the same cube. The general psychological process generally assumed to account for subjects' ability to make correct judgments is called mental rotation. Just and Carpenter (1985) went further, defining several types of possible strategies for solving this task and developing complete simulation models in the form of computer programs. For my intended discussion of the verbal reports on cognitive processes in this task, a brief description of three of these strategies is sufficient.

The first strategy corresponds to mental rotation of the cube along the standard axis of the cube. In order to rotate the cube at the left to overlap with the corresponding cube on the right, one might first rotate the E towards the top and then turn the cube so the E will match in orientation (see Fig. 6.7-I). A second, and in many cases more efficient, strategy would be to select a nonstandard rotation axis as illustrated in Fig. 6.7-II. With such a selection of a rotation axis a *single* rotation is sufficient.

With the third strategy, orientation-free descriptions, subjects encode the information for the presented cube on the left as two symbolic descriptions where

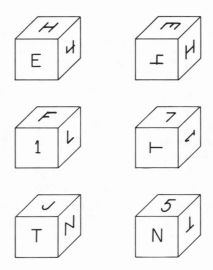

FIG. 6.6.   Examples of three possible test-items from the cube comparison test.

I A sequence of rotation along standard axis

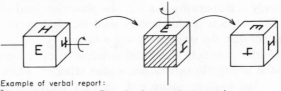

Example of verbal report:
"If you first rotate the E on the front to the top and
then turn the cube so that the E will match (in orientation)."

II A single rotation along non-standard axis

Example of verbal report:
"I spun it around the corner of the three sides until
the letters matched up."

III Orientation - free descriptions

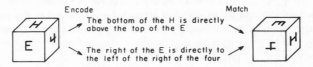

FIG. 6.7.   An illustration of three different strategies for solving items in the cube comparison test.

one of them could be "the bottom of the H is above the top of the E." This encoded information of one of the cubes can be validated or invalidated by comparing it to information provided in the second cube. In comparing the retrospective reports of subjects with high scores on spatial tests to subjects with low scores, Just and Carpenter (1985) found reliable differences in reported cognitive processes. Three of the high-ability subjects used predominantly non-standard rotation axes when applicable, whereas low-ability subjects used standard axes. One of the high-ability subjects relied on orientation-free descriptions.

From analyses of the temporal sequence of eye-fixations, Just and Carpenter (1985) could validate the verbally reported cognitive processes as responsible for the different pattern of latencies for high- and low-ability subjects. In addition, the high-ability subjects using the orientation-free description displayed a different pattern of latencies from subjects using the other two strategies. Just and Carpenter (1985) argued for the importance of determining and describing strategies to better understand spatial ability as measured by psychometric tests. They also noted that "trivial" changes in aspects of cube comparison tests can change the strategies subjects use. Just and Carpenter (1985) collected verbal reports from subjects taking the original Thurstone version of the cube comparison test, which differs only in that arrows, circles, and pluses are used instead of letters. For that version, subjects predominantly used the strategy of orientation-free descriptions rather than the strategies using rotation.

The role of verbal reports in identifying strategies is even more clear in earlier studies of spatial ability. In two earlier studies (Barratt, 1953; French, 1965) subjects were asked to think aloud and verbalize their solution processes to sample items from many psychometric tests, which they had previously taken under standardized conditions. The methods for extracting strategies for solving items from specific tests were only briefly described, but given that high inter-rater agreement of encoding was obtained, the findings should be considered seriously. Barratt (1953) showed that assessed solution methods or strategies were reliably related to performance on several psychometric tests measuring spatial ability. In his original dissertation Barratt (1952) provides more detail about his methods of assessing subjects' strategies. For example, Barratt (1952) identified about half of the subjects as mentally rotating *whole* figures in the Figures Test on the basis of verbal reports like these:

> Subject #18: ". . . . I would look at all these various choices here, and I would take the problem and try to switch it around, turn it around in the same form as these here; after I turn it around, I see that they can be made to coincide. . . ."
>
> Subject #44: "I'm trying to turn the figure around in a way that it is in the same position that the key problem would be. . . ." (pp. 58–59)

Most of the other subjects appeared to rotate only *parts* of the figures as indicated by the following verbal reports:

> Subject #4: ". . . . The semicircle is pointed in one direction, and the V is to the bottom of it, and if the figure were the same way, well, the semicircle would be pointed in the same direction, or if it were laying down or opposite, the semicircle, uh, the V would always be to the left. . . ."
>
> Subject #79: ". . . . I'd look at this V here; I would look for ones that would be this way if turned this way . . . . . I would look at this bar on the bottom; that would be my distinguishing mark here; the bar is turned around in B, etc. . . . "
> (Barratt, 1952, p. 59)

French (1965) divided his subjects into two groups on the basis of their strategy for solving items in a given test. For each group the intercorrelations on all psychometric tests were recomputed separately. Subsequent factor-analysis of each group showed remarkably different factor structures for several of the strategies. French (1965) summarized his findings by saying "Systematizing is a tendency which leads a person to use specialized or symbolic thought processes; this changes what the tests measure, and consequently affects the correlations between the tests" (p. 28).

The research on performance of tasks measuring spatial ability is particularly interesting as it illustrates how quite different sources of data (reaction time, eye-movement data, verbal reports, training studies and experiments) provide converging support for the importance of strategies in accounting for individual differences (Lohman & Kyllonen, 1983; Snow & Lohman, 1984). It also nicely demonstrates the need for information-rich data, like eye-movements and verbal reports, to fully describe complex cognitive entities such as strategies.

EXCEPTIONAL ABILITY vs. ACQUIRED SKILL

Given the reports on successful elicitation of verbal reports on cognitive processes described in the two preceding sections, one might rightfully ask which abilities are basic and yield no or uninformative verbal reports. In the introduction I mentioned that exceptional abilities, like exceptional memory, have consistently been attributed to innate differences in the structure of memory. Implicit in the definition of exceptional basic abilities is the claim that normal subjects cannot attain such abilities even after extensive practice. Furthermore, it is claimed that demonstration of such abilities in, for example, a memory task, will not allow the subject to report any mediating cognitive processes. In the first part of this section I describe some research I conducted with the late Bill Chase examining practice on a specific task. I then discuss analyses of people with alleged exceptional memory.

Effects of Practice on Performance on Memory Tests

Bill Chase and I intentionally selected digit span, because several investigators had proposed that digit span provided the best measure of the *fixed* capacity of short-term memory (STM). The fast rate of presentation of digits was assumed to force subjects to exclusively rely on STM in this memory task.

Our research approach consisted of providing subjects with extensive practice on the digit-span task and monitoring any improvements by requesting retrospective verbal reports from a selected portion of the trials. All significant changes in the reported thoughts were validated by a specially designed experiment (Chase & Ericsson, 1981, 1982; Ericsson, Chase, & Faloon, 1980).

The focus of this account is on our first subject (SF), who discovered the means to improve his memory performance. SF was selected to be a representative and average college student with respect to intelligence and memory ability. His original digit span was about seven.

During each session SF was read random digits at the rate of one digit per second; he then recalled the sequence. If the sequence was reported correctly, the next sequence was increased by one digit; otherwise it was decreased by one digit. The performance on the last sequence in the preceding session determined the length of the digit sequence presented on the first trial on the following session. Figure 6.8 shows SF's average digit span as a function of practice for over 200 practice sessions distributed over 2 years.

Figure 6.8 shows that SF increased his digit span from 7 to over 80 digits. A naive interpretation of this dramatic increase in memory performance is that SF simply extended his short-term memory by a factor of 10. In comparison, subjects with alleged exceptional memory have digit spans of *less* than 20 digits. The relation to exceptional memory is discussed later.

However, after most of the digit-span tests, SF gave a retrospective verbal report on his cognitive processes during the trial. From an analysis of these verbal reports, we find that SF's memory performance can be accounted for in terms of an acquired skill rather than expansion of some basic capacity. The main findings were confirmed by experimental tests.

During the first session with the digit-span task, the verbal reports show that SF relied almost exclusively on rehearsal of all presented digits to remember them. In the second session he started trying to commit the first three digits of a series to memory and to rehearse the remaining digits of the presented series. Once the rehearsed digits had been committed to memory, he would retrieve the first three and initiate recall. The primary mode of encoding was repetition of digits and different numerical relations.

During Session 5, SF reported that he suddenly realized that a 3-digit sequence could be interpreted as a running time for a mile. For example, 418 could be a 4-minute, 18-second mile-time. His average digit span for this session jumped four standard deviations from the session before. SF was a long-distance runner with extensive knowledge of both specific and general categories of

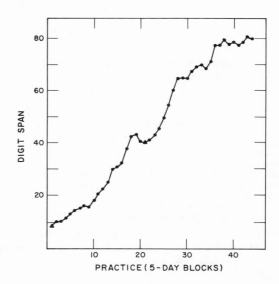

FIG. 6.8.   Average digit span for SF as a function of practice.

running times for a large number of different races. During the following sessions, SF retrieved a set of races (¼-mile, ½-mile, ¾-mile, mile, 2-mile) that would cover the range of most 3-digit numbers from 100 to 959. However, no 3-digit numbers with a middle digit of 6, 7, 8, or 9, (e.g., 483, 873) can be interpreted as meaningful running times. In one experiment we presented digit sequences made up of only such uncodable 3-digit sequences to SF and his memory-span was reduced almost to the level prior to practice. Later SF started to encode 4-digit groups as running times. The different types of encodings are illustrated in a typical retrospective report given by SF shown in Table 6.7.

Finally, SF used an encoding as ages of people for digit groups that could not be meaningfully encoded as running times or dates.

In parallel with the emergence of new and more effective encodings of 3- and 4-digit groups, SF started to store up to four different groups in memory in addition to the four to five digits in the rehearsal buffer. In order to recall these digit groups in their correct order, SF encoded the order of presentation of each digit group as first, middle, or last. At the time of recall, SF could use this as the main cue to retrieve the encoded digit groups in the presented order. The encoding of these additional cues, integrated with memory traces for the purpose of subsequent retrieval, we call *retrieval-structure*. In order to be able to store more groups in memory SF introduced a new level of organization, and used two super-groups to organize encoded digits as either 4-digit groups or 3-digit groups. This hierarchical organization is illustrated in Fig. 6.9, and was evidenced in SF's retrospective verbal reports on how he encoded the digit sequence, as well as in the pauses and intonation patterns of his recall of the digit sequence. Before our experimental study of SF ended, he had extended his retrieval structure to successfully hold 84 digits.

TABLE 6.7
An Example of SF's Retrospective Reports From a Digit-Span Trial

Presented sequence: 4 1 3 1 7 7 8 4 0 6 0 3 4 9 4 8 7 0 9 4 6 2
Segmented digit groups: 4131 - 7784 - 0603 - 494 - 870 - 9462
Retrospective report:
Starting from the beginning.
I made the four thirteen point one a mile time.
I just remembered the seventy-seven eighty-four.
Ok? Ok? Right. Seventy-seven eighty-four.
Then...then...then I...
(Any pattern?)
What?
(Any pattern?)
No. No.Nothing. Just like seventy-seven eighty-four.
Ok. Then I made the oh six oh three, I made that a mile time.
Then I remembered the four nine four and the eight seven oh.
I just had to remember those.
Then I remembered the nine forty-six point...two!
It's definitely point two, two-mile.
I said, so I said to myself "What did you run it in?"
I ran it in nine forty-six point two. Nine forty-six point two. Right.

The digits, presented orally at 1 second/digit, are shown at the top of the table along with SF's segmentation into digit-groups for this trial. Adapted from Chase and Ericsson (1981).

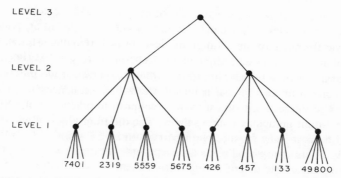

FIG. 6.9.   Proposed hierarchical organization of SF's memory encoding of thirty presented digits. The first level contains mnemonic encodings of digit groups and the second level consists of super-groups, where the relative location of several digit groups are encoded.

SF did not rely on short-term memory for his recall of the digits. His digit span was essentially unaffected by performing other tasks in the interval between the presentation and the recall of a digit sequence, even when these interpolated tasks required the full capacity of short-term memory. More conclusive evidence for storage in long-term memory is obtained from SF's ability to recall about 90% of 200–300 presented digits after the session.

Finally, SF's memory skill did not lead only to an ability to remember a larger number of digits. In a self-paced situation, SF showed that shorter digit lists (10–50 digits) could, after practice, be memorized at more than twice the original presentation rate.

In sum, SF's final performance is based on radically different cognitive processes and capacities than his initial performance prior to practice. In our study of three additional subjects practicing the digit-span task, we found evidence for the same components of skill. Two subjects given fewer practice sessions surpassed the magical limit of 20 digits. The third subject attained a digit span of more than 100 digits and is still improving with further practice. The fact that our subjects could attain digit spans surpassing subjects with alleged exceptional memory after only 50–100 hours of practice raises the possibility that the exceptional subjects were simply misdiagnosed.

Alleged Exceptional Memory Ability

When people attribute to exceptional subjects an innate ability, there is little or no evidence to substantiate such an inference. In fact, such attribution is based on the lack of alternative explanations (Ericsson & Faivre, in press). Some of the affirmative evidence comes from the subject's own verbal descriptions. The famous subject S of Luria (1968) reported storing visual images of matrices without any mediational activity involving meaning. The exceptional memory of

Inaudi was alleged to be based on sound (Binet, 1894). More commonly subjects report a complete lack of mediation, which is often interpreted as evidence for innate basic ability. These general verbal descriptions are quite different from the thinking-aloud protocols and retrospective reports I advocated earlier. Further, there appears to be a conflict of interest that might bias and contaminate the verbal reports from exceptional subjects. In our culture a mysterious ability is deemed more interesting than one that is understood (cf. an act by a magician before and after the detailed steps of the act are explained). If one's livelihood depends on the income from public performances of one's ability, which is the case with several people of alleged exceptional memory, one's willingness to describe any available details of the cognitive processes might be reduced.

First, I report on some comparisons between the memory performance of our trained subjects, whose memory structure is known, and the performance of subjects with alleged exceptional ability. I then describe some analyses of other memory experts using protocol analysis.

Binet (1894) analyzed the digit memory of two mental calculators and a mnemonist. The emphasis on memory for digits was fortunate for Chase and me because it provided an interesting test for our trained subjects (SF and DD). One of the tasks Binet used was memorization of a 25-digit matrix. Luria (1968) reported on memorization of a 50-digit matrix by his subject, S. Ericsson and Chase (1982) compared the trained and the exceptional subjects on time taken to memorize each of these two matrices, and found that the trained subjects could memorize the digits as fast or faster than the exceptional subjects. After the digit matrices were committed to memory, the subjects were asked to recall the digits from the matrix in a wide range of different orders (backward and forward recall of rows, recall of columns of digits starting at the bottom, etc.). It had been argued by Binet (1894) that the observed recall times could differentiate between auditory and visual memory representations. A reanalysis of these recall times showed a remarkable similarity between all exceptional subjects and our two trained subjects. In fact, relying on the retrospective verbal reports of one of our trained subjects, Chase and I constructed a mathematical model of the retrieval, which described the retrieval times of *all* subjects (exceptional or trained) with remarkable accuracy (Ericsson & Chase, 1982).

When Luria (1968) argued that his subject, S, had an exceptional memory, it was based on a combination of performance data and verbal descriptions from S on how he memorized information. A review of a surprisingly large number of case studies of memory experts shows that the subjects showing the most exceptional memory performance do *not* claim to have structurally different memories (Ericsson, 1985). Extensive laboratory studies of Professor Rueckle (Mueller, 1911, 1913, 1917) and of a professional mnemonist, Isahara, (Susukita, 1933, 1934) provide detailed accounts of their methods for memorization directly consistent with the three attributes of acquired memory skill discussed earlier (Chase & Ericsson, 1982). For example, a contemporary analysis of a waiter with exceptional memory for dinner orders showed that thinking-aloud protocols and designed experiments could uncover the mnemonic associations and retrieval structure used to store the information in long-term memory (Ericsson & Polson, in press). The empirical evidence indicates that extraordinary memory performance is due to acquired memory skill regardless of claims for exceptional ability (Ericsson, 1985).

When exceptional memory performance is demonstrated by mentally retarded subjects, such performance is often assumed to reflect "pure" memorization without mediation. From verbal reports of some mentally retarded subjects with exceptionally good memories, however, we find evidence that these retarded subjects are able to use mnemonics in a manner similar to that of trained memory experts. Jones (1926), for instance, analyzed a subjects's (IQ = 75) memorization of digits under laboratory control. The following is a verbal protocol taken from the subject as he memorized the number 30249385274. It bears a striking resemblance to those of our trained digit-span experts.

> 30 is the number of days in a month. 249—if that were 149 it would be the distance from Chicago to Peoria, Illinois. 385—I once paid $3.85 railroad fare going from Cheyenne, Wyoming to Wheatland, Wyoming. 274—I can remember that by putting a 6 in front of it for the time being. 6274 is the seating capacity of the Hippodrome. (Jones, 1926, p. 372.)

On a more general level it appears that most people with remarkable skills are surprisingly unable to describe them and the corresponding cognitive processes. However, the same subjects are able to give detailed concurrent or retrospective verbal reports while performing specific tasks in their domain of expertise. In the beginning of this section I raised the question of what performance or ability is basic, or at least unmediated by reportable cognitive states. At this time I don't know where the boundary will fall, although the documented existence of unmediated retrieval and recognition processes provides a lower bound (Ericsson & Simon, 1984). The clear importance of mediating cognitive processes in perceptual skills and many exceptional abilities in mentally retarded subjects (Ericsson & Faivre, in press) shows that many investigators' intuitions about the location of such a boundary have been incorrect and require a serious reevaluation.

CONCLUDING REMARKS

In this chapter I have shown how data from verbal reports can be represented in the same theoretical framework as traditional performance measures, such as reaction time and correctness of response. The intermediate states of cognitive processes (revealed by encodings of verbal reports) provide detailed descriptions of the processes. The claims that certain tests measure specific cognitive processes can be empirically evaluated by examining verbally reported thought sequences. Drawing on three different areas of research, I have argued for the richness and validity of verbal reports and how the verbal report data have been used to change commonly held views of underlying processes.

The issues of measurement are much broader, and in this final section I describe the relevance of protocol analysis to measurement issues. The arguments in this chapter can easily be extended to apply to the central issue of understanding the correlation between scores on different tests. Understanding what individual tests measure is a prerequisite for understanding the observed correlation between scores on two different tests. Protocol-analysis would allow us to evaluate the importance of two different sources of correlation. The first possibility is that superior test performance is due to the application of the same process or knowledge for both tests. The second and complementary possibility is that superior performance on one of the tests is determined by quite different processes and knowledge from those of the other test. Accounting for correlations due to the second possibility would require an account much different from the first.

In identifying broad issues of future measurement research, I was very influenced by Gene Glass' (1985) recent critique of current measurement research. One of his central arguments was that the information provided by tests was too general and measured abilities on such an abstract level that test scores did not provide any useful or diagnostic information to educators and the people concerned with remedial training. To describe a subjects' cognitive processes for some task requires a lot of information if this description should provide an educator with possible incorrect processes and strategies, lack of relevant knowledge, etc. Such an assessment goal is quite different from the traditional measurement of stable capacities or processing characteristics. In the body of my chapter I have tried to illustrate how protocol data can supply such information. However, the relation between verbally reported knowledge and teachability of the corresponding cognitive processes is more complex than it might appear at first glance.

It is clear that uncovering mediational elements in cognitive processes responsible for some superior or inferior performance on a task raises the possibility of improving the inferior subjects' performance through instruction. This does not, however, imply that subjects following the instruction instantly attain the superior performance of the subjects spontaneously exhibiting that strategy. Furthermore, we know that mediational cognitive processes are involved in many forms of expert performance, which can be attained only after years of practice by highly motivated students. Hence, stable individual differences in tasks are by no means irreconcilable with the existence of mediating cognitive processes. In our earlier discussion of memory skill, we showed that normal, motivated subjects could obtain exceptional memory performance after 50–100 hours of practice. The major obstacle subjects had was the fast presentation rate. To deal with the limited time available to develop retrieval structures, they needed to speed up their encoding processes. This is particularly well-illustrated by our second subject, who was instructed in the cognitive processes used by our first subject.

Given that the second subject was the running partner of the first subject, we can assume that his knowledge about running times was comparable. Although the second subject improved faster during the initial training, the advantage disappeared at a digit span of around 20 digits. This suggests that instruction can effectively guide the subject toward the correct sequence of cognitive processes, but that acquiring the necessary speed and integration requires practice. In this and other respects, mental skills resemble sports and other motor skills.

In the discussion of individual differences in mathematical ability, we noted that global strategies and general heuristics identified by experts did not provide a good conceptual system, either for characterization of individual differences or for instruction. Much better success was obtained with descriptions using domain-specific methods and different types of organization of knowledge.

The realization that any accurate characterization of individual differences in some ability requires a rather detailed description of knowledge and solution methods is important, yet somewhat disappointing. It is important because it should stimulate a closer collaboration between educators and people involved in measurement and assessment. Furthermore, it could lead to the emergence of standardized, individualized testing, with thinking aloud for the purpose of specific assessment of deficiencies as well as computer-based assessment. It is disappointing in that the task of measuring generalizable stable individual differences appears difficult or even impossible. Differences in available specific knowledge and strategies will always confound and cover any basic differences. By extracting information about strategies through verbal reports, we will explicitly address such influence and hence understand better what tests actually measure.

There is, of course, a rather different view, which argues that general individual differences are made up of differences in acquired methods and organized knowledge. The dramatic improvements after practice on all types of tasks (especially simple tasks used to measure basic capacities and processes) appear to provide strong support for this emphasis on skill. The research exploring effects of extensive practice has shown that practice does not simply make the performance quantitatively better but also leads to qualitative changes in performance. This means that many abilities assumed to require such structurally different characteristics might still be a function of practice—extensive practice. Within this skill-based view of individual differences, verbal reports and other descriptions of processes, like eye-fixations, will be absolutely essential in allowing us to characterize the components and organization of performance.

REFERENCES

Anderson, J. R., & Bower, G. H. (1973). *Human associative memory*. Washington, D.C.: V. H. Winston.

Barratt, E. S. (1952). *An analysis of verbal reports of solving spatial problems*. Unpublished doctoral dissertation. University of Texas, Austin.

Barratt, E. S. (1953). An analysis of verbal reports of solving spatial problems as an aid in defining spatial factors. *The Journal of Psychology, 36*, 17–25.

Bellezza, F. S. (1981). Mnemonic devices: Classification, characteristics and criteria. *Review of Educational Research, 51*, 247–275.

Binet, A. (1894). *Psychologie des grands calculateurs et joueurs d'echecs.* Paris: Libraire Hachette.

Bloom, B. S., & Broder, L. J. (1950). *Problem-solving processes of college students.* Chicago, IL: The University of Chicago Press.

Bower, G. H. (1972). Mental imagery and associative learning. In L. W. Gregg (Ed.), *Cognition in learning and memory.* New York: Wiley.

Brown, J. S., & Burton, R. R. (1978). Diagnostic models for procedural bugs in basic mathematical skills. *Cognitive Science, 2*, 155–192.

Brown, J. S., & VanLehn, K. (1980). Repair theory: A generative theory of bugs in procedural skills. *Cognitive Science, 4*, 379–426.

Buswell, G. T., & John, L. (1928). Diagnostic studies in arithmetic. *Supplementary Educational Monographs, 30.*

Chase, W. G., & Ericsson, K. A. (1981). Skilled memory. In J. R. Anderson (Ed.), *Cognitive skills and their acquisition.* Hillsdale, NJ: Lawrence Erlbaum Associates.

Chase, W. G., & Ericsson, K. A. (1982). Skill and working memory. In G. H. Bower (Ed.), *The psychology of learning and motivation* (Vol. 16). New York: Academic Press.

Chi, M. T. H., Feltovich, P. J., & Glaser, R. (1981). Categorization and representation of physics problems by experts and novices. *Cognitive Science, 5*, 121–152.

Deffner, G., & Ericsson, K. A. (1985). *Sprechtempo und Pausen bei lautem Denken.* Paper presented at Tagung experimentell arbeitender Psychologen. Wupperthal, West Germany.

Ebbinghaus, H. (1964). *Memory: A contribution to experimental psychology.* H. A. Ruger and C. E. Bussenius trans. New York: Dover Publications. (Originally published, 1885.)

Einhorn, H. J., Kleinmuntz, D. N., & Kleinmuntz, B. (1979). Linear regression and process-tracing models of judgment. *Psychological Review, 86*, 465–485.

Ericsson, K. A. (1975). Instruction to verbalize as a means to study problem solving processes with the Eight Puzzle: A preliminary study (No. 458). *Reports from the Department of Psychology.* Stockholm: University of Stockholm.

Ericsson, K. A. (1985). Memory skill. *Canadian Journal of Psychology, 39*, 188–231.

Ericsson, K. A., & Chase, W. G. (1982). Exceptional memory. *American Scientist, 70*(6), 507–515.

Ericsson, K. A., Chase, W. G., & Faloon, S. (1980). Acquisition of a memory skill. *Science, 208*, 1181–1182.

Ericsson, K. A., & Faivre, I. A. (in press). What's exceptional about exceptional abilities? In L. K. Obler & D. Fein (Eds.), *Neuropsychology of talent.* New York: Guilford.

Ericsson, K. A., & Polson, P. G. (in press). Memory for restaurant orders. In M. T. T. Chi, R. Glaser, & M. J. Farr (Eds.), *The nature of expertise.* Hillsdale, NJ: Lawrence Erlbaum Associates.

Ericsson, K. A., & Simon, H. A. (1980). Verbal reports as data. *Psychological Review, 87*, 215–251.

Ericsson, K. A., & Simon, H. A. (1984). *Protocol analysis.* Cambridge, MA: MIT Press/Bradford.

Ericsson, K. A., & Simon, H. A. (1985). Protocol analysis. In T. A. van Dijk (Ed.), *Handbook of discourse analysis* (Vol. 2). New York: Academic Press.

Frankel, F., Levine, M., & Karpf, D. (1970). Human discrimination learning: A test of the blank-trials assumption. *Journal of Experimental Psychology, 85*, 342–398.

French, J. W. (1965). The relationship of problem-solving styles to the factor composition of tests. *Educational and Psychological Measurement, 25*, 9–28.

Gimmestad, B. J. (1977). An exploratory study of the processes used by community college students in mathematics problem solving (Doctoral dissertation, University of Colorado at Boulder, 1976). *Dissertation Abstracts International, 37*, 7590A. (University Microfilms No. 77–11300)

Glass, G. V. (1985). Testing old, testing new: Schoolboy psychology and the allocation of intellectual resources. In B. Plake & J. C. Witt (Eds.), *The future of testing* (pp. 9–27). Hillsdale, NJ: Lawrence Erlbaum Associates.

Guilford, J. P. (1967). *The nature of human intelligence.* New York: McGraw-Hill.

Hamilton, J. M. E., & Sanford, A. J. (1978). The symbolic distance effect for alphabetic order judgements: A subjective report and reaction time analysis. *Quarterly Journal of Experimental Psychology, 30,* 33–43.

Heidbreder, E. (1924). An experimental study of thinking. *Archives of Psychology, 11* (Whole No 73).

Hinsley, D. A., Hayes, J. R., & Simon, H. A. (1977). From words to equations: Meaning and representation in algebra word problems. In M. A. Just & P. A. Carpenter (Eds.), *Cognitive Processes in Comprehension.* Hillsdale, NJ: Lawrence Erlbaum Associates.

Hunt, E. (1978). Mechanics of verbal ability. *Psychological Review, 85,* 109–130.

Jones, H. E. (1926). Phenomenal memorizing as a special ability. *Journal of Applied Psychology, 10.* 367–377.

Just, M. A., & Carpenter, P. A. (1985). Cognitive coordinate systems: Accounts of mental rotation and individual differences in spatial ability. *Psychological Review, 92,* 137–171.

Karpf, D., & Levine, M. (1971). Blank-trial probes and introtacts in human discrimination learning. *Journal of Experimental Psychology, 90,* 51–55.

Kennedy, G., Eliot, J., & Krulee, G. (1970). Error patterns in problem solving formulations. *Psychology in the Schools, 7,* 93–99.

Kilpatrick, J. (1968). Analyzing the solution of word problems in mathematics: An exploratory study. Doctoral dissertation, Stanford University, 1967. *Dissertation Abstracts International, 28,* 4380-A (University Microfilms No. 68-6442)

Krutetskii, V. A. (1976). *The psychology of mathematical problem solving.* IL: University of Chicago Press.

Larkin, J. H., McDermott, J., Simon, D. P., & Simon, H. A. (1980). Expert and novice performance in solving physics problems. *Science, 208,* 1335–1342.

Lesgold, A. M. (1984). Acquiring expertise. In J. R. Anderson & S. M. Kosslyn (Eds.), *Tutorials in learning and memory: Essays in honor of Gordon Bower.* San Francisco: W. H. Freeman.

Lohman, D. F., & Kyllonen, P. C. (1983). Individual differences in solution strategy on spatial tasks. In R. F. Dillon & R. R. Schmeck (Eds.), *Individual differences in cognition, Vol. 1.* New York: Academic Press.

Lucas, J. F. (1972). An exploratory study on the diagnostic teaching of heuristic problem-solving strategies in calculus. Doctoral dissertation, University of Wisconsin, 1972. *Dissertation Abstracts International, 32,* 6825A. (University Microfilms No. 72-15368)

Luria, A. R. (1968). *The mind of a mnemonist.* New York: Avon.

Martin, C. J., Boersma, F. J., & Cox, D. L. (1965). A classification of associative strategies in paired-associate learning. *Psychonomic Science, 3,* 455–456.

Miller, K., Perlmutter, M., & Keating, D. (1984). Cognitive arithmetic: Comparisons of operations. *Journal of Experimental Psychology: Learning, Memory and Cognition, 10,* 46–60.

Montague, W. E. (1972). Elaborative strategies in verbal learning and memory. In G. H. Bower (Ed.), *The psychology of learning and motivation* (Vol. 6). New York: Academic Press.

Mueller, G. E. (1911). Zur Analyse der Gedachtnistatigkeit und des Vorstellungsverlaufes: Teil I. *Zeitschrift fur Psychologie, Erganzungsband 5.*

Mueller, G. E. (1913). Neue Versuche mit Rueckle. *Zeitschrift fur Psychologie und Physiologie der Sinnesorgane, 67,* 193–213.

Mueller, G. E. (1917). Zur Analyse der Gedachtnistatigkeit und des Vorstellungsverlaufes: Teil II. *Zeitschrift fur Psycholgie, Erganzungsband 9.*

Newell, A., & Simon, H. A. (1972). *Human problem solving.* Englewood Cliffs, NJ: Prentice-Hall.

Nisbett, R. E., & Wilson, T. D. (1977). Telling more than we can know: Verbal reports on mental processes. *Psychological Review, 84,* 231–259.

Noble, C. E. (1952). An analysis of meaning. *Psychological Review, 59,* 421–430.

Payne, J. W. (1976). Task complexity and contingent processing in decision making: An information search and protocol analysis. *Organizational Behavior and Human Performance, 16,* 366–387.

Polya, G. (1957). *How to solve it.* Garden City, NY: Doubleday-Anchor.

Prytulak, L. S. (1971). Natural language mediation. *Cognitive Psychology, 2,* 1–56.

Schoenfeld, A. H. (1979). Explicit heuristic training as a variable in problem-solving performance. *Journal for Research in Mathematics Education, 10,* 173–187.

Silver, E. A. (1979). Student perceptions of relatedness among mathematical verbal problems. *Journal for Research in Mathematics Education, 10,* 195–210.

Simon, H. A. (1979). *Models of thought.* New Haven, CT: Yale University Press.

Snow, R. E., & Lohman, D. F. (1984). Toward a theory of cognitive aptitude for learning from instruction. *Journal of Educational Psychology, 76,* 347–376.

Sternberg, R. J. (1977). *Intelligence, information processing, and analogical reasoning: The componential analysis of human abilities.* Hillsdale, NJ: Lawrence Erlbaum Associates.

Susukita, T. (1933). Untersuchung eines ausserordentlichen Gedaechtnisses in Japan (I). *Tohoku Psychologica Folia, 1,* 111–154.

Susukita, T. (1934). Untersuchung eines ausserordentlichen Gedaechtnisses in Japan (II), *Tohoku Psychologica Folia, 2,* 14–43.

Svenson, O. (1979). Process descriptions of decision making. *Organizational Behavior and Human Performance, 23,* 86–112.

Varon, E. J. (1935). The development of Alfred Binet's psychology. *Psychological Monographs, 46*(Whole No. 207).

Watson, J. B. (1920). Is thinking merely the action of language mechanisms? *British Journal of Psychology, 11,* 87–104.

Wechsler, D. (1952). *The range of human capacities.* Baltimore: The Williams & Wilkins Co.

Woodworth, R. S. (1938). *Experimental psychology.* New York: Holt.

Young, R. M., & O'Shea, T. (1981). Errors in children's subtraction. *Cognitive Science, 5,* 153–177.

III

METHODOLOGICAL ISSUES

7

Structure and Process in Cognitive Psychology Using Multidimensional Scaling and Related Techniques

Edward J. Shoben
Brian H. Ross
University of Illinois

INTRODUCTION

The goal of cognitive psychology is to provide a general understanding of human cognitive processes through the development of general, formal models of cognition. Although it is clearly true that some areas (such as memory) have been more highly developed than others, it is undeniable that cognitive psychology has witnessed a proliferation of models in the past decade. Perhaps researchers are finding it increasingly difficult to discriminate among competing memory models because the constraints are so weak. One possibility that will be explored in this chapter is the prospect of using multidimensional scaling (MDS) and related procedures as a means of providing constraint for theorizing.

In this chapter, we initially provide a brief description of the problem of the inability to distinguish among models. Subsequently, we sketch some scaling and clustering procedures. We then discuss a number of applications of MDS and related procedures to domains of interest to cognitive psychologists. Particular attention is given to the constraint provided by these techniques on cognitive theorizing. Subsequently, we outline how one might choose the correct procedure and how one might circumvent some problems raised by using these procedures to study cognitive domains. Next, we provide a brief application of these procedures to the domain of cognitive psychology models. Finally, we attempt to provide an assessment of the utility of MDS and related procedures in cognitive psychology.

DISTINGUISHING THEORIES: AN ILLUSTRATIVE EXAMPLE

One particularly salient example of the difficulty in telling seemingly contradictory theories apart is the recent dispute over the viability of the semantic/episodic distinction in human memory. Briefly, Tulving (1983) has proposed that the human memory system can profitably be divided into memory for general world knowledge (semantic) and memory for personal events (episodic). In contrast, other theorists have claimed that a unitary theory of memory provides a better account (Anderson & Ross, 1980; McKoon, Ratcliff, & Dell, in press).

It would certainly seem that two theoretical viewpoints that differ in the desirability of partitioning the memory system along such fundamental lines should be easy to tell apart. In fact, this goal has proven elusive. To date, the most conclusive kind of evidence on this issue is the dissociation experiment in which one examines the effects of an independent variable on an episodic memory task and a semantic one. If we find that the variable has different effects on the two tasks, then according to Tulving (1983) we have evidence for the distinction.

Although one might reasonably believe that these dissociation experiments might resolve this issue, they have not. Proponents of a unitary view argue that when the task changes it is often necessary for the cognitive operations to change also and consequently we should expect these kinds of dissociations. More explicitly, the confusion over the semantic/episodic distinction can best be understood in terms of the distinction between structure and process in cognitive psychology. Basically, any model must specify a set of structural assumptions and a set of processing assumptions. The problem is that whereas one set of assumptions might nicely account for some set of data, it is also the case that a very different set of structural assumptions, usually accompanied by a very different set of processing assumptions, can also account for the same set of data. Compounding the problem is that many models are not sufficiently detailed as to have both an explicit set of structural assumptions and an explicit set of processing assumptions.

In the case of the semantic/episodic distinction, both problems are operative. Proponents of the distinction explain the dissociation by appealing to the different memory structures involved. Unitary theorists claim that different tasks will necessarily involve some different processes and therefore dissociations are far from unequivocal evidence for a structural distinction. Without explicit processing assumptions, it is impossible to determine who has the stronger claim.

One obvious solution to this problem is to require our theorizing to be more precise. McKoon, Ratcliff, and Dell (in press) have made this suggestion quite eloquently and have also proposed a somewhat more detailed version of the unitary theory. However, it would be naive of us to suppose that precision in theorizing will naturally occur because vagueness leads to problems in telling theories apart. What is needed are techniques that enable us to develop more detailed theories. One possibility is any technique that provides some constraint on structure. Although it is not immediately obvious to us that multidimensional scaling will help with making these accounts of the semantic/episodic distinction more distinguishable, we do believe that multidimensional scaling and kindred procedures may, in general, provide this very necessary kind of constraint.

One typically uses MDS to obtain a structural representation of a stimulus domain. It will not provide a process model, although the structure recovered may suggest one. One way to examine the claim that MDS will provide constraint to cognitive theories is to examine some previous uses of the method to determine if its use has provided any constraint on theorizing in the area of application.

KINDS OF MDS AND RELATED PROCEDURES

Before examining the applications of MDS in cognitive psychology, it is useful to make some preliminary distinctions among procedures that correspond to conceptual differences among applications. The most important differences are whether the recovered representation is continuous or discrete and whether individual differences are taken into account.

Carroll and Arabie (1980), in their review of multidimensional scaling propose a detailed taxonomy of MDS methods, of which only a portion will be used here. Two-way MDS is the oldest of these procedures. Originally developed by Shepard (1962a, 1962b) and Kruskal (1964a, 1964b), the original program has evolved considerably over the last 2 decades. In the most modern version, KYST, the input data are a matrix of proximities in which the rows and columns of the matrix represent stimulus objects. KYST uses this type of input matrix that contains the similarity (or dissimilarity) of each object to each other object. The output of the procedure is a graphical depiction of the stimulus objects in k dimensions. In contrast to this continuous measure, there are also discrete two-way procedures. One of the most promising is MAPCLUS, the Arabie and Carroll (1980) algorithm for fitting the Shepard-Arabie ADCLUS (1979) model. This procedure takes the same input data as KYST and returns a solution of k clusters of stimulus objects with a cluster weight (and an additive constant). Goodness-of-fit is measured somewhat differently in the two procedures: MAPCLUS provides variance accounted for whereas KYST reports STRESS, a badness-of-fit measure.

A similar classification can be made of three-way procedures, which take individual differences[1] into account. These procedures all take an input matrix

---

[1]Strictly speaking, the third "way" need not be variation among individuals; it may instead be differences in groups of people or stimulus context, but the most common use is individuals. We employ the most common use here because it is easier to understand.

whose rows and columns represent stimulus objects, as in the two-way matrix, but whose extra third dimension represents individuals. Conceptually, one can think of this matrix as a series of two-way matrices where each individual contributes one two-way matrix. The most common three-way analogue to KYST is INDSCAL, developed by Carroll and Chang (1970), or its faster-running successor SINDSCAL (Pruzansky, 1975). Like KYST, INDSCAL outputs a spatial representation of the stimulus objects in k dimensions. However, in addition to this *object space,* INDSCAL also provides a *subject space,* a plot of the weight that each subject assigns to each dimension.

For discrete models, Arabie and Carroll (1983) have developed an individual differences variant of MAPCLUS named INDCLUS. This procedure takes a three-way matrix of proximities (exactly as in SINDSCAL) and outputs k clusters where each cluster contains elements of the stimulus domain, but INDCLUS also provides a cluster weighting for each individual subject. Thus, just as INDSCAL provided a weighting for each subject on each dimension, so too INDCLUS provides a weighting for each subject on each cluster.

Generally speaking, researchers have employed two-way models when they sought to describe a stimulus structure that was assumed to be common to all individuals and a three-way method when the underlying representation was assumed to vary across individuals. There have been two types of exceptions to this rule. First, because three-way methods can often extract higher dimensionality, some investigators have employed these methods even when variation over individuals was not an issue. Second, there have been several creative uses of three-way methods in which the third way was not individuals, but some other factor, such as age of the particular group of subjects (in developmental studies) or context. Third, three-way methods yield unique orientation of axes, while the axes provided by the two-way methods are usually arbitrary, and so are subject to rotation.

MDS AS A METHOD FOR DETERMINING STRUCTURE

Much of the early work in cognitive psychology that used MDS did so exclusively for descriptive purposes. For example, in one of the largest collections of scaling work, Fillenbaum and Rappaport (1971) used a precursor of KYST to scale a large number of semantic terms ranging from verbs to classes of nouns. Similarly, Clark (1968) scaled a large number of common prepositions. After presenting the graphic solution, the main problem remaining was to label the dimensions. Although we discuss some solutions to this problem below, the standard of 15 years ago was simply to examine the dimensions and label them intuitively. Even under these relatively relaxed standards, it is clear that some of this research was quite fruitful.

One of the most widely analyzed data sets is the confusion matrices collected by Miller and Nicely (1955) on consonant phonemes. Shepard (1972) incorporated the idea of fitting an exponential decay function on the original confusion proportions before performing the MDS analysis. He recovered a two-dimensional solution in which the first dimension distinguished voiced phonemes (za and da) from unvoiced ones (fa and ka). The second dimension separated the nasals (ma and na) from the other consonant phonemes. Within these remaining phonemes, there was also a separation between those that are formed at the front of the mouth (fa and ba) and those that are formed at the rear (ga and zha). These results thus gave considerable support to the featural interpretation of consonant phonemes.

The color domain has also been of long-standing interest to users of MDS (Ekman, 1954). In fact, color was the primary example that Shepard used in his original paper (1962a). Using the judged similarity of the common color names, Shepard found that the data were well fit by a two-dimensional solution in which the names were arranged in a *color circle* in which there was a gap between the color with shortest wavelength (violet) and the one with the longest wavelength (red). In the circle, the points are arranged in terms of their wavelength, such that connecting the points in the circle orders the colors monotonically in terms of their wavelength. In addition, the fact that red and violet are quite close to each other (even though they are maximally different in wavelength) accords quite well with our intuition that these colors are psychologically quite similar.

Semantic.   In contrast to the perceptual and sensory domains, the results of using MDS with semantic domains are generally less clear-cut. There are several possible reasons why the results of MDS analysis are not always salutary with this kind of domain. First, it is the case that most semantic domains are of functionally infinite size (although there are exceptions to this general principle, such as kin terms and English prepositions). Thus, some selection of exemplars from a domain must be made, and, somewhat surprisingly, this selection is often done haphazardly. Different subsets will yield different results. Second, the meaning of various terms can change with the context. This change can be either a function of homonyms or some more subtle change. For a subtle change, the meaning of *eagle* may be different in the context of other birds than is its meaning in the context of other predators. For a radical change the location of *bat* in a multidimensional space is going to be different if *bat* is among other rodents or among other types of sporting equipment. We discuss context effects in greater detail in a later section. Third, semantic domains are potentially more heterogeneous than other domains we have considered. Thus, while all color names can be compared on hue, brightness, and saturation, it is difficult to imagine even a single dimension on which one could relate *drunkenness, lion,* and *chair.* Fourth, some semantic domains, such as categories, that are frequently subjected to MDS analysis may pose technical problems for many of the MDS programs that are presently used. We discuss this issue in a later section.

One of the most commonly scaled semantic domains is categories and one of the most commonly scaled categories is animals. Beginning with Henley (1969), there have been a number of MDS analyses of this particular domain. Henley presented a three-dimensional solution in which the first dimension ordered the animals along the continuum of size. The second dimension, which Henley (1969) labeled ferocity had predators at one pole and domesticated animals at the other. The third dimension was largely uninterpretable. It did seem to set off the anthropoid apes from the other animals, and perhaps for this reason, Henley elected to label it as humanness. However, relatively intelligent animals like the elephant ranked near the bottom of this dimension, and it thus seems that a just conclusion is that this third dimension is uninterpretable.

There has been minor controversy over how many dimensions are appropriate for this domain. Using INDSCAL, Rips, Shoben, and Smith (1973) obtained a satisfactory fit to their data in two dimensions, which they labeled size and predacity. Their second dimension was much like Henley's in that it separated the predators from the farm animals; they felt that ferocity was misleading and therefore employed the obscure term predacity. In addition to the satisfactory fit that Rips et al. (1973) obtained, they also were able to use the distances obtained from the solution to predict categorization latencies. Generally speaking, exemplars that were further in the space from the category label took longer to categorize. Shoben (1976) also found that mammals could be fit in these same two dimensions, although he used only 6 mammal exemplars and 6 bird exemplars. Many other researchers have been unable to obtain an adequate fit without going to a largely uninterpretable third dimension. For example, King, Gruenewald, and Lockhead (1978) argued for a three-dimensional solution, and Rumelhart and Abrahamsen (1973) were unable to use the distances from a two-dimensional solution to generate predictions in an analogies task where distances obtained from a three-dimensional solution provided a very good fit.

Although the results using animal names are certainly not definitive, the results are at least interpretable in terms of plausible, denotative, semantic dimensions. There are many examples to the contrary, and the number extant in the literature probably understates the number of failures considerably because of the difficulty in publishing negative results. Often these negative results are mentioned in a context with results that are more heartwarming to the author. For example, Shoben (1976) was unable to interpret a solution he obtained for fruits and vegetables. Pruzansky, Tversky, and Carroll (1982) report a number of scalings in which the first author was involved, and none of those solutions had readily interpretable dimensions.

Semantic stimuli that are heterogeneous present a different problem. The resulting solution is often interpretable, but usually in terms of connotative dimensions. One example is a study by Arnold (1971) in which his heterogeneous group of concrete and abstract nouns yielded a three-dimensional solution that included the dimensions evaluation, potency, and activation (Osgood, Suci, & Tannenbaum, 1954). In large measure, such an outcome makes sense because it is highly unlikely that a heterogeneous group of objects will have common denotative dimensions. The only common dimensions for such a collection are the connotative attributes.

APPLICATIONS OF MDS TO COGNITIVE TASKS

Although early applications of MDS often took the solution as the end result, some later applications have attempted to use the resulting solution to predict behavior. Rips et al. (1973), for example, used the distances between the exemplars of a category and the category name to predict latencies in a categorization task. In a reaction time (RT) task, subjects were asked to decide if, for example, a duck was a bird. Rips et al. (1973) found that the time to make this judgment could be predicted quite well by the distance between *duck* and *bird* in the multidimensional space produced by INDSCAL.

Shoben (1976) extended this technique in a same-different task. He assumed that short distances should facilitate positive judgments and inhibit negative ones. Shoben used the derived distances to predict both same and different latencies in a task where subjects were presented with pairs of exemplars and decided if the exemplars were from same or different categories. Thus, the correct answer is same for *goose-chicken* and different for *goose-bear*. For same responses, Shoben (1976) found that the distance between each exemplar and the category name contributed significantly to the prediction of Same RT. Interestingly, and in contrast to processing accounts espoused by Schaeffer and Wallace (1970), the distance between the two exemplars had no effect on latency. In a similar way, the distance between the exemplar and the category name also predicted Different RT. Not surprisingly, the distance between the first exemplar and its true category contributed significantly to RT. Somewhat less obviously, the distance between the second exemplar and the *first* category also contributed significantly to RT. Once again, the distance between the two exemplars had no effect. Let us consider the pairs *bear-goose* and *bear-robin*. For both pairs, bear is quite close to its superordinate *mammal* so this aspect of the decision should be quite easy. However, *robin* and *goose* vary in their proximity to the superordinate *mammal*. For a bird exemplar, *goose* is quite close, while *robin* is quite distant. Consequently, we expect *bear-goose* to be more difficult than *bear-robin*.

MDS RESULTS AS A SOURCE OF PROCESSING
EXPLANATIONS

From the regression analyses described above, Shoben (1976) came up with a processing account of performance in the same-different task. He assumed that subjects processed the exemplars sequentially and he presented evidence that people did indeed follow his admonition to read the first word first. Subjects then categorized the first exemplar and the difficulty in performing this operation was a function of the distance between this exemplar and its category name. Subsequently, subjects compared the second exemplar to the category determined in the preceding operation. Here, increasing distance made it more difficult to conclude that the second exemplar was a member of the category, but increasing distance made a negative decision easier. This model thus provides a satisfactory account of performance in a same-different task, and seriously questions the processing explanation offered previously by Schaeffer and Wallace (1970).

Although Shoben (1976) used the MDS analysis to help devise an information processing account of a cognitive task, there are more formal accounts that are tied to scaling data more closely. In particular, the Rumelhart and Abrahamsen (1973) model of analogy is an excellent example. Although more sophisticated theories of analogical reasoning are now available (Sternberg, 1977), Rumelhart and Abrahamsen's theory is one of the best examples of a formal theory derived in large part from MDS analysis.

The task employed by Rumelhart and Abrahamsen (1973) was a 4-term analogy problem. Subjects solved analogies such as fox:horse::chipmunk:_____. They selected the best alternative (in one experiment) from a list of four alternatives: in this example, antelope, donkey, elephant, and wolf, where elephant is the best answer in this case. In spatial terms, Rumelhart and Abrahamsen (1973) noted that the ideal point could be determined by constructing a parallelogram given the three vertices specified by the three given terms of the analogy. In other words, one must determine the relationship between the first two terms of the analogy and then apply those relationships to the third term to determine the ideal point. In this domain (animal names), one must determine these relationships in all three dimensions. For the present example, fox is smaller than horse, somewhat more ferocious than horse, and slightly less human than horse. The ideal point is thus larger than a chipmunk, less ferocious than chipmunk, and slightly more human than chipmunk. Elephant is the closest of the four alternatives to this ideal. It should also be noted that one can rank order the alternatives in terms of proximity to the ideal, as Rumelhart and Abrahamsen did, and one finds that antelope is the second-best completion, donkey is third, and wolf is last.

In addition to predicting subjects' solutions, Rumelhart and Abrahamsen (1973) also leveloped a theory to account for the distribution of responses. They assumed that subjects' choices would be in proportion to their distances from the ideal point. More formally, they suggested that the distribution of responses would follow Luce's (1959) choice rule.

$$\Pr(X_i|X_1, \ldots, X_n) = \frac{v(d_i)}{\sum\limits_j^n v(d_j)} \tag{1}$$

Here, $d_i = X_i - I$: the distance between alternative X_i and the ideal point, and $v(\ )$ is a monotonically decreasing function and $P(X_i|X_1, \ldots, X_n)$ is the probability of selecting the ith item from the n alternatives. Because Shepard (1972) had obtained good fits to recall data by using an exponential decay function, Rumelhart and Abrahamsen (1973) assumed that $v(x) = \exp(-\alpha x)$ where α is constrained to be positive.

Using this one parameter, Rumelhart and Abrahamsen (1973) were able to obtain good fits to the data at both a quantitative and a qualitative level. Even the data for the third and fourth choices show a strikingly good fit. Moreover, this high level of correspondence was invariant when the distances among the alternatives was varied.

The work of Rumelhart and Abrahamsen (1973) is an excellent example of how MDS analysis can lead to a formal processing model. The ability to determine the distances of the alternatives from the ideal was an important prerequisite to the application of Luce's choice rule.

MDS AND CONSTRAINTS ON SEMANTIC MEMORY

Although MDS analysis has certainly proven useful in a number of cases, to what degree are semantic memory models constrained by MDS results? Viewed most negatively, the answer is that MDS analysis has not provided much of a constraint on semantic memory theorizing. Some theorists (Collins & Loftus, 1975) argue that the appropriate metaphor for semantic memory is a network, while others have argued that a set-theoretic account is more appropriate (McCloskey & Glucksberg, 1979). From the perspective of the categorization literature, such fundamental questions as whether prototype models or exemplar models are more appropriate remains an open question (Smith & Medin, 1981). From this account, it seems clear that MDS analysis (or any other kind of analysis) has provided relatively little constraint on theorizing in semantic memory.

However, viewed most positively, MDS has provided considerable constraint. From the work just reviewed, it is clear that there is structure in semantic memory that any model must account for, and that that structure is based on meaning. If, for example, we are interested in the processing of analogies, then, on the basis of Rumelhart and Abrahamsen's (1973) work, we must take into account the similarity in meaning as indicated by the three dimensions derived from Henley's (1969) original scaling of animal names. Although it is correct that this analysis does not specify what form the "correct" model of semantic memory should take, it does specify an important constraint of which any viable model must take notice. This evidence for dimensional processing, for example, is more readily incorporated into set-theoretic accounts than it is into network accounts.

Thus, judging from the semantic memory literature, it is important that the amount of constraint provided by MDS analysis not be oversold. The power to distinguish among broad classes of models is not in the power of the method. In fact, it appears to provide very little in the way of processing constraint. It does, however, provide some index of structure for which any reasonable model must account.

MUSIC PERCEPTION

The area of music perception is a rapidly growing and exciting field within cognitive psychology. Most of the advance has been within the past 6 years and it has been largely concerned with the psychological structure of music. Given this structural emphasis, it is not surprising that the contribution of MDS analysis has been large.

Early work in music perception was largely sensory and focused principally on pitch height (Stevens & Volkmann, 1940). Subsequent work (Shepard, 1964) has indicated a more complicated structure that is characterized by its emphasis on the octave. According to this account, the notes of a musical scale are properly thought of in terms of a chroma circle, analogous to the color circle discussed earlier.

The more recent work on music perception differs from the earlier studies by using an explicit musical context. From the subject's perspective, the more recent studies are examining the perception of music rather than the perception of tones. Some recent studies, for example, have asked subjects to judge the similarity of two tones in the context of a diatonic scale or to judge the similarity of two passages in the context of a melody. The use of richer context has enabled experimenters to recover (using MDS analyses) much more complicated structures.

Perhaps the seminal work of these studies has been performed by Krumhansl (1979). She presented subjects with a variety of musical contexts: a major chord triad, an ascending major scale, or a descending major scale. Subjects in each of these context conditions rated the similarity of a pair of tones in the context.

Differences among these three contexts were slight. Looking first at the raw similarity measures, some very regular results emerge. First, for stimuli in the major triad, other tones in the triad were judged most similar. Diatonic tones were judged next similar, followed by nondiatonics. For the diatonic tones (those not in the major triad), the same pattern was observed. For the nondiatonics, there was little effect of this categorical variable; whether a particular tone was diatonic or nondiatonic mattered little. Pitch height was the primary determinant of similarity between a nondiatonic tone and another tone.

The MDS representation that Krumhansl (1979) obtained is a complicated variant of the chroma circle. In her three-dimensional solution one can see the richness captured by the MDS analysis. The structure resembles an inverted cone. The components of the major triad form the base of the cone. For the C major scale she employed, these components are C, E, G, and high C, reading clockwise around the circle. At the next level are the diatonic tones. Reading clockwise around the circle at this level, we find D, F, A, and B. Finally, at the base of the inverted cone (the circle with the largest diameter) we find the nondiatonic tones. Like the tones at the other two levels, the tones are arranged in ascending order if one reads them in a clockwise order.

Thus it appears that more than a chroma circle emerges when tones are presented in a musical context. Even subjects who had little or no musical training classified tones in the fashion suggested by music theory. Here we have a case where it is difficult to think of a method other than MDS that might have been able to recover this structure.

Krumhansl and her colleagues (Krumhansl, Bharucha, & Kessler, 1982) have generalized this result from tones to chords. In the context of a C major scale, for example, Krumhansl et al. (1982) demonstrated that the major chords (CEG, FAC, and GBD) were central in an MDS representation. For a minor key (Krumhansl et al. used A minor), the corresponding chords were A minor D minor, and E major, respectively. Chords that were not a part of the scale sequence were at the periphery of the space.

More recently, Pollard-Gott (1983) has used MDS analysis to examine the perception of passages of classical music. She had subjects listen repeatedly to a Liszt sonata. Pollard-Gott encouraged her subjects to listen carefully and to take notes. At the end of each session, she gave 28 pairs of stimuli that were constructed from the eight passages from the sonata that she selected. The passages varied in length from 4 to 16 measures.

The similarities were analyzed using SINDSCAL (Carroll & Chang, 1970; Pruzansky, 1975). The data are particularly interesting when examined across sessions. The dimensions extracted, for example, progress from relatively naive and unsophisticated distinctions in the first sessions to a fairly sophisticated one in the final session. More specifically, the dimensions recovered from the similarities obtained after the first session reflected fairly gross physical features of the passages: happy-sad, high-low, simple-complex, and loud-soft. After the second session, however, the more sophisticated dimension of theme emerges. Here, this dimension separates, without any overlap, passages that deal with theme A from those that deal with theme B. This separation is even greater after the third listening session, suggesting that this more sophisticated dimension becomes increasingly important as subjects become more knowledgeable about the composition.

Strong support for this interpretation is provided by the results obtained in an expert condition. Pollard-Gott (1983) obtained the same ratings from a group of subjects who had received extensive musical training. For these subjects, she obtained a SINDSCAL solution that accounted for 84% of the variance in one dimension. This thematic dimension again clustered those passages that dealt with theme A at one end of the dimension and those that dealt with theme B at the other end of the dimension.

At even a higher level, Halpern (1984) has investigated memory organization for familiar songs. She posited that relations between songs could involve extramusical similarity or musical similarity. To assess the organization, she gave subjects 60 songs and asked them to sort them into groups of songs that were similar either in terms of their musical similarity (such as tempo, rhythm, and the like) or in terms of their nonmusical similarity (described simply as on some basis other than how they sound).

Halpern analyzed her results using both KYST and ADDTREE. Her scaling solutions were difficult to interpret and yielded poor fits (though using a maximum dimensionality of three and stress formula two may have contributed to the poor fits she obtained). In any event, the ADDTREE solutions for nonmusical similarity were readily interpretable and accounted for a high proportion (.92) of variance. A number of distinctive clusters emerged. For example, all of the Christmas songs clustered together in the nonmusical solution and these songs were further distinguished into groups of solemn Christmas songs (such as The First Noel) and children's Christmas songs (such as Rudolf the Red-Nosed Reindeer). The musical solution produced neither as satisfactory a fit (.71 of the variance) nor as interpretable a solution. However, some interesting results occurred. The two groups of Christmas songs were no longer classified together; solemn Christmas songs were grouped with patriotic ones (such as God Bless America) while children's Christmas songs were classified with other children's songs (such as Happy Birthday). However, many songs retained similar positions in the tree structure across the two instructions. Although one might argue that this result is an artifact of the experimental procedure in which each subject performed both sets of ratings, it seems more likely to us that songs that are related by topic may simply be inherently more similar musically than pairs of songs not so related. For example, Beatle songs are similar to each other on the basis that they were all recorded by the same artists, yet they are also similar musically.

Halpern (1984) went on to demonstrate that the distance in the tree structure was able to predict performance quite well in two cognitive tasks. In one task, she presented subjects with a song title and the music of a song and asked them to verify that the presented title was correct for the song. When title and song mismatched, she found that the discrimination was more error prone when the two songs were near each other in the tree diagram. In a free recall task, she found that adjacent songs were more likely to be recalled together than songs that were far apart. Halpern's results are consistent with the idea that familiar songs are organized in memory by conceptual (nonmusical) characteristics.

In many respects, music perception is ideally suited to MDS analysis. The research is currently at a stage where it is important to learn how the psychological representation differs from a representation that merely mirrors physical characteristics. In contrast to the research on semantic memory, for example, we really do not have any theories of music perception. Instead, we are searching for constraints on such a theory and MDS analysis has provided us with a number of them. They range from the perception of tones in various contexts to the perception of passages in a piece of classical music to the organization of familiar songs. We have now perhaps reached the point where cognitive psychologists are ready to develop a theory of how people make these judgments of similarity.

MEASUREMENT OF CHANGE IN STRUCTURE

Some of the most impressive applications of MDS analyses have been in demonstrating a change in structure. This change can be the result of a change in conditions, context, or age. By the examination of a set of stimuli in various circumstances, it may also be possible to extract higher dimensionality from the materials in question. At a minimum, it provides good evidence for change.

Perhaps the most obvious place to look for an application of MDS that demonstrates a change in structure is in the area of cognitive development. Several investigators in this area have attempted to show that younger children organize stimuli along perceptual dimensions while older children employ more abstract dimensions. One study that illustrates this point very nicely was performed by Howard and Howard (1977). They selected 10 animal names from Henley's (1969) original set and had their similarity judged by children of varying ages. The subjects were first-graders, third-graders, sixth-graders, and college students. Using Carroll and Chang's (1970) INDSCAL, they obtained a three-dimensional solution in which the three dimensions were size, domesticity, and predativity. Although these last two are usually thought of as equivalent, Howard and Howard make a good case that these dimensions are distinguishable. For the predativity dimension, lion and bear are at one extreme and mouse, rabbit, and deer are at the other. For the domesticity dimension, all five objects are on one side of the dimension, with horse, cow, sheep, pig, and dog at the other.

Howard and Howard (1977) looked for a change in structure by examining the weight assigned to each dimension in the subject space. When they averaged over subjects in each age group, they found that younger children emphasized the perceptual dimension: size. Older children in contrast, emphasized the more abstract dimensions of domesticity and predativity. Sixth-graders, for example, placed equal weight on the size and predativity dimensions and less weight on the domesticity dimension. Younger children placed greater weight on the size dimensions, while college students placed less weight on the size dimension. Thus, it does seem that increasing age leads to increasing reliance on more abstract dimensions, at least with these stimuli.

Miller and Gelman (1983) have recently demonstrated a similar point with a more complicated analysis. They investigated the concept of number in children using techniques developed by Arabie, Kosslyn, and Nelson (1975). Miller and Gelman (1983) obtained similarity judgments for the digits 0 to 9 from groups of kindergartners, third-graders, sixth-graders, and graduate students. They used a modification of the method of triads in which subjects determined which of two digits was more similar to a third. In order to reduce drastically the number of judgments required of very young children, Miller and Gelman used a balanced incomplete sampling procedure developed by Arabie et al. (1975).

Miller and Gelman (1983) obtained two-dimensional solutions for each of the four groups. For the younger children, the solution resembled a semicircle in which the digits were ordered by magnitude. For sixth-graders and adults, there is clearly an odd-even dimension in addition to one based on magnitude. For adults, moreover, a paradoxical finding is that the powers of two (2, 4, and 8) are closer together than they should be in terms of magnitude; the digits 2 and 8 are actually closer than the digits 2 and 7, for example.

Although the results of the MDS analysis were certainly enlightening, Miller and Gelman's most interesting results were observed in their clustering analysis. Using INDCLUS, they obtained seven clusters. Five of them pertained to counting, and the other two were the odd numbers excluding 1 (3, 5, 7, 9) and the powers of two (2, 4, 8). For the children in the two youngest groups, the five counting clusters were all assigned higher weights than these last two clusters. For the adults, however, the powers of two was the cluster with the highest weight, and the odd numbers excluding one was the fourth highest. Sixth-graders were between these two extremes.

The results of the INDCLUS analysis nicely complement the results from the MDS analyses in that both show increasing complexity as a function of age. There is a clear developmental trend away from counting as the sole dimension in digits and toward dimensions that reflect more complex relationships among the digits (such as the powers of two). Methodologically, it is interesting to note that the clustering analysis performed by Miller and Gelman (1983) parallels the scaling analysis done by Howard and Howard (1977). Both sets of authors used a single result, a set of seven clusters for Miller and Gelman, and a three-dimensional solution for Howard and Howard, and then examined the change in weights as a function of age. Both observed that more complex dimensions or clusters tended to be weighted more heavily by older children and adults accompanied by a corresponding decrease in the weighting for more primitive dimensions or clusters. We might also note that the Miller and Gelman (1983) paper is particularly convincing in this respect because these authors also obtained MDS representations for each group of subjects and the analyses of these solutions were highly consistent with this interpretation.

One other unusual application to assess a change in structure has been performed by Schoenfeld and Herrmann (1982). They investigated the perception of the similarity of difficult word problems in mathematics. Earlier studies (e.g., Chi, Feltovich, & Glaser, 1981) had shown a strong, but indirect, relationship between expertise and problem perception, with novices tending to use surface features and experts using deep, structural features. This study examined whether a course in problem solving would lead to changes in problem perception. Each problem was characterized by both a deep structure representation (referring to the principles necessary for solution, such as uniqueness arguments to be proved by contradiction, DeMorgan's Law, or linear dophantine equation) and a surface structure (referring to the salient mathematical objects involved or the subject area, such as polynomials, subset sums, or limits). Schoenfeld and Herrmann asked groups of subjects to sort the problems and then looked at the strongly clustered problems to see whether these problems were more alike in surface structure or in deep structure. Using Johnson's (1967) HICLUS program, they defined strongly clustered pairs as those whose proximity value exceeded .5. The subjects were freshman and sophomores who had completed 1 to 3 semesters of college mathematics. One group subsequently enrolled in a problem solving course and the other group instead enrolled in a computer programming course. The sortings of the two groups did not differ initially. Subsequent to these courses, the same problems were sorted again.

The results were quite striking. Prior to course enrollment, most of the strongly associated clusters (67%) were accounted for by surface similarity. Approximately 11% of the clusters matched the deep structure characterization and approximately 22% matched neither. For the group that took the computer programming course, the percentage changed very little; 64% of the clusters were still similar on the basis of the surface structure (with a deep structure percentage of 9). For the group that took the problem solving course, however, the results changed markedly. Now, 55% of the clusters matched the deep structure characterization, while only 9% matched the surface structure characterization. As a further control, Schoenfeld and Herrmann had these problems sorted by a group of mathematics professors. For these experts, 67% of their strongly clustered pairs were similar in terms of deep structure and 25% were similar in terms of surface structure.

Thus, it seems that taking a course and increasing one's knowledge about a particular domain can have fairly radical effects on one's perception of problems in that domain. It would have been interesting if Schoenfeld and Herrmann had applied MDS techniques to their data and used an analysis similar to the one performed by Miller and Gelman. Even so, they have succeeded in showing a large change in structure in a complex domain.

CONTEXTUAL EFFECTS

One of the most important uses of MDS analysis in cognitive psychology is also one of the most underutilized. MDS analysis provides an excellent means to assess the effects of context. Examining stimuli in a number of contexts may have the corollary benefit of extracting more dimensions.

One straightforward application of this strategy was performed by LaPorte and Voss (1979) in which they presented subjects with a set of nouns taken from one or two simple stories. Initially, subjects rated the similarity of all possible pairs of nouns. For one story, the nouns were: *fields, clouds, vegetation, train, approach, decade, troops, plague, eggs,* and *food*. MDS analysis of this initial similarity matrix yielded a two-dimensional solution in which the first dimension separated man-made objects from natural ones, and the second dimension was interpreted by the authors as separating animals from nonanimals with eggs and food at one extreme and clouds and fields at the other.

Subsequent to this initial rating task, subjects read a story that described how grasshoppers become a pest every 10 years. These subjects then performed the same rating task as before. The first dimension recovered by the MDS analysis was the same as before and reflected the distinction between natural and man-made objects. The second dimension, however, was radically different and reflected the temporal ordering of the objects as they occurred in the story.

Bisanz, LaPorte, Vesonder, and Voss (1978) developed a more extensive framework for studying the effects of prose context. Like LaPorte and Voss (1979), Bisanz et al. were able to demonstrate an effect of context by comparing representations. However, they were also able to recover the thematic structure of the prose context. Finally, and perhaps most importantly, Bisanz et al. were able to show that the recovered representation could also predict memory performance.

Bisanz et al. (1978) presented subjects with pairs of animal names either before or after reading a short story that contained each of these names. When subjects judged the similarity of these animals before reading the story, the resulting MDS solution was very similar to the one obtained by Rips et al. (1973); the two dimensions could be characterized in terms of size and ferocity. Subjects then read a story in which all of the animals were portrayed in terms of their leadership and their helpfulness. Subsequently, they were asked to judge the similarity of the animals in terms of their relationship as expressed in the story. Both themes were recovered as dimensions in the MDS analysis, although, interestingly, these themes were not recovered equally well.

Bisanz et al. (1978) also used this poststory MDS solution to predict performance in a memory task. They presented subjects with pairs of animal names and asked subjects to decide if they were both helpful or both not helpful. At least for affirmative responses, it was clear that the distance between the two animals in the multidimensional space predicted the latencies fairly well. Pairs that were close to each other were responded to more rapidly than pairs that were far apart.

Although Bisanz et al. found a relationship between distance and latency, it might have been possible to obtain greater predictability in their task. The only distance that they examined was the distance between the two stimuli in the pair. It is a reasonable hypothesis to suggest that the distance between each of the items and the point for helpful might influence decision time for affirmative responses. Further, these distances might be even more important for negative responses. Let us assume that lion is helpful and tiger is not. If one also assumes that lion is processed first, then a straightforward processing model suggests that the lion-helpful distance is related to the speed with which one can determine that a lion is a helpful animal. The question then becomes whether or not tigers are helpful. Here, the distance between tiger and helpful is the critical determinant. Because the correct answer is negative, we expect that short distances will make it more difficult to conclude that tigers are not helpful. Thus, small distances are inhibitory and large distances facilitative for negative decisions.

Obviously, this analysis is purely speculative. However, it does explain why Bisanz et al. (1978) obtained better predictability with affirmative responses. Additionally, using a categorization task, Shoben (1976) found that the distance between the exemplars and the appropriate superordinate was always a better predictor than the distance between the two exemplars in a same-different task. It is our contention that similar research could profit from this kind of MDS analysis as it leads to a fairly direct comparison of several alternative processing accounts.

CONTEXT AND INCREASED DIMENSIONALITY

Using several contexts can increase the dimensionality of the solution recovered by MDS. Although increased dimensionality is quite properly not the principal goal in investigating the effects of context, the ability to recover additional dimensions is a byproduct that should not be ignored. Although there is not a hard and fast rule that increasing the number of contexts will increase the number of recoverable dimensions, it is at least suggestive that Howard and Howard (1977) were able to extract three dimensions from their INDSCAL solution (using four contexts) of 10 animal names whereas Rips et al. (1973) could extract only two dimensions from their INDSCAL solution even though they employed 14 animal names.

The most striking example of the higher dimensionality arising from increasing the number of contexts is a study by Soli and Arabie (1979) of consonant phonemes. They used the classic Miller and Nicely (1955) data which Soli and Arabie (1979) transformed to conform better to the INDSCAL model (see Arabie & Soli, 1982, for the justification and details of this procedure). In contrast to earlier analyses of the Miller-Nicely data using scaling techniques, Soli and Arabie (1979) used the full set of confusion matrices, including those where the judgments were made under severe levels of distortion.

Soli and Arabie (1979) obtained a four-dimensional solution that accounted for 69% of the variance. Their first dimension ordered the consonants in terms of periodicity/burst with m/ and n/ at one end of the dimension and p/, t/, k/, f/, and s/ at the other. The second dimension ordered the stimuli in terms of first formants and thus separated the voiced consonants from the voiceless ones. The third dimension similarly ordered the consonants in terms of their second formants. Finally, the fourth dimension ordered the stimuli in terms of spectral dispersion, with two groups of fricatives separated from the other phonemes. This fourth dimension is largely relevant to a particular listening condition.

Soli and Arabie (1979) showed that the salience of a particular dimension varied greatly with the listening condition. In general, increasing levels of degradation increased the reliance on the periodicity/burst and first formant dimensions and decreased the contribution of the second formant and spectral dispersion dimensions. Thus, Soli and Arabie were able to extract additional information out of an old and very well-analyzed data set. By making the data conform more closely to the INDSCAL model, they were able to extract more justifiable dimensions from these data than any prior researchers had been able to do. More importantly, this higher dimensionality enabled them to make some arguments concerning the relative importance of acoustic as opposed to phonemic properties in the underlying representation. From these examples, it appears that MDS can be a very powerful tool in assessing contextual change. In many respects, it is unfortunate that researchers in cognitive psychology have not taken greater advantage of this opportunity. Particularly given the trend in the past decade away from the view that concepts have invariant meanings and toward the view that meanings are flexible, it would seem that these procedures could be put to good use. For example, one of us has been involved in research on context effects in semantic memory. Roth and Shoben (1983) argued that context determined the goodness-of-example of an exemplar for any category. They found that robin was a typical exemplar of the bird category in many contexts, but that it was a poor example in contexts such as "The bird walked across the farmyard" or "The hunter fired too quickly and the bird flew off." Roth and Shoben (1983) even discussed this change in goodness-of-example in terms of a spatial metaphor in which the stimulus space must be completely restructured and not simply refocused. The addition of the different spatial representations would certainly have added weight to Roth and Shoben's argument. If, for example, the solutions obtained for the bird exemplars from MDS analyses were quite different depending on whether the ratings were performed in the context of "The bird sat on a telephone wire" or "John removed the bird from the oven," then one would have very good evidence for the restructuring hypothesis.

Similarly, Cech and Shoben (1985) have argued that linear order judgments in which subjects must determine which of two objects is greater (or lesser) in magnitude are also subject to rather strong contextual effects. They investigated the way in which subjects determined which of two animals was larger or smaller. In a normal context in which the animals varied in size from *flea* to *elephant*, they observed the normal congruity effect (Banks, 1977). For small animals, it was easier to determine the smaller of the pair; for large animals, it was easier to determine the larger of the pair. Cech and Shoben (1985) found that it took less time for subjects to determine the smaller of *rabbit-beaver* than to determine the larger of *rabbit-beaver*. They also found that it was easier to determine the larger of *sheep-crocodile* than the smaller of *sheep-crocodile*.

However, when *rabbit* and *beaver* were the largest items in the study, Cech and Shoben observed that they behaved like large animals; in this context, it was easier to determine the *larger* of *rabbit-beaver* than the smaller of *rabbit-beaver*. A parallel result was obtained for large items.

Although Cech and Shoben employed a number of other contexts to strengthen their contention that memorial size was not invariant, it seems that MDS analysis might also have profitably been applied here as well. According to the claims of Cech and Shoben (1985), animals that are small should behave as large animals in certain contexts. If this claim is correct, then one should be able to compare the MDS solutions from the two different contexts and see a size dimension in both cases. However, if we are comparing only small animals in the restricted context condition, we should find at least some of these small animals on the large side of the neutral point of the dimension. The size dimension for the normal context condition should divide the animals into those that are generally thought of as large and small. Such a result would strengthen Cech and Shoben's more theoretical claim that people recode sizes in order to be able to use the full range of the magnitude scale.

It thus appears that MDS can be very helpful in understanding the effects of context. It can tell us how dimensional weights change as a function of context or age (Bisanz et al., 1978; Miller & Gelman, 1983) and it can also provide us with increased dimensionality in some cases (Howard & Howard, 1977; Soli & Arabie, 1979). We have also argued in the immediately preceding paragraphs that MDS analysis can be used to provide confirmation of many theoretical claims in cognitive psychology.

MDS AND THE UNDERLYING REPRESENTATION

In our discussion of applications of MDS, we have obviously used the term quite broadly. We have included not only two-way and three-way MDS, but also discrete, clustering algorithms such as MAPCLUS. It is a natural question to ask which of these models provides a best fit to data from cognitive experiments.

Although the question may arise naturally, the answer does not. Even if the statistics concerning the goodness-of-fit are nominally identical, it is seldom the case that one can simply compare the numbers and determine which model fits better because the number of parameters is invariably different. In many respects, the advice to be given is similar in spirit to Shepard's counsel on dimensionality: use the one that fits the data the best.

One approach to this problem is theoretically based. If one has a theory that is inherently spatial, then it makes sense to test the viability of the theory by ascertaining whether MDS analysis will provide a satisfactory account. Friendly (1977) has followed this procedure for recall data. A similar approach has been performed by Reitman and Reuter (1980). Although their technique is only peripherally related to MDS, they used their theoretical notions to identify chunks in free recall, which they then converted into a lattice and finally into an ordered tree. Hirtle (1982) has recently extended this line of work.

Perhaps the most ambitious attempt to compare theories directly is the work by Pruzansky, Tversky, and Carroll (1982). They compared the fit of a simple additive tree, as exemplified by Sattath and Tversky's (1979) ADDTREE to MDS as exemplified by KYST. They first demonstrated that each of these algorithms provided a better fit to artificial data when the underlying representation was consistent with the assumptions of the program. Specifically, when the artificial data was generated from a tree, ADDTREE provided a better fit; when the artificial data were generated from a plane, KYST gave a better fit to the data. This relationship held up over many levels of noise in the data and over wide variations in number of stimuli. Thus it seems that there is no uniform advantage of one procedure over the other.

Pruzansky et al. (1982) found two empirical measures that predicted which of the two models would provide a better fit to data (as measured either by product moment correlations or by stress formula 2). The first was skewness, defined in the standard way as the third central moment divided by the cubed standard deviation. The second measure was elongation. Pruzansky et al. defined elongation in terms of triples of nodes. From the nature of binary rooted trees, they observed that it is usually the case that for any triple of nodes, two will form a subcluster. For a triple that includes i, j, and k, assume that i and j form the subcluster. If we look at the triangle formed by connecting these three points, then it is expected that $\Phi_{ij} \leq \Phi_{jk} \leq \Phi_{ik}$. It would similarly be expected that the differences of the distances would have the relationship $\Phi_{ik} - \Phi_{jk} \leq \Phi_{jk} - \Phi_{ij}$. Phrased geometrically, the middle side is closer in length to the long side than it is to the short side. Pruzansky et al. defined elongation as the proportion of triangles in the data where this relationship holds.

Looking at real data, Pruzansky et al. (1982) computed these two measures for 20 data sets. In general, when the elongation measure was high and skewness was low, ADDTREE provided a better fit than did KYST. More explicitly when the elongation measure was .65 or higher and when the skewness was less than $-.4$, ADDTREE provided a better fit; otherwise KYST did. Interestingly, these two measures never conflicted for the data sets that Pruzansky et al. examined and the two measures tended to be negatively correlated.

An important result of this analysis is that data sets whose stimuli could be described as perceptual (colors, forms, and letters) were better fit by KYST, but data sets whose stimuli could be described as conceptual (such as exemplars from semantic categories) were better fit by ADDTREE. Although Pruzansky et al. noted that factorial designs tended to favor KYST and that such designs tended to be employed when perceptual stimuli were investigated, these authors offered no other explanation of this result.

Although there is no doubt that Pruzansky et al.'s (1982) finding is suggestive, we believe that there is reason for caution before concluding that conceptual stimuli are invariably fit better by ADDTREE than by KYST. As we discuss in the next section, there are good reasons to suspect that MDS algorithms have difficulty when category names and exemplars must be represented in the same space. Thus, one difficulty may lie in the particular stimulus sets employed by Pruzansky et al. (1982). Although most of them are unpublished, we have sufficient familiarity with eight of them to offer some speculation. The first seven data sets (referenced by Pruzansky et al as the Mervis et al data sets) consisted of 19 exemplars and one category name. The eighth data set (Henley, 1969) consisted of 30 exemplars and no category name. For the first seven data sets, the superiority of ADDTREE as determined by both of Pruzansky et al.'s (1982) measures of goodness of fit averaged .15 for r^2_L and .07 for r^2_M. The superiority of ADDTREE for the eighth data set was about half these means, .08 and .03 respectively. Only one of the first seven data sets had smaller differences (in the goodness-of-fit measures) than did Henley's data set.

PROBLEMS WITH CATEGORIES

The difficulty that MDS has with categorical data sets may be a result of the way people judge similarities in this context and not an indication of the nature of the underlying representation. We would like to suggest (following Shoben, 1983) that the peculiarities of the similarity judgments may create problems for scaling algorithms and that these problems may have led Pruzansky et al. (1982) to find poorer fits with KYST than with ADDTREE for these types of data sets.

As others have found, Shoben (1976) noted that all members of a category tended to be rated as highly similar to their category name. For example, even an atypical bird such as *goose* was judged to be quite similar to *bird*. In fact, the similarity of these two terms was about as great as the similarity between two very similar exemplars, such as *hawk* and *eagle*. The problem for scaling algorithms arises when one considers that both *robin* and *goose* are highly similar to *bird,* but *robin* and *goose* are quite dissimilar to each other. In an MDS solution, *robin* and *goose* should be quite distant from each other because of their direct similarity rating. However, because of the proximity of each to *bird,* they should be quite close to each other. Put more generally, the distances between exemplars often conflict with the distances between each exemplar and the superordinate. This type of conflict is not present if superordinate terms are not among the test stimuli. Therefore, it is possible that the reason that Henley's (1969) data were fit relatively well by KYST in the study by Pruzansky et al. is that her data did not contain superordinate terms.

Some very recent work by Tversky and Hutchinson (1986) has formalized this generalization. They noted that the situation in which many exemplars are most similar to the superordinate is an example of the Voronoi problem (e.g., Newman, Rinott, & Tversky, 1983) in which only a small number of points in a space can be the nearest neighbor of a particular point. In terms of the spatial representation (using Euclidean distance) of categories, the superordinate can have only five exemplars (in a two-dimensional solution; 11 in a three-dimensional solution) for which it is the nearest neighbor. As their Table 3 indicates, this constraint is violated in many cases in which exemplars are scaled with their superordinates.

One obvious solution to this problem is to omit the superordinate. If one is interested primarily in the relationships among exemplars, then this solution can provide a distinct improvement. As measured by Tversky and Hutchinson, removing the superordinate greatly reduced the nearest neighbor problems in the data (as measured by their statistics of centrality and reciprocity) and subsequent scaling usually showed a decrease in stress when the superordinate term was removed.

It is not clear how one can circumvent the problem of superordinate terms when the relationship between the exemplar and category name is important. In some sense the difficulty for algorithms such as KYST's is to fit the distance between exemplars and the distance between exemplars and the superordinate category name (typicality) at the same time. One possibility is to try to fit these two types of distances separately; another approach is simply to decide that one set of distances is less important than another. We discuss each of these issues in turn.

Krumhansl (1983) attempted to measure the typicality of exemplars (in this case, musical tones) separately. She argued that the similarity of two terms is a function not only of the distance between two objects, but also of the distance between each object and the superordinate. In the absence of explicit context, the stimuli are structured in a chroma circle, as we noted earlier. However, when she varied the context (in terms of which scale was used) she showed that not only did the notes vary in their proximity to the superordinate (vertical structure); they also varied in terms of their relationship to each other (horizontal structure).

Although this structure is certainly an elegant one, it is not clear how general it might be. For musical tones, it appears that context refocuses the horizontal structure; it does not require a radical restructuring. For semantic categories, if we are to take the conclusions of Roth and Shoben (1983) at face value, radical restructuring is at least a possibility, and thus this method developed by Krumhansl (1983) might not be applicable in such circumstances.

An alternative approach is simply to decide that one set of distances is less important than another. For example, Shoben (1976) used MDS analysis to derive distances which he then used to predict RT in a categorization task. To perform the necessary regressions, the distances he needed were the exemplar-superordinate distances. In the initial MDS solution, an examination of the Shepard diagram indicated that the greatest disparity between the fitted distances and the original data occurred with superordinates. Because these distances were precisely the ones that Shoben wanted to use in subsequent analyses, he rescaled the original using the weights option in KYST. This little-known feature of KYST allows the user to specify weights for various similarities. In this particular case, Shoben (1976) weighted the exemplar-superordinate similarities very heavily in order to ensure that the disparity between the original data and the fitted distances would be minimal for these pairs. For his task, the manipulation was highly successful in that these exemplar-superordinate distances predicted RT very well.

SELECTING A REPRESENTATION

There are no hard and fast rules for selecting a single underlying representation. Shepard (1980), among others, has argued that the interpretability of the solution is one important criterion. Clearly, the plausibility of the underlying representation is not enhanced if the solution is not interpretable. However, this criterion is far from objective. We have discussed several solutions based on Henley's (1969) animal data that are readily interpretable. Yet, Sattath and Tversky (1979) have argued that their ADDTREE solution of these data is more interpretable than the ones obtained by MDS.

Moreover, there are often theoretical reasons for preferring one solution to another. Krumhansl (1983), as noted earlier, had excellent theoretical reasons for analyzing her data on musical tones in a particular way. Because she wanted to examine the similarity of the tones to each other and the typicality of each tone with respect to a particular scale separately, her choice of the underlying representation was severely limited. Moreover, there may also be other data that constrain what is the ideal representation.

Thus, the criteria established by Pruzansky et al. (1982) should not be taken too literally. Although their generalization that conceptual data are fit better by an additive tree whereas perceptual data are better represented by a plane is a provocative conclusion, one should not rule out an entire class of models because of this conclusion. Besides the additional criteria of interpretability and other constraints on the representation, there may be peculiarities of particular data sets (such as categories) that may have led to artificially poor fits.

Finally, it should be pointed out that subtle changes in method may make a tremendous difference in the results. The best example of this phenomenon is the reanalysis of the Miller-Nicely data by Soli and Arabie (1979). According to the Pruzansky et al. (1982) classification, both INDSCAL and MDSCAL assume that the underlying representation is a plane, yet Soli and Arabie used the former method and were able to recover four, highly interpretable, dimensions while Shepard used the latter and recovered only two. It thus seems premature to specify any clear set of rules for determining the best underlying representation for any set of data.

MINKOWSKI r METRICS

Most applications of MDS and related procedures in cognitive psychology have assumed that the psychological distances recovered are Euclidean. However, there is good reason to suspect that there are many circumstances where some other, theoretically interesting, metric might provide a better fit to the data. Moreover, the selection of the Euclidean metric also has psychological implications for our conception of the stimuli. More specifically, it has been argued by Shepard (1964) and by Garner (1972) that if the stimuli are best represented in a Euclidean space, then the stimuli are wholistic or integral, rather than analyzable or separable. Unfortunately, many have assumed that their stimuli were integral without a thorough exploration of other possibilities.

In the most general sense, the equation for distance is given in Equation 2. We can restrict our attention to the Minkowski family of metrics when $r \geq 1$.

$$d_{ij} = [\Sigma_k |x_{ik} - x_{jk}|^r]^{1/r} \tag{2}$$

In the case where r is 2, then we have the familiar Euclidean case; the distance between two points is the square root of the sum of the squared differences along all the relevant dimensions.

However, in addition to the Euclidean metric, there are at least two other metrics that are theoretically interesting. The first of these is the city-block metric, so named because distance is computed in the manner in which one measures distance in a city that is laid out in a grid pattern. For example, to go from 42nd Street and 10th Avenue to 32nd street and 6th Avenue in New York is a distance of 14 blocks. One cannot travel along the hypotenuse of the triangle. In terms of dimensions, the distance between the two locations is the sum of their differences on the two dimensions: north-south distance and east-west distance. In terms of Equation 2, city-block metric is obtained when $r = 1$. This metric is particularly interesting to psychologists because it (according to Garner [1972] and Shepard [1964]) indicates that the stimuli are separable rather than integral.

The other theoretically interesting metric is the dominance metric, when r approaches infinity. In this case, the distance between two objects reduces to the maximum distance between them on any dimension. Thus, for example, two objects that differ from each other by a moderate amount on each of three dimensions are closer to each other than another pair of objects that differ only slightly on two dimensions, but differ greatly on a third dimension. Although there have been few applications of this metric in psychology, Arnold (1971) found this metric fit his set of heterogeneous semantic terms better than did either the city-block or Euclidean metrics. Moreover, he argued that the dominance metric was psychologically more plausible than the Euclidean metric.

Although these two non-Euclidean metrics are inherently interesting, there are understandable reasons why they have not received greater attention in applications of MDS in cognitive psychology. The first reason is that numerical problems are much more likely to be encountered with city-block or dominance metrics. When working with Euclidean distances, one can begin with a rational configuration or use some small number of random initial configurations and be reasonably confident that the solution is a minimum. Such a procedure will seldom produce optimal results for non-Euclidean metrics. It appears that local minimum problems are much more severe, and that vastly greater numbers of random initial configurations must be used (Arabie, 1973) when r is other than 2.

Fortunately, Arnold (1971) has devised a method to circumvent most of these problems. As it can be both time consuming and expensive to run large numbers of random initial configurations, Arnold proposed a successive approximation procedure that is neither time consuming nor expensive. One begins by obtaining the best solution when $r = 2$. Approaching city-block metric, one then uses the final configuration for $r = 2$ as the starting configuration for $r = 1.5$. Subsequently, the solution with this metric is used as the starting configuration for $r = 1.25$, and so on. One approaches the dominance metric (with r usually set to 32) is a similar way; one uses the best solution in Euclidean space as the starting configuration for $r = 2.5$, and so on.

When Arnold (1971) employed this procedure on his data, he obtained some striking findings. First, he found that stress declined monotonically as r moved from 2 to 1; it also declined monotonically as r moved from 2 to 32. Second, the solution with the lowest stress was the one employing the dominance metric. To our knowledge, this report is the only application of MDS methods to cognitive psychology that has found evidence for the psychological use of the dominance metric.

As we noted earlier, the question of the appropriate metric is an exceedingly important one from the perspective of cognitive psychology. How the dimensions are processed is nearly as important as what the dimensions are. Models, for example, that assume that pairs of words in a same-different task are compared on all dimensions do not seem terribly plausible if the underlying metric is the dominance metric. Arnold's procedure is seldom cited, but it holds the potential to surmount a formidable obstacle. Cognitive psychologists would do well to become familiar with these methods. There is one important limitation to Arnold's procedure. For some unknown reason, it does not appear to work very well with two-dimensional solutions (Carroll & Arabie, 1980).

MDS AND MEMORY THEORIES

In this chapter, we have discussed a number of different scaling techniques and provided some suggestions for their optimal use to study issues in cognitive psychology. In this section, we illustrate these techniques and suggestions by examining a particular problem. We considered using some well-known data set or gathering some new data on a very specific issue, but we felt that such a specialized topic might be of interest to only a limited group of readers. For broader appeal, we elected to collect and analyze data on a topic that is not usually studied by cognitive psychologists: What is the conceptual organization that cognitive psychologists have of prominent memory theories? Although we hope to learn something about the organization of the field, our main purpose is to allow an illustration of techniques in an interesting context.

Some earlier research has been aimed at analyzing the organization that psychologists have of their field. Coan (1968), by a combination of factor analysis and clustering techniques, examined how basic trends in psychology (e.g., objectivism) have changed historically and how they have been related over time. Fuchs and Kawash (1974; Kawash & Fuchs, 1974) used ratings and then factor analysis to describe six basic schools of psychology (e.g., behaviorism) and summarize their differences. As part of a project examining the learning of the structure of cognitive psychology, Friendly (1981) scaled student and faculty views of the field.

In the present case, two small groups of cognitive psychologists were asked to rate the pairwise similarities of 12 memory theories. (The two groups enabled us to analyze individual differences between groups as well as within groups, to illustrate another use of these scaling techniques.) These 12 theories were chosen from a larger list with the requirements that they be familiar to the subjects, that they not be intimately related to each other, and that they be partially concerned with memory for episodic information. The theories are listed in Table 7.1, with short descriptions and bracketed abbreviations to be used for brevity. Each subject received a random order of all 66 possible pairs of theories and rated them on a scale of 1 (very different) to 9 (very similar). One group consisted of four advanced graduate students at Stanford University and one visiting professor. These ratings were obtained in 1981. The other group consisted of five faculty or visiting faculty at the University of Illinois in 1985. Four of these faculty members have their doctoral degrees from midwestern universities.

There are two basic questions of interest. First, what is the underlying representation of memory theories for these researchers? Second, do the two groups differ?

Before presenting the results, let us go over the form of the data to be analyzed. For each of these ten subjects, we have a lower half matrix (without diagonals) for the pairwise similarities of these 12 theories. In addition, for each group, we have the sum of the five individual matrices for that group, as well as the total matrix of all ten subjects. We analyzed our data first using MDS techniques and then using the more recent clustering techniques.

MDS Analysis.   The most satisfactory answers to the two basic questions we raised earlier are obtained by performing a SINDSCAL analysis, where the two groups are used instead of individual subjects. The two dimensional solution from this scaling is given in Fig. 7.1, accounting for .728 of the variance. Although SINDSCAL does have the advantage of allowing the recovery of higher dimensionality, our third dimension was difficult to interpret. Moreover, the increase in variance accounted for was small: the proportion increased .032 to .760. Our interpretation of Fig. 7.1 is that the X-axis corresponds to the unit of material being analyzed, while the Y-axis corresponds to the degree of formalism or rigor. First, let us consider the abscissa. The two theories furthest to the left are the SCHEMA and MOPS models, followed closely by LNR, KINTSCH, then HAM. The first two theories deal with large units of analysis; groups of scenes, stories, or episodes. LNR and KINTSCH usually apply to slightly smaller units, such as small groups of sentences. HAM also is concerned with small groups of sentences, but much of the well-known work has involved one or a few sentences. The other seven theories usually deal with smaller units, such as sentence fragments or paired-associates. TULVNG and LEVELS often deal with slightly larger units than the other five, but the exact ordering expected by this interpretation for the other theories is unclear.

Second, let us consider the ordinate. The two theories highest on this dimension, RATCLIFF and VECTOR have strong mathematical formulations, as does the distant third theory, SAM. The next two theories, HAM and LNR, have strong computer formulations. The four theories around the origin, although not as strongly formalized, have strong and well-defined structure and processing assumptions. The three theories lowest on this dimension are espoused by psychologists who have concentrated on developing general principles, rather than on developing formal models. Of these three, TULVING has certainly been the most rigorous.

Given this interpretation, we may next ask whether our two groups of subjects differed in their weightings of the dimensions. In fact the two groups weighted both dimensions very similarly (.60 and .63, for the X-axis, and .58 and .55 for the Y-axis). Hence, from this analysis, there appears to be little difference between the two groups. Because the two groups were so similar, SINDSCAL was applied to the ten individual matrices. The object space is similar enough to Fig. 7.1 that it would serve no purpose to present it, but the subject space is presented in Fig. 7.2 for pedagogical purposes. As one can see, two of the subjects appear to weight particular dimensions, but overall the dimensions appear to be used by all subjects. Moreover, it is clear that subjects' group membership is not related to their assignment of weights to dimensions.

TABLE 7.1
Brief Description of Scaled Theories
(Bracketed Names are Used in Figures and Text)

1. James Anderson's (1973; Anderson et al., 1977) Associative Theories [VECTOR]

   Anderson's theory is a distributed memory model with vectors representing patterns of individual neurons. Associations between items are modeled by a reweighting of the synaptic weights between all cells. The model has been applied to various paradigms including item recognition and categorization.

2. HAM - John Anderson & Bower (1973) [HAM]

   In HAM, information is encoded as propositions in an associative network. Queries are answered by an activation search of the network. Most of the experimental work used sentences or small group of sentences as stimuli. Computer simulations and mathematical modeling were used to derive the predictions.

3. Atkinson & Shiffrin (1968) [A&S]

   This theory distinguishes between structure features of memory and control processes. The structural features include the sensory register, STM, and LTM and decay rules. The control processes regulate information flow between the stores. The rehearsal buffer model is a subpart of this theory. Experimental manipulations included all of the main verbal learning techniques.

4. Levels of Processing - Craik & Lockhart (1972) [LEVELS]

   Levels of processing was proposed as an alternative framework to two-store theories. Our memory for an object or event is viewed as a byproduct of the various processing performed upon it. The formulation of the framework rests largely upon common intuitions about the depth of processing required by different tasks.

5. Kintsch (1974) [KINTSCH]

   Kintsch's theory represents text as a list of atomic propositions. The organization of the test is captured by the overlap of propositional elements. His early experiments tested various reading time and memory predictions of his theory. His later work (e.g., Kintsch & Van Dijk, 1978) presents a mathematical model for comprehension and memory of texts.

6. ELINOR - Norman, Rumelhart, & LNR (1975) [LNR]

   Their model contains a network representation, but it emphasizes representations of procedures, called active structural networks. These structures have a case-like quality and use semantic primitives in order to represent relations between verbs. Analyses have been applied to a wide variety of tasks, but most analyses related to memory use a short set of materials.

7. Paivio's (1971) Dual Code Theory   [PAIVIO]

    Paivio argued that verbal and figural information have separate memory structures, which are independent but partially interconnected. Typical tests employ paired-associate learning and various memory measures for single words and pictures.

8. SAM - Raaijmakers & Shiffrin (1980, 1981)   [SAM]

    SAM is a theory of probabilistic search of associative networks with varying strengths of connections. The retrieval processes are modeled mathematically and have been applied to free recall, paired-associate recall, and recognition paradigms.

9. Ratcliff's (1978) Theory of Memory Retrieval   [RATCLIFF]

    Ratcliff's theory of retrieval uses a resonance metaphor. Probe items evoke, in parallel, evidence from related items, which is accumulated in random walk comparison processes. The mathematical model incorporates several response measures and has been applied to item recognition paradigms.

10. SCHEMA - Rumelhart & Ortony (1977)   [SCHEMA]

    "Schemata are data-structures for representing the generic concepts stored in memory. They exist for generalized concepts underlying objects, situations, events, sequences of events, actions, and sequences of actions," (p. 101) and are of primary importance in comprehension. Schemata have variables, can be embedded, and can vary in their level of abstraction and represent knowledge.

11. MOPS - Schank (1980)   [MOPS]

    Schank has proposed MOPS as a flexible version of scripts. MOPS are "memory organizations packets" that are used in understanding and storing the experiences that we have. They provide an organization of the relevant episodes. In addition to theoretical discussion, MOP-like structures have been used in computer simulations of event understanding.

12. Tulving (1972, 1975; Tulving & Thomson, 1973)   [TULVING]

    Tulving has an identifiable orientation towards memory that runs throughout his many publications. Some salient aspects of his orientation are the encoding specificity principle and the semantic-episodic distinction. Tulving generally strives to present general principles rather than formal models. Most of the experimental work used lists of words or paired-associates and measures, recognition, recall, or cued recall. (Most of the subjects were not familiar with the Flexser and Tulving [1978] paper in which a more formal account of recognition failures of recallable words is given.)

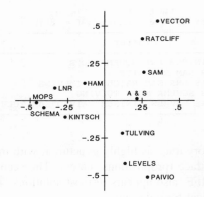

FIG. 7.1. SINDSCAL solution in two dimensions using the two group matrices.

Clustering. In addition to these scalings, a variety of MAPCLUS and IN-DCLUS solutions were generated. We focus on the groups and overall totals. As with the question of ideal number of dimensions, the procedure for choosing the ''correct'' number of clusters is not well-specified, but an examination of a large number of solutions between 3 and 8 clusters convinced us that 5 was the best solution. The variance accounted for increased quite a bit from using just 4 clusters, and did not increase much when we used 6 clusters. In addition, the interpretability of these solutions was good. When groups were used in the INDCLUS procedure, there was usually perfect agreement between the two groups on the order in which to weight the five clusters. However, different runs, with different random starts, seemed to provide quite different solutions. We found that the MAPCLUS solutions were more similar to each other. Because the groups showed only minor differences in their weights of the various clusters, we focus on the MAPCLUS solution. Table 7.2 contains a MAPCLUS solution that accounted for .813 of the variance. In considering each of these clusters, we will also provide information about the other solutions (generated with different initial configurations) to help interpretability. The most weighted cluster in this solution (HAM, KINTSCH, LNR, SCHEMA, MOPS), often emerged as the most heavily weighted cluster in a large number of MAPCLUS and INDCLUS solutions, even when the solutions used different numbers of clusters. These five theories have a number of similar characteristics. As mentioned earlier, they use the largest units of analysis. In addition, they are all symbol-processing models.

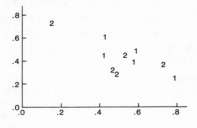

FIG. 7.2. Subject space from the two-dimensional SINDSCAL solution when all often individual subjects are used. Number indicates whether fro first or second group.

TABLE 7.2
MAPCLUS Solution for Five Clusters (VAF = .813)

	Weight	Cluster
(1)	.4447	HAM KINTSCH LNR SCHEMA MOPS
(2)	.4091	VECTOR SAM RATCLIFF
(3)	.2308	HAM A&S LNR SAM RATCLIFF TULVING
(4)	.2162	LEVELS SCHEMA MOPS TULVING
(5)	.1743	HAM A&S LEVELS KINTSCH PAIVIO SAM TULVING

That is, they all view the memory trace as highly structured, with the structure related to the meaning of the trace (propositions, cases). The second cluster, VECTOR, SAM, and RATCLIFF, also appears in most solutions. These three theories have strong mathematical formulations.

The third cluster in Fig. 7.3 varied with different solutions. While it usually contains HAM, A&S, SAM and RATCLIFF, three other theories (LNR, KINTSCH, and TULVING) are sometimes included and sometimes not. The interpretation of this cluster is difficult, because it depends on which of these theories is "really" in the cluster. In some ways, it appears to be excluding the extremes: of units (SCHEMA and MOPS), and of formality (VECTOR at one end, LEVELS and PAIVIO at the other).

The fourth cluster (LEVELS, SCHEMA, MOPS, TULVING) appears in most solutions, though it is not usually weighted very heavily. While the interpretation is arguable, they all appear to be popular theories that have clear general ideas, but rather vague specifics. That is, they all serve as types of frameworks.

The fifth cluster occurs in a large proportion of the solutions, though often it also contains LNR. It appears also to be including a middle portion of the theories, by excluding extremes of units (SCHEMA and MOPS) and formality (VECTOR and RATCLIFF).

Minkowski-metric. In the last section, we discussed the use of metrics other than the Euclidean metric ($r=2$) and claimed that a consideration of different processing possibilities through an examination of different metrics is an important and often neglected use of scaling. With the memory theories data, it is clear that these theories are richly represented in the minds of researchers, but it is not clear how even the major aspects' similarities and differences are used to arrive at a rating. To provide an example of Arnold's procedure, we fit the city-block ($r=1$) and dominance ($r=$infinity, approximated by 32) metrics by starting with the Euclidean configuration. As we mentioned earlier, this procedure works well, but appears to have trouble with two-dimensional solutions. However, our preferred solution was in two dimensions, so we have compared Arnold's procedure with 24 random starts in both metrics.

Let us first consider the dominance metric, in which the distance between two objects is the maximum distance on any dimension. As SINDSCAL (or its progenitor, INDSCAL) does not allow Minkowski metrics other than 2, we used

KYST for this analysis. We found a good KYST solution (similar to Fig. 7.1) and used it as a starting configuration for $r=3$, then used this solution as a starting configuration for $r=4$, then going to 8, 16, and 32. The stress (formula 1) declined from 2 to 16 and then stayed level to 32. (The stress values were .100, .092, .088, .083, .081, and .081 for r's of 2, 3, 4, 8, 16, and 32, respectively). The 24 random configurations used as starts for $r=32$ did not fare nearly as well as the stress of .081 found through Arnold's procedure. The smallest was .091, but only 4 were below .100, and 17 were above .200.

The dominance metric solution is given in Fig. 7.3. Although the purpose of this paper does not allow a lengthy discussion, a brief examination may be useful for understanding the insights gained through the use of other metrics. Overall, the solution is similar to the one in Fig. 7.1 (the SINDSCAL by groups with $r=2$). The Y-axis appears to be related to the formality of the theory. The X-axis is somewhat different from the earlier solution, but for reasons to be mentioned shortly, seems to be well interpreted as before as dealing with the unit of analysis. A second point to mention before discussing specifics, is that both axes are stretched relative to the earlier solution. The Y-axis in particular has a much greater range and appears to be the more important of the two dimensions.

In examining Fig. 7.3, the most striking result is how VECTOR is clearly set apart. With the Euclidean solution, the fact that VECTOR was viewed as different from all the other theories was taken care of by making it a little more extreme on both dimensions. With the dominance metric, we see that VECTOR is set apart on the formality dimension; in every pair involving VECTOR, this dimension has the greater distance. Given this placement, its location on the

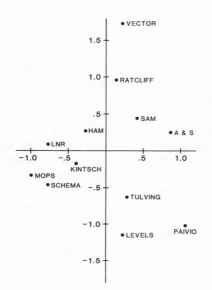

FIG. 7.3. Dominance metric two-dimensional solution using KYST.

other dimension is inconsequential. (In fact, it is likely that its X-coordinate is due to its similarity to RATCLIFF, which in turn is most similar to SAM then HAM, so may have needed to be intermediate.) This major determination by the Y-axis is true to a somewhat lesser extent of RATCLIFF and LEVELS (and to an even lesser extent to PAIVIO, which is extreme on both dimensions). We believe the heavy use of the Y-axis by these theories is what accounts for some of the differences on the X-axis with the earlier solution, as just mentioned for VEC-TOR. As another example, in order to satisfy all the pairwise constraints, the Fig. 7.1 solution has KINTSCH as less formal than SCHEMA or MOPS, when our feeling is that most of the subjects would view it as more formal. The solution of Fig. 7.3 does have KINTSCH as more formal than the other two theories, although it differs from these two theories more on level of unit than formality. We view this result as more satisfactory.

The results for the city-block metric, in which the distance between the two points is the sum of the distances along the dimensions, is not quite so straight-forward. Starting with a configuration from a Euclidean solution, we went to rs of 1.5, 1.25 and then 1.0 with corresponding stress values of .100, .091, .085, and .093. Although the stress with $r<2$ was slightly less than with $r=2$, this decrease was not monotonic. We tried this sequence several times and variations of it several more times and always found this non-monotonicity. A second problem occurred when considering the results from the 24 random starting configurations. Two of these solutions had stress of .071, although the solutions were uninterpretable to us. Of the other 22 solutions, none was below .10 and 18 were above .20. The solution for $r=1$ with stress of .093 is very similar to the $r=32$ solution given in Fig. 7.3. From a visual inspection, the only obvious difference is that TULVING is closer to A&S on both dimensions in the city-block solution.

Summary. As we stated when starting this section, although we hoped to provide some information about the organization of the theories, the principal goal was to illustrate the techniques. From a technical perspective, there are two often neglected procedures that we hope will be used more. First, an important use of these techniques may be to compare groups on their representations and weightings. While our groups showed few differences, we hope the reasoning and procedures were clear. Second, we suggested that the use of other metrics should be considered and we tried to show the additional information that they can provide. In terms of how cognitive psychologists (or a small group of them) view memory theories, two further points may be made. One, degree of for-mality and level of analysis unit appear to be important dimensions. Two, these features are correlated in that theories with high formality often involve mathe-matical treatments and small units, theories with intermediate formality often involve symbol-processing and large units, while theories of low formality are often concerned with characterizing general principles and use intermediate-sized units.

THE PROMISE AND LIMITATIONS OF MDS FOR
COGNITIVE PSYCHOLOGY

In its most straightforward applications, MDS analysis provides us with some ideas about the underlying structure of a domain. Most of the applications that are widely known are fairly simple domains, from a cognitive perspective, such as the Miller-Nicely data on consonant phonemes, or the color circle, or the more recent work on musical tones. However, we have also seen a tendency to deal with more complex phenomena such as semantic categories, prose passages, and musical passages as well. This extension to more complex domains suggests that we have not yet reached the limit where MDS and related procedures become useless. However, it does appear that MDS is able to recover dimensions only when the stimuli have something in common. Although such a point may seem obvious, it is worth mentioning explicitly that the scaling of heterogeneous stimuli is probably not going to be terribly informative. For example, Arnold (1971) scaled a set of unrelated words and recovered the dimensions of the semantic differential: evaluation, potency, and activation. We suspect that the reason these connotative aspects of meaning emerged as the dimensions is that there were no denotative dimensions on which one could order the widely vary-ing terms that Arnold investigated.

Although MDS and related procedure can clearly make an important contribu-tion to our understanding of a structure of a domain, it is less clear what these procedures can offer in terms of an understanding of the process. Strictly speak-ing, MDS tells us nothing about the way in which the stimuli of a domain are processed. In terms of semantic categories, for example, these procedures pro-vide no guidance on whether the concepts in a space are related because of connecting pathways in a semantic network or because of overlapping features. Thus, the kind of fundamental problem that is facing cognitive psychology and that we discussed at the outset of this chapter, is unlikely to be solved by a wider application of MDS. It is not clear to us, for example, how MDS could solve the debate over semantic memory models or the propositional-imagery debate generally.

Although the applicability of MDS to processing questions is far less than its applicability to structural questions, MDS can help, usually indirectly, with processing issues. Perhaps the best example of such assistance is the processing model developed by Rumelhart and Abrahamsen (1973). By invoking some additional assumptions (most notably Luce's choice axiom and an exponential transformation) they were able to come up with a sophisticated processing ac-count of analogical reasoning in a particular domain. Less dramatically, Shoben (1976) developed a processing account of the same-different task (as applied to categorization) that was derived from his multidimensional scaling of the stim-ulus items.

Perhaps the most general way in which to view MDS procedures in the context of cognitive psychology is in terms of constraint. In our introductory remarks, we mentioned the difficulty in distinguishing between dual-store and unitary accounts of the semantic/episodic dispute. The data, at present, seem not terribly constraining in that results that are interpreted as support for one position are quite readily reinterpreted as supporting the opposite view. In some respects, this outcome is a natural course of the progression of science. Its logical conclusion, however, is that we need as much constraint on the domain we are studying as we can possibly get. MDS and related procedures are clearly capable of providing constraint and they are therefore of considerable use to cognitive psychology.

ACKNOWLEDGMENT

Preparation of this chapter was supported in part by NSF Grants (BNS 82-17674 and IST 83-08670) to the authors. The authors would like to thank Phipps Arabie and Lawrence Jones for their helpful comments on an earlier draft of this chapter.

REFERENCES

Anderson, J. A. (1973). A theory for the recognition of items from short memorized lists. *Psychological Review, 80,* 417–438.

Anderson, J. A., Silvestein, J. W., Ritz, S. A., & Jones, R. S. (1977). Distinctive features, categorical perception, and probability learning: Some applications of a neural model. *Psychological Review, 84,* 413–451.

Anderson, J. R., & Bower, G. H. (1973). *Human associative memory.* Washington: Winston.

Anderson, J. R., & Ross, B. H. (1980). Evidence against a semantic-episodic distinction. *Journal of Experimental Psychology: Human Learning and Memory, 6,* 441–466.

Arabie, P. (1973). Concerning Monte Carlo evaluations of nonmetric multidimensional scaling algorithms. *Psychometrika, 38,* 607–608.

Arabie, P., & Carroll, J. D. (1980). MAPCLUS: A mathematical programming approach to fitting the ADCLUS model. *Psychometrika, 45,* 211–235.

Arabie, P., & Carroll, J. D. (1983). INDCLUS: An individual differences generalization of the ADCLUS model and the MAPCLUS algorithm. *Psychometrika, 48,* 157–169.

Arabie, P., Kosslyn, S. M., & Nelson, K. E. (1975). A multidimensional scaling study of visual memory of 5-year-olds and adults. *Journal of Experimental Child Psychology, 19,* 327–345.

Arabie, P., & Soli, S. D. (1982). The interface between the types of regression and methods of collecting proximity data. In R. G. Golledge & J. N. Rayner (Eds.), *Proximity and preference: Problems in the multidimensional analysis of large data sets.* Minneapolis: University of Minnesota Press.

Arnold, J. B. (1971). A multidimensional scaling study of semantic distance. *Journal of Experimental Psychology Monograph, 90,* 349–372.

Atkinson, R. C., & Shiffrin, R. M. (1968). Human memory: A proposed system and its control processes. In K. W. Spence & J. T. Spence (Eds.), *The psychology of learning and motivation: Advances in research and theory, Vol. 2.* New York: Academic Press.

Banks, W. P. (1977). Encoding and processing of symbolic information in comparative judgments. In G. H. Bower (Ed.), *The psychology of learning and motivation* (Vol. 11, pp. 101–159.) New York: Academic Press.

Bisanz, G. L., LaPorte, R. E., Vesonder, G. T., & Voss, J. F. (1978). On the representation of prose: New dimensions. *Journal of Verbal Learning and Verbal Behavior, 17,* 357–358.

Carroll, J. D., & Arabie, P. (1980). Multidimensional scaling. *Annual review of psychology, 31,* 607–649.

Carroll, J. D., & Chang, J. J. (1970). Analysis of individual differences in multidimensional scaling via an N-way generalization of 'Eckard-Young' decomposition. *Psychometrika, 35,* 283–319.

Cech, C. G., & Shoben, E. J. (1985). Context effects in symbolic magnitude comparisons. *Journal of Experimental Psychology: Learning, Memory, and Cognition, 11,* 299–315.

Chi, M. T. H., Feltovich, P. J., & Glaser, R. (1981). Categorization and representation of physics problems by experts and novices. *Cognitive Science, 5,* 121–152.

Clark, H. H. (1968). On the meaning and use of prepositions. *Journal of Verbal Learning and Verbal Behavior, 7,* 421–431.

Coan, R. W. (1968). Dimensions of psychological theory. *American Psychologist, 23,* 715–722.

Collins, A. M., & Loftus, E. F. (1975). A spreading activation theory of semantic processing. *Psychological Review, 82,* 407–428.

Craik, F. I. M., & Lockhart, R. S. (1972). Levels of processing: A framework for memory research. *Journal of Verbal Learning and Verbal Behavior, 11,* 671–684.

Ekman, G. (1954). Dimensions of color vision. *Journal of Psychology, 38,* 467–474.

Fillenbaum, S., & Rappaport, A.(1971). *Structures in the subjective lexicon.* New York: Academic Press.

Flexser, A. J., & Tulving, E. (1978). Retrieval independence in recognition and recall. *Psychological Review, 85,* 153–171.

Friendly, M. L. (1977). In search of the *m*-gram: The structure of organization in free recall. *Cognitive Psychology, 9,* 188–249.

Friendly, M. (1981, November). *Learning the structure of cognitive psychology.* Paper presented at the meeting of the Psychonomic Society, Philadelphia, PA.

Fuchs, A. H., & Kawash, G. F. (1974). Prescriptive dimensions for five schools of psychology. *Journal of the History of the Behavioral Sciences, 10,* 352–366.

Garner, W. R. (1972). Information integration and form of encoding. In A. Melton & E. Martin (Eds.), *Coding processes in human memory.* New York: Wiley.

Halpern, A. R. (1984). Organization in memory for familiar songs. *Journal of Experimental Psychology: Learning, Memory, and Cognition, 10,* 496–512.

Henley, N. M. (1969). A psychological study of the semantics of animal terms. *Journal of Verbal Learning and Verbal Behavior, 8,* 176–184.

Hirtle, S. C. (1982). Lattice-based similarity measures between ordered trees. *Journal of Mathematical Psychology, 25,* 206–225.

Howard, D. V., & Howard, J. H. (1977). A multidimensional scaling analysis of the development of animal names. *Developmental Psychology, 13,* 108–113.

Johnson, S. C. (1967). Heirarchical clustering schemes. *Psychometrika, 32,* 241–254.

Kawash, G., & Fuchs, A. H. (1974). A factor analysis of ratings of five schools of psychology on prescriptive dimensions. *Journal of the History of the Behavioral Sciences, 10,* 426–437.

King, M. C., Gruenewald, P., & Lockhead, G. R. (1978). Classifying related stimuli. *Journal of Experimental Psychology: Human Learning and Memory, 4,* 417–427.

Kintsch, W. (1974). *The representation of meaning in memory.* Hillsdale, NJ: Lawrence Erlbaum Associates.

Kintsch, W., & Dijk, T. A. (1978). Toward a model of text comprehension and production. *Psychological Review, 85,* 363–394.

Krumhansl, C. L. (1979). The psychological representation of musical pitch in a tonal context. *Cognitive Psychology, 11,* 346–374.

Krumhansl, C. L. (1983, August). *Set-theoretic and spatial models of similarity: Some considerations in application.* Paper presented at the Mathematical Psychology meetings, Boulder, CO.

Krumhansl, C. L., Bharucha, J. J., & Kessler, E. J. (1982). Perceived harmonic structure of chords in three related musical keys. *Journal of Experimental Psychology: Human Preception and Performance, 8,* 24–36.

Kruskal, J. B. (1964a). Multidimensional scaling by optimizing goodness of fit to a nonmetric hypothesis. *Psychometrika, 29,* 1–27.

Kruskal, J. B. (1964b). Nonmetric multidimensional scaling: A numerical method. *Psychometrika, 29,* 115–129.

Kruskal, J. B., Young, F. W., & Seery, J. B. (1977). *How to use KYST 2, a very flexible program to do multidimensional scaling and unfolding.* Murray Hill, NJ: Bell Telephone Laboratories.

LaPorte, R. E., & Voss, J. F. (1979). Prose representations: A multidimensional scaling approach. *Multivariante Behavioral Research, 14,* 39–56.

Luce, R. D. (1959). *Individual choice behavior.* New York: Wiley.

McCloskey, M., & Glucksberg, S. (1979). Decision processes in verifying category membership statements: Implications for models of semantic memory. *Cognitive Psychology, 11,* 1–27.

McKoon, G., Ratcliff, R., & Dell, G. (in press). A critical evaluation of the semantic/episodic distinction. *Journal of Experimental Psychology: Learning, Memory and Cognition.*

Miller, G. A., & Nicely, P. E. (1955). An analysis of perceptual confusions among some English consonants. *Journal of the Acoustical Society of America, 27,* 338–352.

Miller, K., & Gelman, R. (1983). The child's representation of number: A multidimensional scaling analysis. *Child Development, 54,* 1470–1479.

Newman, C. M., Rinott, Y., & Tversky, A. (1983). Nearest neighbors and Veronoi regions in certain point processes. *Advances in Applied Probability, 15,* 726–751.

Norman, D. A., Rumelhart, D. E., & The LNR Research Group (1975). *Explorations in cognition.* San Francisco: Freeman.

Osgood, C. E., Suci, G. J., & Tannenbaum, P. H. (1954). *The measurement of meaning.* Urbana: University of Illinois Press.

Paivio, A. (1971). *Imagery and verbal processes.* New York: Holt, Rinehart & Winston.

Pollard-Gott, L. (1983). Emergence of thematic concepts in repeated listening to music. *Cognitive Psychology, 15,* 66–94.

Pruzansky, S. (1975). *SINDSCAL: A computer program for individual difference in multidimensional scaling.* Bell Laboratories Technical Memorandum.

Pruzansky, S., Tversky, A., & Carroll, J. D. (1982). Spatial versus tree representations of proximity data. *Psychometrika, 47,* 3–24.

Raaijmakers, J. G. W., & Shiffrin, R. M. (1980). SAM: A theory of probabilistic search of associative memory. In G. H. Bower (Ed.) *The psychology of learning and motivation, Vol. 14.* New York: Academic Press.

Raaijmakers, J. G. W., & Shiffrin, R. M. (1981). Search of associative memory. *Psychological Review, 88,* 93–134.

Rappaport, A., & Fillenbaum, S. (1972). An experimental study of semantic structures. In A. K. Romney, R. N. Shepard, & S. B. Nerlove (Eds.), *Multidimensional scaling: Theory and applications in the behavioral sciences* (Vol. 2). New York: Seminar Press.

Ratcliff, R. (1978). A theory of memory retrieval. *Psychological Review, 85,* 59–108.

Reitman, J. S., & Reuter, H. H. (1980). Organization revealed by recall orders and confirmed by pauses. *Cognitive Psychology, 12,* 554–581.

Rips, L. J., Shoben, E. J., & Smith, E. E. (1973). Semantic distance and the verification of semantic relationships. *Journal of Verbal Learning and Verbal Behavior, 12,* 1–20.

Roth, E. M., & Shoben, E. J. (1983). The effect of context on the structure of categories. *Cognitive Psychology, 15,* 346–378.

Rumelhart, D. E., & Abrahamsen, A. A. (1973). A model for analogical reasoning. *Cognitive Psychology, 5,* 1–28.

Rumelhart, D. E., & Ortony, A. (1977). The representation of knowledge in memory. In R. C. Anderson, R. J. Spiro, & W. E. Montague (Eds.), *Schooling and the acquisition of knowledge.* Hillsdale, NJ: Lawrence Erlbaum Associates.

Sattath, S., & Tversky, A. (1979). Additive similarity trees. *Psychometrika, 42,* 319–345.

Schaeffer, B., & Wallace, R. (1970). The comparison of word meanings. *Journal of Experimental Psychology, 86,* 144–152.

Schank, R. C. (1980). Language and memory. *Cognitive Science, 4,* 243–284.

Schoenfeld, A. H., & Herrmann, D. J. (1982). Problem perception and knowledge structure in expert and novice mathematical problem solvers. *Journal of Experimental Psychology: Learning, Memory, & Cognition, 8,* 484–494.

Shepard, R. N. (1962a). The analysis of proximities: Multidimensional scaling with an unknown distance function. I. *Psychometrika, 27,* 125–140.

Shepard, R. N. (1962b). The analysis of proximities: Multidimensional scaling with an unknown distance function. II. *Psychometrika, 27,* 219–246.

Shepard, R. N. (1964). Attention and the metric structure of the stimulus space. *Journal of Mathematical Psychology, 1,* 54–87.

Shepard, R. N. (1972). Psychological representations of speech sounds. In E. E. David & P. B. Denes (Eds.), *Human communication: A unified view.* New York: McGraw-Hill.

Shepard, R. N. (1980). Multidimensional scaling, tree-fitting, and clustering. *Science, 210,* 390–398.

Shepard, R. N., & Arabie, P. (1979). Additive clustering: Representation of similarities as combinations of discrete overlapping properties. *Psychological Review, 86,* 87–123.

Shoben, E. J. (1976). The verification of semantic relations in a same-different paradigm: An asymmetry in semantic memory. *Journal of Verbal Learning and Verbal Behavior, 15,* 365–379.

Shoben, E. J. (1983). Applications of multidimensional scaling in cognitive psychology. *Applied Psychological Measurement, 4,* 473–490.

Smith, E. E., & Medin, D. L. (1981). *Categories and concepts.* Cambridge, MA; Harvard University Press.

Soli, S. D., & Arabie, P. (1979). Auditory versus phonetic accounts of observed confusions between consonant phonemes. *Journal of the Acoustical Society of America, 66,* 46–59.

Sternberg, R. J. (1977). Component processes in analogical reasoning. *Psychological Review, 84,* 353–378.

Stevens, S. S., & Volkmann, J. (1940). The relation of pitch to frequency: A relative scale. *American Journal of Psychology, 53,* 329–353.

Tulving, E. (1972). Episodic and semantic memory. In E. Tulving & W. Donaldson (Eds.) *Organization of memory.* New York: Academic Press.

Tulving, E. (1975). Ecphoric processes in recall and recognition. In J. Brown (Ed.), *Recall and recognition.* London: Wiley.

Tulving, E. (1983). *Elements of episodic memory.* London: Oxford Press.

Tulving, E., & Thomson, D. M. (1973). Encoding specificity and retrieval processes in episodic memory. *Psychological Review, 80,* 352–378.

Tversky, A., & Hutchinson, W. J. (1986). Nearest neighbor analysis of psychological spaces. *Psychological Review, 93,* 3–22.

8 New Perspectives in the Analysis of Abilities

John B. Carroll
University of North Carolina at Chapel Hill

INTRODUCTION

One can understandably be skeptical when a "new perspective" is offered on a topic that has been under scientific examination for a very long time. I am not sure that I have any truly new perspectives, but I entertain the notion that my perspectives have the kind of novelty that will last long enough to permit taking a fresh look at some very old problems and getting new insights into their solution. I'm concerned with several such problems: First, what is an "ability"? How can an ability be defined? This is a problem that I believe has never been adequately addressed in the psychometric literature. Second, how can data from ability measurements be best analyzed to help in the definition of the ability, and thus to determine what has often been called the "construct validity" of the measurements? Third, what are the implications for the construction of better measurements of ability? Throughout my presentation, one detects influences from cognitive psychology—influences that I point out, but my primary concern is with psychometric aspects of ability measurements.

Here, I use the term "ability" in a very general sense, so that it covers both the concept of aptitude and the concept of achievement. At the stage of *defining* an ability, the difference between aptitude—thought of as a capacity for some future achievement—and achievement—thought of as the demonstration of some acquired performance—is irrelevant, because, as will shortly be seen, we are concerned in either case with deriving the definition of an ability from observations of performance. The question of the source of the performance (i.e., to what extent it comes through constitutional/genetic factors and to what extent it comes through learned experiences) need not enter discussion.

WHAT IS AN ABILITY?

The *American Heritage Dictionary* defines ability as "the quality of being able to do something; physical, mental, financial, or legal power to perform." We can immediately drop consideration of financial and legal powers; from the standpoint of psychological and educational measurement we can be concerned, however, with physical and mental powers. Nevertheless, even the definition offered by the dictionary has an air of circularity: Ability is defined in terms of "being able to perform something," and ironically enough, the word *able* is defined in terms of "having sufficient ability." I'm afraid the dictionary is of little help in defining "ability," except possibly in the phrase "ability to perform something." What is this *something?* In the context of psychological and educational measurement, must it not refer to some *class* of tasks? If we think of commonly recognized abilities such as athletic ability, or musical ability, the common assumption is that a person with such an ability is able to perform well a variety of tasks that can be called athletic, or musical, as the case may be. When psychologists and educators speak of "mental ability," they are referring to performance in a variety of "mental" tasks. The question is, what is a "mental" task?

We know that abilities are often of a more specialized character. A good basketball player is not necessarily a good 100-yard runner; a good pianist is not necessarily a good composer, or not even a composer at all. Evidence from factor-analytic investigations of mental abilities suggests that there exist a number of somewhat unrelated mental abilities: verbal ability, reasoning ability, spatial ability, numerical ability, and so on. Correlational and factor-analytic evidence is of some use in classifying and identifying abilities, because it yields information on what abilities are likely to go together or to be separate. More precisely, it yields information on the classification of the *tasks* that call for different abilities.

Let us focus on the fact that the tasks that call for a particular ability, whatever it is, can be of considerable variety, perhaps even of infinite variety. How do they vary? One dimension along which they vary is their *difficulty*. One can often diagnose what causes tasks to vary in difficulty. In simple cases, it may be a matter of physics or physiology. In basketball, it is harder to shoot a basket from a long distance than from a short distance. In musical performance, Bach Inventions are generally much easier to play than most of the compositions of, say, Debussy. In fact, it has long been the practice of music educators to assign grades of difficulty to instrumental musical compositions; I do not know whether anyone has analyzed exactly what makes for ease or difficulty of such compositions.

In psychological and educational measurement, the concept of difficulty turns up in the form of information about the proportions of tested samples or populations that are able to "pass" each of the items on a test. Such information is often used in arranging the items of a test in order of difficulty, apparently on the assumption that subjects will be more comfortable in taking the test if they can start with easy tasks. But as in the case of musical compositions, there is usually little concern with what makes items easy or difficult. Test makers often simply take item difficulty data as givens that need not be questioned further. Note, by the way, that "items" on a psychological or educational test are really "tasks" that call for correct performance; the more of these tasks the examinee can perform correctly, the higher the score, and the higher the level of "ability" that is inferred from the score.

A preliminary evaluation of the "construct validity" of a test is often made simply by considering the class of tasks that is involved in the test. If all the items are concerned with English spelling, for example, the test may be regarded as a test of "spelling ability." Or if all the items seem to involve "manipulation of visually presented spatial relationships," the test is regarded as a test of "spatial ability." But intuitive classifications of tasks are often unsatisfactory, perhaps by their very nature. They yield no guarantee that there is only one spelling ability, or only one spatial ability. In the case of spatial ability, at least, the available evidence is to the contrary (Lohman, 1979).

At the same time, it is often pointed out that it is difficult to establish the unitary or nonunitary nature of abilities from correlational studies of items or tasks. The difficulties are technical, stemming from problems with the interpretation of bivariate distributions of item responses. Much of our knowledge about the differentiation of abilities comes from factor-analytic studies using scores on multi-item tests, the tests being composed of series of plausibly similar items. There is now some promise in recently developed techniques for item factor-analysis (Wilson, Wood, & Gibbons, 1984) but as yet these techniques have not been widely applied, and I myself have not yet had the opportunity to use them.

But I am getting off the track. Suppose, for the sake of argument, that we have a set of tasks that can be demonstrated to measure a single ability at different difficulty levels. What might convince us that they measure a single ability would be evidence that there are systematic relationships between characteristics of individuals and the levels of difficulties of the tasks, such that individuals who *can* perform the more difficult tasks have a uniformly higher probability of passing the easier tasks than those who can *not* perform the more difficult tasks, and also, such that individuals who cannot perform the easy tasks also cannot perform the harder tasks. This idea is not new; to my knowledge it was first pointed out by David Walker, a Scottish educational psychologist, in a series of papers published in the *British Journal of Psychology* over the years 1931 to 1940 (Walker, 1931, 1936, 1940). Walker called tests having the above-mentioned property "unig," whereas tests not having this property were called "hig" (from the expression "higgledy-piggledy"). Walker anticipated the idea of what later came to be known as the Guttman scale, and I like to refer to it as the Walker scale, or perhaps the Walker-Guttman scale.

There is much more to this idea, however, I can best illustrate it by referring to data that I collected some years ago on a test that I believe can be shown to measure a single dimension of ability, namely musical pitch discrimination ability. This is the old Seashore Sense of Pitch test; in fact, the data I collected were for the 1919 version of the test. Let me describe this test, in case you are not familiar with it. It consists of 100 items, divided into ten subsets of 10 items each. Each item in a given subset presents, by a phonograph recording, two tones that differ in pitch by a certain amount, constant over the items in the subset; the subject's task is to indicate on the answer sheet whether the second tone is higher or lower than the first. The pitch difference in the easiest subset is 30 cycles per second, or (considering the overall pitch level) about a semitone; the pitch differences in other subsets range down to one-half cycle. Subjects are required to make a response to each item, and thus there is obviously an element of guessing, or success by chance, of 50%. I may note, incidentally, that some years ago Guilford (1941) (while he was in the psychology department at the University of Nebraska) collected and analyzed data with this test and claimed that the test measures three separate abilities. I have recently shown, however (Carroll, 1983) that Guilford was misled by statistical artifacts, and that the test measures essentially only one ability. Imperfections in the 1919 recording add a certain element of response set bias, but this may be ignored for practical purposes.

In a further analysis of the data I collected on about 1100 college students, I wanted to study curves of performance in relation to the pitch differences of the subtests. How did the curves of performance for students with high scores compare with those for students with average and low scores on the test? I divided the total score distribution into deciles and plotted average performance curves for each decile. The results are shown in Fig. 8.1. The baseline is scaled in terms of the logarithm of the pitch difference; the ordinate shows the probability of correct performance. As may be seen, the data are quite systematic. High ability students have practically perfect performance for subtests with large pitch differences; their average performance descends to a threshold only at a pitch difference of about 1.25 Hertz, the limen or threshold being set at 75% correct (halfway between perfect and chance performance). Students in the lowest decile of ability, on the other hand, have on the average a threshold performance at a pitch difference of about 20 Hertz.

The curves have, as one might expect, the general shape of normal ogives, and have approximately the same slope. This slope can be expressed in terms of the logarithm of the pitch difference: one standard deviation of the response curve is about .25 log pitch difference units. I believe that this slope is in fact *characteristic* of pitch discrimination ability. Even with a better-recorded test, and with many more items, this slope would probably not change much. The fact that the slope is not higher, as it would be if the slopes were as represented in Fig. 8.2, puts a certain constraint on the reliability of any test of pitch discrimina-

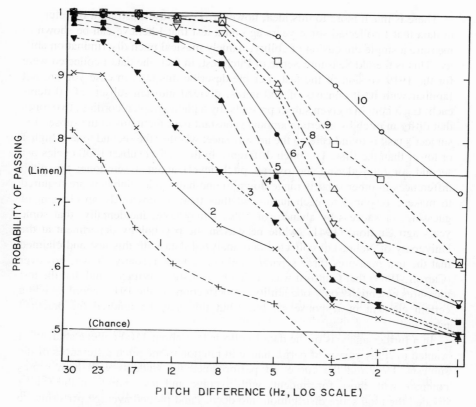

FIG. 8.1.   Person characteristic functions for deciles of the total score distribution, Seashore Sense of Pitch test (*N* = 1082).

tion ability. At least, it puts a constraint on the reliability-per-item, and thus on the reliability of a test of any given length. (It is possible, in fact, to specify the limits on reliability in terms of parameters of the slope function.)

Of even more importance is the fact that these data support the *existence* and *definition* of pitch discrimination ability, in the sense that pitch discrimination ability is revealed in a systematic relation between individual characteristics and performance on subtests of different pitch difference levels. What makes for "difficulty" in pitch discrimination is the smallness of the pitch difference. High ability individuals have much smaller pitch difference thresholds than low ability individuals.

These data illustrate a paradigm that I believe can be transferred or applied to *any* ability. That is, an ability—any ability—can be defined in terms of the relation between individual thresholds of performance and the characteristics of tasks of different degrees of "difficulty." In the case of pitch discrimination

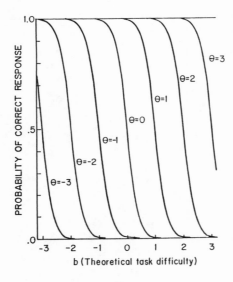

FIG. 8.2. Theoretical person characteristic functions for an ability with a high value of the slope parameter (a = 3).

ability, it is clear that the task characteristics are described in terms of pitch differences, and individual differences can be referred to threshold points on the pitch difference scale. What about other abilities?

To introduce this topic further, I present one other set of data, this time on a Block Counting test that was administered by my colleagues at the University of North Carolina (Johnson & Meade, personal communication) to 10th-grade-children in a study of the development of spatial abilities. The Block Counting test has been regarded as a test of some kind of spatial ability. The test used in this study is a little different from other block-counting tests that appear in some test batteries. Sample items are shown in Fig. 8.3. Each item is a perspective drawing of a pile of blocks; the subject's task is simply to count the blocks and write down the answer. Subjects are told that all blocks in a given drawing are of the same shape. Because the answers are free responses, there is practically no guessing element.

In Fig. 8.4 are shown average probabilities of correct answers for sets of items of varying difficulties, for *ninths* (noniles) of the total score distribution for 119 10th graders. Again, the data are quite systematic. High scoring individuals get correct answers on most of the "easy" items, and have only a little trouble with the hard items. Low scoring individuals have trouble even with the easy items, and have very little chance of passing the hard items. One can specify thresholds of performance for different individuals. Beyond stating it in terms of difficulty level, however, the baseline scale cannot easily be described. We must study, therefore, what makes the items easy or hard, since whatever makes for task difficulty is what gives rise to differences in ability, and thus leads toward a definition of that ability.

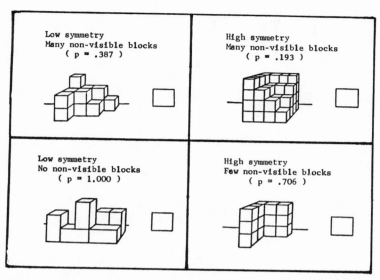

FIG. 8.3.   Sample items from a Block Counting test, arranged to suggest the effect of "symmetry" and of the proportion of nonvisible blocks on item difficulty (*p* = proportion of 10th grade students giving correct answer). Copyright 1986 by Industrial Psychology Inc., 515 Madison Avenue, New York, NY 10022. All rights reserved. Permission granted for limited reproduction in professional psychometric journal in this instance only.

Detailed examination of the items, arranged in order of difficulty (proportion failing), discloses that they vary mainly in two characteristics: (1) the proportion of blocks that are not "visible" because they are hidden by other blocks, and (2) what I call the "symmetry" of the piles, that is, a characteristic such that one can use arithmetic computations to arrive more quickly at the number of blocks. The first of these variables has the greatest influence on item difficulty, but it interacts with the second. In Fig. 8.3 I have arranged the 4 sample items in such a way as to suggest how these task characteristics affect item difficulty. The two items in the bottom row have no or few nonvisible blocks, and are relatively easy, while those in the top row have many nonvisible blocks and are harder. The items in the left column have little "symmetry"; the subject must simply count the blocks more or less one by one. The items in the right column have high symmetry, and counting the blocks can involve some simple arithmetic. For example, the item at the lower right appears to be composed of a wall of 3 × 3 = 9 blocks at the left, plus an adjoining wall of 2 × 3 = 6 blocks, or 15 blocks in all. The items in the left-hand column are somewhat easier than those in the right-hand column.

From this analysis, it appears that the ability chiefly measured by this test is the ability to visualize the positions of blocks that are not immediately visible.

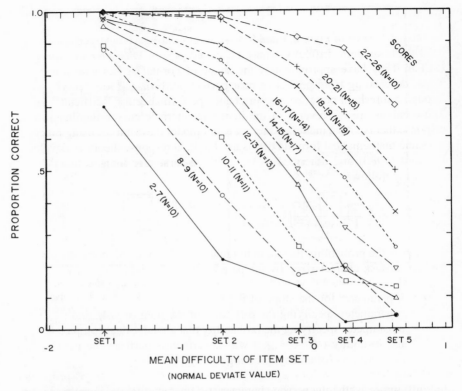

FIG. 8.4.   Person characteristic functions for noniles of the total score distribution for the Block Counting test as given to 119 10th-grade children.

Secondarily, it measures an ability to use simple arithmetical processes in arriving at answers. As a matter of fact, the "symmetry" dimension in this task may tend to distort the assessment of the subject's ability to visualize missing blocks. Possibly a better, purer test of visualization ability could be devised by constructing all items with a minimal amount of symmetry, so as to reduce the possibility of using arithmetical processes.

Suggested by these findings, further questions could arise and be answered by appropriate investigations. Is the ability to visualize hidden blocks specific to the block counting task, or would it be found to be correlated with abilities in other types of visualization tasks, for example, the "surface development" test used by Thurstone (1938) or the mental paper folding test studied by Shepard and Feng (1972)? The answers to such a question could be found by analyzing data for the surface development and mental paper folding tests in the manner I have described, and examining relationships among the task parameters of the several tests.

THE PERSON CHARACTERISTIC FUNCTION (PCF)

The curves shown in Figs. 8.1 and 8.4—curves relating average performance of individuals to item difficulty—may be called *person characteristic functions* (PCFs). They have approximately the shape of normal ogives with a negative slope, descending from perfect or near perfect performance for "easy" items, through a threshold point, to zero or chance performance for "difficult" items. These curves are the reverse of the item characteristic curves familiar in item response theory. As a matter of fact, one can model these curves using precisely the same mathematical formula that is used in item response theory as developed by Lord (1980) and others. This is the three-parameter logistic function expressed as follows:

$$p = c + \frac{1 - c}{1 + \exp\,[-1.7a(\theta - b)]},$$

where p = the probability that an individual with ability θ will correctly perform an item or task characterized by the parameters a, b, and c, where

a = a parameter for the slope of the function;
b = a parameter specifying the difficulty of the item or task; and
c = a parameter specifying the probability that an individual completely lacking in ability ($\theta = -\infty$) will nevertheless perform the item or task correctly, as (often) by guessing.

The difference is that the person characteristic function plots performance *for an individual* (or group of individuals) as a function of item difficulty (the b parameter), whereas the item characteristic function plots performance *for an item* as a function of individual ability (the *theta* parameter θ). Both functions assume that all items measure the same latent ability (or cluster of abilities). Item characteristic functions have well-known uses in test theory, as Lord (1980) has shown. Use of the person characteristic function was first explored by Mosier (1941), although he did not call it that. The advantage I see for it is that it emphasizes the relation between ability and item or task difficulty. When there is a definite relation between ability and item difficulty, one is encouraged to explain that relation in terms of the characteristics of items or tasks.

Item response curves can also be used to look at these relations, but in this case one has to compare the functions for different items. This may be illustrated with data that I developed for vocabulary (opposites) items in the SAT, as shown in Fig. 8.5. (The data available to me did not permit computing person characteristic functions.) What we see in Fig. 8.5 are item characteristic curves for 15 vocabulary items; performance (in terms of percentage correct) is plotted against

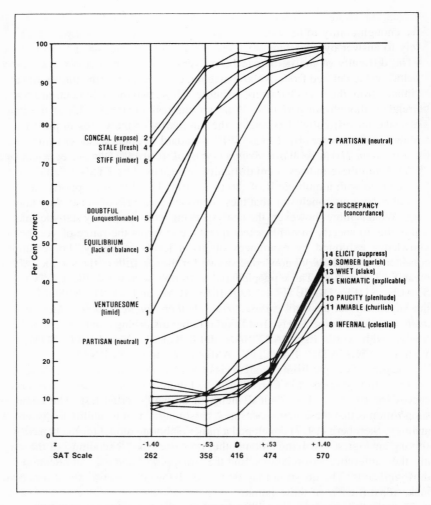

FIG. 8.5.   Item characteristic curves for 15 verbal opposites items from a form of
the SAT-V (from Carroll, 1980).

5 ability levels, actually quintiles (fifths) of an item analysis sample of 1920
cases with a mean SAT score of 416 and a standard deviation of 110. Obviously,
as ability increases, correctness of performance increases; the curves are generally of a normal ogive shape with a positive slope. Note, however, that for most
of the more difficult items, the percentages correct for low-scoring groups are
well below chance levels (chance being 20% since these are 5-alternative items).
The curves tend to have a U-shaped concavity, possibly because it is the low-
average group, at an average SAT-V score of 358, that is most likely to be

seduced into choosing an incorrect alternative. The very low scorers don't even have enough ability to be seduced in this way; they are the ones who are most likely to answer by guessing.

The difficulty of the items can be measured in either of two ways: by the "delta" value derived from overall percentage correct, or by the threshold value estimated from the item characteristic curve. These two measurements are highly correlated, though not perfectly. What are the task characteristics of the items that make for difficulty? I estimated the familiarity of the words in the "lead" and the correct choices by using "SFI" (standard frequency index) values from the *American Heritage Word Frequency Book* (Carroll, Davies, & Richman, 1971). From these indices, item difficulty as measured by ETS's "delta" could be predicted with a multiple R of .80 ($p < .01$). This finding supports, at least, the rather obvious conclusion that these items are measures of vocabulary knowledge. What is more, however, the analysis using word frequency statistics makes it possible to specify in rather exact quantitative terms the range of vocabulary knowledge exhibited by examinees of given levels of ability. For example, consider the vocabulary knowledge shown for the top fifth of the sample, with a mean SAT-V or 570. These people have no trouble with words like CONCEAL, STALE, STIFF, DOUBTFUL, EQUILIBRIUM, and VENTURESOME, and the keyed correct answers *expose, fresh, limber, unquestionable, lack of balance,* and *timid,* respectively. But I find it rather disturbing that they tend to have trouble with words like PARTISAN, DISCREPANCY, ELICIT, SOMBER, WHET, ENIGMATIC, PAUCITY, AMIABLE, and INFERNAL.

One other example from my analysis of SAT items is instructive. (These data are more fully discussed in Carroll, 1980.) Figure 8.6 shows item characteristic curves for 10 "verbal analogies" items of an SAT-Verbal test. The common supposition is that these items measure "reasoning," that is, ability to discern an analogy. Sternberg (1977) developed a rather elaborate model for the behavior of solving analogies, involving among other processes the "encoding" of the stimuli, the "inference" of relations, and the "mapping" and the "application" of those relations. The question may be raised: To what extent do these processes make for difficulty of these items?

There is little evidence here that the examinees have difficulty with the concept and structure of an analogy per se. Even very low-scoring individuals have a fairly good chance of passing a simple analogy like number 27. This suggests that the SAT verbal analogies test does not measure the ability to solve analogies, as such, in the sense that low-scoring individuals would be less able than high-scoring individuals to deal with analogical structures, apart from their content. Instead, the evidence suggests that the harder items involve more difficult encodings, and more difficult and subtle inferences, mappings, and applications than the easy items. To a certain extent, there are vocabulary difficulties; Thus, low-scoring individuals probably have difficulty in encoding concepts represented by words like "slink," "furtive," and "innocuous." But the major difficulty

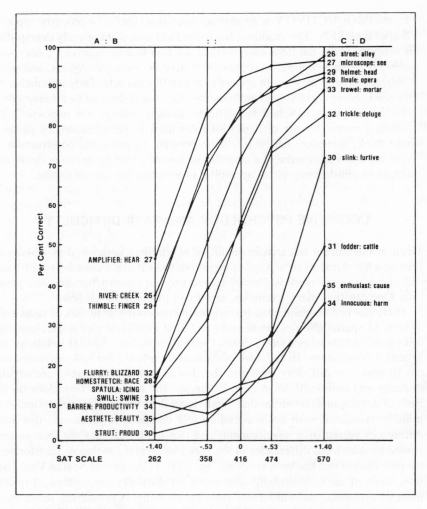

FIG. 8.6.   Item characteristic curves for 10 verbal analogies items from a form of
the SAT-V (from Carroll, 1980).

arises from the complexity of the rules that are the bases of the analogies.
Consider, for example, the hardest of these items:

    34. BARREN:PRODUCTIVITY:: (A) torrid:warmth
         (B) innocuous:harm (C) aberrant:change
         (D) prodigal:reform (E) random:originality

The words in the lead, BARREN and PRODUCTIVITY, are not particularly
difficult words. The rule relating them is fairly complex: BARREN is an adjec-

tive, and PRODUCTIVITY is an abstract noun that signifies a property opposite to that of BARREN. The examinee has to find a choice that correctly exemplifies this relation. From the item analysis data we find that alternative C, *aberrant: change*, is rather tempting, as is also alternative D, *prodigal: reform*, and without careful thought they might appear to exemplify the rule. Only alternative B, *innocuous: harm* correctly exemplifies the rule, but it does so in a fairly subtle way. Unfortunately it would be difficult, though perhaps not impossible, to establish a metric for the difficulty of rules used in verbal analogies items. I would think, however, that it might be possible to make the construction of verbal analogies tests more of a science and less of an art by devoting deliberate attention to constructing items according to a metric for rule-difficulty.

COGNITIVE PSYCHOLOGY AND TASK DIFFICULTY

Much of the current research in cognitive psychology is devoted essentially to finding what elements or aspects of cognitive tasks make them easy or difficult, and in this way the work is directly relevant to test construction and interpretation. One can find many examples, and I can mention only a few.

There has been considerable investigation concerning attributes of tasks used in tests of spatial abilities. Pellegrino and Kail (1982), for example, consider tasks used in tests of two fairly distinct spatial aptitudes—Spatial Relations and Spatial Visualization. In the case of Spatial Relations, the task attributes that chiefly make for difficulty (either in speed or accuracy of response) are angular disparity and familiarity of stimuli. Pellegrino and Kail (1982) conclude on the basis of developmental studies that "individual differences in spatial aptitude are initially associated with basic encoding and comparison processes, that such differences persist over development, and that the differences are then accompanied by additional differences in the speed of mental rotating or transforming the information that has been encoded" (p. 333). In the case of Spatial Visualization, some of the task attributes that make for difficulty are rotation, displacement of elements, and number of stimulus elements. Considering these facts, these authors conclude that "skill in a visualization task such as the form board is related to the speed and quality of the stimulus representation that is achieved" (p. 354).

Another example is the work of Goldman and Pellegrino (1984) on inductive reasoning tasks. They find, among other things, that "the visual or semantic complexity of a particular item affects the degree to which general system characteristics such as working memory and executive monitoring strategies become important cognitive components of performance" (p. 193).

Similarly, I would interpret the work of Rips (1984) on deductive reasoning as an attempt to identify what elements in certain reasoning tasks—verification of arguments containing the connectives *and, or, if . . . then,* and *not*—cause difficulties for subjects. Rips found stable differences between subjects in their handling of rules of reasoning. Although Rips does not present data allowing this direct interpretation, I would speculate that his data suggest that deductive ability can be defined in terms of knowledge of and ability to use an increasingly more complicated set of deductive rules.

APPLICATION OF THE THEORY TO COGNITIVE ABILITY FACTORS

Over the past several years, I have devoted my attention to surveying and in many cases reanalyzing data from the factor-analytic literature in an attempt to determine what the major dimensions of cognitive ability are. I am aware of many of the limitations of factor analysis—they have been pointed out many times. Nevertheless, I have been pursuing my survey on the conviction that if adequate correlational data are uniformly subjected to presently acceptable methods of factor analysis, the results will be more meaningful, consistent, and interpretable than they have appeared to be in the past. I am now approaching the final stages of my survey, and while I am not ready to offer definite conclusions, I now perceive a "light at the end of the tunnel" that appears to confirm my convictions.

One conclusion that now seems evident, however, is somewhat contrary to my initial expectations. My original expectation was that I could identify, from the literature, a fairly large number of factors of ability—not as many as Guilford (1967; Guilford & Hoepfner, 1971) had postulated and claimed to demonstrate— but at least a few more than French (1951) and Ekstrom (1979) had listed in their reviews of the factor-analytic literature. My present view is that there are not more than about thirty distinct, identifiable factors of cognitive ability, and of these, many are of a fairly specific nature and of little importance. The factors that appear over and over in my reanalyses are mostly those originally identified by Thurstone (1938) and other early investigators. Among the first-order "primary" factors that I believe can be confidently identified are Thurstone's Induction, Deductive Reasoning, Verbal Comprehension, Spatial Relations, Visualization, Closure, Perceptual Speed, Associative Memory, Word Fluency, and Memory Span. In addition, there is fairly solid evidence for a series of "second order" broad factors, as identified by Cattell, Horn, and others (e.g., Hakstian & Cattell, 1978): factors of "fluid intelligence," "crystallized intelligence," "general visual perception," "general auditory perception," "general speed," "general memory capacity," and "general idea production." Even some of these factors tend to be correlated, a fact that suggests that Spearman (1927) was correct in asserting the existence and importance of a "general" factor, "g". My analytic procedures assume a hierarchical model such that some factors are of greater generality and applicability than others. The hierarchical model usually results in specifying two or more independent sources of significant variance for a given variable, that is, variance from a primary factor and also variance from a second- or higher-order factor.

Earlier, I suggested that the person characteristic model as illustrated with data from the pitch discrimination test and the block counting test could be transferred or applied to *any* ability. My factorial results, however, pose certain problems for this suggestion.

First, not all factors appear to be characterizable in terms of tasks of varying difficulties. Many, for example, refer mainly to the *speed* of performance of simple cognitive tasks, like, for example, the comparison of stimuli, as in the Perceptual Speed factor. It is not immediately clear how the person characteristic function model can be applied to such factors, unless certain modifications are made in the model. One way of doing this is to utilize individual variation in speed of response over trials as a basis for developing the person characteristic function. A person of a given degree of ability would have an average speed, but the probability of exceeding a given rate would decrease as the baseline value increases. The general idea is illustrated in Fig. 8.7.

The other problem posed by factorial results is the fact that most variables show multiple sources of variance—at least two, as I have mentioned. On the average, I find that about half the common variance of a variable comes from a primary or first-order factor, and the remainder from higher-order factors. This means that many tasks can be supposed to have at least two sources of difficulty—one from a primary factor and one from a higher-order factor, such as a general factor. It would be interesting to work out the implications of this fact for the person characteristic function. I suspect that it means that PCF curves will be somewhat attenuated, i.e., with flatter slopes, when tasks have multiple sources of difficulty. Nevertheless, it may still be possible to separate these effects.

For example, suppose we are concerned, as we should be, with the source of difficulty due to a general factor. That is, independent of the effects of a particular primary factor, what makes a task difficult if it also has a high loading on a

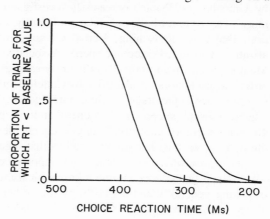

FIG. 8.7. Hypothetical person characteristic curves for three individuals (slow, average, fast) on a speed ability (e.g., choice reaction time).

general factor? If we could find this out, it would contribute to the interpretation of the nature of the general factor. One possibility is deliberately to select tasks that have loadings on different independent primary factors, and then study the person characteristic function for such tasks and the task attributes that function to make them load on a general factor. I am not aware that such an idea has ever been tried. I intend at least to work out the theoretical model by which this might be accomplished, or to determine whether or not it might be accomplished at all.

DISCUSSION

The major points I have been trying to emphasize are the following:

1. The existence of an ability can be demonstrated when it can be shown that for any individual, there is a systematic, monotonic, and close relation between the individual's probability of correct or satisfactory performance and the difficulties of a series of tasks, and when there are variations over individuals in the parameters of this relation.
2. The ability is defined in terms of the attribute or attributes of the tasks that give rise to differences in task difficulty.
3. This formulation, or one closely similar to it, is applicable to any cognitive ability.
4. Cognitive psychology can be of help in the definition of cognitive abilities by investigating what attributes of tasks make for differences in the accuracy or speed with which individuals can perform those tasks, because such attributes are involved in the definition of abilities. Further, knowledge of task attributes can lead to inferences about the psychological processes that are called for in performances, and thus about the psychological processes that underlie a given ability.

A corollary of this formulation is that effects of education, training, or other forms of intervention can be indexed by changes in the position parameter of an individual's person characteristic function. A significantly positive effect of learning or an educational intervention, for example, would be exhibited in a significant increase in the individual's threshold of performance along the task difficulty scale.

The person characteristic function (PCF) model can be shown to apply at least in a number of "simple cases." Probably it could be shown to apply to most of the major types of ability that have been identified. Undoubtedly certain complications would arise in more complex cases. Among these complications are:

1. The possibility that task performance may be a function of more than one ability.

2. The possibility that tasks could be performed through different "strategies" or approaches.

3. The possibility that at least some abilities, especially those representing educational achievements, involve results of specific learning. The fact that individuals may vary in what particular learnings they may have achieved, independent of the overall difficulty of those learnings, may present problems in applying the PCF model to certain kinds of abilities.

No doubt it would be fruitful to study the problems posed by these complications, but I believe that such studies would be appropriate only after considerable success has been achieved in applying the PCF model to "simple cases." Since this has been done thus far to only a limited extent, there is a wide field of problems open for examination.

One final remark: I have only intimated how all this might help in better test construction. I will try to be more explicit: We can make better tests of abilities by paying more attention to the task characteristics that make for item ease or difficulty and to the role of such task characteristics in defining the abilities we seek to measure.

REFERENCES

Carroll, J. B. (1980). Measurement of abilities constructs. In U. S. Office of Personnel Management and Educational Testing Service, *Construct validity in psychological measurement: Proceedings of a Colloquium on Theory and Application in Education and Employment* (pp. 23–41). Princeton, NJ: Educational Testing Service.

Carroll, J. B. (1983). The difficulty of a test and its factor composition revisited. In H. Wainer & S. Messick (Eds.), *Principals of modern psychological measurement: A Festschrift in honor of Frederic M. Lord* (pp. 257–283). Hillsdale, NJ: Lawrence Erlbaum Associates.

Carroll, J. B., Davies, P., & Richman, B. (1971). *The American Heritage word frequency book.* Boston: Houghton Mifflin.

Ekstrom, R. B. (1979). Review of cognitive factors. *Multivariate Behavioral Research Monographs,* No. 79–2, 7–56.

French, J. W. (1951). The description of aptitude and achievement tests in terms of rotated factors. *Psychometric Monographs,* No. 5.

Goldman, S. R., & Pellegrino, J. W. (1984). Deductions about induction: Analyses of developmental and individual differences. In R. J. Sternberg (Ed.), *Advances in the psychology of human intelligence, Vol. 2* (pp. 149–197). Hillsdale, NJ: Lawrence Erlbaum Associates.

Guilford, J. P. (1941). The difficulty of a test and its factor composition. *Psychometrika, 6,* 67–77.

Guilford, J. P. (1967). *The nature of human intelligence.* New York: McGraw-Hill.

Guilford, J. P., & Hoepfner, R. (1971). *The analysis of intelligence.* New York: McGraw-Hill.

Hakstian, A. R., & Cattell, R. B. (1978). Higher-stratum ability structures on a basis of twenty primary abilities. *Journal of Educational Psychology, 70,* 657–669.

Johnson, E. S., & Meade, A. (1982). Personal communication.

Lohman, D. F. (1979). *Spatial ability: Individual differences in speed and level* (Tech. Rep. No. 9). Stanford, CA: Aptitude Research Project, School of Education, Stanford University.

Lord, F. M. (1980). *Applications of item response theory to practical testing problems.* Hillsdale, NJ: Lawrence Erlbaum Associates.

Mosier, C. I. (1941). Psychophysics and mental test theory, II. The constant process. *Psychological Review, 48,* 235–249.

Pellegrino, J. W., & Kail, R., Jr. (1982). Process analyses of spatial aptitude. In R. J. Sternberg (Ed.), *Advances in the psychology of human intelligence,* Vol. 1 (pp. 311–365). Hillsdale, NJ: Lawrence Erlbaum Associates.

Rips, L. J. (1984). Reasoning as a central intellective activity. In R. J. Sternberg (Ed.), *Advances in the psychology of human intelligence,* Vol. 2 (pp. 105–147). Hillsdale, NJ: Lawrence Erlbaum Associates.

Shepard, R. N., & Feng, C. (1972). A chronometric study of mental paper folding. *Cognitive Psychology, 3,* 228–243.

Spearman, C. (1927). *The abilities of man: Their nature and measurement.* New York: Macmillan.

Sternberg, R. J. (1977). *Intelligence, information processing, and analogical reasoning: The componential analysis of human abilities.* Hillsdale, NJ: Lawrence Erlbaum Associates.

Thurstone, L. L. (1938). Primary mental abilities. *Psychometric Monographs,* No. 1.

Walker, D. A. (1931). Answer pattern and score scatter in tests and examinations. *British Journal of Psychology, 22,* 73–86.

Walker, D. A. (1936). Answer pattern and score scatter in tests and examinations. *British Journal of Psychology, 26,* 301–308.

Walker, D. A. (1940). Answer pattern and score scatter in tests and examinations. *British Journal of Psychology, 30,* 248–260.

Wilson, D., Wood, R., & Gibbons, R. D. (1984). TESTFACT [computer program]. Mooresville, IN: Scientific Software.

Author Index

Numbers in italics *indicate pages with complete bibliographic information.*

A

Abrahamsen, A. A., 234, 236, 237, 262, *265*
Ackerman, P. L., 29, *37*
Agrawal, N., 103, *136*
Ahern, S., 121, *136*
Ananda, S. M., 135, *136*
Anastasi, A., 2, *8*, 176, *184*
Anderson, J. A., 19, *38*, 256, *263*
Anderson, J. H., 44, *83*
Anderson, J. R., 31, 36, *37*, 44, *82*, 154, *184*, 195, *223*, 230, 256, *263*
Anderson, R., 54, *82*
Arabie, P., 230, 231, 232, 241, 242, 245, 246, 247, 251, 253, *263*, *264*, *266*
Arnkoff, D. B., 172, *184*
Arnold, J. B., 234, 253, 262, *263*
Atkinson, R. C., 135, *136*, *137*, 256, *263*

B

Bachar-Bassan, E., 63, *82*
Baddeley, A. D., 156, *184*
Bakker, D. J., 157, *184*
Ball, C., 57, *83*

Banks, W. P., 246, *263*
Barclay, C. R., 152, *184*
Barratt, E. S., 215, *223*, *224*
Barrett, P., 105, *137*
Bartholomae, D., 57, *82*
Bartlett, B. J., 155, *184*
Bartlett, F. C., 154, *184*
Bauer, R., 157, *184*
Beatty, J., 121, *136*
Beck, A. T., 172, *184*
Beck, I. L., 53, *82*
Bellezza, F. S., 208, *224*
Belmont, J. M., 49, *82*
Benbassett, J., 63, *82*
Benton, S. L., 161, 164, 166, 167, 168, 169, 174, *184*
Bereiter, C., 164, 173, *188*
Bharucha, J. J., 239, *265*
Biederman, I., 25, *37*
Binet, A., 220, *224*
Bisanz, G. L., 244, 245, 247, *264*
Black, J. B., 154, *184*
Block, J. B., 102, *137*
Blohm, P. J., 164, 166, 174, *184*
Bloom, B. S., 209, *224*
Bluth, G. J., 155, *187*
Bobbitt, B., 135, *138*

285

Bobrow, D. G., 53, *84*
Bock, R. D., 34, *38*
Boersma, F. J., 207, *225*
Boice, R., 172, *184*
Bonar, J., 71, *82*
Borkowski, J. G., 49, *82*
Botwinick, J., 27, *37*
Bower, G. H., 154, *184*, 208, 223, *224*, *233*, 256, *263*
Boyle, C. F., 31, 36, *37*
Braden, W., 105, *137*
Brandt, D. M., 155, *187*
Bransford, J. D., 48, 49, *82*, 150, *184*
Briars, D. J., 175, 177, 178, *184*
Broder, L. J., 209, *224*
Brown, A. L., 48, 49, *82*, 150, 152, *184*, *185*
Brown, J. S., 51, 55, 70, *82*, *83*, 149, 176, *185*, 212, *224*
Bruner, J. S., 153, *187*
Bruning, R. H., 171, *185*
Bryan, A. I., 99, *137*
Bryant, N. T., 177, *188*
Burns, M. S., 48, *82*
Burt, C., 101, 120, *137*
Burton, R. R., 55, 70, *82*, 149, 176, *185*, 212, *224*
Buswell, G. T., 212, *224*
Butterfield, E. C., 49, *82*

C

Campione, J. C., 49, *82*, 150, 152, *184*, *185*
Caramazza, A., 51, 58, *84*
Carbonell, J. G., 31, *37*
Carey, S., 73, *83*
Carlson, J. S., 104, 122, *137*
Carpenter, P. A., 21, *38*, 157, 158, *185*, 213, 214, *225*
Carr, B., 76, *83*
Carroll, J., 15, *37*
Carroll, J. B., 104, *137*, 277, 278, *283*
Carroll, J. D., 231, 232, 239, 241, 251, *263*, *264*, *265*
Carson, R. E., 22, *39*
Cattell, R. B., 15, *37*, 48, *83*, 96, *137*, 280, *283*
Cavanaugh, J. C., 49, *82*
Cech, C. G., 246, 247, *264*
Ceci, S., 33, *37*

Champagne, A., 44, *83*
Chang, J. J., 232, 239, 241, *264*
Chartoff, B. T., 175, 179, *185*
Chase, W. G., 216, 20, *37*, 49, 50, *83*, *85*, 147, *185*, 218, 220, *224*
Chi, M. T. H., 32, *37*, 50, *83*, 147, 150, 152, 180, 182, *185*, 205, *224*, 242, *264*
Chiang, A., 135, 136, *137*
Chiesi, H. L., 20, 30, *37*, 148, *188*
Clark, E. V., 169, *185*
Clark, H. H., 20, *37*, 169, *185*, 232, *264*
Coan, R. W., 254, *264*
Cohen, G., 27, *37*
Cohn, S. J., 104, 122, *137*
Cole, M., 33, *37*
Collins, A. M., 237, *264*
Collins, K. W., 165, *185*
Coltheart, M., 23, *37*
Connon, S., 26, *39*
Conrad, R., 156, *185*
Cooper, L. A., 19, *40*
Corkin, S., 157, *185*
Covington, M. V., 151, *185*
Cox, D. L., 207, *225*
Craik, F. I. M., 256, *264*
Cronbach, L., 11, 12, 34, *37*, 145, 183, *185*
Crutchfield, R. S., 151, *185*
Cunningham, J. W., 164, 165, 166, *187*
Cunningham, P. M., 164, 165, 166, *187*
Curtis, M. E., 52, 53, 54, *83*, *84*

D

Daneman, M., 21, 36, *38*, 157, 158, *185*
Dansereau, D. F., 165, *185*, *187*
Davidson, J., 21, 26, 28, *38*, *39*
Davies, L. B., 151, *185*
Davies, P., 277, *283*
Deffner, G., 197, *224*
de Groot, A. D., 49, *83*
de Kleer, J., 51, *83*
De la Roche, O., 32, *39*
Delclos, V. R., 48, *82*
DeVellis, R. F., 135, *138*
Diekhoff, G., 165, *185*
Donaldson, G., 15, *38*
Donders, F. C., 133, *137*
Dreyfus, H., 36, *38*
Dreyfus, S., 36, *38*
Dugas, J., 135, *138*

E

Eastman, R., 61, *84*
Ebbinghaus, H., 207, *224*
Ehri, L. C., 154, *185*
Einhorn, H. J., 206, *224*
Ekman, G., 233, *264*
Ekstrom, R. B., 280, *283*
Eliot, J., 211, *225*
Emery, G., 172, *184*
Ericsson, K. A., 193, 195, 197, 199, 200, 203, 204, 205, 208, 209, 210, 218, 219, 220, 221, *224*
Ernst, G. W., 151, *185*
Evans, S. H., 165, *185*
Eysenck, H., 11, *38*, 105, 107, 126, 129, *137*

F

Faivre, I. A., 219, 221, *224*
Faloon, S., 216, *224*
Farr, S., 29, *38*
Farrell, R., 31, 36, *37*
Feigenbaum, E. A., 32, *38*
Feltovich, P. J., 45, 50, 52, 63, *83, 84*, 151, 180, 182, *185*, 205, *224*, 242, *264*
Feng, C., 274, *284*
Ferrara, R. A., 49, *82*
Fillenbaum, S., 232, *264, 265*
Finger, E., 154, *187*
Fitts, P. M., 44, *83*
Flavell, J. H., 152, *187*
Flower, L. S., 57, *83*, 163, 164, *186*
Foder, J., 23, *38*
Fogarty, G. J., 117, *137*
Foss, P. J., 27, *38*
Fox, J., 57, *83*
Frankel, F., 194, *224*
Frase, L. T., 154, *186*
Frederiksen, C. H., 155, *186*
Frederiksen, J. R., 154, 156, 157, 159, 160, *186*
French, J. W., 215, *224*, 280, *283*
French, L. A., 48, *82*
Friendly, M. L., 247, 254, *264*
Frost, H., 149, *186*
Frost, N., 14, 36, *38*
Fuchs, A. H., 254, *264*

G

Gagné, E. D., 151, 181, *186*
Gagné, R. M., 176, 179, *186, 187*
Gardner, M. K., 129, 133, 134, *139*
Garland, J., 165, *185*
Garner, R., 162, *186*
Garner, W. R., 252, *264*
Garofolo, J., 178, *187*
Garrett, H. E., 99, *137*
Gehardt, R., 165, *186*
Gelman, R., 241, 242, 247, *265*
Gentner, D., *51, 83*
Gentner, D., 51, *83*
Gibbons, R. D., 269, *284*
Gick, M. L., 31, *38*
Gilford, R., 135, *137*
Gimmestad, B. J., 210, *224*
Gitomer, D., 60, *83*
Glaser, R., 2, *8*, 12, 32, *37, 39*, 45, 47, 50, 52, 54, 63, *83, 84*, 147, 180, 182, *185, 186*, 205, *224*, 242, *264*
Glass, C. R., 172, *184*
Glass, G. V., 2, *8*, 222, *225*
Glenn, C. G., 164, *188*
Glover, J. A., 167, 168, 169, *184*
Glucksberg, S., 237, *265*
Goldman, S. R., 279, *283*
Goldman, T., 157, *189*
Goldstein, I., 76, *83*
Gould, S., 11, 15, *38*
Green, B. F., 34, *38*, 51, 58, *84*
Greeno, J., 32, *39*, 40, 56, *84*
Groen, G. J., 148, 149, *186, 189*
Gruenewald, P., 234, *264*
Guilford, J. P., 15, *38*, 191, *225*, 270, 280, *283*
Gustafsson, J.-E., 97, *137*

H

Hagen, J. W., 150, *186*
Haier, R. J., 105, *137*
Hakstian, A. R., 280, *283*
Halpern, A. R., 239, 240, *264*
Hamilton, J. M. E., 203, *225*
Hammond, K., 53, *84*
Hanna, G. S., 177, *186*
Harris, P. L., 150, 161, 162, *186*
Hasselbring, T. S., 48, *82*

Hawkins, D., 2, *8*
Hayes, J. R., 57, *83*, 163, 164, 175, *186*, 211, *225*
Hayes-Roth, F., 32, 36, *38*
Heidbreder, E., 209, *225*
Heller, J., 32, *40*, 56, *84*
Hemmelgarn, T. E., 104, *137*
Hendrickson, A. E., 129, *137*
Hendrickson, D. E., 22, *38*
Henley, N. M., 233, 234, 237, 249, 251, *264*
Herrmann, D. J., 242, *266*
Herrnstein, R. J., 11, *38*
Hinsley, D. A., *36*, 175, *186*, 211, *225*
Hinton, D., 19, *38*
Hirtle, S. C., 248, *264*
Hoepfner, R., 54, *83*, 280, *283*
Hogaboam, T. W., 53, *84*, 154, *187*
Holden, C., 12, *38*
Holley, C. D., 165, *185*
Holyoak, K. J., 31, *38*
Horn, J. L., 15, 34, *38*, *40*
Howard, D. V., 241, 242, 245, 247, *264*
Howard, J. H., 241, 242, 245, 247, *264*
Hughes, O. L., 132, *137*
Hull, C. L., 45, *83*
Hull, G., 57, *83*
Humphreys, L. G., 34, *38*, 96, 128, *138*
Hunt, E., 12, 14, 17, 21, 26, 27, 28, 29, 32, 34, *38*, *39*, 117, *138*, 149, *186*, 192, *225*
Hutchinson, W. J., 250, *266*

I

Inhelder, B., 58, *83*

J

Jacko, C. M., 165, *186*
Jackson, M. D., 154, *186*
Jensen, A. R., 93, 99, 100, 103, 104, 108, 109, 112, 113, 118, 122, 125, 126, 129, *138*, *139*
Jensen, C. M., 104, *137*
John, L., 212, *224*
Johnson, D., 156, *189*
Johnson, E. S., 272, *283*
Johnson, R. C., 102, *138*

Johnson, S. C., 243, *264*
Johnson, W., 20, *39*
Johnson-Laird, P., 19, *39*
Jones, H. E., 221, *225*
Jones, R. S., 256, *263*
Jorm, A. F., 157, *186*
Juola, J., 135, *137*
Just, M. A., 213, 214, *225*

K

Kail, R., Jr., 18, *40*, 279, *284*
Kaiser, H. F., 94, *138*
Kamin, L., 11, *39*
Kaplan, R., 25, *37*
Karegianes, J. L., 153, *188*
Karpf, D., 194, *224*, *225*
Kawash, G. F., 254, *264*
Kearins, J. M., 28, *39*
Keating, D. P., 14, *39*, 135, *138*, 202, *225*
Kehle, T. J., 104, *137*
Kellas, G., 135, *138*
Kennedy, G., 211, *225*
Kerr, B., 26, *39*
Kessler, E. J., 239, *265*
Kieras, D., 20, *39*
Kiewra, K. A., 161, 169, 171, *184*
Kilpatrick, J., 210, *225*
King, M. C., 234, *264*
Kintsch, W., 27, 32, *39*, *40*, 155, 158, 159, 160, 168, *185*, *186*, 256, *264*
Klein, G. S., 129, *138*
Kleinmuntz, B., 206, *224*
Kleinmuntz, D. N., 206, *224*
Klopfer, D., 44, 45, 52, 63, *83*, *84*
Kolb, B., 15, 20, 26, *39*
Kosslyn, S. M., 241, 242, *263*
Kraft, R. G., 167, 168, 169, *184*
Krech, D., 129, *138*
Kreutzer, M. A., 152, *187*
Kruithos, A., 161, 162, *186*
Krulee, G., 211, *225*
Krumhansl, C. L., 238, 239, 250, 251, *264*, *265*
Kruskal, J. B., 231, *265*
Krutetskii, V. A., 175, *187*, 197, *225*
Kuhl, D. E., 22, *39*
Kuhn, T. S., 44, *83*
Kyllonen, P. C., 216, *225*

L

Laberge, D., 153, *187*
Lansman, M., 26, 28, 29, *38, 39*, 117, *138*
LaPorte, R. E., 243, 244, 245, 247, *264, 265*
Larkin, J., 32, *39*, 44, 50, *84*, 181, *187*, 205, 225
Larson, C. O., 165, *187*
Lave, J., 33, *39*
Lawton, S. C., 152, *185*
Leiman, J. M., 91, *138*
Lenat, D. B., 32, 36, *38*
Leonard, C., 152, *187*
Lesgold, A. M., 45, 52, 53, 63, *84*, 211, 225
Lester, F. K., 178, *187*
Levin, L., 57, *83*
Levine, M., 194, *224, 225*
Lewis, J., 149, *186*
Lidz, C. S., 48, *84*
Light, L. L., 27, *39*
Liker, J., 33, *37*
Lin, R. L., 34, *38*
Lockhart, R. S., 256, *264*
Lockhead, G. R., 243, *264*
Loevinger, J., 128, *138*
Loftus, E. F., 237, *264*
Logan, D., 61, *84*
Lohman, D. F., 16, 17, *39*, 216, *225, 226*, 269, *283*
Longstreth, L. E., 35, *39*
Lord, F. M., 275, *284*
Lucas, J. F., 211, *225*
Lunneborg, C., 14, 36, *38*, 149, *186*
Luria, A. R., 219, 220, *225*

M

Mackworth, N. H., 153, *187*
MacLeod, C., 21, 26, 28, *39*
Macphail, E. M., 120, *138*
Magnus, P., 102, *139*
Markman, E. M., 152, 153, *187*
Marr, D., 19, *39*
Marshalek, B., 16, 17, *39*
Martin, C. J., 207, *225*
Mathews, N., 28, *39*
Maxwell, A. E., 111, *138*
Mazziotia, J. C., 22, *39*

McCauley, C., 135, *138*
McClelland, J. L., 154, *186*
McCloskey, M., 51, 58, *84*, 237, *265*
McCutchen, D., 57, *83*, 163, 164, *187*
McDermott, J., 32, *39*, 50, *84*, 181, *187*, 205, *255*
McDonald, B. A., 165, *185, 187*
McDonald, L. A., 26, *39*
McGee, M. G., 16, *39*
McKeown, M. G., 53, *82*
McKoon, G., 230, *265*
Meade, A., 272, *283*
Medin, D. L., 43, *84*, 237, *266*
Messick, S., 182, 183, *187*
Meyer, B. J. F., 146, 154, 155, 164, 166, *187*
Miller, G. A., 22, *39*, 232, 245, *265*
Miller, K., 202, *225*, 241, 242, 247, *265*
Minsky, M., 19, *39*, 146, *187*
Montague, W. E., 195, 207, *225*
Moore, D. W., 164, 165, 166, *187*
Moore, M., 27, *39*
Moore, S. A., 164, 165, 166, *187*
Mosier, C. I., 275, *284*
Mueller, G. E., 220, *225*
Munro, E., 104, *138*
Murphy, G. L., 43, *84*
Murtagh, M., 33, *39*

N

Nagoshi, C. T., 102, *138*
Nelson, K. E., 241, 242, *263*
Newell, A., 151, *185, 187*, 193, 195, 204, 211, *225*
Newkirk, T., 165, *187*
Newman, C. M., 250, *265*
Nicely, P. E., 232, 245, *265*
Nisbett, R. E., 198, *225*
Noble, C. E., 207, *226*
Norman, D., 1, *8*, 53, *84*, 256, *265*
Nunnaly, J., 14, *39*

O

O'Dell, G., 230, *265*
OKey, J. R., 179, *187*
Ortony, A., 257, *266*

Osgood, C. E., 234, *265*
O'Shea, T., 212, *226*

P

Paivio, A., 257, *265*
Palmer, J., 21, 26, *39*
Papert, S., 19, *39*, 146, *187*
Paradise, N. E., 176, *186*
Parkman, J. M., 149, *186*
Paul, S. M., 115, *138*
Payne, J. W., 206, *226*
Pellegrino, J. W., 12, 18, 34, *39*, *40*, 279,
    283, *284*
Perfetti, C. A., 52, 53, 54, *82*, *84*, 154, 157,
    160, 163, 164, *187*, *188*
Perl, R. E., 99, *137*
Perlmutter, M., 202, *225*
Pflaum, S. W., 153, *188*
Phelps, M. E., 22, *39*
Piaget, J., 58, *83*
Plake, B. S., 167, 168, 169, *184*
Pollard-Gott, L., 239, *265*
Poltrock, S., 29, *39*, 117, *138*
Polya, G., 209, 210, *226*
Posner, M. I., 23, *40*, 121, 134, *138*
Price, B., 109, *138*
Pruzansky, S., 232, 234, 248, 249, 251, *265*
Prytulak, L. S., 207, *226*
Pylyshyn, Z., 19, *40*

R

Raaijmakers, J. G. W., 257, *265*
Rappaport, A., 232, *264*, *265*
Rasher, S. P., 153, *188*
Ratcliff, R., 230, 257, *265*
Raven, J. C., 16, *40*
Reckase, M. D., 34, *38*
Reder, L. M., 154, *184*
Reese, E., 32, *37*, 147, *185*
Reichart, G. J., 49, *82*
Reis, R., 162, *186*
Reiser, B. J., 31, 36, *37*
Reitman, J. S., 247, *265*
Resnick, L. B., 53, *84*, 146, 147, 148, 149,
    188, *189*
Reuter, H. H., 247, *265*
Reynolds, C. R., 93, *138*
Richman, B., 277, *283*

Riley, M. S., 32, *40*, 51, 56, *84*
Rinott, Y., 250, *265*
Rips, L. J., 234, 235, 244, 245, *265*, 279, *284*
Ritz, S. A., 256, *263*
Robinson, D. L., 105, *137*
Ross, B. H., 230, *263*
Roth, E. M., 246, 250, *265*
Roth, S. F., 157, 160, *188*
Rubinson, H., 45, 52, 63, *84*
Rumelhart, D. E., 47, *84*, 234, 236, 237,
    256, 257, 262, *265*, *266*
Rush, J. A., 172, *184*

S

Samuels, S. J., 153, *187*
Sanford, A. J., 203, *226*, *266*
Sattath, S., 248, 251, *266*
Scardamalia, M., 164, 173, *188*
Schaeffer, B., 235, 236, *266*
Schafer, E. W. P., 105, *138*
Schank, R. C., 27, *40*, 257, *266*
Schmid, J., 91, *138*
Schneider, W., 29, *37*, 47, *85*
Schoenfeld, A. H., 178, *188*, 211, 242, *226*,
    266
Scribner, S., 33, *37*
Shannon, C., 19, *40*
Sharan, S., 165, *188*
Shaughnessy, M., 57, *85*
Shaw, B. F., 172, *184*
Shepard, R. N., 19, *40*, 231, 233, 237, 238,
    251, 252, *266*, 274, *284*
Shiffrin, R. M., 256, 257, *263*, *265*
Shoben, E. J., 234, 235, 244, 245, 246, 247,
    249, 250, 251, 262, *265*, *266*
Siegler, R. S., 58, *85*
Silver, E. A., 175, 178, 179, *188*, 211, *226*
Silverstein, J. W., 256, *263*
Simon, D., 32, *39*, 50, *84*, *85*, 181, *187*,
    205, *225*
Simon, H. A., 32, *39*, 49, 50, *83*, *84*, *85*,
    147, 151, 175, 181, *185*, *186*, *187*, 193,
    195, 197, 199, 200, 203, 204, 205, 208,
    209, 210, 221, 211, *224*, *225*, *226*
Sinha, S. N., 103, *136*
Slavin, R. E., 165, *188*
Smith, E. E., 23, 24, *40*, 234, 235, 237,
    244, 245, *265*, *266*
Snow, R. E., 16, 17, *39*, *40*, 216, *226*

Soli, S. D., 245, 246, 247, 251, *263, 266*
Spearman, C., 15, *40*, 90, 95, 119, 120, 126, 127, *138, 139*, 280, *284*
Spence, K. W., 45, *85*
Spiegel, M. R., 177, *188*
Spillich, G. J., 20, 30, *37*, 148, 166, *188, 189*
Spurlin, J. E., 165, *187*
Stallard, C. K., 165, 173, *188*
Stankov, L., 15, 29, 34, *40*, 117, *137, 139*
Stanovich, K. G., 150, *186*
Stein, N. L., 164, *188*
Sternberg, R. J., 2, *8*, 12, 14, 17, 19, 23, *40*, 129, 133, 134, 135, *139*, 145, 149, *188*, 192, *226*, 236, *266*, 277, *284*
Sternberg, S., 135, *139*
Stevens, S. S., 238, *266*
Suci, G. J., 234, *265*
Sundet, J. M., 102, *139*
Susukita, T., 220, *226*
Svenson, O., 206, *226*

T

Tambs, K., 102, *139*
Tannenbaum, P. H., 234, *265*
Taylor, B. M., 155, *188*
Terwogt, M. M., 161, 162, *186*
Thomas, E. L., 153, *188*
Thomson, D. M., 257, *266*
Thomson, G. H., 111, 120, 126, 127, *139*
Thorndike, E. L., 126, *139*
Thorndyke, P. W., 147, 148, 164, *188*
Thurstone, L. L., 15, *40*, 92, 107, *139*, 274, 280, *284*
Tobias, S., 145, *188*
Torgeson, J. K., 150, 157, *189*
Trabasso, T., 164, *188*
Troyka, L. A., 173, *189*
Tulving, E., 230, 257, *264*
Turner, T. J., 154, *184*
Tversky, A., 248, 250, 251, *265, 266*
Tyler, L. E., 128, *139*
Tyler, W., 180, *189*

U

Underwood, B. J., 12, *40*
Undheim, J. O., 107, 128, *139*

V

Van Dijk, T. A., 27, 32, *39, 40*, 155, 158, 159, 160, 168, *185, 186*, 256, *264*
VanLehn, K., 55, *82, 85*, 212, *224*
Varon, E. J., 192, *226*
Vellutino, F. R., 154, *189*
Venezky, R. L., 156, *189*
Vernon, P. A., 104, 109, 118, 125, *139*
Vernon, P. E., 15, *40*, 97, *139*, 146, *189*
Vesonder, G. T., 148, *188, 189*, 244, 245, 247, *264*
Visser, T., 161, 162, *186*
Volkman, J., 238, *266*
Voss, J. F., 20, 30, *37*, 148, 166, 180, *188, 189*, 243, 244, 245, 247, *264, 265*
Vye, N. J., 48, *82*
Vygotsky, L. S., 48, *85*

W

Wade, J. P., 135, *139*
Walberg, H. J., 153, *188*
Walker, D. A., 269, *284*
Wallace, R., 235, 236, *266*
Wang, Y., 45, 52, 63, *84*
Waterman, D., 32, 36, *38*
Watson, J. B., 194, *226*
Weaver, W., 19, *40*
Webster, R. E., 177, *189*
Wechsler, D., 209, *226*
Weinstein, C. E., 162, *189*
Whishaw, I. Q., 15, 20, 26, *39*
Wickens, C. D., 29, *37*
Widaman, K. F., 104, *137*
Wilce, L. C., 154, *185*
Williams, D., 105, *137*
Wilson, D., 269, *284*
Wilson, T. D., 198, *225*
Wood, R., 269, *284*
Woods, S. S., 148, *189*
Woodworth, R. S., 194, *226*

Y

Yengo, L. A., 180, *189*
Young, R. M., 212, *226*

Z

Zelinski, E., 27, *39*

Subject Index

Page numbers followed by n indicate footnotes.

A

Ability, *see also specific type*
  classes of, Cattell-Horn model and, 15
  definition of, 268–274
  exceptional, acquired skill vs., 216–221
  fluid and crystallized, correlation of,
      96–97
  measurement of, 87–88, 267–283
    cognitive ability factors and, 280–282
    definitions and, 268–274
    person characteristic function and,
      275–279
    task difficulty and, 279–280
Academic abilities, 145–183
  cognitive strategies and, 150–152
  control processes and, 149–150
  declarative knowledge and, 146–148
  factors in, 146
  in mathematics, 175–179
  metacognition and, 152–153
  procedural knowledge and, 148–149
  in reading, 153–162, *see also* Reading
  in science, 179–182
  in writing, 163–175, *see also* Writing
Achievement assessment, 41–81
  automaticity and, 44–45
  expert performance and, 49–50

general dimensions for, 77–81
intelligent tutoring systems and, 69–76,
    see also Intelligent tutoring systems
knowledge structures and, 43–44
mental models of, 50–52
metacognitive skills and, 49
practice and, 46–48
proceduralization and, 45–46
proximal development zone and, 48
psychology of learning and, 43
self-regulatory skills and, 49
subject matter acquisition and, 52–60,
    see also Subject matter acquisition;
    specific subject
testing methodology and, 60–69, *see also*
    Testing methodology
Adaptive instruction, tutor architectures
    and, 70–71
ADCLUS, 231
ADDTREE
  music perception and, 240
  underlying representation and, 248–249
Age, metacognition and, 152
Anderson's associative theories, 256
Appearance models, 51, 52
Aptitude layer of knowledge, intelligent
    tutoring systems and, 74–75
Aptitude-treatment interaction research, 145

Arithmetic, achievement in, 55–56
Arithmetic word problems, 56
Armed Services Vocational Aptitude Battery (ASVAB), 112–113
Associative theories, 256
A&S theory, 256
ASVAB (Armed Services Vocational Aptitude Battery), 112–113
Atkinson & Shiffrin theory, 256
Attentional control ability, 29–30
Attentional demands, reduction of, automaticity and, 79
Attention shifting, 29
Automated laboratories, 35
Automaticity, achievement and, 44–45, 79

B

Behavioristic era, 192
Belief systems, mathematical ability and, 178
Between-family correlations, 108–109
Block Counting test, 272–274
Brain function, mental processes and, 22–23
BRIDGE programming tutor, 65–67
BUGGY, 149
Buros-Nebraska Symposium, themes of, 1
Burt's neurophysiological theory of g, 120

C

Categories, multidimensional scaling and, 233–234, 249–251
Cattell-Horn model, 15
Chronometry, 134
City-block metric, 252
  memory theories and, 261
Clustering, memory theories and, multidimensional scaling and, 258–259
Cognition
  brain function and, 22–23
  levels of, 19–21
  modular approach to, 23–27
Cognitive ability, see also Mental ability
  factors in, 280–282
Cognitive correlates, 12
Cognitive development, multidimensional scaling and, 241–242

Cognitive processes
  detailed structure of, 193
  physical mechanisms and, 19
  symbolic processing and
    pure, 19
    referents of, 19
  verbal reports on, see Verbal reports
Cognitive psychology
  academic abilities and, see Academic abilities
  approach of, 18–34
    psychometric issues and, 5–6
  domain of, topics in, 1
  implications of, testing and, 1–8
  psychometrics vs., 2–3
  task difficulty and, 279–280
Cognitive-psychometric connection, 3–5
Cognitive sciences, 12, 18–19
  three levels in, 19
Cognitive strategies
  academic abilities and, 150–152
  mathematical ability and, 178–179
  reading ability and, 158–161
  science ability and, 180–181
  writing ability and, 168–172
Cognitive tasks, 2
  complexity of, g and, 111–118
  elementary, reaction time tasks and, 104–105
  multidimensional scaling and, 235
Color domain, multidimensional scaling and, 233
Competence assessment, see Achievement assessment
Competing tasks, single tasks vs., 117–118
Compiled knowledge, 45
Complexity of task
  experimental manipulation of, 115–118
  g and, 111–118
"Component analysis," 17–18
Component process theories of g, 128–136
Composition, 57
  knowledge compilation and, 45
Computer-assisted instructional systems, see Intelligent tutoring systems
Computer-based menu systems, 65–67
Computers, union of cognitive sciences and psychometrics and, 34–35
Conative speed, 124
Concurrent verbalization model, 196
Confusion matrices, 232–233

Constraints, sensitivity to, 68–69
Context
  effects of, multidimensional scaling
    and, 243–245
  increased dimensionality and, 245–247
Control processes
  academic abilities and, 149–150
  mathematical ability and, 177
  reading ability and, 156–158
  writing ability and, 167–168
Correlational psychology, 145
Correlations, 88–90, see also General factor
Cortical potentials, 105–107
Crystallized ability, 15
  fluid ability and, correlation of, 96–97
Cube comparison test, 213
Curriculum knowledge, intelligent tutor-
    ing systems and, 71–75
Curriculum object structuring, diagnosis
    with, 75–76

D

Decision making, verbal reports and, 206
Declarative knowledge, 44–45
  academic abilities and, 146–148
  intelligent tutoring systems and, 75
  mathematical ability and, 175–177
  reading and, 154–156
  science ability and, 179–180
  writing ability and, 163–167
Deductive reasoning tasks, difficulty of,
    279–280
Development
  actual vs. potential, 48
  cognitive, multidimensional scaling
    and, 241–242
  metacognition and, 152
Dichotic listening, 29
Discourse analysis, 54
Discourse processing, 168–169
Discourse schema knowledge, 164–165
Domain knowledge, intelligent tutoring
    systems and, 71–75
Dominance metric, 252–253
  memory theories and, 260–261
Drive theories of g, 120–121
Dual code theory, 257
Dual tasks, 26, 141–142
  single tasks vs., 117–118

E

Elementary cognitive tasks
  complexity of, 112–113
  reaction time tasks and, 104–105
Episodic memory, semantic memory vs.,
    230
Error variance, 91
Euclidean metric, 252
Euclidean model of mental ability, 14
Evoked cortical potentials, 105–107
Exceptional ability, acquired skill vs., 216–
    221
Exceptional memory, alleged, 219–221
Experimental psychology, 145
Expert performance, 49–50, see also De-
    clarative knowledge

F

Factor analytic studies, 2, 14–15, see also
    General factor
Factor hierarchy, 91, 92
Factor loading, 90
Factors
  cognitive ability, 280–282
  processes vs., 132–133
Family correlations, 102–103
First-order factors, 91
Fisher's variance ratio, 102
Flexible problem solving skill, assessment
    of, 60–64
Fluid ability, crystallized ability and, cor-
    relation of, 96–97
"Fluid intelligence," 15
Fundaments, 88

G

g, see General factor
GATB (General Aptitude Test Battery),
    validity coefficients of, 100
General Aptitude Test Battery (GATB),
    validity coefficients of, 100
General factor (g), 87–142
  Burt's neurophysiological theory of, 120
  characterization of, 94–95
  component process theories of, 128–136
  drive theories of, 120–121

General factor (*g*) (*continued*)
    extraction of, 91–93
    fluid and crystallized ability and, 96–97
    invariance of, 97–99
    motivation theories of, 120–121
    multiprocess theories of, 126–136
    neuronal errors in transmission and,
        121–126
    practical external validity of, 99–100
    processing speed and, 121–126
    "reality" of, 100–107
        evoked cortical potentials and, 105–
            107
        family correlations and, 102–103
        inbreeding depression and, 103–104
        mental processing speed and, 104–
            105
        WAIS subtests and, 102
    refinement of, 107–111
    robustness of, 98–99
    simple structure and, 93–94
    size of, 97–99
    Spearman's "mental energy" theory of,
        119–120
    task complexity and, 111–118
        experimental manipulation of, 115–
            118
    Thomson's sampling theory of, 111,
        126–128
    unitary theories of, 119–126
General Problem Solver (GPS), 151
Generating process, in writing, 163
Genetic inbreeding, 103–104
Genetic variance, WAIS subtests and, 102
Goal-checking strategies, in reading, 161
Goal setting, in writing, 163
GPS (General Problem Solver), 151
Group factors, 91

H

HAM theory, 256
Heritability, of WAIS subtests, 102
Heuristics, 178–179
Hierarchical factor analysis, principal fac-
    tor analysis vs., 92–93
"Hierarchical general factor," 15, *see also*
    General factor
Hierarchical menus, 65–67

I

Inbreeding depression, 103–104
INDCLUS, structure change measurement
    and, 242
Individual differences, assessment of, ver-
    bal reports in, 209–213
INDSCAL, 232
Inductive reasoning tasks, difficulty of,
    279
Information
    manipulation of, writing ability and,
        168
    organization of, reading ability and, 154
Information processing, 19
    modularity and, 24–25
    speed of, as basis of *g*, 121–126
    stages of, 23–24
Information-processing components
    academic abilities and, 149–150
    g and, 128–136
Instruction, testing and, integration of,
    69–76, *see also* Intelligent tutoring
    systems
Intelligence, *see also* Mental ability
    "fluid," 15
    science, technology, and, 11–37, *see also*
        Science
Intelligence tests, 11, *see also* Mental abil-
    ity tests
Intelligent tutoring systems, 69–76
    architectures of, adaptive instruction
        and, 70–71
    curriculum object structuring and, 75–
        76
    knowledge representation and, 71–75
Introspective era, 191–192
Item, definition of, 87

J

"Junk" parameter, 18

K

Kintsch's theory, 256
Knowledge
    declarative, *see* Declarative knowledge

layers of, in intelligent tutoring systems, 71–75
procedural, *see* Procedural knowledge
Knowledge compilation, 45
Knowledge structures
  achievement assessment and, 43–44, 78
  expert, 50
  schemata as, 47n
KYST, 231
  Minkowski-metric and, 260–261

L

Laboratories, automated, 35
Language processing, modularity of, 26–27
Language strategies, 158–161
Learning, *see also* Academic abilities; Achievement assessment; Knowledge *entries*
  metacognitive skills for, achievement assessment and, 80–81
  nature of, achievement assessment and, 41–42
  psychology of, achievement assessment and, 43
  three stages in, 44–48
Learning potential, 48
Levels of processing theory, 256
Lexical access, 153
Lexical knowledge, 165–166
Linguistic processing, modularity of, 26–27
LNR theory, 256
Local coherence strategies, 159–160
  sentence reordering test and, 170
Logic, context-specific, 33
Long-term memory, writing ability and, 163
"Lookback" strategy, 162

M

Macrostrategies, 160–161
  paragraph assembly test and, 170–171
MAPCLUS, 231
Mathematical ability, 175–179
  cognitive strategies used in, 178–179
  components of, 175
  control processes and, 177
  metacognitive strategies used in, 178–179
  prior knowledge and, 175–177
Mathematical orthogonality, 15
Mathematical problem solving, verbal reports and, 209–213
Mathematics, *see also* Arithmetic
  schema of, 32
MDS, *see* Multidimensional scaling
Means-ends analysis, 204–206
Mediating responses, 207–208
Memory
  exceptional alleged, 219–221
  long-term, writing ability and, 163
  mathematical ability and, 177
  reading ability and, 154
  semantic, constraints on, 237–238
  semantic vs. episodic, 230
  short-term
    reading ability and, 21
    writing ability and, 167–168
  verbal ability and, 149–150
  working, writing ability and, 168
Memory retrieval, Ratcliff's theory of, 257
Memory-scanning paradigm, 135
Memory tests, practice and, 216–219
Memory theories, multidimensional scaling and, 254–261, *see also* Multidimensional scaling, memory theories and
Mental ability, Euclidean model of, 14
Mental ability tests, 87–88, *see also* General factor
  facts of nature and, 88–90
"Mental energy" theory of *g*, 119–120
Mental models, 50–52
  quality of, achievement assessment and, 78
Mental processing, speed of, 104–105
Menus, hierarchical, 65–67
Metacognition, 49
  academic abilities and, 152–153
  achievement assessment and, 80–81
  intelligent tutoring systems and, 74–75
  mathematical ability and, 178–179
  reading ability and, 161–162
  writing ability and, 172–174
Metaprocesses, *g* and, 113, 130

Methodological issues, 6–7, *see also* Testing methodology
Metrics, multidimensional scaling and, 252–253
  memory theories and, 259–261
Minkowski *r* metrics, 252–253
  memory theories and, 259–261
Modular processing, 23–27
MOPS theory, 257
Motivation theories of *g*, 120–121
Multidimensional scaling (MDS), 16, 229–263
  categorical data and, problems with, 249–251
  cognitive task applications of, 235
  contextual effects and, 243–245
    increased dimensionality and, 245–247
  limitations of, 262–263
  memory theories and, 254–261
    clustering and, 258–259
    descriptions of, 256–257
    Minkowski-metric and, 259–261
    SINDSCAL analysis of, 255
  Minkowski *r* metrics and, 252–253, 259–261
  music perception and, 238–241
  processing applications and, 235–237
  promise of, 262–263
  representation selection and, 251–252
  semantic memory constraints and, 237–238
  structure change and, measurement of, 241–243
  structure determination with, 232–235
  types of, 231–232
  underlying representation and, 247–249
Multiple-choice technology, 65–67
Music perception, multidimensional scaling and, 238–241

N

Neuronal errors, as basis of *g*, 121–126
Neurophysiological theory of *g*, 120
Neuropsychology, 22
Non-Euclidean metrics, 252–253
  memory theories and, 259–261
Non-*g* variance, 91

O

Objective scoring, 87
Objectivity, 64
Organizing process, in writing, 163
Orthogonality requirement, 15
Overlay approach, in intelligent tutors, 76

P

Paivio's dual code theory, 257
Paper and pencil technology, psychometrics and, 13–14
Paragraph assembly test, 170–171
Parsing, 153
Personal theories
  automation of knowledge and, 46n
  knowledge structures and, 43–44
Person characteristic function, 275–279
Physical level of cognition, 19
Physical mechanisms, cognitive processes and, 19
"Physical symbol manipulating system," 19
Pitch discrimination ability, 270–272
Planning process, in writing, 163
Pleiotropy, 110
Positive manifold, 89
Potential development, zone of, 48
Practice
  achievement and, 46–48
  memory tests and, 216–219
  theory vs., 6–7
Predictive validity, 2
  g and, 99–100
Primary factors, 91
Primary mental abilities, 107
Principal components analysis, 91–92
Problem-solution paths, science ability and, 181
Problem solving
  flexible, 60–64
  mental models in, 50–52
  processes of, awareness of, 178
  representations and, 28
    achievement assessment and, 78
  strategies for, academic abilities and, 150–152
  verbal reports and, 204–206
  of word problems, 56

Procedural efficiency, achievement assessment and, 78–79
Proceduralization
  achievement and, 45–46
  knowledge compilation and, 45
Procedural knowledge
  academic abilities and, 148–149
  achievement assessment and, 79–80
  intelligent tutoring systems and, 75–76
  mathematical ability and, 176
  science ability and, 179–180
Procedural ordering tasks, 68–69
Processes, factors vs., 132–133
Processing, levels of, 256
Processing explanations, multidimensional scaling and, 235–237
Processing speed, as basis of g, 121–126
Process model, procedural knowledge and, 148, 149
Process theories of g, 128–136
Production execution systems, 24–25
Productions
  compiled procedures as, 45
  tuned, 45
Program method, procedural knowledge and, 148
Propositional strategies, 159
  word reordering test and, 169
Protocol analysis, 208–209
  verbal reports and, 194–200
Proximal development, zone of, 48
Psychometric issues, cognitive approaches to, 5–6
Psychometrics, 1
  cognitive psychology vs., 2–3 see also Cognitive-psychometric connection
  definition of, 11n
  levels assessed by, 2
  technology and, paper and pencil, 13–14
  theory of, present status of, 13–18

Q

Qualitative process models, 50–52

R

Ratcliff's theory of memory retrieval, 257
Raven Progressive Matrix Test, 16–17

Reaction time apparatus, 139–142
Reaction time tasks
  complexity of, 112
    Semantic Verification Test and, 116–118
  elementary cognitive tasks and, 104–105
Reading, 153–162
  achievement in, 52–55
  cognitive strategies used in, 158–161
  comprehension in, 153
  control processes in, 156–158
  declarative knowledge in, 154–156
  decoding in, 153
  metacognitive processes used in, 161–162
  processes in, 52
  recoding in, 156
  short-term memory and, 21
Referential level of cognition, 19
Regulatory skills, 80–81
Relational model, 51
Repair theory, 55
Representation
  expert performance and, 50
  problem solving and, 28
  selection of, multidimensional scaling and, 251–252
  underlying, multidimensional scaling and, 247–249
Retrieval, Ratcliff's theory of, 257
Retrieval-structure, 218
Reviewing process, in writing, 163, 173
Rule assessment, 58–59

S

Same-Different tasks, 140–141
Sampling theory of g, 111, 126–128
SAM theory, 257
Schemata, 47n
Schema theory, 257
Science, technology, and intelligence, 11–37
  cognitive psychology approach and, 18–34
  psychometric theory status and, 13–18
  union of scientific psychology camps and, 34–36
Science ability, 179–182
  cognitive strategies used in, 180–181
  prior knowledge and, 179–180

Scientific concepts, achievement in, 57–59
Scoring, objective, 87
Seashore Sense of Pitch test, 270–272
Self-regulatory skills, 49, 80–81
Self-talk, during writing, 172–173
Semantic domains, multidimensional scaling and, 233–235
Semantic memory
    constraints on, multidimensional scaling and, 237–238
    episodic memory vs., 230
Semantic retrieval capability, 53–54
Semantic Verification Test (SVT), g and, 115–117
Sentence integration, 157
Sentence processing, 54
Sentence reordering test, 170
Sentence verification paradigm, 20
Short-term memory
    reading ability and, 21
    tests of, practice and, 216–219
    writing ability and, 167–168
Short-term memory scanning paradigm, 135
Simple structure concept, 93–94
Simplicity, 64
SINDSCAL, 232
    memory theories and, 255
    music perception and, 239
Single tasks, dual tasks, vs., 117–118
Skill, acquired, exceptional ability vs., 216–221
Skill acquisition, see also Achievement assessment
    development of, three stages in, 44–48
Spatial ability, tests of
    assessing strategies in, 213–216
    task difficulty in, 279
Spearman's "mental energy" theory of g, 119–120
Specificity, 91
"Standardized interviews," 11
Sternberg memory scan, 135
Stimulus classification, response production and, 23–24
Strategic discourse processing, 168–169
Structure, change in, measurement of, 241–243
Subject matter acquisition, 52–60
    arithmetic, 55–56
    reading, 52–55
    scientific concepts, 57–59

technical skills, 59–60
word problems and, 56
writing, 57
Subtraction method, 133
SVT (Semantic Verification Test), g and, 115–117
Symbolic processing
    pure, 19
    referents of, 19
Symbol manipulation, 19
    stages of, 23–24
Synonym-Antonym task, 141
Syntactic knowledge, 165–166

T

Task complexity, g and, 111–118
    experimental manipulation and, 115–118
Task difficulty, 279–280
Task environment, 163
Technical skill development, 59–60
Technology
    paper and pencil, psychometrics and, 13–14
    science, intelligence, and, 11–37, see also Science
Testing, see also specific type
    cognitive psychology implications for, 1–8
    computerized, 34–35
    instruction and, integration of, 69–76, see also Intelligent tutoring systems
Testing methodology, see also specific type
    flexible problem solving skill and, 60–64
    hierarchical menus, 65–67
    objectivity in, 64
    procedural ordering task and, 68–69
    simplicity in, 64
Testing technology, 13–14
Text structure, reading ability and, 155–156
Theory(ies)
    distinguishing, 230–231
    practice vs., 6–7
Theory change, procedures for, achievement assessment and, 80
Thinking-aloud protocol, 195–197, see also Verbal reports
Thomson's sampling theory of g, 111, 126–128

Time sharing ability, 29
Trait, definition of, 16–18
Translating process, in writing, 163
   impediments to, 172–173
Troubleshooting skill, 60–64
Tulving theory, 257
Tuned productions, 45
Tutoring systems, intelligent, see Intelligent tutoring systems
Twins, within-pair variance of, 102

V

Validity, g and, 99–100
Validity coefficients, 11
Variance
   genetic, WAIS subtests and, 102
   non-g, 91
Vectors, factor analysis and, 14
Vector theories, 256
Verbal ability, memory and, 149–150
Verbal comprehension
   levels of cognition and, 20–21
   linguistic processing module and, 27
Verbal reports, 191–223
   exceptional ability vs. acquired skill and, 216–221
   implications of, 200–208
   individual differences assessed with, 209–213
   introspective, 191–192
   protocol analysis and, 194–200
   retrospective, 203
   spatial ability and, 213–216
"Visualization" ability, 15
Visual scan, 135

W

Wechsler Adult Intelligence Scale (WAIS)
   evoked cortical potentials and, 105–106
   mental processing speed and, 104
   subtests of, heritability of, 102
Wechsler Intelligence Scale for Children (WISC), inbreeding depression and, 103–104
WEST, 70–71
Why-questions, verbal reports and, 198
WISC (Wechsler Intelligence Scale for Children), inbreeding depression and, 103–104
Within-family correlations, 108–110
Within-pair variance, 102
Word problems, achievement in, 56
Word recognition, 52–53
Word reordering test, 169
Working memory, see also Memory
   writing ability and, 168
Writing, 163–175
   achievement in, 57
   cognitive strategies used in, 168–172
   control processes in, 167–168
   declarative knowledge and, 163–167
   interacting components in, 163
   metacognitive processes used in, 172–174
Writing blocks, 165
Writing processes, 163

Z

Zone of proximal development, 48